# NFT™

## Not For Tourists Guide to
# SEATTLE

**Get more on**
**notfortourists.com**

**Keep connected with:**
**Twitter:**
**twitter/notfortourists**

**Facebook:**
**facebook/notfortourists**

**iPhone App:**
**nftiphone.com**

**Not For Tourists, Inc**

D1490542

**Skyhorse Publishing**

designed by:
**Not For Tourists, Inc**
**NFT<sub>TM</sub>—Not For Tourists<sub>TM</sub> Guide to Seattle**
www.notfortourists.com

| **Publisher** | **Production Manager** | **Research** |
|---|---|---|
| Skyhorse Publishing | Aaron Schielke | Jess Bender |
| **Creative Direction &** | **Writing and Editing** | **Graphic Design and** |
| **Information Design** | Jessica Baxter | **Production** |
| Jane Pirone | Frank Chiachiere | Aaron Schielke |
| | Patricia Glowinski | Katherine Yaksich |
| **Director** | Craig Nelson | |
| Stuart Farr | Scott Sendrow | **Information Systems** |
| | | **Manager** |
| **Managing Editor** | **City Editor** | Juan Molinari |
| Scott Sendrow | Jessica Baxter | |

Printed in China
ISBN# 978-1-62636-056-3  $21.95
ISSN 2163-9191
Copyright © 2014 by Not For Tourists, Inc.
6th Edition

Every effort has been made to ensure that the information in this book is as up-to-date as possible at press time. However, many details are liable to change—as we have learned. Not For Tourists cannot accept responsibility for any consequences arising from the use of this book.

Not For Tourists does not solicit individuals, organizations, or businesses for listings inclusion in our guides, nor do we accept payment for inclusion into the editorial portion of our book; the advertising sections, however, are exempt from this policy. We always welcome communications from anyone regarding ANYTHING having to do with our books; please visit us on our website at www.notfortourists.com for appropriate contact information.

Skyhorse Publishing books may be purchased in bulk at special discounts for sales promotion, corporate gifts, fund-raising, or educational purposes. Special editions can also be created to specifications. For details, contact the Special Sales Department, Skyhorse Publishing, 307 West 36th Street, 11th Floor, New York, NY 10018 or specialsales@skyhorsepublishing.com.

www.skyhorsepublishing.com

10 9 8 7 6 5 4 3 2 1

Dear NFT User:

Ever since the city's humble beginnings, we've been a transient's town, full of sailors on leave, gold rush/dot-com/grunge rock hopefuls, and gentlemen loafers sleeping beneath the stars. Microsoft, Starbucks, Amazon, and Sub Pop changed all that, and suddenly the city's reputation changed in the eyes of the world and itself, becoming an international hub of commerce, technology, and youth culture. The dot-com bust punctured the economy but not Seattle's upwardly mobile self-image, so we steadfastly cling to the notion that we can reclaim our former glory (even if many of us are working in bars or writing code instead of selling out the Paramount or playing golf with Bezos and Gates).

You might need to be a millionaire to buy a house here, but you only need a couple of bucks to buy this book. So while you wait for whatever big break you seek, there is a vibrant music scene, great food, amazing art, incredible libraries, quirky landmarks, and thousands of eccentric panhandlers willing to accept any spare change that's weighing you down. And this sixth edition of NFT is here to help you navigate it all!

So whether you were born in Ballard or just moved from Boston, beginning a start-up venture or squandering your venture capital, you need this book. You'll find each and every one of Seattle's neighborhoods represented within, with full details on all the essential nightlife, restaurants, shopping spots, and coffee shops—hell, we've even included a whole section on…gulp…the Eastside.

The 2014 NFT Seattle is full of hundreds of new listings and updates, but if there's still something amiss or missing, by all means let us know. Your feedback is essential in helping us make this the ultimate guide to Seattle. Dig www.notfortourists.com to give us pro or con feedback. We can take it! And check out our nifty mobile app, for the latest up-to-date information on the go.

—Jane, Scott, Jessica, Frank, et al.

# Table of Contents

The formerly seedy Belltown now bursts with condos, boutique eateries, and noisy nightlife destinations. But don't fret, heroin can still be scored on the proper street corners. Homeless shelters and public health centers neighbor the rock clubs, art galleries, and sushi joints, making for an occasionally jarring mix of people. To escape the craziness, take a stroll through SAM's fabulous **Olympic Sculpture Park**.

## Landmarks

- **Cinerama** • 2100 4th Ave
206-448-6680
One of three theaters in the world showing three-panel Cinerama films. Amazing.
- **The Edgewater Hotel** • 2411 Alaskan Way
206-728-7000
Yes, Virginia, you really can fish from your hotel window.
- **Olympic Sculpture Park** • 2901 Western Ave
206-654-3100
Ambitious venue for the SAM's sculpture collection.
- **Seattle P.I. Globe** • 101 Elliott Ave W
800-542-0820
Is it the Post-Intelligencer or the Daily Planet?

##  Coffee

- **Bedlam Coffee** • 2231 2nd Ave
206-910-2300
Coffeehouse or community center: you decide.
- **Cherry Street Coffee House** • 2719 1st Ave
206-441-5489
Good coffee, nice staff, but the owner added a sick leave surcharge to protest a city mandate. Not cool.
- **Cherry Street Coffee House** • 2621 5th Ave
206-812-1298
Good coffee, nice staff, but the owner added a sick leave surcharge to protest a city mandate. Not cool.
- **Dimitrou's Jazz Alley Coffee** • 2203 6th Ave
206-441-9729
They'll get you jazzed, alright.
- **Midtown Espresso** • 2133 5th Ave
206-443-9070
Best breakfast sandwiches in town.
- **Street Bean Espresso** • 2702 3rd Ave
206-708-6803
Good coffee for a great cause: Helping kids get off the streets.
- **Uptown Espresso** • 2801 Alaskan Way
206-770-7777
Self-proclaimed "Home of the Velvet Foam" but the coffee underneath is just so-so.

- **Uptown Espresso** • 2504 4th Ave
206-441-1084
Self-proclaimed "Home of the Velvet Foam," but the coffee underneath is just so-so.
- **Wheelhouse Coffee** • 2113 Westlake Ave
206-467-0160
Serving Lighthouse coffee with a smile is totally in their wheelhouse.

##  Nightlife

- **101 Restaurant & Lounge** • 101 Denny Way
206-448-3035
Emphasis on the word "lounge."
- **The 5 Point Café** • 415 Cedar St
323-467-1175
Start and finish your Belltown adventure at this all-night joint.
- **Amber** • 2214 1st Ave
206-728-8500
If Maxim Magazine owned a bar.
- **Ampersand Lounge** • 113 Bell St
206-230-0830
Aaaaand it's another Belltown meat market you'd be wise to avoid.
- **Belltown Billiards & Lounge** • 90 Blanchard St
206-420-3146
It's all about balls.
- **Black Bottle** • 2600 1st Ave
206-441-1500
Damned if it ain't noisy, though the list is decent, and the flatbreads rule.
- **The Crocodile** • 2200 2nd Ave
206-441-4618
Legendary venue where some of Seattle's biggest names got their start.
- **Cyclops Café and Lounge** • 2421 1st Ave
206-441-1677
A tip of the fedora to old Belltown lounge days.
- **Far Eats** • 2301 5th Ave
206-770-3287
Above-average Indian tucked away in the quiet part of Belltown.
- **Foundation Nightclub** • 2218 Western Ave
206-535-7285
Top 40 and blurred lines galore.

- **Frontier Room** • 2203 1st Ave
206-956-7427
Cheap beer and BBQ happy hour. Addictive.
- **Henry and Oscar's** • 2525 4th Ave
206-448-2444
The Mad Men at SCDP would love it here, despite having to smoke outside.
- **Hula Hula** • 106 1st Ave N
206-284-5003
Drink BOWLS full of rum in this ultra tiki lounge.
- **Karma** • 2318 2nd Ave
206-838-6018
Karma can be good or bad. It just depends on the time of day.
- **Lava Lounge** • 2226 2nd Ave
206-441-5660
Free shuffleboard and a great '80s jukebox offer a refuge from Belltown yuppies.
- **List** • 2226 1st Ave
206-441-1000
Terrific weeknight happy hour. Typical B-Town douchery on weekends.
- **Palace Kitchen** • 2030 5th Ave
206-448-2001
Just getting started at midnight? Eat fine grub until 1 am, drink 'til 2 am.
- **Queen City Grill** • 2201 1st Ave
206-443-0975
Decent Northwest fare and loud Belltown crowd.
- **Rabbit Hole** • 2222 2nd Ave
206-956-4653
Worth jumping down, depsite squandered theme potential. Hush puppies.
- **Rendezvous** • 2322 2nd Ave
206-441-5823
Dive bar with a touch of old Hollywood class.
- **Rob Roy** • 2332 2nd Ave
206-956-8423
Linda's rather impressive attempt at swank. Two-fist Cristal with High Life.

- **Rocco's** • 2228 2nd Ave
206-448-2625
Pizza and cocktails from the crazy alcoholics who brought you Noc Noc.
- **Sarajevo Lounge** • 2332 1st Ave
206-448-9000
Party like the Bosians and/or Herzegovinians.
- **Shorty's** • 2222 2nd Ave
206-441-5449
Pinball, hot dogs, and booze: the Holy Trinity of Awesome.
- **Some Random Bar** • 2604 1st Ave
206-745-2185
Inventive menu, gorgeous decor, WORST NAME EVER.
- **Spitfire** • 2219 4th Ave
206-441-7966
"Urban sports bar" pleases all sorts with awesome happy hour.
- **Tia Lou** • 2218 1st Ave
206-733-8226
Happy hour patio: Muy bonita. Night crowd: El Douche.
- **Tini Bigs** • 100 Denny Way
206-284-0931
Be so very new millennium by heading back to the '50s at this martini lounge.
- **Twist** • 2313 1st Ave
206-448-9478
The twist is that you're the meat.
- **Umi Sake House** • 2230 1st Ave
206-374-8717
Late-night sushi happy hour in indoor zen garden!
- **The Upstairs** • 2209 2nd Ave
206-441-4013
A Hipstamatic wet dream.
- **Wasabi** • 2311 2nd Ave
206-441-6044
"Bistro" is Japanese for "Yuppie."
- **The Whiskey Bar** • 2122 2nd Ave
206-443-4490
Guess what their specialty is.

**Shorty's** is the closest thing to heaven in Seattle with pinball, booze, and hot dogs. **Cinerama** is a close second, offering one of the best movie-going experiences in the world. Other highlights include the Polynesian-tastic happy hour at **Ohana**, the Rat Pack drink experience at the **Rendezvous**, and a rock show at the legendary **Crocodile**.

# Restaurants

- **The 5 Point Café** • 415 Cedar St
  323-467-1175 • $
  24-hour bar/diner with decent food. Just don't piss off the wait staff.
- **Anthony's Bell Street Diner** • 2201 Alaskan Way
  206-448-6688 • $$$
  Casual (and affordable) offshoot of the popular Anthony's chain.
- **Anthony's Pier 66** • 2201 Alaskan Way
  206-448-6688 • $$$$
  Pacific Northwest chain on Elliott Bay.
- **Assaggio Ristorante** • 2010 4th Ave
  206-441-1399 • $$$$
  If you don't mind the tourists, some of the food is pretty good.
- **Bell Thai** • 2211 4th Ave
  206-441-8488 • $$
  Great lunch deals. Otherwise uninspiring.
- **Bellini Italian Bistro** • 2302 1st Ave
  206-441-4480 • $$
  Napoli-style pizza and pasta with the full Italian dining experience. You're too skinny.
- **Black Bottle** • 2600 1st Ave
  206-441-1500 • $$
  Fill your jowls with flatbread and wine to drown out the noise.
- **Boat Street Café** • 3131 Western Ave
  206-632-4602 • $$
  Traditional French selections with an unabashed use of cream.
- **Buffalo Deli** • 2123 1st Ave
  206-728-8759 • $
  Pretty much determined to have the best French dip in town.
- **Cafe Casbah** • 2219 2nd Ave
  206-728-1771 • $
  Coffee with a Mediterranean flair. Yes, the Casbah does rock.

- **CJ's Eatery** • 2619 1st Ave
  206-728-1648 • $$
  Delicious omelettes and amazing homemade chicken noodle soup.
- **The Crocodile** • 2200 2nd Ave
  206-441-4618 • $
  Serving wood-fired pizza late in the Back Bar.
- **Dahlia Lounge** • 2001 4th Ave
  206-682-4142 • $$$$
  Another gem in Tom Douglas's juggernaut. Great for dates.
- **El Camion** • 1021 Occidental Ave S
  206-659-0236 • $
  Amazing truck tacos and tamales you can trust.
- **El Gaucho** • 2505 1st Ave
  206-728-1337 • $$$$
  Super-luxurious surf and turf, best for impressing the pants off someone.
- **Far Eats** • 2301 5th Ave
  206-770-3287 • $$
  Above-average Indian tucked away in the quiet part of Belltown.
- **Flying Fish** • 2234 1st Ave
  206-728-8595 • $$$$
  Fish for the fresh-faced younger set.
- **Frontier Room** • 2203 1st Ave
  206-956-7427 • $$
  A welcome dive in the midst of Cosmo-laden Belltown.
- **The Grill from Ipanema** • 2313 1st Ave
  206-457-4885 • $$$
  A carnivore's paradise if you can get past the name and annoying website.
- **Holy Cannoli** • 2720 3rd Ave
  206-841-8205 • $
  Your Italian pastry & stromboli prayers have been answered.
- **Hook & Plow** • 2100 Alaskan Way
  206-256-1040 • $$
  Lackluster hotel (Marriott) restaurant disguised as a trendy gastropub.
- **Icon Grill** • 1935 5th Ave
  206-441-6330 • $$$
  Kitchsy-crazy interior and familiar favorites bumped up a notch.

- **The Innkeeper** • 2510 1st Ave
206-441-7817 • $$
You don't have to go home, but you can't stay here.
- **La Fontana Siciliana** • 120 Blanchard St
206-441-1045 • $$
Much-loved Sicilian spot.
- **La Vita E Bella** • 2411 2nd Ave
206-441-5322 • $$
Among the most deliciousest pizza crusts in town—crisp, chewy, perfect.
- **Local 360** • 2234 1st Ave
206-441-9360 • $$
Appealing to any degree of Seattlite, from kid to drunken foodie.
- **Lola** • 2000 4th Ave
206-441-1430 • $$
Always hoppin', so service can be spotty. Food's a little Greek and a lot delicious.
- **The Lucky Diner** • 2630 1st Ave
206-805-0133 • $$
Ultra-modern diner. Just a little too clean to be a greasy spoon.
- **Macrina Bakery & Café** • 2408 1st Ave
206-448-4032 • $$
Macrina's baked goods will make breakfast your most important meal.
- **Madhu Cuisine of India** • 2330 2nd Ave
206-441-7017 • $$
Indian restaurant with a hip, obscure DJ bar in the back.
- **Mama's Mexican Kitchen** • 2334 2nd Ave
206-728-6262 • $$
Kitschy Mexican cooking with a thing for Elvis (and cheese).
- **Marrakesh Moroccan Restaurant** • 2334 2nd Ave
206-956-0500 • $$$
Belly Dancer Had a Little Lamb.
- **Ohana** • 2207 1st Ave
206-956-9329 • $$
Pu-pus that are far from poo poo.
- **Palace Kitchen** • 2030 5th Ave
206-448-2001 • $$$
Gourmet late-night dining in Seattle? This is your spot.
- **Queen City Grill** • 2201 1st Ave
206-443-0975 • $$$$
Seafood's the focus, unless you count the horndogs hoping to score.

- **Restaurant Zoe** • 2137 2nd Ave
206-256-2060 • $$$
The brown butter-bathed ricotta gnudi is now officially Seattle legend.
- **Rocco's** • 2228 2nd Ave
206-448-2625 • $$
Pizza and cocktails from the crazy alcoholics who brought you Noc Noc.
- **Serious Pie** • 316 Virginia St
206-838-7388 • $$$
Truly amazing crust in tiny quarters.
- **Shiro's Sushi** • 2401 2nd Ave
206-443-9844 • $$$
Wait to sit at the bar, chat with Shiro, be utterly delighted.
- **Six Seven** • 2411 Alaskan Way
206-269-4575 • $$$$
Northwest seafood classics.
- **Some Random Bar** • 2604 1st Ave
206-745-2185 • $$
Inventive menu, gorgeous decor, WORST NAME EVER.
- **Tavolata** • 2323 2nd Ave
206-838-8008 • $$
Fantastically sexy space with handmade pastas to match.
- **Tilikum Place Café** • 407 Cedar St
206-282-4830 • $$
Euro flavors with a delightfully NW twist. Also sexy waitstaff.
- **Top Pot Doughnuts** • 2124 5th Ave
206-728-1966 • $
Top Pot is tops!
- **Two Bells** • 2313 4th Ave
206-441-3050 • $$
A rare old soul in trendy Belltown. Tasty burgers.
- **Wasabi** • 2311 2nd Ave
206-441-6044 • $$$$
Sushi rolls usually involving avocado or cream cheese. Not for purists.
- **The Yellow Leaf Cupcake Co.** • 2209 4th Ave
206-441-4240 • $
The next evolution of cupcakes.
- **Zeek's Pizza** • 419 Denny Way
206-285-8646 • $$
Pizzas with pizzazz, like the Thai version with peanut sauce.

Eating-wise, indulge on tasty baked goods at **Macrina**. For something a little more upscale, try the cozy and inventive flavors of **Tilikum Place Cafe**. And of course there are all those Tom Douglas places: **Dahlia Lounge**, **Lola**, **Serious Pie**, and **Palace Kitchen**—it seems like the list goes on and on. For more in the Top Chef vein, visit Ethan Stowell's **Tavolata**. Elsewhere, all the romance and intrigue of Morocco comes alive in the mysterious-looking **Marrakesh Moroccan Restaurant** And if 24-7 greasy grub is all you're after, try **The 5 Point Café**.

# Shopping

- **Boston St** • 1902 Post Alley
206-634-0580
The children's (somewhat smart ass, sometimes endearing) everything store.
- **Champion Party Supply** • 124 Denny Way
206-284-1980
From slutty nurse costumes to slutty werewolf costumes. And party supplies!
- **Dahlia Bakery** • 2001 4th Ave
206-441-4540
Take a hot steaming loaf of Tom Douglas home with you.

- **Kuhlman** • 2419 1st Ave
206-441-1999
Your friends Ben Sherman and Fred Perry live here.
- **Peter Miller Books** • 2326 2nd Ave
206-441-4114
Top-notch selection of architecture and design books.
- **Rudy's Barbershop** • 89 Wall St
206-448-8900
Absolute best cheap haircut.
- **Singles Going Steady** • 2219 2nd Ave
206-441-7396
Terrific range of new/used punk and indie music sold by friendly crusties.

What do you get the man who has everything? How about a neighborhood? For years, Paul Allen sought to make this warehouse wasteland into a destination. Once Amazon.com moved in, he finally succeeded. Tom Douglas followed with a handful of restaurants and condos sprung up to house the young professionals the 'hood is designed to ensnare. Naturally, these people will shop at Whole Foods. However, you still won't catch anyone local riding the S.L.U.T.

## ○ Landmarks

- **Elephant Car Wash** • 616 Battery St
  206-441-6776
  That giant pink elephant in the sky.

## Coffee

- **Espresso Vivace** • 227 Yale Ave N
  206-388-5164
  Coffee so good it makes you purr.
- **Motore Coffee** • 1904 9th Ave
  206-388-2803
  A coffee house for those that ride a scootere.
- **Zoka Coffee Roaster & Tea Company** •
  351 Boren Ave
  206-545-4277
  A true Seattle original.

## Nightlife

- **13 Coins** • 125 Boren Ave N
  206-682-2513
  Sometimes you just gotta blow $50 on steak and lobster at 3 am.
- **Brave Horse Tavern** • 310 Terry Ave N
  206-971-0717
  Get blotto the Tom Douglas way.
- **Dimitriou's Jazz Alley** • 2033 6th Ave
  206-441-9729
  Seattle's longstanding jazz venue. Let them entertain you.
- **El Corazon** • 109 Eastlake Ave E
  206-262-0482
  If you like your punk and metal with a little teenager.
- **Feierabend** • 422 Yale Ave N
  206-340-2528
  Grab a bier and make new friends. Prost.
- **The Hurricane Café** • 2230 7th Ave
  206-682-5858
  For the show after the show.
- **Lo-Fi** • 429 Eastlake Ave E
  206-254-2824
  A dance club for grownups and young folks with refined musical taste.
- **Re-Bar** • 1114 Howell St
  206-233-9873
  Fringe theater, live music, and decidedly drag-friendly. Experience the unexpected.
- **Soul Wine** • 401 Westlake Ave N
  206-436-2350
  Fill up on vino while you wait for your table at Serious Pie.

## Restaurants

- **13 Coins** • 125 Boren Ave N
206-682-2513 • $$$
Sometimes you just gotta blow $50 on steak and lobster at 3 am.
- **314 Pie** • Boren Ave
206-701-9233 • $$
Aussie pies by locally based Aussiephiles will ensure you a g'day.
- **The Berliner Döner Kebab** • 428 Westlake Ave N
206-838-5032 • $
A very Seattle gyrocery with tofu instead of falafel.
- **Cactus** • 350 Terry Ave N
206-913-2250 • $$
Legendary local chain, serving outstanding mojitos and Mexican.
- **Café Suisse** • 2008 Westlake Ave
206-633-3876 • $
This bona fide Swiss cafe is not to be missed.
- **Caffè Torino** • 422 Yale Ave N
206-682-2099 • $
Helping Seattle to keep its superior coffee reputation.
- **Cuoco** • 301 Terry Ave N
206-971-0710 • $$$
Italian food with bellissimo results.
- **FareStart** • 700 Virginia St
206-267-7601 • $$
Eat well, feel great: FareStart trains the disadvantaged to launch new lives as chefs.
- **Happy Grillmore** • Harrison & Boren Ave N
206-486-0797 • $
Fatty burgers that are way better than Adam Sandler's last 10 movies..
- **Hot Dog King** • 400 Westlake Ave
206-327-4847 • $
Long live the king!
- **The Hurricane Café** • 2230 7th Ave
206-682-5858 • $
24-hour diner with full bar. Start or end your day with cheap, greasy eggs.
- **Kaosamai Thai Cook Truck** • 970 Denny Way
206-349-6533 • $
Exactly what you would expect: Thai food out of a truck.
- **La Lot** • 925 Stewart St
206-682-8812 • $$
If you're into Vietnamese fusion, you'll like this place la lot.
- **La Toscanella Bakery & Paninoteca** • 116 Westlake Ave N
206-682-1044 • $
An authentic-as-hell Italian bakery and cafe with cannoli and everything!
- **Lunchbox Laboratory** • 1253 Thomas St
206-621-1090 • $
Stunning burger specimens—the "dork" is a thing of beauty.
- **Mio Sushi** • 120 Westlake Ave N
206-971-0069 • $$
Franchise sushi that will do in a pinch.
- **Mistral Kitchen** • 2020 Westlake Ave
206-623-1922 • $$$
Got cash? Splurge for the 8 course menu.
- **Off the Rez** • Boren & Harrison
206-414-8226 • $
The Native American flatbread tacos that will change your life. Fatter, maybe. But blissfully satiated.
- **Outside the Box** • 411 Fairview Ave S
425-272-5361 • $$
Since that Paleo thing doesn't seem to be going away, here's a food truck that parks outside Crossfit gyms.
- **Portage Bay Cafe** • 391 Terry Ave N
206-462-6400 • $$
Local organic breakfasts and lunches.

If you like Tom Douglas restaurants (and what's not to like?), you'll be pleased as hand-crafted locally made punch to dine here. Experience a welcome re-invention of Italian cuisine at **Cuoco**, take in a sporting match at the **Brave Horse Tavern** or brunch with the family at **Portage Bay Café**. If you're hiding tattoos under your work shirt, you may be more comfortable at **Hurricane Café**.

- **Re:public** • 429 Westlake Ave N
  206-467-5300 • $$$
  A republic worth standing for.
- **Serious Pie** • 401 Westlake Ave N
  206-436-0500 • $$
  It's worth the potentially long wait. SERIOUSLY.
- **Serious Biscuit** • 401 Westlake Ave N
  206-436-0050 • $
  Leave it to Tom Douglas to make the breakfast sandwich more decadent.
- **Shilla Restaurant** • 2300 8th Ave
  206-623-9996 • $$
  Menu is a crash-course in Korean Food 101. Impressive panchan.
- **Skinny Phoenix** • Harrison & Boren Ave N
  253-293-9226 • $
  I don't know how the phoenix stays so skinny eating breakfast pizza.
- **Top Pot Doughnuts** • 590 Terry Ave N
  206-995-8296 • $
  Top Pot is tops!
- **Tutta Bella** • 2200 Westlake Ave
  206-624-4422 • $$
  Excellent pizza for new condo owners.
- **Veggie Grill** • 446 Terry Ave N
  206-623-0336 • $$
  Santa Monica-based chain offers up the ultimate in vegetarian comfort food.
- **Venik Lounge** • 227 9th Ave N
  206-223-3734 • $
  The Russians know vodka and caviar. Swanky.
- **Xplosive Mobile Food Truck** • 425 Terry Ave
  206-612-4739 • $$
  Asian fusion taste explosions.
- **Zaw** • 434 Yale Ave N
  206-623-0299 • $$
  It's not delivery. It's artisan take-and-bake.

## Shopping

- **Eurostyle Your Life** • 2008 Westlake Ave
  206-633-3876
  Cool products from Europe and the US.
- **Play it Again Sports** • 1304 Stewart St
  206-264-9255
  Used sports equipment, check here before walking the block to REI.
- **REI** • 222 Yale Ave N
  206-223-1944
  The granola flagship store with an impressive rock wall.

Like most downtowns, Seattle's mainly caters to tourists, consumers, and the work-a-day crowd. Therefore department stores, happy hours, and Starbucks are plentiful. But fancy condos are starting to spring up on every block, and more people are calling this 'hood home. You can get your culture on at **Benaroya Hall** or the **Seattle Art Museum**. Westlake Center is flavor country in terms of colorful characters, religious zealots, and the occasional "Personality Test" booth.

## ○ Landmarks

- **5th Avenue Theatre** • 1308 5th Ave
  206-625-1900
  Lavish Chinese-inspired interior. Cheesy shows.
- **The Blade** • 2nd Ave & Pike St
  Used to be crack and coke. Now it's condos and coffee.
- **Columbia Center** • 701 5th Ave
  Tallest building in Seattle with an observation deck on the 73rd floor.
- **Freeway Park** • 700 Seneca St
  206-684-4075
  Unique urban park. Bonus points for making it out alive.
- **Giant Rotating Shuttlecock** •
  Western Ave & Lenora St
  Officially known as Angie's Umbrella.
- **The Great Wheel** • 1301 Alaskan Way
  206-623-8600
  Buy tickets online to save yourself an hour+ wait before you wait some more. And keep in mind it's just a ferris wheel.
- **The Hammering Man** • 100 University St
  206-654-3100
  Jonathan Borofsky's mechanized sculpture looms over the SAM.
- **Paramount Theatre** • 911 Pine St
  206-682-1414
  Former vaudeville theater houses a rare Wurlitzer organ.
- **Pike Place Market** • 1501 Pike Pl
  206-682-7453
  So authentic even locals shop here!
- **Pike Place Market Gum Wall** •
  Lower Post Alley & Pike St
  The most unlikely public art created by thousands of wads of masticated gum.
- **Rachel the Piggy Bank** • Pike St & Pike Pl
  Meeting point for internet daters.

- **Rainier Tower** • 1301 5th Ave
  Architect Minoru Yamasaki also designed the World Trade Center in NYC.
- **Seattle Art Museum Downtown** • 1300 1st Ave
  206-654-3100
  A museum named SAM.
- **Seattle Central Library** • 1000 4th Ave
  206-386-4636
  Koolhaas designed. Stunning inside and out. Free tours.
- **Starbucks** • 1912 Pike Pl
  206-448-8762
  Original store (but not original location); where it all began.

##  Coffee

- **Ancient Grounds** • 1220 1st Ave
  206-749-0747
  Part art gallery, part coffee joint.
- **Caffe Appassionato** • 801 Alaskan Way
  206-264-2500
  Classic Seattle coffee shop vibe at this small-ish local chain. Frasier would love it here.
- **Caffe D'Arte** • 1625 2nd Ave
  206-728-4468
  Italian-style espresso.
- **Caffe Ladro** • 108 Union St
  206-267-0600
  Strong coffee for the strong coffee drinker.
- **Caffe Ladro** • 801 Pine St
  206-405-1950
  Strong coffee for the strong coffee drinker.
- **Cherry Street Coffee House** • 1212 1st Ave
  206-264-9372
  Good coffee, nice staff, but the owner added a sick leave surcharge to protest a city mandate. Not cool.
- **Cherry Street Coffee House** • 103 Cherry St
  206-621-9372
  Good coffee, nice staff, but the owner added a sick leave surcharge to protest a city mandate. Not cool.

- **Cherry Street Coffee House** • 808 3rd Ave
  206-442-9372
  Good coffee, nice staff, but the owner added a sick leave surcharge to protest a city mandate. Not cool.
- **Diva Espresso** • 401 5th Ave
  206-682-2173
  Local chain with unpredictable service. I guess it's kind of like ordering coffee from a diva.
- **Espresso Caffe Dior** • 725 Pike St
  206-624-0814
  Also sandwiches.
- **Ghost Alley Espresso** • 1499 Post Alley
  206-805-0195
  Have a spiritual coffee experience next to the infamous wall of masticated gum corpses.
- **Monorail Espresso** • 520 Pike St
  206-625-0449
  Their product is a whole hell of a lot more useful than the actual monorail. Tastier too.
- **Moore Coffee Shop** • 1930 2nd Ave
  206-728-5668
  Nutella latte. Need I say Moore?
- **Nordstrom eBar** • 500 Pine St
  206-628-2111
  Nothing special, but hey, it's right there.
- **Pegasus Coffee Bar** • 711 3rd Ave
  206-682-3113
  Bainbridge Island roasters' downtown location.
- **Pegasus Coffee Bar** • 1218 3rd Ave
  206-292-3013
  Bainbridge Island roasters' downtown location.
- **Phoenix Cafe** • 1017 3rd Ave
  206-466-1906
  Serving Fonte coffee with their own fiery twist.
- **Seattle Coffee Works** • 107 Pike St
  206-340-8867
  To these guys, making coffee is not work.
- **Simon's Espresso Cafe** • 925 4th Ave
  206-957-4545
  The best thing going in this particular office building. May even some of the surrounding ones.
- **Voxx Coffee** • 1200 6th Ave
  206-682-1242
  A welcoming shop with tons of outlets. Take off your coat and stay a while.

##  Nightlife

- **Alibi Room** • 85 Pike St
  206-623-3180
  Dark, underground bar with a lounge feel.
- **Athenian** • 1517 Pike Pl
  206-624-7166
  Drink with other Pike Place Market alcoholics.
- **BOKA** • 1010 1st Ave
  206-357-9000
  Terrific happy hour food. Otherwise a boka bore.
- **Can Can** • 94 Pike St
  206-652-0832
  1940s cabaret is alive and well. Make reservations EARLY.
- **Contour** • 807 1st Ave
  206-447-7704
  Ongoing mix 'em up of live and DJ'd music.
- **The Diller Room** • 1224 1st Ave
  206-467-4042
  Cozy booths and cozier food with an Italian flare.
- **Fado Irish Pub** • 801 1st Ave
  206-264-2700
  More like Frat-O.
- **The Forge Lounge** • 65 Marion St
  206-623-5107
  Grab a sandwich and a drink to help you stomach ferry travel.
- **GameWorks** • 1511 7th Ave
  206-521-0952
  Another dateless Friday night.
- **Kells** • 1916 Post Alley
  206-728-1916
  Where everybody gets a little Irish in them.
- **The Lobby Bar** • 916 Pike St
  206-328-6703
  You won't mind hanging around in a lobby this nice.
- **Moore Theatre** • 1932 2nd Ave
  206-467-5510
  Architecturally stunning performance hall.
- **Nitelite Lounge** • 1926 2nd Ave
  206-443-0899
  Lethal drinks and Johnny Cash comfort lonely hearts and ironic hipsters.

No national telecast is complete without the requisite fish-flinging shot from **Pike Place Market**. Less heralded, but just as impressive, is the mastication celebration of the **Gum Wall** there. If you're going to patronize a Starbucks, it might as well be the coffee behemoth's original Pike Place store. Rem Koolhaas' **Seattle Central Library** is as advertised, and provides a satisfying architectural counterpoint to the Space Age nostalgia just north of here.

Map

- **Oliver's Lounge** • 405 Olive Way
  206-623-8700
  Feel wealthier and classier by buying overpriced martinis in a posh hotel scene.
- **The Owl & Thistle** • 808 Post Ave
  206-621-7777
  In true Irish fashion, you'll probably witness a fight.
- **Paramount Theatre** • 911 Pine St
  206-682-1414
  Opulent theater showcasing big-name musicals, concerts, and events.
- **Purple Café & Wine Bar** • 1225 4th Ave
  206-829-2280
  Dramatic in size, selection, and ambiance. Suits abound.
- **Showbox at the Market** • 1426 1st Ave
  206-628-3151
  Superb sight lines and crystalline sound on the city's biggest nightclub stage.
- **Suite 410** • 410 Stewart St
  206-682-4101
  For those who miss pretentious L.A. bars.
- **Trace Bar** • 1112 4th Ave
  206-264-6060
  A bit of New York swank, if you're into that.
- **The Triple Door** • 216 Union St
  206-838-4333
  Live music venue with a Vegas nightclub slant.
- **Virginia Inn** • 1937 1st Ave
  206-728-1937
  A one-drink destination.
- **Von's Gustobistro** • 1225 1st Ave
  206-621-8667
  Red meat, Manhattans, and Martinis.
- **White Horse Trading Company** • 1908 Post Alley
  206-441-7767
  Top-secret English pub and bookstore. Enjoy a hearthside ale.
- **Yard House** • 1501 4th Ave
  206-682-2087
  Cheesecake Factory-themed pub tries to be all things to all people and falls short.
- **Zig Zag Café** • 1501 Western Ave
  206-625-1146
  Fitzgerald-esque cocktail lounge.

# 🍴 Restaurants

- **Andaluca** • 407 Olive Way
  206-382-6999 • $$$$
  Tasty upscale tapas will have you exclaiming "¡Qué sabroso!"
- **Bakeman's** • 122 Cherry St
  206-622-3375 • $
  The plump turkey sandwiches are dirt-cheap, and damn tasty.
- **Belle Epicurean** • 1206 4th Ave
  206-262-9404 • $
  Inspired French pastries served with snooty attitude.
- **Blueacre Seafood** • 1700 7th Ave
  206-659-0737 • $$$
  Steelhead proprietor successfully branches out to the water.
- **The Brooklyn** • 1212 2nd Ave
  206-224-7000 • $$$$
  Gulp down the oysters (the specialty here) in old-Seattle elegance.
- **Cafe ABoDegas** • 1303 6th Ave
  206-624-9999 • $
  They aim to please even the gluten-freest among you.
- **Café Campagne** • 1600 Post Alley
  206-728-2233 • $$$
  Campagne's more laid-back sister. And the absolute best brunch downtown.
- **Cafe Fonté** • 1321 1st Ave
  206-777-6193 • $$
  Lovely cafe across from the SAM serving locally sourced everything.
- **Cafe Zum Zum** • 823 3rd Ave
  206-622-7391 • $
  Giant affordable lunch that is yum yum.
- **Caffe Lieto** • 1909 1st Ave
  206-441-7999 • $
  Weekend nights, mannered Lieto becomes the Biscuit Bitch. And that's a bitch you DO want to trifle with.

- **Campagne** • 86 Pine St
206-728-2800 • $$$$
Frenchified Northwest loved for 20 years by tourists and locals alike.
- **Coffee and…A Specialty Bakery** •
1500 Western Ave
206-280-7946 • $$
The ellipsis stands for gluten free baked goods galore.
- **The Crumpet Shop** • 1503 1st Ave
206-682-1598 • $
Fresh, buttery crumpets with sweet or savory toppings. Not just for Brits!
- **Dilettante Mocha Cafe** • 400 Pine St
206-903-8595 • $$
Just skip dinner and indulge in a chocolate dessert orgy. You deserve it.
- **Dilettante Mocha Café** • 1300 5th Ave
206-223-1644 • $$
Just skip dinner and indulge in a chocolate dessert orgy. You deserve it.
- **Dragonfish** • 722 Pine St
206-467-7777 • $$
Pop-culture Asian that takes a ride around the Pacific Rim.
- **El Borracho** • 1521 1st Ave
206-538-0440 • $$
Mellow Mexican cafe with plenty of tequila to get you borracho. (There's a family section too).
- **El Puerco Lloron** • 1501 Western Ave
206-624-0541 • $
Cafeteria-style served carnitas and corn tortillas, which are fantastico.
- **Elliot's Oyster House** • 1201 Alaskan Way
206-623-4340 • $$$
Get messy with the cioppino.
- **Emmett Watson's Oyster Bar** • 1916 Pike Pl
206-448-7721 • $$
Seattle's very first oyster bar, appropriately shabby—in a good way.
- **Etta's** • 2020 Western Ave
206-443-6000 • $$$
Fresh seafood from Tommy D.
- **Fonte Cafe & Wine Bar** • 1321 1st Ave
206-777-6193 • $$
Fontastic coffee and gourmet eats.
- **Gelatiamo** • 1400 3rd Ave

206-467-9563 • $
Some tasty pastries and heavenly gelato.
- **The Georgian** • 411 University St
206-621-7889 • $$$$$
For impressing the spouse, the in-laws, or your boss.
- **Hard Rock Cafe** • 116 Pike St
206-204-2233 • $$
Party like it's 1994.
- **Il Bistro** • 93 Pike St
206-682-3049 • $$$$
Decent Italian off the Market; nice scotch selection
- **Il Fornaio** • 600 Pine St
206-264-0994 • $$
If you must eat in a mall, this place has edible Italian.
- **Jack's Fish Spot** • 1514 Pike Pl
206-467-0514 • $
No-nonsense counter that embodies the soul of the Market—for better or worse.
- **Japonessa Sushi Cocina** • 1400 1st Ave
206-971-7979 • $$$
If you've ever wondered what Asian Tapas tasted like, mystery solved.
- **Katsoori Grill** • 94 Stewart St
206-441-5456 • $$
A lunch buffet that tastes like fine dining.
- **La Creperie Voila** • 707 Pike St
206-447-2737 • $$
In the eating wasteland that is the Convention Center, Voila is your warm, buttery salvation.
- **Le Panier** • 1902 Pike Pl
206-441-3669 • $$
Win popularity by doling out their macaroons— they will blow you away.
- **Le Pichet** • 1933 1st Ave
206-256-1499 • $$
Eat roast chicken. Drink beaujolais. Pretend you're in Paris. Save airfare.
- **Lecosho** • 89 University St
206-623-2101 • $$
If you like eating pig, they provide numerous ways to do it.
- **Library Bistro** • 92 Madison St
206-624-3646 • $$
Swanky yet unfussy, and the food is equally lovely
- **Long Provincial Vietnamese Restaurant** •

Grab a bar stool at the **Zig Zag** for a stiff cocktail. **The Showbox** and the **Moore** have top-notch music calendars, and the **Paramount Theatre** hosts all things to all people, big and small. Jazz it up with the cool kats at **Can Can**. Disregard the hipsters and glass-gaze the lethal drinks at the **Nitelite**.

1901 2nd Ave
206-443-6266 • $$
Modern Vietnamese cuisine in a dark, posh hole.

• **Mae Phim Thai Restaurant** • 94 Columbia St
206-624-2979 • $
Enormous portions of slightly authentic Thai for not much more than a fiver.

• **Marché** • 86 Pine St
206-728-2800 • $$
A portal to Paris, right down to the snooty attitude.

• **Market Grill** • 1509 Pike Pl
206-682-2654 • $
Homemade chowder and blackened salmon sandwiches are worth the wait.

• **Matt's in the Market** • 94 Pike St
206-467-7909 • $$$
Market-fresh produce and fish tossed up to the second floor window? It's magic.

• **Maximilien** • 81 Pike St
206-682-7270 • $$$
Classic French in all its butter-sauced glory; classy and cheap happy hour.

• **Maximus Minimus** • 2nd Ave & Pike St
206-601-5510 • $
Yummy BBQ served out of a giant metal pig.

• **McCormick & Schmick's** • 1103 1st Ave
206-623-5500 • $$$
Corporate club vibe and an unparalleled $1.95 happy hour burger.

• **McCormick's Fish House & Bar** • 722 4th Ave
206-682-3900 • $$$
Corporate club vibe with weekly oyster specials.

• **Mee Sum Pastry** • 1526 Pike Pl
206-682-6780 • $
Marvelous buns.

• **Metropolitan Grill** • 820 2nd Ave
206-624-3287 • $$$$$
Martinis, mahogany and meat.

• **Morton's The Steakhouse** • 1511 6th Ave
206-223-0550 • $$$$$
Yet another dark-wood, clubby, pricey steakhouse. Tableside service.

• **Osaka Grill** • 128 Pike St
206-340-1793 • $
Worth braving the grime for tasty teriyaki.

• **The Pink Door** • 1919 Post Alley
206-443-3241 • $$

Acceptable Italian, cranky servers. And sometimes people swing from trapezes.

• **Place Pigalle** • 81 Pike St
206-624-1756 • $$$$
Great views highlight a nice seafood menu.

• **Potbelly Sandwich Shop** • 1429 4th Ave
206-623-0099 • $
Decent sandwich chain, giving Specialities a run for their money.

• **Potbelly Sandwich Shop** • 1111 3rd Ave
206-204-0079 • $
Decent sandwich chain, giving Specialities a run for their money.

• **Purple Café & Wine Bar** • 1225 4th Ave
206-829-2280 • $$$
Tome-like wine list can be intimidating; food is upscale café fare.

• **Rachel's Ginger Beer** • 1530 Post Alley
206-467-4924 • $
A craft soda fountain with a booze option. Finally, something that's truly fun for the whole family.

• **RN74** • 1433 4th Ave
206-456-7474 • $$$
The highway to fancy pants.

• **Rview** • 515 Madison St
206-583-0300 • $$$
Seafood and a view that would make Frasier jealous.

• **Sazerac** • 1101 4th Ave
206-624-7755 • $$$$
Trendy twists on Southern classics. Upscale-tacky interior.

• **Seatown** • 2010 Western Ave
206-436-0390 • $$
Snacks a la Tom Douglas: You either love him or are an idiot.

• **Shuckers** • 411 University St
206-621-1984 • $$$$
Slick business-y types slurp oysters and sign deals.

• **Steelhead Diner** • 95 Pine St
206-625-0129 • $$
Pitch-perfect dishes exude the essence of Seattle and the Northwest.

• **Street Donuts** •
206-414-7410 • $
Donuts made fresh in front of your face! On the street!

Map 3

# Downtown

- **Sullivan's Steakhouse** • 621 Union St
206-494-4442 • $$$
Steaks, martinis and jazz…if you're into that sort of thing.
- **Sweet Iron Waffles** • 1200 3rd Ave
206-682-3336 • $$
Like the waffle house. But only waffles.
- **Tap House Grill** • 1506 6th Ave
206-816-3314 • $$
160 beers on tap. We repeat: 160 beers. On tap.
- **Three Girls Bakery** • 1514 Pike Pl
206-622-1045 • $
The sandwiches are classic, no frills, and the hands-down favorite.
- **Top Pot Doughnuts** • 720 3rd Ave
206-454-3694 • $
Top Pot is tops!
- **Trace** • 1112 4th Ave
206-264-6060 • $$$$
Find your culinary center piled high and gorgeous on the plate. Renowned.
- **Tulio Ristorante** • 1100 5th Ave
206-624-5500 • $$$$
Fancified Italian dishes loved by businesspeople. Great service.

- **Turkish Delight** • 1930 Pike Pl
206-443-1387 • $
Brave the Market crowd for the 3-buck lentil soup.
- **Urbane** • 1639 8th Ave
206-676-4600 • $$$$
Hit the happy hour or convince the boss to bring the corporate card.
- **Von's Gustobistro** • 1225 1st Ave
206-621-8667 • $$
Red meat, Manhattans, and Martinis.
- **Wild Ginger** • 1401 3rd Ave
206-623-4450 • $$$
Wildly overrated, but still remains an eternal favorite.
- **Wild Rye Cafe Bakery** • 806 Pike St
206-694-5049 • $
Where you can find quiet neighborhood feeling right smack in downtown.
- **Yard House** • 1501 4th Ave
206-682-2087 • $$
Cheesecake Factory-themed pub tries to be all things to all people and falls short.
- **Zaccagni's** • 97 Pike St
206-765-6605 • $
Italian hot sandwiches with a small but solid menu. Eggplant parm for the herbivores.

As far as seafood goes, and as far as highbrow is concerned, **Matt's in the Market** gives a true taste of Pike Place while Tom Douglas serves up calamari and Copper River salmon for his adoring fans at **Etta's Seafood**. If thy lower brow, gorge thee at **Emmett Watson's** or **Jack's**. For the landlubber, the best ginger beer you ever tasted, guaranteed, is at **Rachel's**.

##  Shopping

- **American Apparel** • 1504 6th Ave
  206-381-3400
  Soft t-shirts and free porn!
- **Baby and Company** • 1936 1st Ave
  206-448-4077
  Want to pay to dress like you live in Manhattan?
  Try here.
- **BB Ranch** • 94 Pike St
  206-299-8486
  Where happy farm animals died for your dinner.
- **Beecher's Handmade Cheese** • 1600 Pike Pl
  206-956-1964
  Stop in everyday for a free sample and then buy
  the place out.
- **Bergman Luggage** • 1901 3rd Ave
  206-448-3000
  Serious baggage for serious travelers.
- **Bottega Italiana** • 1425 1st Ave
  206-343-0200
  Seattle's best gelato.
- **Chocolate Box** • 108 Pine St
  206-443-3900
  Think Willy Wonka's Chocolate Factory.

- **The Confectional** • 1530 Pike Pl
  206-257-6597
  The real sin is skipping dessert.
- **DeLaurenti Specialty Food & Wine** • 1435 1st Ave
  206-622-0141
  Euro-snacks that you craved during that summer
  abroad.
- **Diva Dollz** • 624 1st Ave
  206-652-2299
  Bettie Page would have loved this place.
- **Don & Joe's Meats** • 85 Pike St
  206-682-7670
  Old-school butcher shop.
- **Dragon's Toy Box** • 1521 1st Ave
  206-652-2333
  If you don't believe in magic, this place will make
  you wish you did.
- **First and Pike News** • 93 Pike St
  206-624-0140
  Classic Pike Place Market newstand.
- **Gian DeCaro Sartoria** • 2025 1st Ave
  206-448-2812
  Gian transforms your Polartek boy into a suave
  Italian lover.

- **Golden Age Collectibles** • 1501 Pike Pl
206-622-9799
Essential geek merchandise.
- **The Good Coffee Company** • 818 Post Ave
206-622-5602
Stock up on your at-home caffeinated needs.
- **Hair Fair Wig Shop** • 124 Pike St
206-623-9430
The Blade's best and only wig shop. RIP Wigland.
- **Ian** • 1919 2nd Ave
206-441-4055
I don't know who this Ian person is, but he must
be loaded.
- **Isadora's** • 1601 1st Ave
206-441-7711
The queen of vintage. Prices to match.
- **Left Bank Books Collective** • 92 Pike St
206-622-0195
Anarchist, revolution, Chomsky—everything that
made the '60s great.
- **Leroy Mens' Wear** • 201 Pike St
206-682-1033
Classy duds for classy dudes.
- **Market Magic** • 1501 Pike Pl
206-624-4271
Make your social life magically disappear.
- **Market Optical** • 1906 Pike Pl
206-448-7739
Contact lenses are so yesterday. Whack out with
really expensive frames.
- **Marketspice** • 85 Pike St
206-622-6340
This is one of those times when you should believe
the hype. Marketspice Tea is the shiz.

- **Metsker Maps** • 1511 1st Ave
206-623-8747
A geographer's paradise.
- **Mt. Townsend Creamery** • 89 Pike St
206-743-9059
You'll need to climb a mountain to burn off all that
cheesy goodness.
- **Nordstrom** • 500 Pine St
206-628-2111
It all began here: The legendary customer service,
the fine designer goods.
- **Nordstrom Rack** • 400 Pine St
206-448-8522
Nordstrom stuff, a half season later and much
cheaper. Go for the shoes.
- **Paris Grocery** • 1418 Western Ave
206-682-0679
That's a baguette in my pocket AND I'm glad to
see you.
- **Perennial Tea Room** • 1910 Post Alley
206-448-4054
All tea all the time. Stock up for your favorite tea
addict.
- **Pike Place Market Creamery** • 1514 Pike Pl
206-622-5029
Who can resist Nancy Nipples' dairy products?
- **Pure Food Fish Market** • 1515 Pike Pl
206-622-5765
No flying fish, just great seafood and service.
- **Rachel's Ginger Beer** • 1530 Post Alley
206-467-4924
It's a tad pricey, but guaranteed to be the best
ginger beer you've ever tasted.

Get up early, brave the tourists, and shop like a local at **Pike Place Market**. The fresh food and flowers are all worth sticking out the crowds. That said, if you really can't bear the thought of seeing your dinner marched on the aquacultural perpwalk that is the **Pike Place Fish Market**, go to **Harry at Pure Food Fish**. Raise your cholesterol levels at **Beecher's Handmade Cheese**. And return your old car tires at the original **Nordstrom**.

- **Sandylew** • 1408 1st Ave
  206-903-0303
  Clothes for offbeat cougars and independent ladies.
- **Schmancy** • 1932 2nd Ave
  206-728-8008
  Coolest stuffed animals ever.
- **Seattle Art Museum Shop** • 1300 3rd Ave
  206-654-3100
  Rent art for your new condo. Reasonable prices on contemporary art for rent.
- **Seattle Mystery Bookshop** • 117 Cherry St
  206-587-5737
  It's all here. Detective fiction, suspense, thrillers, true crime.
- **Sephora** • 415 Pine St
  206-624-7003
  All the make-up you can dream-up in one store.
- **Sneaker City** • 110 Pike St
  206-621-7923
  Fill your proverbial wazoo full of sneakers.
- **The Spanish Table** • 1426 Western Ave
  206-682-2827
  Catherine sends you home with fine sherries and fixings for tapas.
- **Sway & Cake** • 1631 6th Ave
  206-624-2699
  Fun, flirty LA labels for the ladies. Cake not included.
- **Teavana** • 600 Pine St
  206-623-3581
  Come as you are. But bring your credit card.

- **Tenzing Momo** • 93 Pike St
  206-623-9837
  Herbs, teas, incense, tarot readings. Get your hippie supplies here.
- **Top Ten Toys** • 600 Pine St
  206-623-1370
  Classic, teaching, affordable toys that won't bum a kid out either.
- **Twist** • 600 Pine St
  206-315-8080
  Gorgeous jewelry, eclectic ceramics, and other fine, expensive breakables.
- **Uli's Famous Sausage** • 1511 Pike Pl
  206-839-1712
  Tasty sausagefest.
- **Vain** • 2018 1st Ave
  206-441-3441
  Hair. Shop. Art.
- **Watson Kennedy Fine Home** • 1022 1st Ave
  206-652-8350
  Their largest shop dedicated to an eclectic mix of fun goods.
- **Watson Kennedy Fine Living** • 86 Pine St
  206-443-6281
  Swanky Frenchy things your lady friends will like.
- **Zanadu Comics** • 1923 3rd Ave
  206-443-1316
  The best place to satisfy the new comics Wednesday jones.

If you absolutely have to get sick, try to do it on "Pill Hill," where numerous hospitals, medical centers, and private practices make having a heart attack or getting injured downright convenient. Meanwhile, the nearby Pike/Pine corridor is the epicenter of Seattle hipster culture, where twenty-something bohemians waste their youth in assorted tattoo parlors, carefully-designed dive bars, and vintage clothing stores. Stop by **Stumptown**, **Victrola**, or **Bauhaus** for your caffeine fix.

#  Landmarks

- **The Elliott Bay Book Company** • 1521 10th Ave
206-624-6600
Flagship establishment of the Seattle literary scene.
- **Jimi Hendrix Statue** • Broadway & E Pine St
Tribute to the wailing guitar god.

# 🎮 Coffee

- **Bauhaus Books & Coffee** • 414 E Pine St
206-625-1600
A little pretentious but so worth it.
- **Black Coffee** • 501 E Pine St
347-541-8694
A vegan cafe with a mission (shocking, I know). But they're also pretty cool and make good grub.
- **Broadcast Coffee** • 1623 Bellevue Ave
206-467-4717
Broadcasting the best of Seattle products including Stumptown, Mighty O and Macrina.
- **Caffe Vita** • 1005 E Pike St
206-709-4440
The best of the local chains.
- **Cherry Street Coffee House** • 1223 E Cherry St
206-454-3592
Good coffee, nice staff, but the owner added a sick leave surcharge to protest a city mandate. Not cool.
- **Cupcake Royale/Verite Coffee** • 1111 E Pike St
202-883-7656
Coffee and cupcakes go well together.
- **Diva Espresso** • 502 9th Ave
206-724-0658
Local chain with unpredictable service. I guess it's kind of like ordering coffee from a diva.
- **Elliott Bay Cafe** • 1521 10th Ave
206-436-8482
A cafe so nice they built it twice.
- **Kaladi Brothers Coffee** • 517 E Pike St
206-388-1700
Alaskan coffee pioneers behind something amazing called the Sivetz Air Roasting method.
- **Pettirosso** • 1101 E Pike St
206-324-2233
Gem of a coffeehouse.

- **Porchlight Coffee & Records** • 1318 E Pike St
206-329-5461
Herkimer Coffee and new & used vinyl.
- **Stumptown Coffee Roasters** • 616 E Pine St
206-329-0115
Puddletown favorite heads north.
- **Stumptown Coffee Roasters** • 1115 12th Ave
206-323-1544
Puddletown favorite heads north.
- **Uncle Elizabeth's Internet Café** • 1123 Pike St
206-381-1600
Kind of a dying breed but the name is funny.
- **Victrola Roastery and Cafe** • 310 E Pike St
206-624-1725
From a time before coffee was good.

# 🍸 Nightlife

- **611 Supreme** • 611 E Pine St
206-328-0292
Crepes by day, DJs at night.
- **95 Slide** • 722 E Pike St
206-328-7666
A sports bar for socially conscious hipsters who love their M's and S's.
- **Artusi** • 1535 14th Ave
206-678-2516
Small food menu & disappointing beer selection. As the Italians say, "Meh."
- **Auto Battery** • 1009 Union St
206-322-2886
Sports and drink where car batteries were once sold.
- **Baltic Room** • 1207 Pine St
206-625-4444
Fashionable dance spot with the big velvet drapes.
- **Bar Ferd'nand** • 1531 Melrose Ave
206-623-5882
Continue your pleasant (and pretenious) evening at this wine bar.
- **Barboza** • 925 E Pike St
206-709-9442
A live music club in the basement of Neumos. Password not required.
- **Barca** • 1510 11th Ave
206-325-8263
Bitchy wait staff serve you drinks in the dark.

- **Canon: Whiskey & Bitters Emporium** •
928 12th Ave
A canon you'll want to shoot yourself INTO.
- **Century Ballroom** • 915 E Pine St
206-324-7263
Lindy, swing, salsa, tango anyone? Do it here in style, lessons available for klutzes.
- **Cha Cha Lounge** • 1013 E Pike St
206-322-0703
High-attitude tiki bar for hipsters.
- **The Chieftain Irish Pub** • 908 12th Ave
206-324-4100
Dime-a-dozen Irish pub.
- **Chop Suey** • 1325 E Madison St
206-324-8005
Alt-rock club with the ethnically insensitive moniker.
- **Clever Dunne's Irish House** • 1501 E Olive Way
206-709-8079
Best pub quiz ever.
- **The Cobra Lounge** • 1122 E Madison St
Smoke out of a hookah and not get the least bit high.
- **Comet Tavern** • 922 E Pike St
206-322-9272
Order an Oly and get into a fight!
- **Crescent Lounge** • 1413 E Olive Way
206-726-1774
Divey gay bar with karaoke seven nights a week.
- **The Cuff** • 1533 13th Ave
206-323-1525
Try (or try not) to get cuffed in the men's room.
- **Elysian Brewing Company** • 1221 E Pike St
206-860-1920
Super food and micros but lacks atmosphere. Bring interesting company.
- **Fireside Room** • 900 Madison St
206-622-6400
Where Thurston Howell, III would hang if he weren't stuck on that island.
- **Garage Billiards & Bowl** • 1130 Broadway
206-322-2296
Getting drunk and bowling is obviously a wise combination.
- **Grim's** • 1512 11th Ave
206-324-7467
Fancy pub food specifically designed for the inebriated palate.

- **Havana** • 1010 E Pike St
206-323-2822
Kick it like Castro.
- **The Hideout** • 1005 Boren Ave
206-903-8480
Drink tasty cocktails amidst paintings inspired by fever dreams.
- **John John's Game Room** • 1351 E Olive Way
206-696-1613
Pinball and alcohol. What's not to like?
- **Knee High Stocking Co** • 1356 E Olive Way
206-979-7049
A pioneer of the post-prohibition speakeasy movement.
- **Linda's Tavern** • 707 E Pine St
206-325-1220
Hipsters vie for seniority.
- **Lost Lake Cafe & Lounge** • 1505 10th Ave E
206-323-5678
Seattle's own Twin Peak's style diner complete with damn fine coffee and pie 24 hours a day
- **Madison Pub** • 1315 E Madison St
206-325-6537
Eat, drink, and be gay.
- **Manhattan** • 1419 12th Ave
206-325-6574
Apparently, Manhattanites are addicted to bourbon and $50 steak.
- **Marjorie** • 1412 E Union St
206-441-9842
Fresh cocktails in a Euro-style ambiance.
- **Mercury @ Machinewerks** • 1009 E Union St
Private club for people who know goth people.
- **Moe Bar** • 1425 10th Ave
206-709-9951
Convenient for shows at Neumo's. Inconvenient for fun.
- **Montana** • 1506 E Olive Way
206-422-4647
Much like its namesake, it's a place for drinking.
- **Narwhal** • 1118 E Pike St
206-325-6492
The Unicorn's basement-dwelling cousin. Same carnival decor + video games.

Map 4

If you're under 30 (or never stopped partying), you'll have a blast at the bars along Pike and Pine. **Linda's** has a great jukebox and a heated back patio. Over 30? Try the awesome **Melrose Market** for all your foodie needs. Meet some ladies at the **Wild Rose**, take a date to **Anchovies & Olives**, score some late night tacos (**Rancho Bravo**) or fish n' chips (**Pike Street Fish Fry**), or kick it old school grungy at the **Comet**.

- **Neighbours** • 1509 Broadway
  206-324-5358
  Straight-friendly all-night dance parties for the fabulous people.
- **Neumos** • 925 E Pike St
  206-709-9442
  Music club that welcomes Seattle's legions of hip-hoppers and punk rockers.
- **Oddfellows Cafe & Bar** • 1525 10th Ave
  206-325-0807
  The odds are good and the goods are also good.
- **The Old Sage** • 1410 12th Ave
  206-557-7430
  Smoked meats galore by the speakeasy gurus behind Tavern Law.
- **Pie Bar** • 1361 E Olive Way
  206-257-1459
  Two great words that taste great together. Everything pie from drink to dessert.
- **The Pine Box** • 1600 Melrose Ave
  206-588-0375
  With 34 microbrew taps, it just may be your funeral.
- **Poco Wine + Spirits** • 1408 E Pine St
  206-322-9463
  Intimate and contemporary; Northwest emphasis with traveling international list.
- **Pony** • 1221 E Madison St
  206-324-2854
  The stallion of gay bars.
- **Purr** • 1518 11th Ave
  206-325-3112
  Martini bar for classy cats.
- **Quarter Lounge** • 909 Madison St
  206-332-0772
  Cheap drinks and pool. Not much else. You get what you pay for.
- **R Place** • 619 E Pine St
  206-322-8828
  Karaoke, dancing, and all-male underwear contests.
- **Redwood** • 514 E Howell St
  206-329-1952
  Hunting lodge chic. Vegetarians and Nuge fans come together!
- **Richard Hugo House** • 1634 11th Ave
  206-322-7030
  Pretend you like poetry, get laid.

- **Rock Box** • 1603 Nagle Pl
  206-302-7625
  For those about to rock…behind closed doors.
- **The Saint** • 1416 E Olive Way
  206-323-9922
  Cleanse your soul with 80 different tequilas and super-fresh fare.
- **Saint John's Bar and Eatery** • 719 E Pike St
  206-245-1390
  Rock n' roll restaurateurs head up a hard rock cafe that's worthwhile.
- **Seattle Eagle** • 314 E Pike St
  206-621-7591
  Quintessential leather bar.
- **Six Arms** • 300 E Pike St
  206-223-1698
  Dude. They have tater tots.
- **Still Liquor** • 1524 Minor Ave
  206-467-4075
  Another Seattle speakeasy provides that old-timey drunk feeling.
- **Sun Liquor Distillery** • 514 E Pike St
  206-720-1600
  A micro-boozery from the wonderful folks at Sun Liquor.
- **Tango** • 1100 Pike St
  206-583-0382
  Awesome if you're not paying.
- **Tavern Law** • 1406 12th Ave
  206-322-9734
  Speakeasy Chic: Cos Seattle's alcohol laws aren't puritanical enough.
- **Unicorn** • 1118 E Pike St
  206-325-6492
  A peek inside the dreams of hipsters.
- **Vito's** • 929 9th Ave
  206-397-4053
  The historic lounge of ill-repute is back and classier than ever.
- **Von Trapp's** • 912 12th Ave
  206-325-5409
  Indoor bocce court, a bazillion beers and brats and a line out the door every weekend.
- **Wild Rose** • 1021 E Pike St
  206-324-9210
  Friendly and fun lesbians. $1 Taco Tuesdays aren't (just) a euphemism.

# Restaurants

- **611 Supreme** • 611 E Pine St
  206-328-0292 • $$
  Crepes for hipsters.
- **8 Oz. Burger Bar** • 1401 Broadway
  206-466-5989 • $$
  Micro-chain that sells…guess what…8 oz burgers.
- **Anchovies & Olives** • 1550 15th Ave
  206-838-8080 • $$$$
  Ethan Stowell's fishy enterprise. So fresh and so clean clean.
- **Annapurna Café** • 1833 Broadway
  206-320-7770 • $$
  Warm, nourishing food from Nepal, Tibet, and India served in a cozy basement.
- **Arabica Lounge** • 1550 E Olive Way
  206-347-6093 • $
  It's the kind of place that pluralizes "toast."
- **Ayutthaya Thai Cuisine** • 727 E Pike St
  206-324-8833 • $$
  Unbelievably fresh and satisfying Thai. Dubious musical accompaniment.
- **Ba Bar** • 550 12th Ave
  206-328-2030 • $
  Enjoy Vietnamese street food indoors and pretty much whenever you want.
- **Baguette Box** • 1203 Pine St
  206-332-0220 • $
  Amazing, super-fresh sandwiches. The tofu 'wich, especially delish.
- **Ballet** • 914 E Pike St
  206-328-7983 • $
  Cheap Asian fusion with a vast selection.
- **Bar Ferd'nand Coffee** • 1531 Melrose Ave
  206-623-5882 • $$
  A snack bar, Sitka & Spruce style.
- **Big Mario's NY Style Pizza** • 1009 E Pike St
  206-922-3875 • $
  East Coast expats, here's your precious NY pizza. Now shut up.
- **Bill's Off Broadway** • 725 E Pine St
  206-323-7200 • $
  Line your stomach with satisfying grease after a night of debauchery.
- **Bimbo's Cantina** • 1013 E Pike St
  206-322-9950 • $
  If Hunter S. Thompson opened a burrito joint.
- **Black Coffee** • 501 E Pine St
  347-541-8694 • $
  A vegan cafe with a mission (shocking, I know). Bu they're also pretty cool and make good grub.
- **Boom Noodle** • 1121 E Pike St
  206-701-9130 • $$
  Japanese izakaya spot with flavors that explode i your mouth. Boom!
- **Café Presse** • 1117 12th Ave
  206-709-7674 • $$
  Authentic French bistro serving food until 2 am. Très magnifique!
- **Cedars on Broadway** • 500 Broadway
  206-325-3988 • $
  Indian food that's naan-stop delicious. Many clair its dominance.
- **Chatterbox Café** • 1100 12th Ave
  206-324-2324 • $
  Dubious service, but there aren't a whole lot of other Singaporean cuisine options in town.
- **Chungee's Drink & Eat** • 1830 12th Ave
  206-323-1673 • $$
  Self-explanatory late-nite Chinese.
- **Coffee Tree** • 905 8th Ave
  206-387-7545 • $
  Maybe they should look into finding a good service tree to go along with that coffee.
- **Cure** • 1641 Nagle Pl
  206-568-5475 • $$
  The cure for the common meat, cheese and booz deficiency.
- **Dinette** • 1514 E Olive Way
  206-328-2282 • $$$
  Come for the lovely, fancy toast—it's more delicious and filling than it sounds.
- **Elliott Bay Cafe** • 1521 10th Ave
  206-436-8482 • $$
  A cafe so nice, they built it twice.
- **Fogón Cocina Mexicana** • 600 E Pine St
  206-320-7777 • $$
  This sweet Mexican family is kind enough to shar their transcendent food with Seattleites. Gracias!

Map 4

Go casually upscale with the farm-to-plate genius of **Terra Plata**. Matt Dillon's **Sitka & Spruce** and **Bar Ferd'nand** lend a Toply Cheffed gravitas to the 'hood. Impress vegetarian friends---or those who love them---at **Plum Bistro**. Elsewhere, Hill trolls swear by **Hot Mama's Pizza**, and **Mamnoon** will hook you on their Syrian and Lebanese flavors.

- **Freddy Junior's** • 1513 Broadway Ave
$
Freddy of Rancho Bravo fame tries his hand at a slider joint. He does tacos better.
- **High 5 Pie** • 1400 12th Ave
206-695-2284 • $
Move over, cupcakes. Pies are the new It Dessert.
- **Hot Mama's Pizza** • 700 E Pine St
206-322-6444 • $
Everything looks hotter with beer goggles on.
- **Hunt Club** • 900 Madison St
206-343-6156 • $$$$
Doesn't the name just ooze pretension? So do the setting and the prices.
- **In the Bowl Vegetarian Noodle Bistro** •
1554 E Olive Way
206-568-2343 • $
Another example of fake meat made delicious. And they deliver.
- **Jimmy John's** • 1221 Madison St
206-812-1043 • $
Like Subway but with delivery.
- **Kafe Berlin** • 613 9th Ave
206-623-4242 • $
Vaguely German cafe which serves pretzels alonside panini.
- **La Bête** • 1802 Bellevue Ave
206-329-4047 • $$$
Local food done right. And without pretension.
- **La Cocina Oaxaquena** • 1216 Pine St
206-623-8226 • $$
The Bizzaro cousin of the insanely popular Carta de Oaxaca in Ballard. Same great food, different crowd.
- **La Spiga Osteria** • 1429 12th St
206-323-8881 • $$$
Gorgeous pastas and sandwiches. Emilia-Romagna comes to Seattle.
- **Lark** • 926 12th Ave
206-323-5275 • $$$$
Little plates never had it so good. Casual elegance epitomized.
- **Little Uncle** • 1509 E Madison St
206-329-1503 • $
The best Thai food you can get from a little window. Online ordering!

- **Lost Lake Cafe & Lounge** • 1505 10th Ave E
206-323-5678 • $$
Seattle's own Twin Peak's style diner complete with damn fine coffee and pie 24 hours a day.
- **Machiavelli** • 1215 Pine St
206-621-7941 • $$$
Canoodle over some noodles in this hip, affordable Italian favorite.
- **Mamnoon** • 1508 Melrose Ave
206-906-9606 • $$$
This ain't your daddy's seasonal Middle Eastern food (unless your daddy is Lebanese).
- **Marination Station** • 1412 Harvard Ave
$
The stationary version of the food truck.
- **Marjorie** • 1412 E Union St
206-441-9842 • $$$
Eclectic is an understatement. Nice patio.
- **Mediterranean Express** • 1417 Broadway
206-860-3989 • $$$
Garlicky Greek goodness.
- **Mediterranean Kitchen** • 1009 Boren Ave
206-467-5046 • $
Garlicky Greek goodness.
- **Mesob** • 1325 E Jefferson St
206-860-0403 • $
Arguably the best Ethiopian joint in Seattle. Ignore the sketchy exterior.
- **Momiji** • 1522 12th Ave
206-457-4068 • $$$
You'll want to make a night of their speciality sushi rolls and cocktails.
- **My Sweet Lil Cakes** • 1208 Pine St
206-351-0356 • $
MF-ing waffles on a stick! Sweet AND savory; meat AND veg; gluten AND not. Nailed it.
- **Octo Sushi** • 1621 12th Ave
206-805-8998 • $$$
Sushi sushi joy joy.
- **The Old Sage** • 1410 12th Ave
206-557-7430 • $$
Smoked meats galore by the speakeasy gurus behind Tavern Law.
- **The Other Coast Cafe** • 721 E Pike St
206-257-5927 • $
A proudly Northwestern delicatessen.

- **Pho Le's** • 720 E Pike St
206-322-1818 • $
More pho for your salty soup satisfaction.
- **Pie Bar** • 1361 E Olive Way
206-257-1459 • $$
Two great words that taste great together.
Everything pie from drink to dessert.
- **Piecora's** • 1401 E Madison St
206-322-9411 • $$
The best NY-style pizza in town, whole or by the
slice.
- **Pike Street Fish Fry** • 925 E Pike St
206-329-7453 • $$
Unbelievably fresh fish and chips: a revelatory,
late-night godsend on Cap Hill.
- **Pinto Thai Bistro & Sushi Bar** • 408 Broadway
206-724-0559 • $$
All your Asian favs under one roof, plus extra
special specials.
- **Plum Vegan Bistro** • 1429 12th Ave
206-838-5333 • $$$
Vegan food doesn't have to be made by crusty
punks. It can get dressed up once in a while!
- **Po Dog Hot Dogs** • 1009 Union St
206-325-6055 • $
If this is po, I don't wanna be rich.
- **Poco Wine + Spirits** • 1408 E Pine St
206-322-9463 • $$
Small plates of cold duck and local cheeses pair
exquisitely with the top-notch wines.
- **Poquitos** • 1000 E Pike St
206-453-4216 • $
- **Primo** • 1106 8th Ave
206-547-7466 • $
Italian carb heaven.
- **Quinn's** • 1001 E Pike St
206-325-7711 • $$
Farm food meets fine dining. Get the wild boar
sloppy joes and leave the vegetarians at home.
- **Rancho Bravo Tacos** • 1001 E Pine St
206-322-9399 • $
The popular taco truck has finally found a
permanent home.
- **Regent Bakery & Cafe** • 1404 E Pine St
206-743-8866 • $$
Family-run Chinese bakery well known for their
massive selection of cakes.

- **Restaurant Zoë** • 1318 E Union St
206-256-2060 • $$$
A gastropub without the pub.
- **Saley** • 800 Olive Way
206-405-3444 • $
A sweet, small one-woman crepe shop.
- **Sitka & Spruce** • 1531 Melrose Ave
206-324-0662 • $$$
The freshest local ingredients. Tiny, busy, worth it
- **Skillet Diner** • 1400 E Union St
206-512-2000 • $$
Now you don't have to chase their food truck to
score some bacon jam.
- **Tacos Guaymas** • 1415 Broadway
206-860-3871 • $$
Cheap and filling.
- **Tango** • 1100 Pike St
206-583-0382 • $$$$
Posh yet cozy; come for the half-price wine bottle
on Mondays.
- **Terra Plata** • 1501 Melrose Ave
206-325-1501 • $$
Mindblowing local, seasonal and sustainable fare,
some from the restaurant's rooftop.
- **Via Tribunali** • 913 E Pike St
206-322-9234 • $$
One bite of the pizza will transport you back to
Napoli.
- **Von Trapp's** • 912 12th Ave
206-325-5409 •
Indoor bocce court, a bazillion beers and brats and
a line out the door every weekend.
- **Vostok Dumpling House** • 1416 Harvard Ave
206-687-7865 • $$
The Russians really know how to eat. Fortunately,
they're willing to share.
- **Zaw** • 1424 E Pine St
206-325-5528 • $$
It's not delivery. It's artisan take-and-bake.
- **zpizza** • 1620 Broadway
206-432-9158 • $
Organic toppings and vegan/GF options. Seattle
hipster pizza heaven.

Map 4

Shopping is plentiful in the Pike/Pine Corridor. For retro gear, or if you are looking for pieces for a Halloween costume, try **Atlas Clothing Co.** After you're dudded up, hit **Rain Shadow** for the best in locally farmed meatware. And Pioneer Square's loss will forever be Pike/Pine's gain now that Seattle's premier bookseller **Elliott Bay** has relocated here.

#  Shopping

- **35th North** • 1100 E Pike St
206-320-1252
Comprehensive selection of goods for co-ed skaters.
- **Atlas Clothing Co.** • 1419 10th Ave
206-323-0960
Retro treasures, new and used.
- **Babeland** • 707 E Pike St
206-328-2914
A sex shop you can be proud to visit, staffed by enlightened women.
- **Bootyland** • 1317 E Pine St
206-328-0636
Because your baby really needs a Ramones t-shirt.
- **The Calf & Kid** • 1531 Melrose Ave
206-467-5447
Artisan cheese on Cap Hill. I kid you not.
- **City Market** • 1722 Bellevue Ave
206-323-1715
Thanks to South Park, everyone calls it Shitty Market. It's anything but.
- **Le Frock** • 613 E Pine St
206-623-5339
Swanky vintage clothing for dudes and dolls.
- **Lifelong Thrift Store** • 1017 E Union St
206-957-1655
Proceeds help people affected by AIDS.
- **Lucky Devil Tattoo Parlor** • 1407 E Madison St
206-323-1637
Personable, versatile artists help you piss off your parents for a reasonable price!
- **Marigold and Mint** • 1531 Melrose Ave
206-682-3111
Organic flowers end edible plants from a Snoqualmie farm. So quaint!
- **Melrose Market** • 1501 Melrose Ave
Indoor farmer's market. Why didn't we think of that before?
- **Molly Moon's** • 917 E Pine St
206-708-7947
Fresh, local, sustainably organic ice cream.
- **NuBe Green** • 921 E Pine St
206-402-4515
Sustainable gifts for the friend with more than one dreamcatcher.

- **Oola Distillery** • 1314 E Union St
206-709-7909
Local booze-makers offer samples of their goods. And the goods are good.
- **Platinum Records** • 915 E Pike St
206-324-8032
DJ equipment and vinyl.
- **Rain Shadow Meats** • 1531 Melrose Ave
206-467-6328
Making Cap Hill feel even smaller with locally farmed meats.
- **Rudy's Barbershop** • 614 E Pine St
206-329-3008
Absolute best cheap haircut!
- **SugarPill** • 900 E Pine St
206-322-7455
An old timey apothecary for all your chocolate and tonic needs.
- **Throwbacks Northwest** • 1205 E Pike St
206-402-4855
Look dope in old-school Sonics, Mariners, and Seahawks gear.
- **Twice Sold Tales** • 1833 Harvard Ave
206-324-2421
Buy and sell used books whilst petting kitties.
- **Wall of Sound** • 315 E Pine St
206-441-9880
An honest to god record store. With records and everything!
- **Westlake Center** • 400 Pine St
206-467-1600
Maybe, if every other store in Seattle goes out of business. Maybe.
- **Yogurtland** • 1620 Broadway
206-860-1386
Rule over your own froyo fairy tale with endless flavor/topping combos.
- **Zero Zero Hair** • 1525 Summit Ave
206-568-3996
The best hipster hairstyling bang for your buck.
- **Zion's Gate Records** • 1100 E Pike St
206-568-5446
Turntables, wide range of vinyl, smoking accessories.

Map 5

The north side of the Central District is an Ethiopian and African-American community being swallowed by new developments. Family-owned groceries and restaurants sit quietly between the busy streets of Adler, 23rd Avenue, MLK, and Union where the Garfield Community Center and the Martin Luther King, Jr. Mural are located.

## oLandmarks

- **AM/PM Gas Station** • E Cherry St & 23rd Ave
  Panhandlers' address.
- **Black Panther Headquarters** • 2111 E Union St
  Power to the people.
- **Martin Luther King Jr. Mural** • 2726 E Cherry St
  A painting of his contemplation.
- **Medgar Evers Swimming Pool Mosaic Art** •
  500 23rd Ave
  Beautiful child-like art.
- **Polish Home** • 1714 18th Ave
  206-322-3020
  Pierogies and bison grass vodka every Friday night.

## Coffee

- **Cortona Cafe** • 2425 E Union St
  206-327-9728
  Serving espresso, waffles and beer. It's up to you whether or to order all 3 at once.
- **Tougo Coffee Co.** • 1410 18th Ave
  206-860-3518
  Stick your kids in the play area and get a coffee ToStay.

## Nightlife

- **CC Attle's** • 1701 E Olive Way
  206-726-0565
  Feed the bears!
- **Central Cinema** • 1411 21st Ave
  206-328-3230
  Drink beer and watch a cult or classic film. So simple yet so brilliant.
- **The Neighbor Lady** • 2308 E Union St
  206-695-2072
  Vegetarian bar and grill with a sexy brothel vibe.
- **The Twilight Exit** • 2514 E Cherry St
  206-324-7462
  Where hipsters go to avoid other hipsters.

## Restaurants

- **Assimba Ethiopian Cuisine** • 2722 E Cherry St
  206-322-1019 • $
  Ethiopian utopia.
- **The Barbeque Pit** • 2515 E Cherry St
  206-724-0005 •
  Sometimes a "pit" isn't a bad place to eat lunch.
- **Cafe Selam** • 2715 E Cherry St
  206-328-0404 • $
  This hole-in-the-wall Ethiopian is a favorite with cabbies.
- **Catfish Corner** • 2726 E Cherry St
  206-323-4330 • $
  Like fried bottom feeders? This is the place.
- **Central Cinema** • 1411 21st Ave
  206-328-3230 • $
  Forget popcorn. Pair a movie with good beer and decent grub.
- **El Gallito** • 1700 20th Ave
  206-329-8088 • $
  Easy to overlook, but so perfect before a night of boozin'. Huge portions.
- **Ezell's Famous Chicken** • 501 23rd Ave
  206-324-4141 • $
  Oprah's had Ezell's chicken FedExed straight from Seattle to her mouth. Really.
- **Meskel Ethiopian Restaurant** • 2605 E Cherry St
  206-860-1724 • $
  You'll need lots of napkins. And beer.
- **The Neighbor Lady** • 2308 E Union St
  206-695-2072 • $$
  Vegetarian bar and grill with a sexy brothel vibe.
- **Tougo Coffee Co.** • 1410 18th Ave
  206-860-3518 • $
  Stick your kids in the play area and get a coffee ToStay.

# Map 6 • Madrona

1

2

E John St

E Denny Blaine Pl

Hassen Ln E

34th Ave E

35th Ave

E Florence Ct

Madrona Pl E

Madison Ln E

E Denny Way

E Denny Way

38th Ave

**19**

33rd Ave E

3000

3400

E Howell St

Madrona Dr

E Howell St

**A**

28th Ave E

27th Ave

29th Ave

E Schubert Pl

Howell Pl

Howell Park

E Olive St

1600

38th Ave

39th Ave

Evergreen Pl

40th Ave

E Olive Ln

Martin Luther King Jr Way E

E Pine St

3000

3400

1600

39th Ave

Grand Ave

Madrona Dr

E Pine St

E Pike St

**◄ 5**

E Union St

3000

30th Ave

31st Ave

32nd Ave

33rd Ave

34th Ave

35th Ave

38th Ave

E Pike St

37th Ave

Newport Way

**B**

E Spring St

1100

3400

1100

Parkside Pl

E Madrona
Playground

E Marion St

3400

Madrona
Park

E Marion St

E Columbia St

E Columbia St

Randolph Pl

Spectrum
Dance
Theater

39th Ave

E Arlington Pl

3000

E Cherry St

3400

700

Norwood Pl

Randolph Ave

38th Ave

Washington Ave

Fullerton Ave

Temple Pl

27th Ave

28th Ave

29th Ave

E James St

E James St

E Conover Ct

E Jefferson St

E Jefferson St

**C**

Martin Luther King Jr Way

Powell
Barnett
Park

E Terrace St

35th Ave

34th Ave

Randolph Ave

E Terrace St

Ellis Ave

*Lake Washington*

Lake Washington Blvd E

E Spruce St

Lake Dell Ave

E Alder St

**10**

E Spruce St

| 1/4 mile | .25 km |

E Superior St

What's steeper? Madrona's rising home values or the walk from the lake? A short bus ride from downtown Seattle, this lovely area on Lake Washington is home to staid matriarchs, gay couples, artists, and multi-generational families residing in everything from Seattle big-money mansions to shabby cottages. Locals covet life on the beach with astounding views of Mount Rainier, but it's the variety of food and drink on 34th Avenue that's the real draw.

Map

# ○ Landmarks

- **Spectrum Dance Theater** •
  800 Lake Washington Blvd
  206-325-4161
  Beautiful old brick building is a rare waterfront venue for dance performances

 Coffee

- **Cupcake Royale/Verite Coffee** • 1101 34th Ave
  206-883-7656
  Cupcakes and coffee go well together.
- **Hi Spot Café** • 1410 34th Ave
  206-325-7905
  Locals love this place.

 Nightlife

- **Bottlehouse** • 1416 34th Ave
  206-708-7164
  A house party of a higher calibre.
- **Madrona Eatery & Ale House** • 1138 34th Ave
  206-323-7807
  Great bar food. Bring the whole family.

# 🍴 Restaurants

- **Bistro Turkuaz** • 1114 34th Ave
  206-324-3039 • $$$
  Awesome Turkish food.
- **Café Soleil** • 1400 34th Ave
  206-325-1126 • $$
  Laid-back breakfast mornings and spicy Ethiopian nights.
- **Hi Spot Café** • 1410 34th Ave
  206-325-7905 • $$
  Locals love this place.
- **Lalibela** • 2800 E Cherry St
  206-322-8565 • $
  Standard Ethiopian; great combo platter.
- **Madrona Eatery & Ale House** • 1138 34th Ave
  206-323-7807 • $$
  Great bar food. Bring the whole family.
- **St. Clouds** • 1131 34th Ave
  206-726-1522 • $$$
  Upscale neighborhood joint with style and late-night dining.

# 🛍 Shopping

- **Conley Hats** • 913 27th Ave
  206-322-1868
  Made to order hats. Now that's old-school.
- **Décor on 34th** • 1421 34th Ave
  206-571-0094
  Stylish home décor shop.
- **Hitchcock Madrona** • 1406 34th Ave
  206-838-7173
  Cool little store: jewelry, clothes, etc.
- **Juniper** • 3314 E Spring St
  206-838-7496
  The very definition of boutique.
- **Molly Moon's** • 1408 34th Ave
  206-324-0753
  Organic ice cream with unusual flavors that sells like…cold ice cream.

Elliott Bay

Bainbridge Island
Bremerton

**PIONEER SQUARE**

Pioneer Sq Park

Smith Tower

The Underground Tour

Yesler Way

Occidental Park

Fallen Firefighters Memorial

Waterfall Garden

City Hall Park

Kobe Terrace Park

**A**

**B**

**C**

Seneca

Spring St

Madison St

Marion St

3rd Ave

Columbia St

Cherry St

James St

Jefferson St

4th Ave

Columbia St

5

Terrace St

Dining Way

Prefontaine Pl S

Western Ave

Alaskan Way

S Washington St

S Main St

S Jackson St

S King St

Occidental Ave S

1st Ave S

2nd Ave S

3rd Ave S

4th Ave S

5th Ave S

6th Ave S

Maynard Ave S

S Washington St

S Main St

S Jackson St

S King St

S Weller St

S Lane St

King Street Station

**PAGE 220**

S Railroad Way

S Dearborn St

99

Alaskan Way S

CenturyLink Field

**PAGE 216**

CenturyLink Field Events Center

S Dearborn St

Airport Way S

5th Ave S

S Vermont St

S Royal Brougham Way

Utah Ave S

1st Ave S

Occidental Ave S

Colorado Ave S

Safeco Field

**PAGE 271**

3rd Ave S

4th Ave S

6th Ave S

S Atlantic St

**SODO**

S Atlantic St

Edgar Martinez Dr

39

S Massachusetts St

S Massachusetts St

S Massachusetts St

2nd Avenue Ext S

3

4

5

8

1/4 mile    .25 km

As the city's oldest neighborhood, there's a mystique about Pioneer Square, the nation's original "Skid Road" where the early settlers toiled through harsh conditions. Today, Pioneer Square entertains a tenuous mix of tourists, art galleries, and frat bars around its community living room, Occidental Square. Start your day at **Grand Central Bakery** for homemade pastries.

## ○ Landmarks

- **CenturyLink Field** • 800 Occidental Ave S
  206-381-7555
  Get tossed in the CLink while you cheer on the Sounders or Seahawks.
- **Fallen Firefighters' Memorial** •
  Occidental Ave S & S Main St
  Bronze firemen amid the pigeons and the homeless.
- **Safeco Field** • 1250 1st Ave S
  206-628-0888
  Lovable M's keep losing here, but you can drown your sorrows in $11 pints of beer.
- **Smith Tower** • 506 2nd Ave
  206-622-4004
  View from 1914 tower is cheaper (and maybe better) than the Space Needle.
- **Waterfall Garden** • S Main St & 2nd Ave S
  This tranquil urban haven commemorates the birth of UPS.

## ☕ Coffee

- **Caffe Umbria** • 320 Occidental Ave S
  206-624-5847
  Big-time roaster's Pioneer Square flagship.
- **Caffe Vita** • 125 Prefontaine Pl S
  206-652-8331
  The best of the local chains.
- **Grand Central Bakery** • 214 1st Ave S
  206-622-3644
  Caffe Vita brew served here.
- **Trabant Coffee & Chai** • 602 2nd Ave
  Dude. This chai rocks.
- **Zeitgeist** • 171 S Jackson St
  206-583-0497
  Not as revolutionary as they'd have you believe, but not bad.

## ▼ Nightlife

- **Central Saloon** • 207 1st Ave S
  206-622-0209
  Frat boys have been drinking here since 1892.
- **Collins Pub** • 526 2nd Ave
  206-623-1016
  Craft and Belgian beers to the nth degree.
- **Cowgirls Inc.** • 421 1st Ave S
  206-340-0777
  Like Coyote Ugly, but sluttier.
- **Double Header** • 407 2nd Ave S
  206-464-9918
  Friendly old dudes who like dudes.
- **Easy Joe's American Pub** • 704 1st Ave
  206-623-3440
  It's like if one of the cool Top Chef guys opened a diner.
- **Elysian Fields** • 542 1st Ave S
  206-382-4498
  Stadium-size brewery a home-run shot from Safeco Field.
- **Last Supper Club** • 124 S Washington St
  206-748-9975
  Three-tiered thumping nightclub attracting the skimpily-clad set.
- **New Orleans Creole** • 114 1st Ave S
  206-622-2563
  Blues and jazz in old hipster setting.
- **Pyramid Alehouse** • 1201 1st Ave S
  206-682-3377
  Get sh*t-faced like the Egyptians used to do.
- **Temple Billiards** • 126 S Jackson St
  206-682-3242
  Great pizza and very little competition for a table.
- **Triangle Pub** • 553 1st Ave S
  206-628-0474
  Great spot for a Rainier before you watch the M's lose again.
- **Trinity Nightclub** • 111 Yesler Way
  206-447-4140
  Different action in three spacious rooms. Be twenty something, wear less, enjoy more.

# Restaurants

- **Al Boccalino** • 1 Yesler Way
206-622-7688 • $$$$
Nice Southern Italian in a historic building.
- **Bar Sajor** • 323 Occidental Ave S
206-682-1117 • $$$
Famed Chef Matt Dillon's attempt at classing up
Pioneer Square.
- **The Berliner Döner Kebab** • 221 1st Ave S
206-838-0339 • $
A very Seattle gyrocery with tofu instead of falafel.
- **Café Paloma** • 93 Yesler Way
206-405-1920 • $
Lovingly made meze-style food and delicious pita.
- **Delicatus** • 103 1st Ave S
206-623-3780 • $$
Latin for Seattle Deli. Sea-town themed
sandwiches.
- **Easy Joe's American Pub** • 704 1st Ave
206-623-3440 • $$
It's like if one of the cool Top Chef guys opened a
diner.
- **Grand Central Bakery** • 214 1st Ave S
206-622-3644 • $
Great lunch spot with amazing pastries.
- **Green Leaf Vietnamese Restaurant** •
418 8th Ave S
206-340-1388 • $
Fresh, fantastic Vietnamese. One of the best and
busiest in town.
- **Il Corvo Pasta** • 217 James St
206-538-0999 • $
Nothing like a pasta lunch to get you through the
rest of your work day.
- **Il Terrazzo Carmine** • 411 1st Ave S
206-467-7797 • $$$
Classic, well-executed Italian.

- **Jimmy John's** • 102 1st Avenue South
206-621-9500 • $
Like Subway but with delivery.
- **The London Plane** • 322 Occidental Ave S
206-624-1374 • $$
A brilliant combo of foodie shop and wine cafe.
Possibly too classy for Pioneer Square.
- **Marcela's Creole Cookery** • 106 James St
206-223-0042 • $$
Down-home grub, N'awlins style. Try the
muffuletta.
- **New Orleans Creole** • 114 1st Ave S
206-622-2563 • $$
Hush puppies, live jazz and blues every night—
and even vegetarian options!
- **The People's Burger** • 922 Occidental Ave S
206-471-5781 • $
A burger revolution.
- **Pizzeria Napoletana** • 125 Prefontaine Pl S
206-652-8331 • $$
A tiny taste of Napoli conveniently located inside
a coffee shop.
- **Rain Shadow Meats Squared** •
404 Occidental Ave S
206-467-4854 • $$
Enjoy your acquisitions straight away in the deli
portion of this unmatched butcher shop.
- **Salumi Artisan Cured Meats** • 309 3rd Ave S
206-621-8772 • $
Mario Batali's dad makes damn good salami.
- **Tat's Delicatessen** • 159 Yesler Way
206-264-8287 • $
Big, sloppy sammies to stink up your big meeting
or office party.
- **Thai Curry Simple** • 406 5th Ave S
206-327-4838 • $
Simply amazing curry and breakfast. (Yes,
breakfast!)

It has old-fashioned charm in spades, even if it's hidden under the grimy veil of homelessness, petty crime, and drunken revelers. It's also a refuge for men's men seeking cheap booze and thrills at bars like **Central Saloon**, while Mariners and Seahawks fans crowd into **Triangle Pub**. Meanwhile, Matt Dillon classes things up at **Bar Sajor** and foodies flock to **Salumi** to indulge in heavenly pork products. **Rain Shadow Meats Squared** is the quintessential Northwest meat emporium with a deli so that you don't have to wait till you get home to chow down.

## Shopping

- **Ebbets Field Flannels** • 408 Occidental Ave S
  206-382-7249
  Finest maker of historic and authentic baseball uniforms.
- **Magic Mouse Toys** • 603 1st Ave
  206-682-8097
  We think it's run by elves.

- **Rain Shadow Meats Squared** •
  404 Occidental Ave S
  206-467-4854
  Even the drunks of Pioneer Square like farm fresh meat.
- **Salumi Artisan Cured Meats** • 309 3rd Ave S
  206-621-8772
  Mario Batali's dad makes damn good salami. Take home some gnocchi on Tuesdays.

# Map 8 · **International District**

N

**1** ··· **2**

Seattle University

Seattle University Gymnasium

E Jefferson St

Marion St

Columbia St

Columbia St

Cherry St

5th Ave

4th Ave

Jefferson St

James St

7th Ave

8th Ave

9th Ave

Terry Ave

Jefferson St

Boren Ave N

Terrace St

Cherry St

E Barclay Ct

E Remington Ct

**4**

E Terrace St

E Terrace St

E Alder St

Broadway

10th Ave

11th Ave

12th Ave

14th Ave S

15th Ave S

17th Ave S

E Spruce St

E Spruce St

E Fir St

E Fir St

E Yesler Way

Boren Ave

13th Ave

1200

800

Yesler Way

Exit 165

**5**

S Washington St

S Washington St

Kobe Terrace Park

S Main St

S Main St

6th Ave S

8th Ave S

500

S Jackson St

S Jackson St

S Jackson Pl

Site of the Former Wah Mee Club

Wing Luke Asian Museum

5th Ave S

Maynard Ave S

Canton Alley

8th Ave S

9th Ave S

1200

S King St

S King St

S King St

12th Ave S

4th Ave S

Maynard Ave S

7th Ave S

S Weller St

S Weller St

**7** ◀ ··· ▶ **9**

Rainier Ave S

S Lane St

S Lane St

S Lane St

10th Ave S

Corwin Pl

Dearborn Pl S

3rd Ave S

S Dearborn St

S Dearborn St

S Dearborn St

6th Ave S

S Charles St

S Dean St

Exit 2B

S Charles St

S Charles St

S Vermont St

S Plummer St

**90**

S Charles St

Golf Dr S

Sturgus Park

S Norman St

Poplar Pl S

Sturgus Ave S

S Bush Pl

Exit 2A

S Royal Brougham Wy

Dr Rizal Park

Airport Way S

4th Ave S

6th Ave S

Exit 164B

S Judkins St

Sander Rd S

16th Ave S

**39**

S Atlantic St

11th Ave S

S Atlantic St

18th Ave S

3rd Ave S

Martinez Dr S

S Massachusetts St

S Massachusetts St

12th Ave S

S State St

S State St

S Grand St

S Holgate St

| 1/4 mile | | .25 km |

This historic neighborhood has provided a cultural hub for Seattle's sizable Asian-American population since the 19th century. Home to Filipino, Vietnamese, Cambodian, Japanese, and Chinese businesses of every stripe, the International District truly feels, well, international. It's hardly the most glamorous area of the city, but strolling through the ID is highly recommended.

# ☉ Landmarks

- **Site of the Former Wah Mee Club •**
  S King St & Maynard Alley S
  Site of 1983 gang massacre.
- **Wing Luke Museum •** 719 S King St
  206-623-5124
  A gem of a museum in the heart of the ID.

# Coffee

- **Gossip Espresso & Tea •** 651 S King St
  206-624-5402
  Bubble tea.
- **Oasis Tea Zone •** 519 6th Ave S
  206-447-8098
  Bubble tea and other Asian junk food. In other words, delicious.
- **Panama Hotel Tea & Coffee House •** 607 S Main St
  206-515-4000
  Lavazza beans.

# 🍸 Nightlife

- **Bush Garden •** 614 Maynard Ave S
  206-682-6830
  Drunken late-night karaoke. Beware of bachelorettes.
- **Fort St. George •** 601 S King St
  206-382-0662
  Japan meets the UK at this pub that also serves decent food.
- **Venus Karaoke •** 601 S King St
  206-264-1779
  Rent a room and get lost in translation.

Map 8

# Restaurants

- **663 Bistro** • 663 S Weller St
  206-667-8760 • $
  Chinese with a rare, incomparably light touch. A shining highlight in the ID.
- **Fuji Bakery** • 526 S King St
  206-623-4050 • $
  Gorgeous Asian-inspired patries, which shame the entire nation of France.
- **Hing Loon** • 628 S Weller St
  206-682-2828 • $$
  The smoked duck: primal, carnivorous pleasure.
- **Honey Court Seafood Restaurant** •
  516 Maynard Ave S
  206-292-8828 • $$
  Late night Chinese for your drinking and dumpling pleasure.
- **House of Hong** • 409 8th Ave S
  206-622-7997 • $$
  Great food, even better name.
- **Hue Ky Mi Gia** • 1207 S Jackson St
  206-568-1268 • $
  Ooddles of tasty noodles.
- **Jade Garden** • 704 S King St
  206-622-8181 • $$
  Some argue it's Seattle's best dim sum; honestly, it probably is.
- **Loving Hut** • 1226 S Jackson St
  206-299-2219 • $
  Comfort food just like your militant vegan Grandma used to make.
- **Malay Satay Hut** • 212 12th Ave S
  206-324-4091 • $$
  Three cuisines unite under one roof, with delicic results.
- **Maneki** • 304 6th Ave S
  206-622-2631 • $$
  Tasty traditional Japanese food. A Seattle institution.
- **Mikado Teppanyaki** • 1306 S King St
  206-860-1556 • $$$
  Like Benihana, but classier.
- **Phnom Penh** • 660 S King St
  206-748-9825 • $
  Cambodian noodle joint.
- **Pho Bac** • 415 7th Ave S
  206-621-0532 • $
  A reliable pho filling station. Try the banh mi and spring rolls too.
- **Ping's Dumpling House** • 508 S King St
  206-623-6764 • $
  If a house full of dumplings sounds good to you, it's hard to go wrong here.
- **Saigon Vietnam Deli** • 1200 S Jackson St
  206-328-2357 • $$
  Some of the best banh mi you'll find. Cheap, fast and so good.
- **Samurai Noodle** • 606 5th Ave S
  206-624-9321 • $
  If your experience has been more Top Ramen th top notch, prepare to get your mind blown.
- **Sea Garden** • 509 7th Ave S
  206-623-2100 • $$$
  You can stay til 3 am and watch your food get snatched from the aquarium.

Uwajimaya Village features an awesome food court, a bookstore, apartments, and even a bank—you could move in and never leave. But hit the streets of the ID for the real eats. **Maneki**, a Seattle gem, has been dishing up sushi and traditional Japanese for over 100 years. For Malaysian fare, check out **Malay Satay Hut** and if you want to try Cambodian, head to **Phnom Penh**. Or grab a super cheap bahn mi at **Saigon Deli**.

- **Shanghai Garden** • 524 6th Ave S
  206-625-1688 • $$
  Delicious hand-shaved barley noodles and at least 100 other options.
- **Spring Garden** • 1032 S Jackson St
  206-859-6998 • $
  Chow down and pretend you can get vitamin D from a sky-painted ceiling.
- **Szechuan Noodle Bowl** • 420 8th Ave S
  206-623-4198 • $
  Perfect scallion pancakes. Perfect noodle soups. Perfect dumplings.
- **Tai Tung** • 655 S King St
  206-622-7372 • $$
  Sit at the counter with the regulars and soothe yourself with one of many comforting soups.
- **Tamarind Tree** • 1036 S Jackson St
  206-860-1404 • $
  Exotically droolworthy Vietnamese cuisine.
- **Tea Garden** • 708 Rainier Ave S
  206-709-9038 • $$
  The dim sum flows freely, and it is fantastic. One of Seattle's best.
- **Tsukushinbo** • 515 S Main St
  206-467-4004 • $
  Hidden Japanese gem is a favorite of local chefs.
- **Uwajimaya** • 600 5th Ave S
  206-624-6248 • $
  Hawaiian, Filipino, Korean, and more. All food courts should be this tasty.
- **World Pizza** • 672 S King St
  206-682-4161 • $
  Bringing a little vegetarian Italian flair to the I.D.

## Shopping

- **Big John's Pacific Food Importers** •
  1001 6th Ave S
  206-682-2022
  Primarily Meditteranean grocery. Bulk and otherwise.
- **International Model Toys** • 601 S King St
  206-682-8534
  Pac Man belt buckles for the kids…or, ya know, you.
- **Kinokuniya Bookstore** • 525 S Weller St
  206-587-2477
  If NFT was available in Japanese, it would be sold here.
- **Pink Gorilla** • 601 S King St
  206-264-2434
  You'll love this place if you played video games in the 80's…or still do.
- **RE-PC** • 1565 6th Ave S
  206-623-9151
  Bins and bins of computer stuff.
- **Star Tea Shop** • 616 S Jackson St
  206-382-7827
  A beautiful collection of tea and tea accessories. Sample before you buy.
- **Tsue Chong Company** • 800 S Weller St
  206-623-0801
  Giant bags of fortune cookies.
- **Uwajimaya** • 600 5th Ave S
  206-624-6248
  Asian superstore with groceries, gifts, restaurants, even apartments.

Map 9 • **Central District (South)**

1

2

E Terrace St
E Terrace St
5
E Alder St
E Spruce St
E Fir St

20th Ave
21st Ave S
22nd Ave
23rd Ave
24th Ave
25th Ave
26th Ave
27th Ave

Martin Luther King Jr Way

28th Ave

Pow
Barn
Pa

A

14th Ave E
15th Ave E

E Yesler Way

Pratt
Park

S Washington St
S Washington St
S Washington St

22nd Pl S

Dr Blanche
Lavizzo
Park

23rd Ave

S Main St
S Main St
S Main St

S Main St

16th Ave S
17th Ave S
18th Ave S
19th Ave S

S Jackson St

21st Ave S
22nd Ave S

S Jackson St

S Jackson Pl

S King St

20th Pl S

S King St

S King St

28th Ave S

10

8

S Weller St

S Lane St
S Lane St

S Lane St

20th Ave S
20th Pl S

26th Ave S

B

Colwell Pl S

Dearborn Pl S

S Dearborn St

S Dearborn St

Fowler Pl S

S Dean St

S Nye Pl

19th Ave S

20th Pl S

22nd Ave S

S Charles St

23rd Ave

S Charle

S Charles St

Hiawatha Pl S

Davis Pl S

1800

1800

S Ingersoll Pl

2300
S Charles St

S Norman St
S Norman St
S Norman St

S Elmwood Pl

Sturgis
Park

Rainier Ave S

S Norman St

20th Ave S

21st Ave S

25th Ave S

26th Ave S

Brandner Pl S

Sturgis Pl S

S Bush Pl

Judkins
Park

S Judkins St
S Wadsworth Pl
S Irving St

26th Ave S

C

16th Ave S
Sturgis Pl S

Exit 3

Exit 3B

Exit 3A

90

S Atlantic St
16th Ave S
18th Ave S

19th Ave S
Valentine Pl S

21st Ave
22nd Ave

S Atlantic St

25th Ave S
26th Ave S

28th Ave S

39

40

S Massachusetts St

1/4 mile          .25 km

Can you say gentrification? Well, promenade along the main streets of CD's south side and experience the word itself. The high traffic streets of Martin Luther King, 23rd Avenue, Massachusetts, and Yesler contain a regurgitated version of Pleasantville. But at least parks are pretty green respites from the irreality.

#  Coffee

- **Broadcast Coffee** • 1918 E Yesler Way
  206-322-0807
  Broadcasting the best of Seattle products including Stumptown, Mighty O and Macrina.
- **Café Weekend** • 851 Hiawatha Pl S
  206-860-0727
  Have your weekend between Monday and Saturday, because they're closed Sundays.

# Restaurants

- **Cheeky Cafe** • 1700 S Jackson St
  206-322-9895 • $
  International comfort food to fill out those cheeks.
- **Judkins Street Cafe** • 2608 S Judkins St
  206-322-1091 • $
  Quintessential quaint neighborhood cafe.
- **Moonlight Cafe** • 1919 S Jackson St
  206-322-3378 • $
  Good vegan Vietnamese options in a shabby setting.
- **San Fernando Roasted Peruvian Chicken** •
  900 Rainier Ave S
  206-331-3763 • $
  Lynnwood favorite comes to Seattle. Guess what they serve.
- **Taco del Mar** • 2309 S Jackson St
  206-329-8383 • $
  Fast food tacos that suffice—they're fresher than most.
- **Umai-Do Japanese Sweets** • 1825 S Jackson St
  206-325-7888 • $
  Delectable Japanese treats for happy mouth-making.

# Shopping

- **Africa Braids and Jewelry** • 2506 S Jackson St
  206-860-7235
  Your hair will thank you.
- **Flowers Just For You** • 2216 S Jackson St
  206-324-1440
  Family owned, friendly, and helpful staff.
- **Two Big Blondes** • 2501 S Jackson St
  206-762-8620
  Phat shirts, phat pants, phat skirts, etc for those livin' large.
- **Western Beauty Supply** • 2301 S Jackson St
  206-329-2582
  Disney World for beauticians.

Map 10

Gee, Toto, there's no place like Leschi. The neighborhood rises quietly above the shores of Lake Washington, boasting spectacular views of Mt. Rainier, the Cascade Range, Mt. Baker, the screaming Blue Angels in August, and decorated Christmas ships during December. The packed retail core is home to throngs of weekend cyclists, kayakers, and boaters, but there's plenty of room to toss Frisbees and chase kids in the spacious parks.

# Restaurants

- **A La Bonne Franquette** • 1421 31st Ave S
  206-568-7715 • $$$
  As French as French can be.
- **Bluwater Bistro** • 102 Lakeside Ave
  206-328-2233 • $$
  Pricey but perfect seafood and meat for appeasing the carnivore in your life.
- **Daniel's Broiler** • 200 Lake Washington Blvd
  206-329-4191 • $$$$
  Fancy folk (or those whose parents are paying) head here for decent steak.
- **Pert's Deli** • 120 Lakeside Ave
  206-325-0277 • $
  Pick up a turkey and swiss before heading to the park.
- **That's Amore** • 1425 31st Ave S
  206-322-3677 • $$
  A real gem in the restaurant doldrums of Mt. Baker, despite the clichèd name.

# Shopping

- **Leschi Market** • 103 Lakeside Ave
  206-322-0700
  Amazing wine selection.

# Map 11 • **Magnolia / Interbay**

**1**

**2**

*Shilshole Bay*

NW 70th St

NW 69th St

NW 67th St

NW 67th St

NW 65th St

34th Ave NW

NW 64th St

NW 63rd St

NW 62nd St

NW 61st St

NW 60th St

NW 59th St

15th Ave NW

NW 58th St

NW 57th St

NW Market St

NW 53rd St

28

NW 49th St

*Salmon Bay*

23

NW Leary Way

**A**

W Sheridan St

W Parry Way

W Cramer St

W Sheridan St

W Cramer St

47th Ave W

W Hooker St

PAGE 180

W Commodore Way

Discovery Park

W Lawton St

W Lawton St

W Mccord Pl

Kiwanis Memorial Preserve Park

W Fort St

Fort Lawton Military Reservation

Fort Lawton Cemetery

W Fort St

W Government St

W Harley St

W Jameson St

W Government Way

W Jameson St

Ballard Brdg

Shilshole Ave NW

W Mansell St

W Elmore Pl

W Elmore St

W Elmore St

W Thurman St

W View Pl

W Emerson Pl

Gilman Ave W

W Thurman St

W Ewing St

36th Ave W

Lawton Park

W Emerson St

W Emerson St

W Emerson St

W Emerson St

12

**B**

*Puget Sound*

W Ruffner St

W Ruffner St

W Tilden St

W Tilden St

W Ruffner St

W Ruffner St

W Ruffner St

W Bertona St

W Prosper St

W Dravus St

W Bertona St

W Grover St

W Bertona St

Magnolia Blvd W

34th Ave W

W Dravus St

W Dravus St

Thorndyke Ave W

15th Ave W

20th Ave W

W Barrett St

W Barrett St

W Barrett St

W Barrett St

W Barrett St

W Fulton St

W Fulton St

W Armour Pl

W Armour St

28th Ave W

24th Ave W

W Raye St

Bayview Playground

Interbay Athletic Field

W Raye St

W Raye St

Interbay Family Golf Center

W Bothwell

West Magnolia Playfield

W Smith St

W Halladay St

W Wheeler St

W Smith St

Gilman Dr W

E Magnolia Plgd

W Mcgraw St

W Mcgraw St

W Mcgraw St

W Lynn St

W Lynn Pl

National Guard Armory

W Lynn St

W Boston St

W Boston St

Kinnear Park

Condon Way W

Magnolia Blvd W

W Newton St

W Crockett St

W Plymouth St

W Howe St

W Blaine St

W Hayes St

14

W Garfield St

W Eaton St

W Garfield St

12th Ave W

14th Ave W

11th Ave W

W Galer St

W Martina Pl

W Galer St

Smith Cove Park

Elliott Ave W

**C**

W Lee St

W Prospect St

*Elliott Bay*

1/2 mile    .5 km

Since it's on a peninsula, Magnolia residents rely on a trio of bridges to connect them to the rest of the city (unless landslides or earthquakes interfere). However, the relative isolation suits this quiet, family-friendly community. Dominated by the 500-acre **Discovery Park** and surrounded by Shilshole Bay and Puget Sound, Magnolia is prime real estate, boasting some of Seattle's most expensive homes. Interbay is an industrial strip useful mostly for getting to and from other neighborhoods.

##  Landmarks

- **Discovery Park** • 3801 Discovery Park Blvd
  206-386-4236
  534 acres of honest-to-goodness nature.

##  Coffee

- **Caffe Appassionato** • 4001 21st Ave W
  206-281-8040
  Classic Seattle coffee shop vibe at this small-ish local chain. Frasier would love it here.
- **Discovery Espresso & Juice** • 3103 W Jameson St
  206-286-1481
  Neighborhood joint convenient to Discovery Park.
- **Gilman Ave Coffee & Doughnuts** •
  4211 Gilman Ave W
  206-397-3784
  Conduit coffee and a bevy of local doughnuts to go with your bevy-erage.
- **Uptown Espresso** • 3223 W McGraw St
  Self-proclaimed "Home of the Velvet Foam" but the coffee underneath is just so-so.

## Farmers Markets

- **Magnolia Farmers Market** •
  33rd Ave W & W McGraw St
  Saturdays, 10-2, early June to late Sept

##  Restaurants

- **Bay Café** • 1900 W Nickerson St
  206-282-3435 • $$
  Waterfront diner doin' it right: breakfast all day and malted milkshakes.
- **Caffe Appassionato** • 4001 21st Ave W
  206-281-8040 • $$
  Classic Seattle coffee shop vibe at this small-ish local chain. Frasier would love it here.
- **Chinook's at Salmon Bay** • 1900 W Nickerson St
  206-283-4665 • $$
  Perfect for getting out of the halibut/salmon rut.

- **The Highliner** • 3909 18th Ave W
  206-216-1254 • $
  Historic pub with new, fishy veneer.
- **Josefina's Mexican Grill** • 2818 Thorndyke Ave W
  206-216-1078 • $$
  The commercial-style Mexican restaurant that Magnolia has been waiting for.
- **Mondello Ristorante** • 2435 33rd Ave W
  206-352-8700 • $$
  Real Sicilian trattoria, run by merry Mamma Enza.
- **Palisade** • 2601 W Marina Pl
  206-285-1000 • $$$$$
  Fancy seafood dishes that range from so-so to spectacular.
- **Queen Margherita** • 3111 W McGraw St
  206-548-4908 • $
  Pizza ovens made from Mount Vesuvius bricks = Bona fide.
- **Red Mill Burgers** • 1613 W Dravus St
  206-284-6363 • $
  The undisputed best burger in Seattle. And possibly, the best onion rings.
- **Serendipity Cafe** • 3222 W McGraw St
  206-282-9866 • $$
  Stick your kids in the back play area while you take a load off.
- **Szmania's** • 3321 W McGraw St
  206-284-7305 • $$$$
  Colorful, kind of crazy-looking food. Bring the platinum card.
- **Tanglewood Supreme** • 3216 W Wheeler St
  206-708-6235 • $$
  Seafood date night for Magnolians who can't be bothered to leave the hood.
- **Where Ya At Matt** • W Dravus St & 16th Ave W
  $
  If you find them, you'll eat po boys & beignets. Fridays in Interbay.

##  Shopping

- **Wild Salmon Seafood Market** •
  1900 W Nickerson St
  206-283-3366
  How fresh is this? Dockside store gets fish right off the boats.

This neighborhood perched atop Queen Anne Hill, the highest point in Seattle, is a magnet for yuppie families, millionaires, and thrifty octogenarians. Dead people also love Queen Anne North, as the Mt. Pleasant Cemetery's booming business conclusively proves.

# Coffee

- **Bustle** • 535 W McGraw St
  206-453-4285
  Serving unusual twists on traditional coffee drinks. Get the Spanish Mocha.
- **Java Jazz** • 3457 15th Ave W
  206-282-232
  Drive thru.
- **Muse Coffee Co.** • 1907 10th Ave W
  206-282-2711
  They didn't write the book on coffee, but they do teach a class.
- **Q Café** • 3223 15th Ave W
  206-352-2525
  Brewing Stumptown Coffee beans.

# Restaurants

- **Cheese Wizards** • 210 Nickerson St
  $
  The best way to level up your grilled cheese intake.
- **La Palma** • 3456 15th Ave W
  206-284-1001 • $$
  Delicious and cheap Mexican of the lardy, salty, cheesy variety.
- **Macrina Bakery** • 615 W McGraw St
  206-283-5900 • $$
  Macrina's baked goods will make breakfast your most important meal.
- **Yasuko's Teriyaki** • 3200 15th Ave W
  206-283-9152 • $
  Seattleites love teriyaki. Go figure.

When the young urban professionals of LQA decide to marry and breed, they buy a house here. When you're deep inside this little suburban chimera, you can easily forget how close you are to the unsavory big city. There aren't many ways for kids or adults to get into trouble in these parts, unless your idea of trouble is having one-too-many mimosas with brunch. Make sure to grab a Mexican hot chocolate from the lovely ladies at **El Diablo**.

Map

## Coffee

- **Caffe Appassionato** • 1417 Queen Anne Ave N
206-270-8760
Classic Seattle coffee shop vibe at this small-ish local chain. Frasier would love it here.
- **Caffe Ladro** • 2205 Queen Anne Ave N
206-282-5313
Strong coffee for the strong coffee drinker.
- **Cederberg Tea House** • 1417 Queen Anne Ave N
206-285-1352
South African tea house that offers a passport to deliciousness. Get the malva pudding if it's not sold out.
- **El Diablo Coffee Company** •
1811 Queen Anne Ave N
206-285-0693
The devil must be in their amazing Mexican hot chocolate.
- **Vienna Mae Coffee** • 318 Nickerson St
206-769-5333
Cute drive-thru that specializes in hemp milk lattes.

## Nightlife

- **Hilltop Ale House** • 2129 Queen Anne Ave N
206-285-3877
Neighborhood pub.

55

Map 1

# Restaurants

- **5 Spot** • 1502 Queen Anne Ave N
  206-285-7768 • $$
  Rotating, regional experiments with spotty results, but the fans are die-hard.
- **The Book Bindery** • 198 Nickerson St
  206-283-2665 • $$$
  An instant classic.
- **Café de Lion** • 1629 Queen Anne Ave N
  206-913-2125 • $$
  French-inspired pastries which are (almost) too beautiful to eat. Rowr!
- **Canlis** • 2576 Aurora Ave N
  206-283-3313 • $$$$
  Sure, it'll cost you. But the food is as astounding as the legendary view.
- **Cederberg Tea House** • 1417 Queen Anne Ave N
  206-285-1352 • $$
  If you're not already familiar with South African baked goods and coffee, you're about to have your mind blown.
- **China Harbor** • 2040 Westlake Ave N
  206-286-1688 • $$
  Lakeside dining.
- **Chinoise Café** • 12 Boston St
  206-284-6671 • $$
  Modern sushi joint with a Pan-Asian flair and a heap of noodle dishes.
- **Elliott Bay Pizza Co.** • 2115 Queen Anne Ave N
  206-285-0500 • $$
  Combining meat, sauce, cheese and bread in nearly endless combinations.
- **Grub** • 7 Boston St
  206-216-3628 • $$
  A fine dining diner with dishes like lamb burgers and…get ready…an eggs benedict biscuit breakfast sandwich. Whuuuut?
- **Hilltop Ale House** • 2129 Queen Anne Ave N
  206-285-3877 • $$
  Not your average pub grub. Baked goat cheese salad and curry cashews!
- **Homegrown Sustainable Sandwich Shop** • 2201 Queen Anne Ave N
  206-217-4745 • $
  It is what it is.
- **How to Cook a Wolf** • 2208 Queen Anne Ave N
  206-838-8090 • $$$
  Another iteration of Ethan Stowell's clean, composed dishes.
- **La Luna** • 2 Boston St
  206-282-2511 • $$
  Serving Seattle-style Mexican to the Queen Anne boozers of the night.
- **Le Rêve Bakery & Cafe** • 1805 Queen Anne Ave N
  206-623-7383 • $$
  Dreamy Parisian pastries and sandwiches. Feel free to pinch yourself.
- **LloydMartin** • 1525 Queen Anne Ave N
  206-420-7602 • $$
  It sounds like a bank, but it's a restaurant. A really good one, at that.

This neighborhood is designed for people who plan to be in bed by 11 and like to pay too much for groceries. The **Hilltop Ale House** is decent and your only real nightlife option. **How to Cook a Wolf** will blow you away at dinner time, and for breakfast you can't do better than the **5 Spot**. If it's a special occasion, try **Book Bindery**, which resides in (you guessed it) an old book bindery, or impress your date with a pants-dropping view of Lake Union at the worth-every-penny **Canlis**.

- **Mezcaleria Oaxaca** • 2123 Queen Anne Ave N
  206-216-4446 • $$
  Sister to La Carta in Ballard and every bit as pretty.
- **Orrapin Thai Cuisine** • 10 Boston St
  206-283-7118 • $
  Mellow, candlelit Thai.
- **Ponti Seafood Grill** • 3014 3rd Ave N
  206-284-3000 • $$$$
  A very good seafood restaurant, and not overflowing with tourists.
- **Portage** • 2209 Queen Anne Ave N
  206-352-6213 • $$$
  Worthy of respect. Reservations recommended.
- **Queen Anne Café** • 2121 Queen Anne Ave N
  206-285-2060 • $$
  Absolutely superb breakfast dishes; dinner, however, is spotty.
- **Six Coins Japanese Food Truck** • 2121 8th Ave
  206-395-5785 • $
  They serve something called a "rice box" that you definitely want to eat.
- **Twirl Cafe** • 2111 Queen Anne Ave N
  206-283-4552 • $$
  For moms who want to relax and kids who don't.
- **Zaw** • 1635 Queen Anne Ave N
  206-787-1198 • $$
  It's not delivery. It's artisan take-and-bake.
- **Zeek's Pizza** • 41 Dravus St
  206-285-8646 • $$
  Pizzas with pizzazz, like the Thai version with peanut sauce.

## Shopping

- **A & J Meats & Seafood** • 2401 Queen Anne Ave N
  206-284-3885
  Great neighborhood butcher and fish monger.
- **Chocolopolis** • 1527 Queen Anne Ave N
  206-282-0776
  Over 220 bars of chocolate from 20 different countries. Yep.
- **Eat Local** • 2400 Queen Anne Ave N
  206-328-3663
  Local, organic health market.
- **Menchie's** • 2101 Queen Anne Ave N
  206-216-1650
  Serving approximated candy bars & cheesecake for housewives by the pound.

Map 14

Like the rest of Queen Anne, this section caters to the upwardly mobile---meaning condos and attractive views. Speaking of which, Kinnear Park provides fine views of the Seattle skyline and Puget Sound from its upper tier, while the lower section appears welcoming until you stumble upon overgrown shrubs and the makeshift hobo camp.

## ○ Landmarks

- **Kerry Park** • 211 W Highland Dr
  206-684-4075
  All those scenic Seattle postcards? This is the vantage point.
- **Parsons Garden** • 7th Ave W & W Highland Dr
  206-684-4081
  Secret garden for non-tourists.

## Coffee

- **Caffè Fiorè** • 224 W Galer St
  206-282-1441
  Makes the bold claim of being Seattle's first organic coffee.
- **Gourmet Latté** • 540 Elliott Ave W
  206-352-2633
  Gourmet is a relative term, but the coffee at this unassuming roadside shack is A-OK.

## ▼ Nightlife

- **Targy's** • 600 W Crockett St
  206-352-8882
  Time travel back to the old Queen Anne. Lovely.

## Restaurants

- **Betty** • 1507 Queen Anne Ave N
  206-352-3773 • $$
  Comforting bistro dishes, not-so-cozy space. Still, locals are adoring.
- **Chopstix** •
  425-610-7388 • $
  Food truck that combines Asian flavors in inspired ways. Peking duck taco!
- **Top Pot Doughnuts** • 325 W Galer St
  206-631-2120 • $
  Top Pot is tops!

## ⦿ Shopping

- **Icebox Grocery** • 1903 10th Ave W
  206-708-6742
  A really nice fridge that charges you for raiding it.
- **Molly Moon's** • 321 W Galer St
  206-457-8854
  Organic ice cream with unusual flavors that sells like…cold ice cream.

# Map 15 · **Lower Queen Anne / Seattle Center**

N

**1**

**2**

99

W Galer St

Galer St

2nd Ave W

1st Ave W

Orange Pl N

2nd Ave N

3rd Ave N

Galer Pl N

Nob Hill Ave N

4th Ave N

W Lee St

Lee St

Lee St

**13**

Comstock Pl

W Comstock St

Tower Pl

Warren Pl

Bigelow Ave N

Comstock St

A

W Highland Dr

Highland Dr

Highland Dr

Kerry
Park

Prospect St

Prospect St

Aurora Ave

**16**

Highland Dr

Ward St

1st Ave N

Ward Pl

Aloha St

2nd Ave N

3rd Ave N

Nob Hill Ave N

4th Ave N

5th Ave N

Taylor Ave N

6th Ave N

**14**

W Queen Anne Dr

Valley St

W Roy St

Roy St

P

W Mercer St

Queen Anne Ave N

B

2nd Ave W

Mercer St

1st Ave W

Warren Ave N

Republican St

PAGE
**266** McCaw Hall

Republican St

N Broad St

W Republican St

Republican St

PAGE
**215**

International
Fountain

PAGE
**192**

Harrison St

Key Arena

Harrison St

Seattle Center

Experience
Music Project

Broad St

W Thomas St

Thomas St

Monorail

Thomas St

1st Ave N

Warren Ave N

2nd Ave N

5th Ave N

Taylor Ave N

6th Ave N

**2**

W John St

John St

Pacific Science
Center

The Space Needle

C

Western Ave W

4th Ave N

5th Ave N

W Denny Way

Denny Way

Elliott Ave

Bay St

Eagle St

5th Ave

4th Ave

Myrtle
Edwards
Park

**1**

3rd Ave

Wall St

Battery St

| 1/4 mile | .25 km |

The residents of the LQA are mostly single, urban professionals in their mid-twenties to early thirties who enjoy a healthy nightlife and unassuming upscale residences. The neighborhood retains a slightly more economical Belltown vibe. Plus, sometimes they have an express train (some call it a "Monorail") to Westlake Center.

## ○ Landmarks

- **Experience Music Project** • 325 5th Ave N
  206-770-2700
  A billionaire's rock memorabilia collection and a public eyesore.
- **International Fountain** • 305 Harrison St
  206-684-7200
  Water show set to music.
- **Key Arena** • 305 Harrison St
  206-281-5800
  The former home of the Seattle Sonics is now dominated by ladies sports.
- **Pacific Science Center** • 200 2nd Ave N
  206-443-2001
  You're never too old for a Floyd or Zeppelin laser show.
- **Seattle Monorail** • 5th Avenue & Pine Street
  206-905-2620
  90 thrilling seconds zipping through Seattle (if it's actually running).
- **Space Needle** • 400 Broad St
  206-905-2100
  Like so many things in life, it's not as big as you'd expect.

##  Coffee

- **Caffe Ladro** • 600 Queen Anne Ave N
  206-282-1549
  Strong coffee for the strong coffee drinker.
- **Caffe Vita** • 813 5th Ave N
  206-285-9662
  The best of the local chains.
- **Caffé Zingaro** • 127 Mercer St
  206-352-2861
  Lighthouse Roasters plus food.
- **Espresso Elegance** • 122 Elliott Ave W
  206-282-8155
  Worth a trip off the beaten path for their $2 espresso happy hour.
- **Forza Coffee Company** • 100 4th Ave N
  206-404-3679
  Come for the coffee. Leave for the food.
- **Uptown Espresso** • 525 Queen Anne Ave N
  206-285-3757
  Self-proclaimed "Home of the Velvet Foam" but the coffee underneath is just so-so.

# Lower Queen Anne / Seattle Center

## Nightlife

- **Buckley's On Queen Anne** • 232 1st Ave W
  206-691-0232
  A fine, friendly neighborhood pub with tasty eats.
- **Crow Restaurant and Bar** • 823 5th Ave N
  206-283-8800
  Good food and cocktails, but make a reservation or don't bother.
- **Jabu's Pub** • 174 Roy St
  206-284-9093
  A friendly, comfortable place to get drizunk.
- **Mecca Café** • 526 Queen Anne Ave N
  206-285-9728
  Visit the Queen Anne of olden days.
- **Ozzie's** • 105 W Mercer St
  206-284-4618
  Where frat boys go to sing karaoke and bust the occasional head.
- **Peso's** • 605 Queen Anne Ave N
  206-283-9353
  If you like your meat market with a side of guac.
- **Plaza Garibaldi** • 129 1st Ave N
  206-397-4088
  Veg-friendly Mex turns LQA karaoke bar on weekends, becomes less friendly.
- **The Sitting Room** • 108 W Roy St
  206-285-2830
  Warm and orange. You'll see what I mean.
- **Solo Bar** • 200 Roy St
  206-213-0080
  Faith No More (remember them?) serves up some cocktails.
- **Spectator Bar & Grill** • 529 Queen Anne Ave N
  206-599-4263
  Typical sports bar transforms into epic punk rock karaoke party at week's end.
- **Sport** • 140 4th Ave N
  206-404-7767
  A place where intellectuals debate existential theory. Just kidding!
- **Teatro Zinzanni** • 222 Mercer St
  206-802-0015
  A fine night out. If someone else is paying.
- **Ten Mercer** • 10 Mercer St
  206-691-3723
  You'll think you've died and gone to a Bret Easto Ellis novel.
- **The Tin Lizzie Lounge** • 600 S 244th St
  206-282-7407
  The MarQueen's gorgeous hotel bar might want see the Wizard for a heart.
- **The Vera Project** • 305 Harrison St
  206-956-8372
  Keeping the kids out of trouble in the coolest wa possible.

## Restaurants

- **Bamboo Garden** • 364 Roy St
  206-282-6616 • $$
  Chinese vegetarian spot that makes fake meat taste unnaturally good.
- **Bigfood** • 305 Harrison St
  206-719-5549 • $
  Mobile S'quatch-themed food truck now has a stationary spot in the Armory.
- **Blue Water Taco Grill** • 515 Queen Anne Ave N
  206-352-2407 • $
  Cheap Ameri-Mexican that's at least pretty fresh.
- **Citizen** • 706 Taylor Ave N
  206-284-1015 •
  Delicious crepes and sandwiches that'll make yo count as two citizens.
- **Collections Cafe** • 305 Harrison St
  206-753-4935 • $$
  The Chihuly Museum's highfalutin eatery decorated with crap from Dale's attic.
- **Crow Restaurant and Bar** • 823 5th Ave N
  206-283-8800 • $$
  Scoff at the small plate trend and indulge in hearty, sausage-stuffed lasagna.
- **Dick's Drive-In** • 500 Queen Anne Ave N
  206-285-5155 • $
  A local obsession, specializing in cheap burgers and shakes. Perfect at 1 am.

The hub of LQA is contained in the several blocks near the Seattle Center that are packed with restaurants and bars. Relish delectable Indian at **Roti**. Even carnivores appreciate the faux-meat delights at **Bamboo Garden**. In terms of nightlife, **Ozzie's** and **Peso's** draw the biggest crowds and chiefly deal in meat-marketing. Start or end your night at the classic dive **Mecca Café**.

- **Kidd Valley** • 531 Queen Anne Ave N
  206-284-0184 • $
  Like a slightly fancier Burger King with not much more to offer.
- **Laredos Grill** • 555 Aloha St
  206-218-1040 • $$
  Queso and tacos till 1am. Ole!
- **Mecca Café** • 526 Queen Anne Ave N
  206-285-9728 • $
  Your taste buds will thank you. Your heart and liver will disown you.
- **The Melting Pot** • 14 Mercer St
  206-378-1208 • $$$$
  Gimmicky and retro, perhaps, but dipping things in cheese can never be bad.
- **New York Pizza & Bar** • 500 Mercer St
  206-913-2565 • $$
  A family house of junk food where mom and dad can also get plastered.
- **Obasan** • 11 Mercer St
  206-282-2333 •
  Casual Japanese spot.
- **Oskar's Kitchen** • 621 Queen Anne Ave N
  206-402-3375 • $$
  Shawn Kemp's sexy-fish-themed barstraunt.
- **Pagliacci Pizza** • 550 Queen Anne Ave N
  206-726-1717 • $
  Local favorite pizza chain makes crispy-chewy delights with seasonal ingredients.
- **Peso's** • 605 Queen Anne Ave N
  206-283-9353 • $$$
  Mexican with substance. Same can be said for the margaritas but not the patrons.
- **Pie** • 305 Harrison St
  206-428-6312 • $
  This sweet/savory hand pie-oneer (sorry) now has a stall at Seattle Center.
- **Plaza Garibaldi** • 129 1st Ave N
  206-397-4088 • $$
  Vast and varied Mexican menu made from "family recipes."
- **Plum Juice Bar** • 305 Harrison St
  206-428-6337 • $
  Contributing to the classing up of the Armory with vegan lunch food.

- **Racha** • 23 Mercer St
  206-281-8883 • $$$
  Safe bet for pad thai, once you get past the yuppies.
- **Roti Cuisine of India** • 530 Queen Anne Ave N
  206-216-7684 • $$
  Tasty, reasonably priced lunch buffet. Guaranteed food coma.
- **Shiki Japanese** • 4 W Roy St
  206-281-1352 • $$
  One of the only places in the state to get fugu. Non life-threatening dishes available, too.
- **Skillet Counter** • 305 Harrison St
  206-428-6311 • $$
  Great organic meal if you can withstand their cutesy menu and city prices.
- **SkyCity** • 400 Broad St
  206-905-2100 • $$$
  Ridiculously overpriced, mediocre food—but what a view. For tourists.
- **Solo Bar** • 200 Roy St
  206-213-0080 • $$
  ItalEthioSpaBulgarian cuisine. And tapas.
- **Spectator Bar & Grill** • 529 Queen Anne Ave N
  206-599-4263 • $$
  Typical sports bar transforms into epic punk rock karaoke party at week's end.
- **Sushi Land** • 803 5th Ave N
  206-267-7621 • $
  Fun, cheap sushi.
- **Ten Mercer** • 10 Mercer St
  206-691-3723 • $$$$
  Hip bar and romantic upstairs area—heavy on the meat options.
- **Toulouse Petit** • 601 Queen Anne Ave N
  206-432-9069 • $$
  From the guy who brought you Peso's. Different food, same attitude.
- **Uptown China** • 200 Queen Anne Ave N
  206-285-7710 • $$
  Efficient, spice-a-licious Chinese, best complemented by a Tsingtao.

Map 10 • **Westlake / South Lake Union**

N

1

2

Dexter Way N
Waverly Pl N
8th Ave N
Crockett St

△ 13

Newton St

A

Westlake Ave N

Red Ave E
Fairview Ave E
Minor Ave E

E New

△ 20

E Galer St

Hayes St
8th Ave N

Garfield St

Garfield St

Dexter Ave N

Galer St        Galer St

WESTLAKE

*Lake Union*

B

Westlake Ave

Comstock St

Dexter Cn N

17▶

◀ 15
Highland Dr

Aurora Ave N

Fairview Ave N
Eastlake Ave E

6th Ave N

99

Prospect St

Yale Ave N

Ward St

○
Museum
of History
and
Industry

Fairview
& Campus Drive

8th Ave N

9th Ave N

Minor Ave N

Aloha St

Dexter Ave

Valley St

Lake
Union
Park

Fairview N

Valley St

Center For
Wooden Boats

○

C

E Roy St

○      Valley St

Lake Union Park

Eastlake Ave E

Exit 166

N Broad St

E Roy St

SOUTH LAKE
UNION

Roy St

5

Westlake Ave

Terry Ave N

Boren Ave N

Fairview Ave N

Minor Ave N

Pontius Ave N

Yale Ave N

Melrose Ave E

6th Ave N

N Broad St

Westlake
& Mercer

Mercer St

Terry
& Mercer

2
▽

Republican St

1/4 mile          .25 km

Once a light industrial area on sweet little Lake Union, Paul Allen is still putting the finishing touches on the top half of his pet 'hood. The jewel at the center is the 12-acre waterfront park. Completed in 2010, plans for the park were originally proposed 100 years ago. Seattleites don't like to rush into anything. Beware the novelty streetcar that ends its tedious two-mile journey here.

##  Landmarks

- **The Center for Wooden Boats** • 1010 Valley St
  206-382-2628
  Free boat rides on Lake Union every Sunday!
- **Museum of History and Industry** •
  860 Terry Ave N
  206-324-1126
  Experience all of Seattle's history from inception to present day.

## Coffee

- **Uptown Espresso** • 500 Westlake Ave N
  206-621-2045
  Self-proclaimed "Home of the Velvet Foam" but the coffee underneath is just so-so.

## Nightlife

- **Jillian's Billiard Club** • 731 Westlake Ave N
  206-223-0300
  A club that only frat boys want to be a part of.

## Restaurants

- **1Hundred Bistro & Bar** • 1001 Fairview Ave N
  425-455-4278 • $$
  A little bit of Bellevue in South Lake Union.
- **Chandler's Crabhouse** • 901 Fairview Ave N
  206-223-2722 • $$$$
  Not-bad crabs with an excellent view of Lake Union.
- **Compass Café** • 860 Terry Ave N
  206-324-1126 • $
  This excellent cafe upstages the Museum of History & Industry in which it resides
- **Daniel's Broiler** • 809 Fairview Ave N
  206-621-8262 • $$$$
  Fancy folk (or those whose parents are paying) head here for decent steak.
- **I Love My GFF** • 1016 Republican St
  $
  Piles of healthy goodness. Arch Nemesis of the Famous Bowl.
- **I Love Sushi** • 1001 Fairview Ave N
  206-625-9604 • $$
  Sushi with a water view.
- **McCormick & Schmick's Harborside** •
  1200 Westlake Ave N
  206-270-9052 • $$$
  Corporate club vibe and an unparalleled $1.95 happy hour burger.
- **Raney Brothers BBQ** •
  206-371-5078 • $
  Suicide food at its most suicidal.
- **Shanik** • 500 Terry Ave N
  206-486-6884 • $$$
  Vij's, the Vancouver BC restaurant with a cult following, brings their legendary grub southward.

Lake Union

E Galer St 1

E Galer St 2

E Highland Dr

E Highland Dr

**20**

St. Marks Cathedral

E Highland Dr

Volunteer Park

PAGE 202

Seattle Asian Art Museum

Fairview Ave N

Eastlake Ave E

E Nelson Pl

Lakeview Blvd E

**◄16**

A

Lakeview Blvd E

Exit 167

E Prospect St

E Prospect St

Summit Ave E

Bellevue Pl E

Belmont Ave E

Bellevue Ct E

Boylston Ave E

Harvard Ave E

Broadway E

10th Ave E

Federal Ave E

Volunteer Park Rd

12th Ave E

13th Ave E

E Ward St

E Aloha St

E Aloha St

E Aloha St

E Valley S

Exit 166

Roy St

10th Ave E

E Roy St

E Roy St

11th Ave E

13th Ave E

14th Ave E

E Roy St

Eastlake Ave E

Top Pot Donuts

E Mercer St

Broadway E

E Mercer St

**18►**

B

Melrose Ave E

Bellevue Ave E

Summit Ave E

Belmont Ave E

Boylston Ave E

E Republican St

E Republican St

**5**

E Harrison St

Boylston Ave E

10th Ave E

Federal Ave E

E Harrison St

Malden Ave E

E Thomas St

10th Ave E

11th Ave E

12th Ave E

13th Ave E

14th Ave E

E Thomas St

**◄2**

Harvard Ave E

Williams Ct E

C

Eastlake Ave E

E John St

E Olive Way

Belmont Ave E

Boylston Ave E

E Olive Way

Spooky Coke Machine

E John St

E Denny Way

Public Toilet on Broadway

E Denny Way

E Loretta Pl

Cal Anderson Park

PAGE 176

E Denny Way

E Howell St

Summit Ave E

Belmont Ave E

**4**

Broadway E

Nagle Pl

E Olive Pl

E Olive Way

Harvard Ave E

Seattle Central Community College

E Howell St

E Olive St

| 1/4 mile | .25 km |

Seattle's a gay-friendly city and there's no neighborhood pinker than Capitol Hill, particularly along the main drag, Broadway. Rainbow flags festoon the lampposts, bold displays of affection are commonplace, and leather daddies can be spotted strolling grocery store aisles in full regalia. Meanwhile, runaway street urchins make themselves at home and new condos are beginning to sprout up on every corner. Oh, and by 2016 that gaping hole at Broadway and John will have become a Light Rail station. Get an espresso at **Espresso Vivace** and contemplate it all.

## o Landmarks

- **Public Toilet on Broadway** • 115 Broadway E
  A crap capsule of sex and drugs.
- **Saint Mark's Cathedral** • 1245 10th Ave E
  206-323-0300
  Colossal cathedral on the hill; compline choir attracts yuppies, grannies, and street kids alike.
- **Seattle Asian Art Museum** • 1400 E Prospect St
  206-654-3100
  Gorgeous Art Deco building with a superb collection of Asian art.
- **Spooky Coke Machine** • E John St & Broadway E
  Press the mystery button if you dare.
- **Top Pot Doughnuts** • 609 Summit Ave E
  206-323-7841
  The planet's best donut shop.

## Coffee

- **Analog Coffee** • 235 Summit Ave E
  A sweet little neighborhood coffee joint that, luddite moniker aside, totally allows lap tops.
- **Espresso Vivace** • 532 Broadway E
  206-860-2722
  The ultimate coffee hut.
- **Espresso Vivace** • 321 Broadway E
  Watch the beautiful Broadway freak show stroll by.
- **Joe Bar** • 810 E Roy St
  206-324-0407
  Solid joe from Joe.
- **Roy Street Coffee & Tea** • 700 Broadway Ave E
  206-325-2211
  Another incognito Starbucks.
- **TNT Espresso** • 324 Broadway Ave E
  206-323-9151
  You could get better coffee, but probably not as fast.

## Farmers Markets

- **Broadway Farmers Market** • 400 Pine St
  Sundays, 11-3, mid-May to Mid-December

## Nightlife

- **Bait Shop** • 606 Broadway E
  206-420-8742
  Linda Derschang brings her hipster revolution to the Seafood world.
- **Captain Black's** • 129 Belmont Ave E
  206-327-9549
  Here be booze, chicken, waffles, and a patio.
- **Dilettante Mocha Café** • 538 Broadway E
  206-329-6463
  Premium chocolate orgy.
- **Highline** • 210 Broadway E
  206-328-7837
  Valhala for vegan punks. Plus Cake-aroke!
- **The Stumbling Monk** • 1635 E Olive Way
  206-860-0916
  Discuss the waning political climate over Belgian beers. NFT fav.
- **Summit Public House** • 601 Summit Ave E
  206-324-7611
  The quintessential neighborhood pub.
- **Sun Liquor** • 607 Summit Ave E
  206-860-1130
  What's better than freshly-juiced cocktails and warm nuts? Not a damn thing.
- **Theory Vodka Lounge** • 715 Olive Way
  206-915-2852
  Theorize about which of their 75+ vodkas gets you the drunkest.
- **Tommy Gun** • 1703 E Olive Way
  206-323-4866
  The most conspicuous of the Seattle speakeasies.

Map 1

# Restaurants

- **Altura** • 617 Broadway E
  206-402-6749 • $$$$
  Occasion dining with the full Italian treatment, from aperitif to dolce.
- **Aoki Japanese Grill & Sushi Bar** • 621 Broadway E
  206-324-3633 • $$$
  Japanese owned, Japanese served.
- **Bait Shop** • 606 Broadway E
  206-420-8742 • $$
  Linda Derschang brings her hipster revolution to the Seafood world.
- **Barriga Llena** • 219 Broadway E
  206-782-1220 • $
  Tortas are Mexican food in sandwich form. These are really good versions of that concept.
- **Charlie's Bar & Grill** • 217 Broadway E
  206-323-2535 • $$
  Bar food that tastes like home cookin'. Or tries to.
- **Crumble & Flake Patisserie** • 1500 E Olive Way
  206-329-1804 • $$
  Aptly-named bakery which sells out of its popular treats every single day.
- **Deluxe Bar & Grill** • 625 Broadway E
  206-324-9697 • $$
  Kitchen stays open late, and the fries will leave you begging for mercy.
- **Dick's Drive-In** • 115 Broadway E
  206-323-1300 • $
  A local obsession, specializing in cheap burgers and shakes. Perfect at 1 am.

- **Dilettante Mocha Café** • 538 Broadway E
  206-329-6463 • $$
  Just skip dinner and indulge in a chocolate desse orgy. You deserve it.
- **Glo's** • 1621 E Olive Way
  206-324-2577 • $
  Almost puts Grandma's biscuits and gravy to shame. Great on a rainy morning.
- **Irwin's Cafe Hydro House** • 1201 Eastlake Ave E
  206-623-1510 • $$
  Quaint cafe with great pastries and a carb-heavy lunch menu.
- **Jai Thai** • 235 Broadway E
  206-322-5781 • $
  Consistently good Thai; the curries are always kickin', and the happy hour menu is tops.
- **Noah's Bagels** • 220 Broadway E
  206-720-2925 • $
  Better to wait for your next trip to New York.
- **Pagliacci Pizza** • 426 Broadway E
  206-324-0730 • $$
  Local favorite pizza chain makes crispy-chewy delights with seasonal ingredients.
- **Panevino Trattoria** • 416 Broadway E
  206-328-7187 • $$
  A good Italian joint.
- **Pho Cyclo** • 406 Broadway E
  206-329-9256 • $
  Super-tasty bowls of pho. Not the cheapest, but one of the yummiest.

For Vietnamese pho, try **Pho Cyclo** or the **Capitol Hill Than Brothers**. **Aoki** pulls off good quality sushi and a wide selection of sakes. Feed your Broadway posse at **Dick's Drive-In** late Friday night after sipping a divine cocktail at **Sun Liquor**. **The Stumbling Monk** is a comfy spot for Belgian beers and good conversation. If you don't have Netflix, get your movies at **Broadway Video**. **Glo's** is the place for breakfast (now open late!), but be prepared to wait.

- **Pho Than Brothers'** • 516 Broadway E
  206-568-7218 • $
  Three words: free cream puff.
- **Poppy** • 622 Broadway E
  206-324-1108 • $$$
  Fine dining in an IKEA show room.
- **Queen Sheba** • 916 E John St
  206-322-0852 • $
  Finger-lickin' spicy goodness to mop up with injera bread. Bring friends.
- **Rom Mai Thai** • 613 Broadway E
  206-726-9058 • $
  Friendly people and top-notch Thai; one of the best on Broadway.
- **Table 219** • 219 Broadway E
  206-328-4604 • $$
  Same brunch classics from the El Greco days; dinner's got new creative touches.
- **Tacos Chukis** • 219 Broadway E
  206-328-4447 • $
  What they do to your meat with a pinepple is illegal several states.
- **Thomas Street Bistro** • 421 E Thomas St
  206-323-0914 • $$
  Euro dining without the need to learn a foreign language.
- **Top Pot Doughnuts** • 609 Summit Ave E
  206-323-7841 • $
  Top Pot is tops!
- **Zhivago's Café** • 416 Broadway E
  206-328-0500 • $
  Delicious piroshkies. No Bolshevik.

## 🛍 Shopping

- **American Apparel** • 200 Broadway E
  206-709-8100
  Soft t-shirts and free porn!
- **Broadway Video** • 512 Broadway E
  206-328-5023
  With five-day specials and reservations, who needs Netflix?
- **Castle Megastore** • 206 Broadway E
  206-204-0126
  An adult mega-store.
- **The Confectional** • 618 Broadway E
  206-282-4422
  The real sin is skipping dessert.
- **Crossroads Trading Co.** • 325 Broadway E
  206-328-5867
  Buys and sells only fashionable designer clothing.
- **Metro Clothing Company** • 231 Broadway E
  206-726-7978
  Goth Wear. Costumes for some. Business Casual for others.
- **Mishu Boutique II** • 321 Broadway E
  206-802-8022
  Unique, affordable clothing made by folks in Asia who get lunch breaks.
- **Pretty Parlor** • 119 Summit Ave E
  206-405-2883
  Vintage and locally designed couture that make you feel pretty.
- **Red Light Vintage Clothing** • 312 Broadway E
  206-329-2200
  Vintage clothing for people with 10 inch waists.
- **Spin Cycle** • 321 Broadway Ave E
  206-971-0267
  As lovingly stocked as that shop in "High Fidelity" but without all the attitude.
- **Urban Outfitters** • 401 Broadway E
  206-322-1800
  Fashionable and affordable clothes for faux-city dwellers.
- **Vino Verite** • 208 Boylston Ave E
  206-324-0324
  These guys love wine even more than you do.

# Map 18 · Capitol Hill (East) / Madison Valley

While the western side of Capitol Hill caters directly to the young and decadent, the eastern portion of the neighborhood is more of a, well, neighborhood. Still, there's no shortage of pink pride or nightlife, so it's not utter culture shock. Nearby Madison Valley is even homier, with numerous parks, public schools, and escalating real estate values—a far cry from the down-and-out neighborhood it once was.

## o Landmarks

- **Singles Apartment Complex** • 1820 E Thomas St
No, Matt Dillon doesn't live here anymore.
- **Volunteer Park** • 1247 15th Ave E
206-684-4075
Climb to the top of this Victorian-era conservatory and water tower.

##  Coffee

- **Caffe Ladro** • 435 15th Ave E
206-267-0551
Strong coffee for the strong coffee drinker.
- **Coffee Pronto** • 312 15th Ave E
206-322-9693
Breakfast, too.
- **El Portal Coffee Roasters** • 2310 E Madison St
206-860-6923
El portal goes to Mexico where the coffee is muy bueno.
- **Fuel** • 610 19th Ave E
206-329-4700
Now this is a type of fuel that actually has a future
- **Victrola Coffee & Art** • 411 15th Ave E
206-325-6520
From a time before coffee was good.

## Nightlife

- **The BottleNeck Lounge** • 2328 E Madison St
206-323-1098
Come meet your new neighbors at this cozy spot.
- **Hopvine Pub** • 507 15th Ave E
206-328-3120
100% Pacific Northwest right down to the beer and fleece.
- **Liberty** • 517 15th Ave E
206-323-9898
Sushi and cocktails served by people who are more hip than you.
- **Smith** • 332 15th Ave E
206-709-1900
Linda's winning combination of animal heads and hipster pub fare.

## Restaurants

- **Bamboo** • 345 15th Ave E
  206-567-3399 • $$
  Pho house with veggie-loaded menu.
- **Coastal Kitchen** • 429 15th Ave E
  206-322-1145 • $$$
  A quarterly rotating menu focusing on a different global cuisine. And blunch!
- **Crush** • 2319 E Madison St
  206-302-7874 • $$
  Gorgeous food pops against the modern, sexy interior. Service to write home about.
- **The Essential Baking Company** •
  2719 E Madison St
  206-328-0078 • $
  You'll think you're in a European bakery.
- **Gyro Cafe** • 107 15th Ave E
  206-324-6435 • $
  Hit-or-miss gyrocery.
- **The Harvest Vine** • 2701 E Madison St
  206-320-9771 • $$
  Gorgeous, perfect tapas.
- **Jamjuree** • 509 15th Ave E
  206-323-4255 • $
  Another competent Thai restaurant.
- **The Kingfish Cafe** • 602 19th Ave E
  206-320-8757 • $$
  The place for comforting soul food. Eat up, get f be grateful.
- **Monsoon** • 615 19th Ave E
  206-325-2111 • $$$
  Sublimely elegant Vietnamese, and oh-so-affordable. Great dim sum brunch.
- **The Patio Fine Thai** • 524 15th Ave E
  206-328-2406 • $
  Doing their part to keep Thai food ubiquitous in Sea-town.

# Capitol Hill (East) / Madison Valley

Capitol Hill East is home to plenty of laid-back restaurants and pubs. If Linda's is the hipster starter bar, Derschang's **Smith**, with its rotating taps and charcuterie plates, is where they graduate to once they've settled into steady-paycheck adulthood. Try **Liberty** for sushi in a stylish setting. The **Kingfish Café** serves up tasty soul food and fries a mean chicken. Madison Valley is known for fancy four-star eateries like **Crush** and **The Harvest Vine** for folks in ties and polished shoes.

- **Remedy Teas** • 345 15th Ave E
  206-323-4832 • $$
  150 incredible loose teas, the friendliest staff, lovely treats, and a clean, modern interior.
- **Rione XIII** • 401 15th Ave E
  206-838-2878 • $$
  Ethan Stowell brings you wood fired pizza, 13th District Rome style.
- **Smith** • 332 15th Ave E
  206-709-1900 • $$
  Perfect sweet potato fries and brunch make for elegantly eclectic pub fare.
- **Vios Café & Marketplace** • 903 19th Ave E
  206-329-3236 • $
  Beautiful Greek dishes. Wines for the adults, play area for the kiddies.
- **The Wandering Goose** • 403 15th Ave E
  206-323-9938 • $$
  A great place to wander into, goose or otherwise.

Shopping

- **Henrietta's Hats** • 2707 E Madison St
  206-322-8169
  Need a custom Kentucky Derby hat? Here you go.
- **North Hill Bakery** • 518 15th Ave E
  206-325-9007
  Popular local bakery.
- **Shoprite** • 432 15th Ave E
  206-328-5138
  Sort of like a dollar store, but better—and more random.

Map 18

Polar opposite extremes of wealth and health. Families living in mansions on Lake Washington recreate at the Seattle Tennis Club's waterfront courts and privately educate prodigal youth at the elite Bush School. Nearby, at a gritty city intersection, Seattle's Bailey-Bouche provides housing for people living with terminal diseases and public schools get the axe due to budget cuts. Gotta love the commonalities— Seattle Tennis Club, Bush School, and Bailey-Bouche House all have exclusive admission criteria.

## ○ Landmarks

- **Japanese Garden** • 1075 Lake Washington Blvd E
  206-684-4725
  Renowned formal Japanese garden; check out the periodic tea ceremonies.
- **Seattle Tennis Club** • 922 McGilvra Blvd E
  206-324-3200
  A venerable Madison Park institution. Country clubbish.

## 🍴 Restaurants

- **Belle Epicurean** • 3109 E Madison St
  206-466-1320 • $
  Inspired French pastries served with approriately snooty attitude.
- **Café Flora** • 2901 E Madison St
  206-325-9100 • $$
  Eat fancy vegetarian (one of the country's best) in a Zen garden.
- **Nishino** • 3130 E Madison St
  206-322-5800 • $$$
  One of the premier sushi places in town. Reservations requisite.
- **Voilà ! Bistrot** • 2805 E Madison St
  206-322-5460 • $$$
  Classic French in a classy setting. Stupid name.

## 🛍 Shopping

- **City People's Garden Store** • 2939 E Madison St
  206-324-0737
  Yes, you too can have flowers blooming and veggies growing year round in Seattle.
- **Fury Extraordinary Women's Consignment** •
  2810 E Madison St
  206-329-6829
  Got-bucks women consign clothing onto the racks of Fury.
- **The Lavender Heart** • 2812 E Madison St
  206-568-4441
  Walk into the store, breathe in the creative mind of owner Holly Henderson, exhale.

Map 20 · **Eastlake / Montlake / Portage Bay**

N

1
2

NE Boat St

NE Pacific St

Eastlake Av Ramp

Portage Bay Pl E

26

PAGE
198

University of
Washington

Meridian Ave N

N Pacific St

N Northlake Way

A

25

Eastlake Ave E

E Martin St

Broadway E

Fairview Ave E

E Allison St

E Allison St

E Allison St

E Gwinn Pl

1800

E Shelby St

E Shelby St

10th Ave E

5

Exit 168A

Boylston Ave E

Portage Bay

E Hamlin St

E Hamlin St

Harvard Ave E

Broadway E

10th Ave E

E Edgar St

E Edgar St

Yale Ter

Yale Ave E

Franklin Ave E

1700

Roanoke
Park

1000

E Roanoke St

520

B

Fairview Ave E

Minor Ave E

Yale Ave E

Eastlake Ave E

Rogers
Playground

E Louisa St

Franklin Ave E

Exit 168B

Boylston Ave E

Harvard Ave E

10th Ave E

E Miller St

Delmar Dr E

Boyer Ave E

Everett Ave E

21

Mo
Pla

19th Ave E

16th Ave E

3 Ave E

E Calhoun St

14th Ave E

E Miller St

E Mcgraw St

E Lynn St

E Lynn St

12th Ave

13th Ave

Reid Ave E

Franklin Ave E

2200

E Boston St

E Boston St

11th Ave

12th Ave

Broadway E

18th Ave E

Lake Union

Boylston Ave E

100

E Newton St

2100

E Newton St

E Crockett St

Everett Ave E

Federal Ave E

1200

Grand
Army
Cemetery

14th Ave E

15th Ave E

E Boston Ter

Interlaken Blvd

Interlaken Dr E

Harvard Ave E

Yale Pl E

Franklin Pl E

Eastlake Ave E

E Howe St

C

E Blaine St

E Blaine St

10th Ave E

Lake View
Cemetery

E Clay Pl

E Garfield St

15th Ave E

Grandview Pl E

Auburn Pl E

E Garfield St

Fairview Ave E

E Garfield St

E Galer St

E Galer St

1000

1100

Lakeview Blvd E

E Galer St

17

Volunteer
Park

PAGE
202

15th Ave E

E Galer St

E Highland Dr

E Highland Dr

1/4 mile

.25 km

Map 20

Eastlake is one gem of a neighborhood with an ideal location—a short bus ride from the U District and a hop-skip-jump from downtown. Being nuzzled up to Lake Washington makes the 'hood that much more desirable. It's old, funky, and a touch European, with its brightly painted homes and homespun shops. Once a more industrial section of town, residential buildings have sprung up near Eastlake's idyllic and thriving houseboat community.

# Coffee

- **Voxx Coffee** • 2245 Eastlake Ave E
  206-324-2778
  A welcoming shop with tons of outlets. Take off your coat and stay a while.

# Nightlife

- **Eastlake Zoo Tavern** • 2301 Eastlake Ave E
  206-329-3277
  Those grizzled old bartenders also own the joint.
- **Roanoke Park Place** • 2409 10th Ave E
  206-324-5882
  Drown another Husky football loss in their good beer selection.
- **Ship Canal Grill** • 3218 Eastlake Ave E
  206-588-8885
  Nautical-themed sports bar. Nothing says "football" like "fish n' chips."

# Restaurants

- **14 Carrot Café** • 2305 Eastlake Ave E
  206-324-1442 • $$
  Typical breakfast fare that's, well, typical. Popular anyway.
- **Abay Ethiopian Cusine** • 2359 10th Ave E
  206-257-4778 • $$
  Probably the best Ethiopian food you've ever tasted, unless your mother is Ethiopian.
- **Blind Pig at Eastlake Teriyaki** •
  2236 Eastlake Ave E
  206-329-2744 • $
  Day-time lunch annex for the unassuming but decadent Blind Pig Bistro serving seasonal sandwiches from multiple genres.

- **Blind Pig Bistro** • 2238 Eastlake Ave E
  206-329-2744 • $$
  Chalkboard foodie place, classing up that weird Eastlake mini strip mall.
- **Little Water Cantina** • 2865 Eastlake Ave E
  206-397-4940 • $$
  Mediocre, overpriced "modern" Mexican. And such small portions.
- **Louisa's Café & Bakery** • 2379 Eastlake Ave E
  206-325-0081 • $
  Baked goods, espresso, counter service.
- **Ravish** • 2956 Eastlake Ave E
  206-913-2497 • $$
  Wine bar with small plates.
- **Sebi's Bistro** • 3242 Eastlake Ave E
  206-420-2199 • $$
  Did you hear the one about the Polish restaurant?
- **Serafina** • 2043 Eastlake Ave E
  206-323-0807 • $$
  Rustic and charming Italian. A very loyal Eastlake following.
- **Sushi Kappo Tamura** • 2968 Eastlake Ave E
  206-547-0937 • $$$
  Fancy pants sushi that's worth conning someone into paying for.

# Shopping

- **Everyday Music** • 1520 10th Ave E
  206-568-3321
  Two floors of used CDs, DVDs, and LPs. Your wallet is screwed.
- **The Flower Lady** • 3230 Eastlake Ave E
  206-325-5751
  Finally out of the parking lot and into her own shop—delightful flowers within budget.

# Map 21 · Montlake

1

2

PAGE 198

University of Washington

Union Bay

A

E Allison St

E Shelby St

Portage Bay

E Hamlin St

Lake Washington Canal

26

E Shelby St

West Montlake Park

Montlake Blvd

E Park Dr

East Montlake Park

E Edgar St

E Hamlin St

Seattle Yacht Club

24th Ave

520

E Lake Washington Blvd

E North St

Montlake Playfield

E Roanoke St

E Louisa St

2400

Road Ct E

26th Ave E

Delmar Dr E

Everett Ave E

15th Ave E

Boyer Ave E

14th Ave E

19th Ave E

W Montlake Pl E

20th Ave E

22nd Ave E

24th Ave E

25th Ave E

E Miller St

E Calhoun St

E Foster Island Rd

E Miller St

12th Ave E

13th Ave E

E Calhoun St

2600

B

E Crockett St

E McGraw St

1600

E Lynn St

E McGraw St

20

E Interlaken Blvd

18th Ave E

E Newton St

E Howe St

E Boston St

22

E Newton St

25th Ave E

Everett Ave E

14th Ave E

15th Ave E

E Boston Ter

E Blaine St

19th Ave E

20th Ave E

21st Ave E

22nd Ave E

23rd Ave E

2400

26th Ave E

E Newton St

E Newton St

E Newton St

E Boston St

1700

Grand Army Cemetery

E Newton St

1500

E Howe St

Boyer Ave E

PAGE 203

Lake Washington Blvd E

Washington Park Arboretum

O

Lake View Cemetery

Elm Pl E

Interlaken Dr E

Interlaken Park

Interlaken Pl E

24th Ave E

C

E Garfield St

Grandview Pl E

Auburn Pl E

15th Ave E

Interlaken Dr E

20th Ave E

Peach Pl E

E Crescent Dr E

28th Ave E

29th Ave E

E Interlaken Blvd

E Garfield St

2300

2400

Volunteer Park

PAGE 202

18

15th Ave E

16th Ave E

17th Ave E

18th Ave E

19th Ave E

20th Ave E

21st Ave E

22nd Ave E

23rd Ave E

E Galer St

E Lee St

26th Ave E

E Highland Dr

Arboretum Dr E

1/4 mile

.25 km

This classy, educated neighborhood borders the bucolic Arboretum, the wooded ravines of Interlaken Park, and the Montlake Cut connecting Lake Union and Lake Washington. The venerable **Seattle Yacht Club** presides west of the bridge. The spiffy Montlake Branch Library attracts local brainiacs, and regattas draw rowers to May's raucous first day of boating season. Beware—traffic chokes Montlake on Husky game days and during drawbridge openings.

## ○ Landmarks

- **Lake View Cemetery** • 1554 15th Ave E
  206-322-1582
  Bruce Lee for Kung Fu enthusiasts. Brandon Lee for the Goths.
- **Seattle Yacht Club** • 1807 E Hamlin St
  206-325-1000
  Sorry little buddy. Members only.

## Coffee

- **Fuel** • 2300 24th Ave E
  206-405-3835
  Now this is a type of fuel that actually has a future.

## Nightlife

- **Montlake Ale House** • 2307 24th Ave E
  206-726-5968
  Features a kid pit for weary parents who need a drink. Their food needs work.

## Restaurants

- **Café Lago** • 2305 24th Ave E
  206-329-8005 • $$$
  Heartbreakingly wonderful neighborhood Italian.
- **Volunteer Park Cafe and Marketplace** •
  1501 17th Ave E
  206-328-3155 • $
  Stop by after a stroll through Volunteer Park to grab a light-as-air scone.

## Shopping

- **Mont's Market** • 2350 24th Ave E
  206-860-7876
  Gourmet goods for the 'hood.
- **Montlake Bicycle Shop** • 2223 24th Ave E
  206-329-7333
  Used bikes rentals, and sales. Knowledgeable staff.
- **Mr. Johnson's Antiques** • 2315 24th Ave E
  206-322-6033
  Fair prices, some negotiable.

1

2

A

East
Montlake
Park

Union Bay

520

Everdreen Point Brdg

E Roanoke St

E Edgewater Pl

E Miller St

E Mcgilvra St

3800

Canterbury Ln E

4100

E Calhoun St

E McGraw St

E Mcgraw St

E Lynn St

38th Ave E

38th Ave

39th Ave

40th Ave E

E Lynn St

41st Ave E

42nd Ave E

43rd Ave E

3300

Foster Island Rd

E Boston St

B

PAGE
203

Broadmoor Dr E

E Shorr Dr

E Crockett St

3800

37th Ave

38th Ave

39th Ave

42nd Ave E

Washington
Park
Arboretum

Washington
Park Arboretum

E Newton St

4100

Mcgilvra Blvd

3800

E Howe St

Madison
Park

Waverly Way

21

Arboretum Dr E

Parkside Dr

E Howe St

37th Pl E

37th Ave

38th Ave

39th Ave

Broadmoor
Golf
Club

Sherwood Dr

Broadmoor Dr

E Blaine St

41st Ave E

4100

Madison
Park
Beach

26th Ave

28th Ave

Boyer Ave

Lake Washington Blvd E

Lake Washington Blvd E

E Blaine St

3800

Windermere Dr E

Emerson Ave

E Garfield St

42nd Ave E

37th Ave

E Madison St

Mcgilvra Blvd

C

Woodrow Pl E

E Galer St

1400

19

E Lee St

26th Ave

E Prospect St

Lexington Way E

St Andrews Way

38th Ave

E Morley Way

E Highland Dr

E Highland Dr

E Highland Dr

Lake Washington

E Helen St

Mcgilvra Blvd E

E Prospect St

E Prospect St

31st Ave E

32nd Ave E

33rd Ave

34th Ave E

36th Ave

Knox Pl E

42nd Ave E

Washington Pl E

E Ward St

E Ward St

1/4 mile

.25 km

Transferred here from Connecticut and miss the East Coast? Move to Madison Park and fork over serious dough for a cozy bungalow. Or for a few million more, you'll feel right at home in Broadmoor, a gated community established long before anyone knew gates from Gates. Waterfront condos have mountain and lake views, and the Madison Park hub will offer you those trendy little shops and cliquey, smug, safe neighborhood feel you've been missing since moving from Darien.

## ⊙ Landmarks

- **Washington Park Arboretum** •
  2300 Arboretum Dr E
  206-543-8100
  A haven for tree-huggers, bird-watchers, and botanists.

##  Coffee

- **East Madison Street Coffee Bar & Deli** •
  2818 E Madison St
  206-327-9242
  You'll go here because you have little other choice.
- **Harbour Pointe Coffeehouse** • 2818 E Madison St
  206-420-1187
  It's totally one of your options in Madison Park!

##  Nightlife

- **Attic Ale House & Eatery** • 4226 E Madison St
  206-323-3131
  Serving up the brews since '53.

##  Restaurants

- **Arosa Cafe** • 3121 E Madison St
  206-324-4542 • $
  It's a waffle cafe. I'll let that sink in…
- **Bing's** • 4200 E Madison St
  206-323-8623 • $$
  Madison Park's go-to burger joint. Mainly because it's there.
- **Cactus** • 4220 E Madison St
  206-324-4140 • $$$
  Outstanding mojitos and Mexican.
- **Cafe Parco** • 1807 42nd Ave E
  206-328-4757 • $$
  Up-and-comer in the generally lacking upscale Italian scene.
- **The Independent Pizzeria** • 4235 E Madison St
  206-860-6110 • $
  A classy family pizza joint with a DIY attitude.
- **Madison Kitchen** • 4122 E Madison St
  206-557-4640 • $$
  A decent lunch counter conveniently located near one of the prettiest parks in Seattle.
- **Madison Park Conservatory** • 1927 43rd Ave E
  206-324-9701 • $$$
  A culinary celebration of those animals unlucky enough to be lower on the food chain.

## 🛍 Shopping

- **Madison Cellars** • 4227 E Madison St
  206-323-9333
  Artistic postcard of a wine store—the tiny cellar boasts an eclectic selection.
- **Scoop du Jour** • 4029 E Madison St
  206-325-9562
  32 flavors of ice cream and a deli!

A Scandinavian fishing village at the turn of the 20th century and until relatively recently considered a nice place for seniors, Ballard has reinvented and reinvigorated itself as one of Seattle's most desirable 'nabes. Life's necessities are never hard to track down in this triangle-shaped hub hugging Salmon Bay, and a recent boom in condo development certainly doesn't hurt.

## ○ Landmarks
- **Bergen Place Park** • 5420 22nd Avenue Northwest
  206-684-4075
  Seuss-like tree sculptures and Scandinavian flags.

 ## Coffee
- **Anchored Ship Coffee Bar** • 5306 Ballard Ave NW
  206-484-5143
  Hole-in-the-wall that will keep you anchored.
- **B&O Espresso** • 5404 Leary Ave NW
  206-322-5028
  The Cap Hill legend has settled into its new home where they're less likely to get turned into condos.
- **Ballard Coffee Works** • 2060 NW Market St
  206-340-8867
  The coffee here definitely works.
- **Caffè Fiorè** • 5405 Leary Ave NW
  206-706-0421
  Makes the bold claim of being Seattle's first organic coffee.

- **Cupcake Royale/Verite Coffee** •
  2052 NW Market St
  206-883-7656
  Cupcakes and coffee go well together.
- **Equal Exchange Espresso Bar** • 1400 NW 56th St
  206-783-4955
  They're all about the free trade, so you can feel extra smug about your latte.
- **Java Bean** • 5819 24th Ave NW
  206-788-9677
  Since 1989: organic, shade grown, fair trade.
- **Java Jahn** • 1428 NW Leary Way
  206-789-9441
  They'll be your Jahnny on the spot for your caffeine fix.
- **Sip & Ship** • 1752 NW Market St
  206-789-4488
  Like a home office with an espresso bar.
- **Slate Coffee Bar** • 5413 6th Ave NW
  206-240-7174
  The perfect place for a clean slate.
- **The Way Station** • 336 NW 40th St
  206-789-5900
  When you're short on will, try the Way.

# Nightlife

- **The 2 Bit Saloon** • 4818 17th Ave NW
206-708-6917
Stiff drinks, filthy bathrooms.
- **Ballard Annex Oyster House** •
5410 Ballard Ave NW
206-783-5410
The fun seafood party that Red Lobster ads promised and couldn't deliver.
- **Ballard Loft** • 5105 Ballard Ave NW
206-420-2737
The place in Ballard to watch the game. Any game.
- **Ballard Smoke Shop** • 5439 Ballard Ave NW
206-784-6611
A smokey taste of Old Ballard.
- **Ballard Station Public House** •
2236 NW Market St
206-906-9040
Super chill Ballard scene specializing in local brews and spirits.
- **BalMar** • 5449 Ballard Ave NW
206-486-5449
Plenty of places to sit to avoid some of the more annoying clientele.
- **Hattie's Hat** • 5231 Ballard Ave NW
206-784-0175
Still gritty, but we're no longer afraid to eat there.
- **Hazelwood** • 2311 NW Market St
206-783-0478
Classy but not snooty, with two levels of dimly-lit ambiance.
- **Jolly Roger Taproom** • 1111 NW Ballard Way
206-782-6181
Bigger location with a subdued pirate theme. Fried pickles: Aarr!
- **Kangaroo & Kiwi** • 2026 NW Market St
206-297-0507
Where homesick Australians get pissed with New Zealand ex-pats.
- **Kickin' Boot Whiskey Kitchen** •
5309 22nd Ave NW
206-783-2668
Ballardites can get their kicks with whiskey and modern southern cuisine.

- **King's Hardware** • 5225 Ballard Ave NW
206-782-0027
Uber-hip bar with unhip crowd on weekends. Brought to you by Linda.
- **The Leary Traveler** • 4354 Leary Way NW
206-783-4805
Frites and beer! Rest your barking dogs here.
- **Lock & Keel Tavern** • 5144 Ballard Ave NW
206-781-8023
A boat graveyard with booze.
- **The Market Arms** • 2401 NW Market St
206-789-0470
Fine footie pub from the blokes behind the George & Dragon.
- **Matador** • 2221 NW Market St
206-297-2855
Lots of tequila. Lots.
- **Ocho** • 2325 NW Market St
206-784-0699
Like having an office party in your walk-in closet.
- **The People's Pub** • 5429 Ballard Ave NW
206-783-6521
Like grandma's dining room, with late-night schnitzel and wurst.
- **The Sexton** • 5327 Ballard Ave NW
206-829-8645
Southern comfort tapas and comfort booze to match.
- **Shelter Lounge** • 4910 Leary Ave NW
206-829-8568
An urban ski lodge.
- **The Sunset** • 5433 Ballard Ave NW
206-784-4880
Opium den-themed bar and concert venue for local bands.
- **The Tractor Tavern** • 5213 Ballard Ave NW
206-789-3599
Live alt twang.
- **Urban Family Public House** • 5329 Ballard Ave NW
206-861-6769
25 taps for people who consider beer their family.
- **Zayda Buddy's** • 5405 Leary Ave NW
206-783-7777
Fhaux-dive with Leinenkugel's!

# Ballard

Map 23

| 33 | 34 |
| 29 | 30 | 31 | 32 | 27 |
| 23 |
| 24 | 25 | 26 |
| 12 | 13 |
| 20 | 21 | 22 |

Spots like **Hattie's Hat**, **Tractor Tavern**, **King's Hardware**, and the **People's Pub** have the bases covered for great neighborhood nightlife. The **Tractor Tavern** is your home for live alt-country. Discover your new favorite band at the **Sunset**.

 Restaurants

- **Ann's Teriyaki** • 2246 NW Market St
  206-789-5838 • $
  Huge menu, gigantic portions, quick. And cheap!
- **Ballard Annex Oyster House** •
  5410 Ballard Ave NW
  206-783-5410 • $$$
  The fun seafood party that Red Lobster ads promised and couldn't deliver.
- **Ballard Mandarin Chinese Restaurant** •
  5500 8th Ave NW
  206-782-5531 • $$
  I wouldn't do it…unless it were on a bet.
- **Ballard Pizza Company** • 5107 Ballard Ave NW
  206-659-6033 • $$
  Ethan Stowell furthers his Ballard conquest with pizza & gnocchi.
- **Bastille Cafe & Bar** • 5307 Ballard Ave NW
  206-453-5014 • $$
  The French invade Little Norway with haute cuisine. Hipsters rejoice.
- **Belle Clementine** • 5451 Leary Ave NW
  206-257-5761 • $$
  Break bread with other foodies at this farm-to-table supper club.
- **Bitterroot** • 5239 Ballard Ave NW
  206-588-1577 • $$
  Even vegetarians don't have much to be bitter about at this transcendent BBQ spot.
- **The Blue Dog Kitchen** • 5905 15th Ave NW
  206-462-6083 • $$
  There is no way that dog is blue in the kitchen.
- **Café Besalu** • 5909 24th Ave NW
  206-789-1463 • $
  Beautifully crafted pastries, quiches, cookies, brioches…
- **Cafe Mox** • 5105 Leary Ave NW
  206-436-0540 • $
  Gamer cafe with way better food than your D.M. would provide.
- **Cafe Munir** • 2408 NW 80th St
  206-783-4190 • $$
  A nice family Lebanese restaurant that also serves liquor. We don't have enough of these.

- **Cupcake Royale/Verite Coffee** •
  2052 NW Market St
  206-883-7656 • $
  Cupcakes and coffee go well together.
- **The Dish** • 4358 Leary Way NW
  206-782-9985 • $$
  Probably one of the best tofu scrambles of all the local hippie-dippies.
- **El Camion** • 5314 15th Ave NW
  206-297-1124 • $
  Amazing truck tacos and tamales you can trust.
- **El Camión Adentro** • 6416 15th Ave NW
  206-784-5411 • $
  Brick-and-mortar version of Tom Douglas' (understandably) favorite taco truck.
- **Fez on Wheels** • 1550 NW 49th St
  206-432-0415 • $
  The hummus is a must.
- **Floating Leaves Tea** • 1704 NW Market St
  206-276-9542 • $
  Tea is the new coffee.
- **Flying Squirrel Pizza Co** •
  5433 Ballard Avenue Northwest
  206-784-4880 • $$
  Imaginative pies made from local organic ingredients. So very Seatown.
- **The Gerald** • 5210 Ballard Ave NW
  206-432-9280 • $$
  Upscale comfort fare perfect for the inebriated foodie.
- **Golden Beetle** • 1744 NW Market St
  206-706-2977 • $$
  An exotic flavor excursion brought to you by Maria Hines of Tilth fame.
- **Hale's Ales Pub** • 4301 Leary Way NW
  206-706-1544 • $$
  Seattle's oldest microbrewery with unfortunate corporate-like atmosphere.
- **The Hi-Life** • 5425 Russell Ave NW
  206-784-7272 • $$
  Breakfast, lunch, dinner, and quart-sized Bloody Marys in a 1911 firehouse.
- **Hot Cakes Molten Chocolate Cakery** •
  5427 Ballard Ave NW
  206-420-3431 • $$
  Decadent dessert cafe. Known for molten cakes and boozy milkshakes.

Map 23

# Ballard

- **India Bistro** • 2301 NW Market St
206-783-5080 • $$
Perfectly spiced entrees with excellent seafood.
- **Jolly Roger Taproom** • 1111 NW Ballard Way
206-782-6181 • $$
Yes, it's a brewery, but to call it pub food would be sacrilegious.
- **Kickin' Boot Whiskey Kitchen** •
5309 22nd Ave NW
206-783-2668 • $$
Ballardites can get their kicks with whiskey and modern southern cuisine.
- **La Carta de Oaxaca** • 5431 Ballard Ave NW
206-782-8722 • $$
Authentic Oaxacan—think deep, dark sweet mole—at bargain prices.
- **La Isla** • 2320 NW Market St
206-789-0516 • $$
A half-dozen Puerto Rican platos that are addictive and satisfying.
- **Louie's Cuisine of China** • 5100 15th Ave NW
206-782-8855 • $$
Chinese comfort food since 1930-something.
- **Matador** • 2221 NW Market St
206-297-2855 • $$
If you can't get a table at Oaxaca.
- **Mr. Gyros** • 5522 20th Ave NW
206-782-7777 • $
It's almost like he was born to make Gyros.
- **Nick's Off Market** • 1556 NW 56th St
206-783-0131 • $$
Local everything served in a casually upscale living room.
- **The Other Coast Café** • 5315 Ballard Ave NW
206-789-0936 • $
Sloppy sammies and super subs like they slather up way out east.
- **Pasta Bella** • 5913 15th Ave NW
206-789-4933 • $$$
Your run-of-the-mill romantic Italian restaurant.
- **Pho Big Bowl** • 2248 NW Market St
206-588-1249 • $
Pho-tastic. And big as advertized.
- **Pho Thân Brothers'** • 2021 NW Market St
206-782-5715 • $
Cheap, fast, and filling, with a free cream puff to boot.
- **Plaka Estiatorio** • 5407 20th Ave NW
206-829-8934 • $$
Opa! Hands down best Greek food in town.
- **Po Dog Hot Dogs** • 2014 NW Market St
206-783-3647 • $
If this is po, I don't wanna be rich.
- **Root Table** • 2213 NW Market St
206-420-3214 • $$
Menage-a-Thai.
- **Savour** • 2242 NW Market St
206-789-0775 • $$
If shopping for gourmet foodstuffs exhausts you, treat yourself to a glass of wine and charcuterie.
- **Senor Moose** • 5242 Leary Ave NW
206-784-5568 • $
Ballard breakfast institution. The guac is already legend.
- **Staple & Fancy Mercantile** • 4739 Ballard Ave NW
206-789-1200 • $$$
For a special night out, try the supper in 4 courses.
- **Stoneburner** • 5214 Ballard Ave NW
206-695-2051 • $$
Upscale pizza that you don't have to be a stoned burner to enjoy.
- **Tall Grass Bakery** • 5907 24th Ave NW
206-706-0991 • $
Bring extra bread to pay for these award-winning loaves.
- **Top Pot Doughnuts** • 1416 NW 46th Street
206-728-1986 • $
Top Pot is tops!
- **Vera's** • 5417 22nd Ave NW
206-782-9966 • $
Good old breakfast with crusty regulars.
- **Volterra** • 5411 Ballard Ave NW
206-789-5100 • $$$
Lovely Italian specialties with contemporary flair.
- **The Walrus and The Carpenter** •
4743 Ballard Ave NW
206-395-9227 • $$$
Stylish and transcendent oyster bar tucked behind a bike shop.
- **Yozen** • 2038 NW Market St
206-257-4658 • $
This froyo thing is not over. Not by a long shot.
- **Zayda Buddy's** • 5405 Leary Ave NW
206-783-7777 • $$
Midwestern comfort food and Schlitz. Burn in hell, Wisconsin, for sending us more hipsters.

The two main and navigable drags—vibrant Market Street and historic Ballard Avenue—feature tons of restaurants. **La Carta de Oaxaca** is well worth the wait, while **Vera's** is one of the last true old-school dining spots left in the city. Go big at Ethan Stowell's **Staple & Fancy** or Maria Hines' **Golden Beetle**. Have an oyster-gasm at **The Walrus and the Carpenter**. Finally, don't miss the **Ballard Market** every Sunday.

##  Shopping

- **Anchor Tattoo** • 2313 NW Market St
  206-784-4051
  You'll be in good, (and clean) hands here.
- **Ballard Farmers Market** • 5330 Ballard Ave NW
  Organic farmers, restauranteurs, and sidewalk buskers.
- **Ballard Town & Country Market** •
  1400 NW 56th St
  206-783-7922
  Local produce, wine and desserts.
- **Blackbird** • 5410 22nd Ave NW
  206-547-2524
  Hot designer clothes which you totally can't afford.
- **Bop Street Records** • 5219 Ballard Ave NW
  206-297-2232
  Huge basement full of vinyl. Certain piles off limits.
- **Buffalo Exchange** • 2232 NW Market St
  206-297-5920
  Second-hand clothes for girls who drink Zima.
- **Card Kingdom** • 5105 Leary Ave NW
  206-523-2273
  The ultimate destination for Lawful Good times.
- **Dutch Bike Co.** • 4741 Ballard Ave NW
  206-789-1678
  Super fancy bikes and espresso. Only in Seattle.
- **Electric & Folding Bikes Northwest** •
  4810 17th Ave NW
  206-547-4621
  Electric bicycle sales and repairs.
- **Fred Meyer** • 915 NW 45th St
  206-297-4300
  Just like Target but with groceries too!
- **Full Tilt Ice Cream** • 5453 Leary Ave NW
  206-297-3000
  Ice cream, beer & pinball. Sweet.
- **Greener Lifestyles** • 5317 Ballard Ave NW
  206-545-4405
  Interesting, eco-friendly (re: expensive) goods. Appointment Only.
- **Hilliard's Taproom** • 1550 NW 49th St
  206-257-4486
  Taste the local craft beer that has become an instant classic.
- **Jo Ann Fabrics** • 2217 NW 57th St
  206-782-6242
  Fabrics supplies and fun decorations at excellent prices.

- **La Tienda Folk Art Gallery** • 2050 NW Market St
  206-297-3605
  The difference between "folk art" and "tourist trap" is location.
- **NW Peaks Brewery** • 4912 17th Ave NW
  206-853-0525
  Limited-edition micro-brews inspired by the ice-cold Cascades.
- **Pink Ginger** • 5334 Ballard Ave NW
  206-285-2629
  Fashionable clothes for the ladies Mix-A-Lot sang about.
- **The RE Store** • 1440 NW 52nd St
  206-297-9119
  Funky reused building material and all the cheap knick-knacks you could possibly want.
- **Re-Soul** • 5319 Ballard Ave NW
  206-789-7312
  Where one goes to blow a paycheck on a pair of shoes.
- **Savour** • 2242 NW Market St
  206-789-0775
  Buy groceries like the Europeans with a selection of local cheeses and meats and a glass of wine.
- **Second Ascent** • 5209 Ballard Ave NW
  206-545-8810
  New and used sporting equipment.
- **Sonic Boom Records** • 2209 NW Market St
  206-297-2666
  National and international acts perform free live sets at the Ballard location.
- **Space Oddity Vintage Furniture** •
  5318 22nd Ave NW
  206-322-6704
  Ground control to major deals.
- **Sweet Mickey's** • 2230 NW 57th St
  206-402-6272
  Old fashioned sweets shop serving shakes, malts and candy rarities.
- **Vain** • 5401 Ballard Ave NW
  206-706-2707
  Hair. Shop. Art.
- **Velouria** • 2205 NW Market St
  206-788-0330
  Friendly boutique featuring indie designers.

# Map 24 • Fremont

Once a haven for counterculture in Seattle, Fremont has gentrified in recent years. Getty Images, Adobe, and Google all have offices near the ship canal and the famous naked cyclists of the Solstice Parade now bike past high-end boutiques and a Peet's Coffee. Vladimir Lenin still glowers in mute disdain over yuppies and hippies alike.

## ○ Landmarks

- **Archie McPhee** • 1300 N 45th St
206-297-0240
Legendary novelty toy shop filled with bacon and mustache-emblazoned items.
- **Aurora Bridge** • Aurora Ave N & N 34th St
Affectionately known as "Suicide Bridge."
- **Fremont Rocket** • 601 N 35th St
1950s rocket fuselage bearing the motto, "De Libertas Quirkas," or Freedom to Be Peculiar.
- **Fremont Troll** • N 36th St & Troll Ave N
Monstrous public art, crushing a real VW.
- **Vladimir Lenin Statue** • 600 N 36th St
The irony grows stronger with every new condo.
- **Waiting for the Interurban** •
Fremont Ave N & N 34th St
The 1979 sculpture of commuters is the victim of frequent "art attacks" by locals.
- **Woodland Park Zoo** • 5500 Phinney Ave N
206-548-2500
Too much fun despite the cute animals behind bars.
- **Woodland Skatepark** • 5201 Green Lake Way N
You know…for kids!

## ☕ Coffee

- **Caffe Ladro** • 452 N 36th St
206-675-0854
Strong coffee for the strong coffee drinker.
- **Caffe Vita** • 4301 Fremont Ave N
206-632-3535
The best of the local chains.
- **Diva Espresso** • 4615 Stone Way N
206-632-7019
Local chain with unpredictable service. I guess it's kind of like ordering coffee from a diva.
- **ETG Coffee** • 3512 Fremont Pl N
206-633-3685
These people treat coffee like a fine wine. And you'll feel classier drinking it.
- **Fremont Coffee Company** • 459 N 36th St
206-632-3633
Fair trade roasters.
- **Lighthouse Roasters** • 400 N 43rd St
206-634-3140
Well-liked roasters' cafe.
- **Lucca Espresso** • 3623 Leary Way NW
206-297-7752
For coffee-addicted statuary enthusiasts.
- **Milstead & Co.** • 770 N 34th St
206-659-4814
Hipster coffee, but in the best possible way.

# Nightlife

- **Backdoor at Roxy's** • 462 N 36th St
  206-632-7322
  Finally! A hipster speakeasy with an all-you-can-eat prime rib special.
- **The Barrel Thief** • 3417 Evanston Ave N
  206-402-5492
  Party like a grown-up with fancy wines, cocktails and truffle-infused snacks. Wine and beer tastings to boot.
- **Brouwer's Café** • 400 N 35th St
  206-267-2437
  Could double as an S&M dungeon; amazing selection of beer but the food is torture.
- **El Camino** • 607 N 35th St
  206-632-7303
  Mexican frou-frou with covered outdoor seating.
- **George & Dragon Pub** • 206 N 36th St
  206-545-6864
  They call it football here.
- **High Dive** • 513 N 36th St
  206-632-0212
  BBQ and bands.

- **LTD Bar & Grill** • 309 N 36th St
  206-632-7876
  Every sporting event on TV plus Golden Tee.
- **Nectar Lounge** • 412 N 36th St
  206-632-2020
  Good cheap happy hour pizza. Terrible piped-in music.
- **Norm's Eatery and Ale House** • 460 N 36th St
  206-547-1417
  Enjoy a beer with your dog after eating dinner elsewhere.
- **Pacific Inn Pub** • 3501 Stone Way N
  206-547-2967
  When you need a break from the Fremont yuppie
- **Smash** • 1401 N 45th St
  206-547-3232
  Accessible wine bar operated by former sommelier; international list.
- **The White Rabbit** • 513 N 36th St
  206-588-0155
  Books live local acts of the "whatever" variety. Don't forget your hookah.
- **Woodsky's** • 303 N 36th St
  206-547-9662
  Ski lodge-themed bar.

Though it lacks quite a few practical amenities, Fremont has more cool shops than you have fingers and seemingly more Thai restaurants per capita than Bangkok. Rare and precious, however, are the meaty Cuban sandwiches at **Paseo** and the low-brow Britishness of the **George & Dragon**. Have a beer with the canine townies and the people who love them at dog-friendly **Norm's Eatery & Alehouse**.

# Restaurants

- **Agrodolce** • 709 N 35th St
  206-547-9707 • $$$
  Maria Hines' inspired Italian food will make you anything buy agro.
- **Art of the Table** • 1054 N 39th St
  206-282-0942 • $$$$
  A true culinary experience with harmonic pairings and intimate company. You won't forget it.
- **Bamboo Village** • 4900 Stone Way N
  206-632-8888 • $$
  With the addition of this Dim Sum place, this 'hood is finally complete.
- **The Barrel Thief** • 3417 Evanston Ave N
  206-402-5492 • $$
  Upscale bar bistro with a weekend waffle brunch and tons of local alcohol.
- **Bizzarro Italian Café** • 1307 N 46th St
  206-632-7277 • $$
  Tasty pasta dishes in a funky, yet intimate, setting.
- **Blue C Sushi** • 3411 Fremont Ave N
  206-633-3411 • $
  What's cooler than a selection of cheap sushi on a conveyer belt?
- **Blue Moon Burgers** • 703 N 34th St
  206-547-1907 • $
  Tremendous burgers that might make you fat, but certainly not blue.
- **Blue Star Café** • 4512 Stone Way N
  206-548-0345 • $$
  Stellar breakfast menu.
- **Brad's Swingside Café** • 4212 Fremont Ave N
  206-633-4057 • $$
  Very Seattle. Very Italian. Very NFT.
- **Brouwer's Café** • 400 N 35th St
  206-267-2437 • $$
  Belgian cuisine and a staggering beer menu.
- **Chillies Paste** • 119 N 36th St
  206-633-1433 • $
  Delicious curries, wide noodle dishes, and a fantastic seafood soufflé.
- **Chiso** • 3520 Fremont Ave N
  206-632-3430 • $$$
  Sushi served up chic.

- **Dot's Delicatessen** • 4262 Fremont Ave N
  206-687-7446 • $$
  Local meats and cheeses that really hit the dot.
- **El Camino** • 607 N 35th St
  206-632-7303 • $$
  Flavorful Mexican food with patio dining. Few veg options.
- **Homegrown** • 3416 Fremont Ave N
  206-453-5232 • $
  Sustainable sandwich shop with killer updates of old favs.
- **Jai Thai** • 3423 Fremont Ave N
  206-632-7060 • $
  The curries are always kickin', and the happy hour menu is tops.
- **Joule** • 3506 Stone Way N
  206-632-5685 • $$$
  Inspired small plates pack a punch, fusing Korean spice with French precision.
- **Kaosamai** • 404 N 36th St
  206-925-9979 • $
  Generally run-of-the-mill food truck with exceptional spring rolls.
- **Kidd Valley** • 4910 Greenlake Way N
  206-547-0121 • $
  Hey, at least they have veggie burgers.
- **Kwanjai Thai** • 469 N 36th St
  206-632-3656 • $
  Cheap, reliable, lightning-fast.
- **Mama's Brown Bags** • 770 N 34th St
  206-633-2247 • $$
  Let Mama bring the office lunch! Of course, you'll have to pay her…
- **Musashi's** • 1400 N 45th St
  206-633-0212 • $$
  Cozy up to the Japanese regulars and chow down on a bento box.
- **Paseo** • 4225 Fremont Ave N
  206-545-7440 • $
  Restaurant the size of a garage, and so is the pork sandwich. So damn good.
- **Pecado Bueno** • 4307 Fremont Ave N
  206-457-8837 • $
  Celebrating the naughtiness of good Mexican food and tequila.

- **Pel'Meni** • 3516 Fremont Pl N
  206-588-2570 • $
  In Center of Universe, Russian Dumplings eat you.
- **Perche No Pasta & Vino** • 1319 N 49th St
  206-547-0222 • $
  Housemade pasta (!); high on faux brick and friendliness.
- **Pie** • 3515 Fremont Ave N
  206-436-8590 • $
  Pie till 2am on weekends! Like that dream you had, without the mama issues.
- **Qazis Indian Curry House** • 473 N 36th St
  206-632-3575 • $$
  When you're sick of all the Thai places in Fremont.
- **Red Door** • 3401 Evanston Ave N
  206-547-7521 • $
  A better class of pub grub.
- **Restaurant Roux** • 4201 Fremont Ave N • $$
  Let the good times (and excellent food) roll at Where Ya At Matt's highly anticipated brick n' mortar joint.
- **Revel** • 403 N 36th St
  206-547-2040 • $$
  All the mindblowingness of a food truck without the pesky traveling.
- **RockCreek Seafood & Spirits** • 4300 Fremont Ave N
  206-557-7532 • $$$
  Ex-Toulouse Petit chef's local sustainable seafood miracle.
- **Rocking Wok** • 4301 Interlake Ave N
  206-545-4878 • $
  Not the prettiest place to look at, but the bargain-priced dim sum is true Taiwanese.
- **RoRo BBQ & Grill** • 3620 Stone Way N
  206-954-1100 • $$
  A dozen ways to eat BBQd meat, including piled into a bowl.
- **Roxy's Diner** • 462 N 36th St
  206-632-3963 • $
  As close to Katz's as Seattle's going to get. The best is the pastrami on rye.
- **Silence-Heart-Nest** • 3508 Fremont Pl N
  206-633-5169 • $
  Delectable vegetarian dishes made with love by Sri Chinmoy devotees.

- **Simply Desserts** • 3421 Fremont Ave N
  206-633-2671 • $
  Simply the best chocolate cake. Anywhere.
- **Sinbad Express** • 3526 Fremont Pl N
  206-632-7426 • $
  Cheap middle-eastern grub to keep you sated on "high" seas.
- **Smash** • 1401 N 45th St
  206-547-3232 • $$
  Accessible wine bar operated by former sommelier; international list.
- **Solsticio** • 1100 N Northlake Way
  206-547-0404 • $
  Nice atmosphere and extensive menu. for a coffee shop.
- **Tacos Guaymas** • 100 N 36th St
  206-547-5110 • $
  Delicious tacos of all kinds including braaaaiiiins for your zombie friends.
- **Tawon Thai** • 3410 Fremont Ave N
  206-633-4545 • $
  Pad Thai here is a beacon in the sea of Fremont's Thai restaurants.
- **Tilth** • 1411 N 45th St
  206-633-0801 • $$$
  The definition of seasonal, organic, local cooking. And it's delicious to boot.
- **Trattoria Roma** • 4705 Aurora Ave N
  206-547-9992 • $$
  Pizza place that does better with the sides than the pizza.
- **Tutta Bella Neopolitan Pizzeria** • 4411 Stone Way N
  206-633-3800 • $$
  Their pizza has been certified by the Italian government. 'Nuff said.
- **Uneeda Burger** • 4302 Fremont Ave N
  206-547-2600 • $$
  Ted Nugent's dream upscale burger joint.
- **Vif** • 4401 Fremont Ave N
  206-557-7357 • $
  Locally-conscious cafe and wine bar with an Sea-town-tastic organic menu.
- **Zaw** • 4612 Stone Way N
  206-297-1334 • $$
  It's not delivery. It's artisan take-and-bake.

Get your pastrami fix at **Roxy's Diner**; it's as close to Katz's as Seattle's going to get. On the other end of the spectrum, Maria Hines' **Agrodolce** and **Tilth** both make for destination dining. Meanwhile, **Chiso** takes sushi for a spin in a hip, modern setting. And what started out as a weekend supper club has grown into a hospitable and unforgettable celebration of food at **Art of the Table**.

# Shopping

- **Archie McPhee** • 1300 N 45th St
  206-297-0240
  For all your potato gun and monster finger puppet needs.
- **Bliss** • 3501 Fremont Ave N
  206-632-6695
  Small clothing boutique with designer duds mixed in.
- **Blue Video** • 4100 Aurora Ave N
  206-632-9886
  No one is surprised that this adult video rental store is on Aurora.
- **Bluebird Ice Cream** • 3515 Fremont Ave N
  206-588-1079
  Beer ice cream? Yes you can.
- **Book Larder** • 4252 Fremont Ave N
  206-397-4271
  Specialty cookbook store for Top Chefing it in your home kitchen.
- **Destee Nation Shirt Co.** • 3412 Evanston Ave N
  206-632-7874
  T-shirts emblazoned with logos of local bars and record shops.
- **Flying Apron Bakery** • 3510 Fremont Ave N
  206-442-1115
  Vegan, gluten-free, wheat-free, funny-tasting bakery.
- **Fremont Sunday Street Market** • Phinney Ave N & N 34th St
  206-781-6776
  The world's most fabulously bizarre bazaar.
- **Fremont Vintage Mall** • 3419 Fremont Pl N
  206-329-4460
  Huge antique store where you're sure to find your next favorite piece.
- **Fusion Beads** • 3830 Stone Way N
  206-782-4595
  A well-organized bead store that also offers classes.
- **Hub and Bespoke** • 513 N 36th St
  206-547-5730
  Cyclists need to be seen, so they may as well look cool.
- **The Indoor Sun Shoppe** • 160 N Canal St
  206-634-3727
  When you don't have a garden, they'll help you create one, inside.

- **Jive Time Records** • 3506 Fremont Ave N
  206-632-5483
  Rare vinyl, used CDs, 99Â¢ bins.
- **Les Amis** • 3420 Evanston Ave N
  206-632-2877
  Out-of-this-world clothes at astronomical prices.
- **Marketime Foods** • 4416 Fremont Ave N
  206-632-8958
  The TARDIS of convenience stores. It's bigger on the inside!
- **Mishu Boutique** • 465 N 36th St
  206-802-8022
  Unique, affordable clothing made by folks in Asia who get lunch breaks.
- **Not a Number Cards & Gifts** • 720 N 35th St
  206-784-0965
  Fun, random stuff you never knew you needed.
- **Ophelia's Books** • 3504 Fremont Ave N
  206-632-3759
  Large collection of books for the non cat allergic.
- **PCC Natural Markets** • 600 N 34th St
  206-632-6811
  One-stop shopping for overpriced organic groceries.
- **Piece of Mind** • 315 N 36th St
  206-675-0637
  It's a water pipe…for tobacco.
- **Portage Bay Goods** • 621 N 35th St
  206-547-5221
  Eclectic gifts for babies, children, and adults in a range of prices.
- **Private Screening** • 3504 Fremont Pl N
  206-548-0751
  When you want to look like Jackie O. or Frank Sinatra.
- **Rudy's Barbershop** • 475 N 36th St
  206-547-0818
  Absolute best cheap haircut!
- **Show Pony** • 702 N 35th St
  206-706-4188
  Pretty things for your pony. Or, you know, yourself.
- **Theo Chocolate** • 3400 Phinney Ave N
  206-632-5100
  Delicious free-trade, organic chocolate, without the ramped up price.
- **Vintage Angel Company** • 3519 Fremont Pl N
  206-499-1811
  Your childhood is considered vintage now, so you may as well get used to it.

Thanks to the enormous sign atop the local QFC supermarket (a nod to the old Food Giant sign), visitors know when they reach Wallingford. With Woodland Park and Green Lake to the north and **Gas Works Park** to the south, the neighborhood has a Sunday afternoon vibe all week long. This somewhat sleepy residential neighborhood hosts multiple summer food festivals and is home to the original **Dick's Drive-In**.

## Landmarks

- **Blue Moon Tavern** • 712 NE 45th St
  206-675-9116
  Countless artistic luminaries have passed out there.
- **Dick's Drive-In** • 111 NE 45th St
  206-632-5125
  A little bit nostalgia, a little bit cholesterol.
- **Gas Works Park** • 2101 N Northlake Way
  206-684-4075
  Industrial site turned America's strangest park. Amazing view.
- **Sadako and the Thousand Cranes Peace Park** •
  NE 40th St & NE Pacific St
  A tribute to a young girl that died of leukemia after the atomic bombing of Nagasaki.

 Coffee

- **Caffe Appassionato** • 1218 N 45th St
  206-549-9149
  Classic Seattle coffee shop vibe at this small-ish local chain. Frasier would love it here.
- **Chocolati Cafe** • 1716 N 45th St
  206-633-7765
  Coffee, yes. But it's really more about the chocolate.
- **Fuel** • 1705 N 45th St
  206-634-2700
  Now this is a type of fuel that actually has a future.
- **Mosaic Coffeehouse** • 4401 2nd Ave NE
  206-369-0326
  Community coffee shop with a pay-what-you-can business model and an amazing indoor playground.
- **Palazzo** • 1906 N 34th St
  206-634-0922
  Plus baked goods.

- **Seattle Espresso** • 4405 Wallingford Ave N
  206-632-7178
  Fortunately, they put a lot more effort into their coffee than they did their name.
- **Teahouse Kuan Yin** • 1911 N 45th St
  206-632-2055
  Bulk tea plus cafe.
- **Uptown Espresso** • 2300 N 45th St
  206-812-0404
  Self-proclaimed "Home of the Velvet Foam" but the coffee underneath is just so-so.

 Nightlife

- **Al's Tavern** • 2303 N 45th St
  206-545-9959
  Divey and lovable.
- **Blue Moon Tavern** • 712 NE 45th St
  206-675-9116
  Kerouac, Roethke, and other artists have fallen over drunk here.
- **The Grizzled Wizard** • 2317 N 45th St
  206-395-4749
  At last, a place for the cool gothy gamer geeks.
- **The Iron Bull** • 2121 N 45th St
  206-453-3901
  The place to get your sports on in Wallingford.
- **Kate's Pub** • 309 NE 45th St
  206-547-6832
  Hidden gem. Specials and games galore. Easy on the Jaeger.
- **May Restaurant and Lounge** • 1612 N 45th St
  206-675-0037
  Pricey but delicious Thai bar food served late and sluggishly.
- **Moon Temple** • 2108 N 45th St
  206-633-4280
  Everyone loves stiff drinks.
- **Murphy's Pub** • 1928 N 45th St
  206-634-2110
  Drinks for Hibernians.

# 🍴Restaurants

- **Boulangerie** • 2200 N 45th St
206-634-2211 • $
Even a Frenchman would admit les croissants sont authentiques.
- **Chocolati Cafe** • 1716 N 45th St
206-633-7765 • $$
You haven't lived till you've eaten a chocolate-covered potato chip.
- **Chutney's Bistro** • 1815 N 45th St
206-634-1000 • $$
Curry cuts across the socioeconimc divide.
- **Dick's Drive-In** • 111 NE 45th St
206-632-5125 • $
A local obsession, specializing in cheap burgers and shakes. Perfect at 1 am.
- **Djan's Modern Thai Restaurant** • 264 NE 45th St
206-633-3526 • $$
Solid Thai delivery.
- **The Essential Baking Company** • 1604 N 34th St
206-545-0444 • $
You'll think you're in a European bakery.
- **Fainting Goat Gelato** • 1903 N 45th St
206-327-9459 • $
Don't tell the Italians, but the Turks can make a damn good gelato.
- **Irwin's Neighborhood Bakery & Cafe** •
2123 N 40th St
206-675-1484 • $$
Quaint cafe with great pastries and a carb-heavy lunch menu.
- **Ivar's Salmon House** • 401 NE Northlake Way
206-632-0767 • $$
It's all about the chowdah at this Seattle seafood institution.
- **Julia's** • 4401 Wallingford Ave N
206-633-1175 • $$
Quirky space, awesome breakfast. And your mom will like it, too.
- **Kabul Afghan Cuisine** • 2301 N 45th St
206-545-9000 • $$
Warm family setting with a traditional Afghan menu.

- **May Restaurant and Lounge** • 1612 N 45th St
206-675-0037 • $$
Refreshing, subtly balanced Thai dishes that are utterly devoid of ketchup.
- **Miyabi 45th** • 2208 N 45th St
206-632-4545 • $$$
A soba restaurant you can take your date to without looking cheap.
- **Molly Moon's** • 1622 N 45th St
206-547-5105 • $
Fresh, local, sustainably organic ice cream—down to the dairy and the compostable dishes.
- **Pinky's Kitchen** • 210 NE 45th St
206-257-5483 • $
Bravo for a late-night BBQ truck (with veggie options).
- **Rancho Bravo Tacos** • 211 NE 45th St
206-830-2657 • $
Mexican served out of a silver trailer. Locals are fanatical for the tacos.
- **Satay** • 1711 N 45th St
206-547-0597 • $
Simple menu. Complex food.
- **Shima** • 4429 Wallingford Ave N
206-632-2583 • $$
Classically trained sushi chef serves it up, Hawaiia style.
- **Sutra** • 1605 N 45th St
206-547-1348 • $$$$
High-end prix-fixe vegetarian.
- **Tiny Ninja Cafe** • 3510 Stone Way N
206-632-0647 • $
Named after the shop's mascot: a diminutive woo ninja who apparently likes live music.
- **TNT Taqueria** • 2114 N 45th St
206-322-0124 • $
Dino-mite tacos made from local, happy farm animals. Plus churros for breakfast!
- **Varsity Inn** • 1801 N 34th St
206-547-2161 • $
Friendly, unassuming diner that becomes a delicious taco place by night.
- **The Whale Wins** • 3506 Stone Way N
206-632-9425 • $$
A great addition to Seattle's slow food movement

While Wallingford's portion of 45th Street isn't much of a weekend destination, there are more than enough bars, restaurants, and cafès to make a night of it. **Miyabi 45th** is a fine-dining soba noodle house. **Al's** is our favorite little hole in the wall with **Moon Temple** running a close second. Happily spend your entire paycheck at **Bottleworks**—the beer selection is incredible. Or fill your backpack at **Wide World of Books & Maps**, a Seattle institution since the '70s.

#  Shopping

- **Bottleworks** • 1710 N 45th St
206-633-2437
The world's finest beers ripe for the six-packing.
- **Comics Dungeon** • 319 NE 45th St
206-545-8373
Preventing geeks from getting girlfriends since the early '90s!
- **The Erotic Bakery** • 2323 N 45th St
206-545-6969
What a lovely flower cake…er…oh MY!
- **Fainting Goat Gelato** • 1903 N 45th St
206-327-9459
Don't tell the Italians, but the Turks can make a damn good gelato.
- **Golden Oldies Records Tapes & CDs** •
201 NE 45th St
206-547-2260
45s like mad and 99 cent CDs.
- **Hawaii General Store** • 258 NE 45th St
206-633-5233
For all your next luau needs.
- **I Do Bridal** • 2206 N 45th St
206-633-7926
Small bridal shop with a broad range of dress sizes and prices.

- **Molly Moon's** • 1622 N 45th St
206-547-5105
Fresh, local, sustainably organic ice cream—down to the dairy and the compostable dishes.
- **Open Books: A Poem Emporium** • 2414 N 45th St
206-633-0811
One of the few poetry-only bookstores in the nation.
- **Sugar on Top Salon** • 1601 N 45th St
206-427-9377
You'll be pretty pleased.
- **Trophy Cupcakes** • 1815 N 45th St
206-632-7020
The perfect combo: cute & tasty.
- **Wide World Books & Maps** •
4411 Wallingford Ave N
206-634-3453
The nation's first travel-only bookstore is now 30 years old.
- **Wine World and Spirits** • 400 NE 45th St
206-402-6086
Show me more, spirits!
- **Yogurtland** • 2320 N 45th St
206-634-2900
Rule over your own froyo fairy tale with endless flavor/topping combos.

Map

Map 26

U-Dub boasts an impeccable reputation as a bastion of higher learning—after all, Bruce Lee once studied here. The campus is as charming as enrollment brochures suggest, but the surrounding area is an unlikely collision of thug-lifers, rah-rah collegiate types, meth-damaged street hustlers, and stubborn eccentrics. The U District has been designated an "alcohol impact zone," banning certain types of beverages from package stores, so plan ahead if you need some fortified wine for a sorority party.

## ○ Landmarks

- **Former Location of TUBS** •
4750 Roosevelt Way NE
Who knew bathing could be so dirty?
- **Red Square** • NE Pacific St
Home of the Barnett Newman's sculpture, *Broken Obelisk*.
- **Scarecrow Video** • 5030 Roosevelt Way NE
206-524-8554
Best video store in the universe.
- **Wall of Death** • Burke Gilman Trail Under the University Bridge
A tribute to the carnival motor domes of the early 20th century.

##  Coffee

- **Burke Museum Cafe** • NE 45th St & 17th Ave NE
206-543-9854
Nimble, young coed pick-up bar, er, cafe.
- **Café Allegro** • 4214 University Way NE
206-633-3030
Since 1975.
- **Café on the Ave** • 4201 University Way NE
206-632-6001
Serving Caffé Vita; lunch and dinner options.
- **Oasis Tea Zone** • 4508 University Way NE
206-547-9967
Bubble tea and other Asian junk food. In other words, delicious.
- **Sureshot Cafe** • 4505 University Way NE
206-632-3100
Vegan pastries and paninis accompany competent beverages.
- **Trabant Coffee & Chai** • 1309 NE 45th St
206-675-0668
Dude. This chai rocks.
- **VHSpresso** • 5030 Roosevelt Way NE
206-524-8554
Enjoy a fresh cup of coffee whilst perusing the dusty film selection of Scarecrow Video.
- **Yunnie Bubble Tea** • 4511 University Way NE
206-547-9648
Bubble tea on the Ave.

##  Farmers Markets

- **University District Farmers Market** •
NE 50th St & University Way NE
Saturdays 9-2, year-round

## ▼ Nightlife

- **Big Time Brewery & Alehouse** •
4133 University Way NE
206-545-4509
Laid back college pub for a brew and a slice of pizza.
- **College Inn Pub** • 4006 University Way NE
206-634-2307
Best thing about the College Inn: You get older, they stay the same age.
- **Dante's** • 5300 Roosevelt Way NE
206-525-1300
Seattle's only Satanic college-themed sports bar.
- **The District** • 4507 Brooklyn Ave NE
206-634-2000
Great for a romantic date. Especially if you aren't the one paying.
- **Earl's on the Ave** • 4333 University Way NE
206-535-4493
Pints of liquor at closeout prices. Don't make any plans after that.
- **Finn MacCool's** • 4217 University Way NE
206-675-0885
Great if you like hanging with loud co-eds. Awful if you don't.
- **Flowers Bar & Restaurant** •
4247 University Way NE
206-633-1903
Vegetarian buffet by day, laid back bar by night.
- **The Kraken Bar & Lounge** •
5257 University Way NE
206-522-5334
Let loose at the Kraken. You'll be glad you did.
- **Monkey Pub** • 5305 Roosevelt Way NE
206-523-6457
Frat-free oasis in U District.
- **Neptune Theatre** • 1303 NE 45th St
206-781-5755
Indie concerts and comedy shows in a theater worthy of the gods.

Map 26

# U District

## 🍴 Restaurants

- **50 North** • 5001 25th Ave NE
206-397-3939 • $$
Vashon's Hardware Store brings its delicious island secret to the big city.
- **Agua Verde** • 1303 NE Boat St
206-545-8570 • $$
Eat authentic Baja-style Mexican cuisine. Then rent a kayak.
- **Aladdin Falafel Corner** • 4541 University Way NE
206-548-9539 • $
Perfect for those times when you're too drunk to stumble the extra 2 blocks to Aladdin Gyro-Cery.
- **Aladdin Gyro-Cery** • 4541 University Way NE
206-632-5253 • $
Best falafel on the Ave. Standing room only.
- **Araya's Vegetarian Place** •
5420 University Way NE
206-524-4332 • $$
We can't believe it's not meat.
- **Blue C Sushi** • 4601 26th Ave NE
206-525-4601 • $
Enjoy the same fast sushi as the Fremont location, but with yuppies.
- **Burger & Kabob Hut** • 4142 University Way NE
206-632-0324 • $
A good place to stumble into for onion rings after the bars kick you out.
- **Burke Museum Cafe** • NE 45th St & 17th Ave NE
206-543-9854 • $
Nimble, young coed pick-up bar, er, cafe.
- **Cafe Solstice** • 4116 University Way NE
206-675-0850 • $
Overrun with students but worth getting food to go.
- **Cedars on Brooklyn** • 4759 Brooklyn Ave NE
206-527-4000 • $$
Indian food that's naan-stop delicious. Plus, a nice view of the Safeway parking lot.

- **Chaco Canyon Organic Café** • 4757 12th Ave NE
206-522-6966 • $
An amazing voyage into the raw-food universe; the mocha shakes rock!
- **China Village** • 3224 NE 45th Street
206-523-0772 • $$
Above average. Don't let the stock Chinese Restaurant name fool you.
- **Coffee Drop Cafe** • 4915 25th Ave NE
206-525-5442 • $
Neighborhood coffee goodness. Have a drop of sandwich while you're at it.
- **Delfino's Chicago Style Pizzeria** •
2631 NE University Village St
206-522-3466 • $$
You may have to wait, but the thickly gooey Chicago-style 'zas are worth it.
- **Flowers Bar & Restaurant** •
4247 University Way NE
206-633-1903 • $$
Mediterranean veggie buffet may be the best lunch deal in Seattle.
- **Guanaco's Tacos Pupuseria** •
4106 Brooklyn Ave NE
206-547-2369 • $
There's nothing funny about a good pupuseria.
- **Jimmy John's** • 4141 University Way NE
206-548-9500 • $
Fast sandwiches that can be delivered within the U District.
- **Kai's Bistro & Lounge** • 1312 NE 43rd St
206-547-2784 • $
Side-street bistro with quality cocktails and great happy hour.
- **Memo's Mexican Food** • 4743 University Way NE
206-729-5071 • $
If a 24-hour Taco Bell had real Mexican names for food.
- **Morsel** • 4754 University Way NE
206-268-0154 • $
Picking up where the beloved Nook left off with genius biscuit dishes and perfect espresso.

Kai's makes the best Manhattan in the city, but for serious drinking, head over to **Earl's**, that place with the black facade and chicken wire instead of windows; during their happy hour, a PINT of well booze is unconsciously cheap. The **Kraken Bar & Lounge** is very metal, very dirty and your best bet on the Ave for avoiding students. Also try the karaoke at **Monkey Pub**, a beloved dive with the gritty, punk rock vibe.

**Map**

- **Orange King** • 1411 NE 42nd St
206-632-1331 • $
A UW student's wet dream. Burgers and teriyaki under one roof.
- **Pagliacci Pizza** • 4529 University Way NE
206-726-1717 • $
Local favorite pizza chain makes crispy-chewy delights with seasonal ingredients.
- **Pam's Kitchen** • 5000 University Way NE
206-696-7010 • $
A taste of the Caribbean arrives on The Ave.
- **Pasta & Co** • 4622 26th Ave NE
206-523-8594 • $$
One-stop gourmet chain has fresh bread, wine, and risotto cakes to go.
- **Pho Thân Brothers'** • 4207 University Way NE
206-632-7272 • $
Cheap, fast, and filling, with a free cream puff to boot.
- **Pho Vietnam** • 4235 University Way NE
206-547-1709 • $
Lots of love for the noodle soup here, pho good reason.
- **Pizza Ragazzi** • 5201 University Way NE
206-525-1700 • $
At 4 am, who cares what the pizza tastes like?
- **Portage Bay Café** • 4130 Roosevelt Way NE
206-547-8230 • $$
Local organic breakfasts and lunches.
- **Ristorante Doria** • 4759 Roosevelt Way NE
206-466-2380 • $$
A little bit of Italy in the U.D. Stuff yourself silly and regret nothing.
- **Samurai Noodle** • 4138 University Way NE
206-547-1774 • $
Top notch Top Ramen.
- **Shultzy's Sausage** • 4114 University Way NE
206-548-9461 • $
Purveyors of fine encased meats, plus a great beer menu.
- **Starlife on the Oasis Cafe** • 1405 NE 50th St
206-729-3542 • $
A cozy oasis for the long lap-top lunch.
- **Tandoor Indian Restaurant** •
5024 University Way NE
206-523-7477 • $
Consistently excellent, and the best pakora $2.50 can buy.
- **Tea Republik** • 4527 University Way NE
206-497-7631 • $
More tea than you can shake a stik at.
- **Thai 65** • 4214 University Way NE
206-632-6542 • $
Another of the U District Thai favorites. Lots of seating.
- **Thai Tom** • 4543 University Way NE
206-548-9548 • $
Come for the best open kitchen show in Seattle. Always busy.
- **Thaiger Room** • 4228 University Way NE
206-632-9299 • $
If by Thaigers they mean cockroaches.
- **Ugly Mug Cafe** • 1309 NE 43rd St
206-547-3219 • $
"Ugly" is an ironic name. Oh, and the sandwiches aren't bad either.
- **Veggie Grill** • 2681 NE University Village St
206-523-1961 • $$
Santa Monica-based chain offers up the ultimate in vegetarian comfort food.
- **Village Sushi** • 4741 12th Ave NE
206-985-6870 • $$
Amazing sushi, funky jazz and weird paintings.
- **Wing Central** • 4524 University Way NE
206-634-9464 • $
Ellensburg's beloved college wing joint goes to the Dawgs.

# Shopping

- **American Apparel** • 4345 University Way NE
  206-547-0399
  Non-sweatshop basics.
- **Anthropologie** • 2520 NE University Village St
  206-985-2101
  Higher end clothing and home accessories.
- **Buffalo Exchange** • 4530 University Way NE
  206-545-0175
  Second-hand clothes for girls who drink Zima.
- **Bulldog News** • 4208 University Way NE
  206-632-6397
  Pick up a copy of *Obscure French Cinema Monthly* and *People* simultaneously.
- **Cinema Books** • 4753 Roosevelt Way NE
  206-547-7667
  Reel literature.
- **The Confectionary** • 4608 26th Ave NE
  206-523-1443
  If this place doesn't make you happy, you have no soul.
- **Crossroads Trading Co.** • 4300 University Way NE
  206-632-3111
  Vintage. Cheap.

- **Fireworks** • 2617 NE Village Ln
  206-527-2858
  Eclectic gift shop.
- **Full Tilt Ice Cream** • 4759 Brooklyn Ave NE
  206-524-4406
  No pinball or beer at this half-tilt location. But sti
  ice cream!
- **Gargoyles Statuary** • 4550 University Way NE
  206-632-4940
  For all your gothic, home decorating needs.
- **Half Price Books** • 4709 Roosevelt Way NE
  206-547-7859
  Books, music, video, magazines.
- **Hardwick's** • 4214 Roosevelt Way NE
  206-632-1203
  An adventure in hardware.
- **Lucky Vintage** • 4742 University Way NE
  206-523-6621
  Come in looking like Hilary Clinton, leave like Bettie Page.
- **Magus Books** • 1408 NE 42nd St
  206-633-1800
  Used bookstore with a friendly, helpful, and knowledgeable staff.

Thai food reigns supreme, with seemingly dozens of joints on every block varying wildly in quality and price. **Thai Tom** is worth the long wait for a seat, but check out the slightly less delicious **Thai 65** if you're in a hurry. **Memo's** slings burritos 24/7. **Pho Thàn Brothers'** namesake soup blows away the copious competition. **Village Sushi** and **Blue C Sushi** are both dependable—the latter even features one of those silly-but-fun conveyor belt systems.

Map

- **Menchie's** • 4609 Village Court NE
  206-525-4445
  Serving approximated candy bars & cheesecake for housewives by the pound.
- **Recycled Cycles** • 1007 NE Boat St
  206-547-4491
  Comprehensive bike store specializing in used and DIY bikes.
- **Red Light Vintage Clothing** •
  4560 University Way NE
  206-545-4044
  Vintage clothing for people with 10 inch waists.
- **Rudy's Barbershop** • 4738 University Way NE
  206-527-5267
  Absolute best cheap haircut!
- **Scarecrow Video** • 5030 Roosevelt Way NE
  206-524-8554
  Best video store in Seattle? No, best in the world.
- **Sephora** • 2618 NE University Village St
  206-526-9110
  All the make-up you can dream-up in one store.
- **Shiga's Imports** • 4306 University Way NE
  206-633-2400
  Decorate your dorm room like an opium den.
- **Something Silver** • 4628 Village Ct NE
  206-523-7545
  Unique silver jewelry.

- **Trophy Cupcakes** • 2612 Village Ln
  206-632-7020
  The perfect combo: cute & tasty.
- **University Book Store** • 4326 University Way NE
  206-634-3400
  Huge bookstore and gift shop. Don't go there the first week of any quarter.
- **University Village** • 2623 NE University Village St
  206-523-0622
  What the rich housewives do with their husband's money.
- **Valley of Roses** • 4748 University Wy NE
  206-522-6887
  You don't need a lot of green to shop in this valley.
- **Weaving Works, Inc** • 4717 Brooklyn Ave NE
  206-524-1221
  Complete explosion of colors and textures, skilled advice for Seattle's needleworkers.
- **The Woolly Mammoth** • 4303 University Way NE
  206-632-3254
  Sensible shoes for the masses.
- **Yogurtland** • 4334 University Way NE
  206-547-2900
  Rule over your own froyo fairy tale with endless flavor/topping combos.

Map 27 • **Laurelhurst / Wedgwood / Sand Point** (N)

The half-dozen 'hoods northeast of UW make up "Seattle's First Suburb": a nice, quiet place that's good for, um, raising kids. Its identity mimics the UW profs who live here: homogeneous, overly intellectual, and passive. Seattle's second-largest Jewish community (after Rainier Beach) dwells in Wedgwood/View Ridge, which explains the synagogues, temples, Jewish Library, Jewish Community Center, bagels, and Universalist Unitarians.

## ○ Landmarks

- **Sound Garden** • 7400 Sand Point Way NE
Sonorous art installation from which a certain grunge band lifted its name.

## Coffee

- **Cafe Javasti** • 8617 35th Ave NE
206-204-0255
It's all about the crepes.
- **Coffee Crew** • 3614 NE 45th St
206-525-2883
Solid morning option.
- **Gretchen's Place** • 5432 Sand Point Way NE
206-403-1426
Brewing Caffé Vita beans.
- **Van Gogh Coffeehouse** • 8210 35th Ave NE
206-523-1466
Unmatched coffee and customer service from cutie pies.

## ● Nightlife

- **Wedgwood Alehouse** • 8515 35th Ave NE
206-527-2676
Everyone who frequents this place went to high school together.

## ● Restaurants

- **Black Pearl** • 7347 35th Ave NE
206-526-5115 • $$
Great housemade noodles and noticeably ungreasy food.
- **Cafe Javasti** • 8617 35th Ave NE
206-204-0255 • $
It's all about the crepes.
- **Jak's Grill** • 3701 NE 45th St
206-985-8545 • $$$$
Best place for a classy, meaty, potatoey night out.
- **Top Pot Doughnuts** • 6855 35th Ave NE
206-525-1966 • $
Top Pot is tops!
- **Zaw** • 7320 35th Ave NE
206-658-2929 • $$
It's not delivery. It's artisan take-and-bake.

## ● Shopping

- **City People's Mercantile** •
5440 Sand Point Way NE
206-524-1200
Yes, you too can have flowers blooming and veggies growing year round in Seattle.
- **Metropolitan Market** • 5250 40th Ave NE
206-938-6600
High end groceries, high end prices.
- **PCC Natural Markets** • 6514 40th Ave NE
206-526-7661
A great natural market that will leave your wallet unnaturally empty.

This 'hood is on the rise, as newfangled restaurants and merchants have begun to hobnob with austere industrial firms and revered maritime showrooms. What has remained unchanged are two of Seattle's trademark hotspots: the **Hiram M. Chittenden Locks**, where a canal joins the city's freshwater lakes with the saltwater of Puget Sound, and the waterside Golden Gardens Park, with its sandy beaches, bonfires, and sunsets over the Olympics.

## Landmarks

- **Hiram M. Chittenden Locks** • 3015 NW 54th St
  Industrial-age marvel; watch the local salmon
  populations dwindle before your very eyes!
- **Leif Erikson Statue** • Seaview Ave NW
  Famous viking explorer surrounded by rune-
  stones in the shape of a Viking ship.

 Coffee

- **Caffè Fiorè** • 3125 NW 85th St
  206-706-7580
  Makes the bold claim of being Seattle's first
  organic coffee.
- **Firehouse Coffee** • 2622 NW Market St
  206-784-2911
  Kid and dog friendly just like a real firehouse.

 Nightlife

- **Percy's & Co** • 5233 Ballard Ave NW
  206-420-3750
  An Apothecary style restaurant and bar with food
  and cocktails to cure what ails you.
- **Sloop Tavern** • 2830 NW Market St
  206-782-3330
  Get drunk cheaply with enormous beers.

 Restaurants

- **Anthony's HomePort Shilshole Bay** •
  6135 Seaview Ave NW
  206-783-0780 • $$$
  Pacific Northwest chain with an impressive view.
- **Caffè Fiorè** • 3125 NW 85th St
  206-706-7580 • $$
  Makes the bold claim of being Seattle's first
  organic coffee.
- **Paseo** • 6226 Seaview Ave NW
  206-789-3100 • $
  Legendary Cuban sandwiches (with veggie
  options) that can't be overhyped.
- **Percy's & Co** • 5233 Ballard Ave NW
  206-420-3750 • $$
  An Apothecary style restaurant and bar with food
  and cocktails to cure what ails you.
- **Portage Bay Cafe** • 2821 NW Market St
  206-783-1547 • $$
  Local organic breakfasts and lunches.
- **Ray's Café** • 6049 Seaview Ave NW
  206-782-0094 • $$$
  Venerable institution that's been doing seafood
  right for decades. Watch out for tourists.
- **Red Mill Totem House** • 3058 NW 54th St
  206-784-1400 • $
  Fish & Chips by the locks in an awesome Totem
  House! How can you go wrong?
- **The Scoop @ Walter's** • 6408 32nd Ave NW
  206-782-3920 • $
  Walter serves the best of the local ice creams.

## Shopping

- **Kick It Boots & Stompwear** • 2607 NW Market St
  206-784-3399
  These boots are made for stompin'.

Map 29

The residential focus of Loyal Heights means family green areas like Salmon Bay and Baker Parks and a half-dozen learning institutions, including Seattle's coolest, Ballard High School. But one blockbuster drive from 85th Street (where Mt. Rainier looms over the city like a giant ice cream cone) down the ever-active 15th Avenue Northwest, and Ballard's long-lost neighborhood brother is found again.

# Coffee

- **Grumpy D's Coffee House** • 7001 15th Ave NW
  206-783-4039
  If you're still grumpy after their coffee, you might be a D.
- **Jumpin' Jimmy's** • 6501 15th Ave NW
  206-783-7786
  Solid drive-through espresso in a jumpin' jim flash!

# Nightlife

- **Chuck's Hop Shop** • 656 NW 85th St
  206-297-6212
  With 38 beers ON TAP and rotating food trucks outside, its the only convenience store that makes sense as a hangout.
- **The Dray** • 708 NW 65th St
  206-453-4527
  Beer on tap. Beer to go in growlers. Beer soaked raisins on the grilled cheese.
- **Waterwheel Lounge** • 7034 15th Ave NW
  206-784-5701
  A rumpus room where you have to pay for drinks.

# Restaurants

- **Delancey** • 1415 NW 70th St
  206-838-1960 •
  Orangette blogger's Ballard pizza venture.
- **The Fat Hen** • 1418 NW 70th St
  206-782-5422 • $$
  Enough delicious pastries and sammies to turn you into a big fat hen.
- **Honore Artisan Bakery** • 1413 NW 70th St
  206-706-4035 • $
  Their macaroons will make you swoon.
- **Kasbah Authentic Moroccan** • 1471 NW 85th St
  206-788-0777 • $$
  Your heart will be still for the b'stilla. And belly dancers are always fun.

- **The Original Pancake House** • 8037 15th Ave NW
  206-781-3344 • $$
  Homemade batter! A dozen types of flapjacks! It's breakfast heaven.
- **Smokin' Pete's BBQ** • 1918 NW 65th St
  206-783-0454 • $$
  All meat, all the time. Stacks of napkins requisite.
- **Thai Siam** • 8305 15th Ave NW
  206-784-5465 • $
  Skip the pad thai; go for the huge, droolworthy steak salad.
- **Wild Mountain Café** • 1408 NW 85th St
  206-297-WILD • $$$
  Tasty, funky, spirited home-grown food.

# Shopping

- **Cascioppo Bros. Meats** • 2364 NW 80th St
  206-784-6121
  You can't beat their meat!
- **Chuck's Hop Shop** • 656 NW 85th St
  206-297-6212
  The convenience store of your dreams with 38 rotating beer taps and plenty of reasons to stay a while.
- **Fresh Fish Company** • 2364 NW 80th St
  206-782-1632
  Truth in naming conventions.
- **Goodwill** • 6400 8th Ave NW
  206-957-5544
  Make sure to check for stains.
- **Larsen's Danish Bakery** • 8000 24th Ave NW
  206-782-8285
  Danish bakery with all the Scandinavian flavor you've come to expect!
- **Laura Bee Designs** • 6418 20th Ave NW
  206-789-4044
  If you're gonna pay $80 for a purse, it may as well be made locally.
- **Top Banana** • 6501 15th Ave NW
  206-783-7786
  This cheap, family-owned produce vendor is more than just bananaz.

Map 30 · **Greenwood / Phinney Ridge** Ⓝ

NW 89th St

NW 88th St

1

N 89th St

2

NW 87th St

NW 87th St

Phinney Ave N

N 87th St

NW 86th St

N 86th St

N 86th St

33

NW 83rd St

Dayton Ave N

N 85th St

N 84th St

A

NW 82nd St

1st Ave NW

83rd

N 83rd St

N 82nd St

Stone Ave N

Interlake Ave N

Ashworth Ave N

8th Ave NW

NW 82nd St

NW 81st St

Green Lake Dr N

Dibble Ave NW

GREENWOOD

N 80th St

NW 79th St

3rd Ave NW

Greenwood Ave N

99

31

NW 78th St

NW 77th St

29

NW 76th St

N 75th St

Aurora Ave N

Winona Ave N

NW 74th St

NW 73rd St

W Green Lake Dr N

Stone Ave N

Ashton Way N

NW 72nd St

N 72nd St

B

N 71st St

7th Ave NW

2nd Ave NW

Sycamore Ave NW

1st Ave NW

N 70th St

Francis Ave N

N 68th St

Linden Ave N

Cleopatra NW Pl

N 67th St

PHINNEY RIDGE

N 66th St

PAGE 182

N 65th St

Phinney Ave N

Francis Ave N

N 64th St

Linden Ave N

Green Lake

Dibble NW

Division Ave NW

6th Ave NW

4th Ave NW

3rd Ave NW

Palatine Ave N

N 63rd St

Evanston Ave N

Fremont Ave N

Woodland Pl N

N 62nd St

N 61st St

NW 60th St

N 60th St

N 60th St

W Green Lake Way N

NW 59th St

N 59th St

1st Ave NW

N 59th St

C

NW 58th St

Greenwood Ave N

Woodland Park Loop

PAGE 206

Woodland Park Zoo

Woodland Park

Ashworth Ave N

23

7th Ave NW

6th Ave NW

4th Ave NW

3rd Ave NW

NW 57th St

N 57th St

1st Ave NW

N Argyle Pl

N 56th St

N 56th St

N 56th St

24

N Clopston Way

NW 55th St

N 55th St

NW 54th St

2nd Ave NW

1st Ave NW

N 54th St

NW 53rd St

N 53rd St

1/4 mile    .25 km

The tree-lined corridor at Phinney and Greenwood Avenues is one of the better places to raise a family in Seattle, while the blocks along Aurora will show your kids what will happen to them if they don't stay in school. Right around Green Lake the area turns downright affluent, but all the best shopping, eating, and drinking can be found where the regular folk live.

##  Landmarks

• **Woodland Park** • Aurora Ave N & N 59th St
206-684-4075
Here you'll find a zoo, a rose garden, and a veritable metropolis of bunny rabbits.

## Coffee

• **Cafe Bambino** • 405 NW 65th St
206-706-4934
Look for the buddha and charming neon sign.
• **Caffe Vita** • 7402 Greenwood Ave N
206-588-1519
The best of the local chains.
• **Diva Espresso** • 7916 Greenwood Ave N
206-781-1213
Local chain with unpredictable service. I guess it's kind of like ordering coffee from a diva.
• **Green Bean Coffeehouse** •
8515 Greenwood Ave N
206-706-4587
A community coffeehouse with tons of events and a pay-what-you-will menu.
• **Herkimer Coffee** • 7320 Greenwood Ave N
206-784-0202
Roasting their own. Awesome space.
• **Makeda Coffee** • 153 N 78th St
206-782-1489
Asian-inspired and artsy vibe make this a cool stop during Greenwood Art Walk.
• **Monkey Grind Espresso Bar** • 518 N 85th St
206-782-6100
Le Fournil & Alki bakery pastries go perfectly with their no-monkey-business coffee drinks.
• **Neptune Coffee** • 8415 Greenwood Ave N
206-599-8822
Trivia theme nights + coffee + alcohol = out-of-this-world good time.

## Farmers Markets

• **Phinney Farmers Market** •
Phinney Ave N & N 67th St
Fridays, 3pm–7pm, late May through early October

## Nightlife

• **418 Public House** • 418 NW 65th St
206-783-0418
Apparently, "pub" can now mean Mexican food and vegan options.
• **Alibi Room** • 10406 Holman Rd NW
206-623-3180
Equally dark sister lounge to Pike Place Market's clandestine DJ spot.
• **The Angry Beaver** • 8412 Greenwood Ave N
206-782-6044
Poutine flights and hockey for Canucks and those who love them.
• **Barking Dog Alehouse** • 705 NW 70th St
206-782-2974
The dog barks for Belgian beer.
• **Duck Island Ale House** • 7317 Aurora Ave N
206-783-3360
The friendliest beer connoisseurs in Seattle.
• **El Chupacabra** • 6711 Greenwood Ave N
206-706-4889
Frighteningly delicious Mexican munchies and margaritas.
• **Molly Maguire's** • 610 NW 65th St
206-789-9643
Requisite neighborhood Irish pub, only with real Irish people!
• **The Park Public House** • 6114 Phinney Ave N
206-789-8187
Extra pubbish Public House with friendly service and delicious grub.
• **Prost!** • 7311 Greenwood Ave N
206-706-5430
Small German-themed bar with a friendly attitude.
• **Sully's Snow Goose Saloon** • 6119 Phinney Ave N
206-782-9231
Quaint country pub.
• **Sweet Lou's** • 851 N 85th St
206-782-9690
Formerly the Sundown. Lou's got BBQ, beer, and local flavor for yous.

Map 30

- **Tin Hat Bar & Grill** • 512 NW 65th St
  206-782-2770
  Even the jukebox has tattoos.
- **Uber Tavern** • 7517 Aurora Ave N
  206-782-2337
  Enjoy a cold brew at this small hangout.
- **The Yard Cafe** • 8313 Greenwood Ave N
  206-588-1746
  As comfortable as your own back yard, but with way more booze.

## Restaurants

- **74th St Ale House** • 7401 Greenwood Ave N
  206-784-2955 • $$
  Serious about food and beer.
- **A La Mode Pies** • 5821 Phinney Ave N
  206-383-3796 • $$
  Fresh, seasonal pie delivered directly to your face.
- **Barking Dog Alehouse** • 705 NW 70th St
  206-782-2974 • $$
  Cozy dinners, weekend brunch, and generous beer selection.
- **Beth's Café** • 7311 Aurora Ave N
  206-782-5588 • $
  12-egg omelets, all-u-can eat hashbrowns. You'll die and go to heaven, or just…die.
- **The Blue Glass** • 704 NW 65th St
  206-420-1631 • $$
  Upscale pub food that will make you feel superior about getting fat.
- **El Chupacabra** • 6711 Greenwood Ave N
  206-706-4889 • $
  Hearty Mexican, loud music, wacky interior.
- **Four Spoons Cafe** • 850 N 85th St
  206-297-6384 • $
  French bistro atmosphere.
- **Gorditos** • 213 N 85th St
  206-706-9352 • $
  Burritos bigger than a newborn baby.

- **Gorgeous George's Mediterranean Kitchen** •
  7719 Greenwood Ave N
  206-783-0116 • $$
  Even if the food sucked (it doesn't) you'd still co
  back for George.
- **Kalbi Grill Express** • 8202 Greenwood Ave N
  206-457-5930 • $$
  A fam-friendly introduction to Korean food (grill
  fast).
- **Mr. Gyros** • 8411 Greenwood Ave N
  206-706-7472 • $
  It's almost like he was born to make Gyros.
- **Now Make Me a Sandwich** • 85th St NW
  206-714-5090 • $
  Finally, a way to carry out your misogynistic foo
  fantasies without jail time.
- **The Olive and Grape** • 8516 Greenwood Ave N
  206-724-0272 • $$
  They have other stuff too.
- **Pete's Egg Nest** • 7717 Greenwood Ave N
  206-784-5348 • $
  Sure, it's just breakfast. But it is SOLID.
- **Phinney Market Pub & Eatery** •
  5918 Phinney Ave N
  206-219-9105 • $$
  The pub for the fancy NW family. The kids menu
  features risotto.
- **Pho Thân Brothers'** • 7714 Aurora Ave N
  206-527-5973 • $
  Cheap, fast, and filling, with a free cream puff to
  boot.
- **Picnic : A Food & Wine Boutique** •
  6801 Greenwood Ave N
  206-453-5867 • $$
  Buy gourmet items for your fancy-pants picnic
  or have your picnic right there in the store if it's
  raining.
- **Razzi's Pizzeria** • 8523 Greenwood Ave N
  206-782-9005 • $
  A pizza joint the whole, dietary-restricted famil
  can enjoy.
- **Red Mill Burgers** • 312 N 67th St
  206-783-6362 • $
  The undisputed best burger in Seattle. And
  possibly, the best onion rings.

Map 30

Stumbling Goat Bistro brings casual elegance to the neighborhood, while **Gordito's**, **Beth's Café**, and **Red Mill** feed the happy masses. The crack-house chic of Aurora gives way to two of the most comprehensive beer bars in Seattle---**Duck Island Ale House** and **Über Tavern**. Wash your pint down with some good eats at **74th Street Ale House**. The younger, grungier crowd is at **Tin Hat**.

- **The Ridgeback Cafe** • 500 NW 65th St
  206-783-4073 • $
- **The Santa Fe Café** • 5910 Phinney Ave N
  206-783-9755 • $$$
  Nuevo Mexican/Southwestern improvisations like blue-corn crepes. Â¡Delicioso!
- **Stacia's** • 305 NW 85th St
  206-781-0292 • $$
  Free cookies with your pizza!
- **Stumbling Goat Bistro** • 6722 Greenwood Ave N
  206-784-3535 • $$$
  As a bistro should be: Simple, uncomplicated, romantic.
- **Taquería Tequila Authentic Mexican Food** •
  301 NW 85th St
  206-784-4699 • $
  99 cent tacos, dudes.
- **Thaiku** • 6705 Greenwood Ave N
  206-706-7807 • $$
  Aphrodisiac drinks the are main draw—limit one per person.
- **Yanni's** • 7419 Greenwood Ave N
  206-783-6945 • $$$
  Great place to convert Greek food naysayers. Exceptional dolmathes.
- **Zeek's Pizza** • 6000 Phinney Ave N
  206-285-8646 • $$
  Pizzas with pizzazz, like the Thai version with peanut sauce.

## Shopping

- **Better Meat Co.** • 305 NW 82nd St
  206-783-0570
  Old-timey, new-timey meat.
- **Couth Buzzard Books** • 8310 Greenwood Ave N
  206-436-2960
  General used books.
- **Fred Meyer** • 100 NW 85th St
  206-784-9600
  Just like Target but with groceries too!
- **Greenwood Hardware** • 7201 Greenwood Ave N
  206-783-2900
  Makes you really, really, really hate Home Depot.

- **Greenwood Space Travel Supply Co.** •
  8414 Greenwood Ave N
  206-725-2625
  Space travel (and raising money to benefit 826 Seattle) is all they do!
- **Insurrection** • 8403 Greenwood Ave N
  206-782-5752
  Leather gear for riding horses, steel otherwise.
- **Ken's Market** • 7231 Greenwood Ave N
  206-784-3470
  Last of the old-fashioned neighborhood markets.
- **Lil Paisley** • 6500 Phinney Ave N
  206-784-5255
  Accessorize like Liz Taylor and find the jewels that will always bring you luck.
- **New Roots Organics** • 4544 Leary Way NW
  206-261-2500
  Fruits and vegetables till the cows come home. Recipe suggestions, too.
- **PCC Natural Markets** • 7504 Aurora Ave N
  206-525-3586
  One-stop shopping for overpriced organic groceries.
- **Picnic : A Food & Wine Boutique** •
  6801 Greenwood Ave N
  206-453-5867
  Specialty meats and cheese for your fancy-pants picnic. Plus 400 wines to get your date nice and sloppy.
- **Rudy's Barbershop** • 6415 Phinney Ave N
  206-782-9861
  Absolute best cheap haircut!
- **The Sneakery** • 612 NW 65th St
  206-297-1786
  Hipsters will notice your cool shoes, not your jacked-up ingrown toenail.
- **Top Ten Toys** • 124 N 85th St
  206-782-0098
  Classic, teaching, affordable toys that won't bum a kid out either.
- **Zuma Grocery** • 129 NW 85th St
  206-781-8600
  These Ethiopian foods and ingredients are ZOMG good!

Seattle's singletons and families alike flock to Green Lake on rare sunny days for outdoor fun and frolic, jogging, rollerblading, and paddle boat rentals. The pedestrian-friendly lake and surrounding park are true gems for those without private waterfront access or million-dollar houseboats. Nearby Roosevelt, smaller and less popular than its sister 'hood, is a quiet, tree-lined residential enclave on the outskirts of Ravenna Park.

## ○ Landmarks

- **Bettie Page Mural** • 700 NE 59th St
  Giant Bettie seduces commuters from the side of a house.

##  Coffee

- **72nd Street Cafe** • 308 NE 72nd St
  206-523-5623
  Very locally-focused and laid back folks. Enjoy Green Lake no matter how crappy the weather is.
- **Bus Stop Espresso** • 800 NE 65th St
  206-528-5997
  Not quite near enough to your bus stop.
- **Cafe Javasti** • 8410 5th Ave NE
  206-985-9903
  It's all about the crepes.
- **Café Lulu** • 6417 Latona Ave NE
  206-465-4800
  Open until early afternoon.
- **Cafe Momo** • 7119 Woodlawn Ave NE
  206-985-6900
  Vaguely French home of the iSalad and a to-die-for tofu sandwich.
- **Cafe Racer** • 5828 Roosevelt Way NE
  206-523-5282
  The heart of the community and just the coolest people ever.
- **Forza Coffee Company** • 6900 E Green Lake Way N
  206-453-4279
  Forza is a franchise. This is one of the better ones because they were smart enough to add beer and live music.
- **Peet's Coffee & Tea** • 6850 E Green Lake Way N
  206-267-1440
  Bay Area interlopers.
- **Revolutions Espresso** • 7012 Woodlawn Ave NE
  206-527-1908
  Also bakery.
- **Wayward Coffeehouse** • 6417 Roosevelt Way NE
  206-525-5191
  Vegetarian/vegan-focused joint. Not a bad way to go wayward.
- **Zoka Coffee Roaster & Tea Company** •
  2200 N 56th St
  206-545-4277
  One of the Seattle originals.

## ♀ Nightlife

- **Atlantic Crossing** • 6508 Roosevelt Way NE
  206-729-6266
  No need to cross the pond for that Euro pub feeling!
- **Burgundian** • 2253 N 56th St
  206-420-8943
  Craft beer and all-day breakfast for the barflies who get a late start.
- **Die Bierstube** • 6106 Roosevelt Way NE
  206-527-7019
  German beers the size of a German head.
- **Elysian Tangletown** • 2106 N 55th St
  206-547-5929
  Elysian micros in a cozy neighborhood pub.
- **Little Red Hen** • 7115 Woodlawn Ave NE
  206-522-1168
  Serious honky-tonk for urban cowboys. Slummers get bounced.
- **Mojito** • 7545 Lake City Way NE
  206-525-3162
  Mojitos are just the Tip of the Plantain.
- **Mutiny Hall** • 1205 NE 65th St
  206-524-5020
  Their insanely long, rare beer list will keep you plenty subdued.
- **Pies and Pints** • 1215 NE 65th St
  206-524-7082
  Great concept. Poor execution.

Map 31

# Restaurants

- **Bengal Tiger** • 6510 Roosevelt Way NE
  206-985-0041 • $$
  This Indian food is grrrrreat!
- **Cafe Momo** • 7119 Woodlawn Ave NE
  206-985-6900 • $
  Vaguely French home of the iSalad and a to-die-for tofu sandwich.
- **Cafe Racer** • 5828 Roosevelt Way NE
  206-523-5282 • $
  The heart of the community and just the coolest people ever.
- **Cake Envy** • 7900 East Green Lake Dr N
  206-453-3337 • $$
  The cupcake will not die. This one stays up till midnight on weekends.
- **Casa Patron** • 805 NE 65th St
  206-923-7680 • $$
  Sounds like a good place to get shit-faced, but families eat here too.
- **COA Mexican Eatery & Tequileria** •
  7919 Roosevelt Way NE
  206-522-6179 • $$
  A perfectly serviceable place to eat Mexican food and drink tequila.
- **Diggity Dog Hotdog & Sausage Co.** •
  5421 Meridian Ave N
  206-633-1966 • $
  You'll diggity these hot dogs.
- **Duke's Chowder House** • 7850 Green Lake Dr N
  206-522-4908 • $$
  For all you chowda' heads.
- **Eva** • 2227 N 56th St
  206-633-3538 • $$$
  An elegant meal (ties, high heels, expense accounts not necessary).
- **Flying Squirrel Pizza Co** • 8310 5th Ave NE
  206-524-6345 • $$
  Imaginative pies made from local organic ingredients. So very Seatown.
- **Jodee's Desserts** • 7214 Woodlawn Ave NE
  206-525-2900 • $
  Fairy godmother to sweet-toothed people with dietary restrictions.
- **Krittika's Noodles & Thai Cuisine** •
  6411 Latona Ave NE
  206-985-1182 • $$
  Touch-and-go Thai—some people scarf it up, others barf it up. You decide.
- **Latona Pub** • 6423 Latona Ave NE
  206-525-2238 • $$
  Refuel after a loop around Greenlake with a supe beef pot pie.
- **Mighty-O Donuts** • 2110 N 55th St
  206-547-5431 • $
  Spoiler alert: That damn fine donut you're enjoyi is vegan!
- **Mutiny Hall** • 1205 NE 65th St
  206-524-5020 • $$
  Their insanely long, rare beer list will keep you plenty subdued.
- **Nell's Restaurant** • 6804 E Green Lake Way N
  206-524-4044 • $$
  Subtle, lovely dishes showcasing tip-top local ingredients.
- **Pies and Pints** • 1215 NE 65th St
  206-524-7082 • $
  Buttery, flaky, savory pies and, um…pints.
- **Salvatore Ristorante** • 6100 Roosevelt Way NE
  206-527-9301 • $$$$
  Straightforward and spensy Italian.
- **Savatdee Thai** • 5801 Roosevelt Way NE
  206-331-9666 • $$
  Another Thai place? Luckily, it's really good.
- **Spud Fish & Chips** • 6860 E Green Lake Way N
  206-524-0565 • $
  This place has been around for 75 years for a goo reason.
- **Sunlight Café** • 6403 Roosevelt Way NE
  206-522-9060 • $
  Super-crunchy vegetarian place—aptly named, too.
- **Sushi Tokyo** • 6311 Roosevelt Way NE
  206-526-2935 • $$
  Sushi + teriyaki = yum.
- **Tacos Guaymas** • 6808 East Green Lake Way N
  206-729-6563 • $$
  Delicious tacos of all kinds including braaaaiiiins for your zombie friends.
- **Taste of India** • 5517 Roosevelt Way NE
  206-528-1575 • $$
  A decidedly better buffet, with above-average Indian standards.

Before enjoying a lap or three around the lake, the avid cyclist should check out **Gregg's Cycle** for expert service and superior selection. By contrast, Roosevelt offers a less athletic and more hippie vibe for those of the mellower persuasion. Establishments like **East West Bookshop**, Whole Foods, and **Sunlight Café**, Seattle's oldest vegetarian restaurant, define the neighborhood's shopping district. **Nell's** is one of Seattle's best secrets: pitch-perfect Euro/New American dishes that are elegant but not ostentatious.

#  Shopping

- **Derby Salon** • 6315 Roosevelt Way NE
  206-526-1470
  Great haircuts you won't need a derby to cover up.
- **East West Bookshop** • 6500 Roosevelt Way NE
  206-523-3726
  When you feel like some new-age reading, or learning how to meditate.
- **The Fish Store** • 6109 Roosevelt Way NE
  206-522-5259
  Specialized equipment for the aquarium enthusiast.
- **Gregg's Cycle** • 7007 Woodlawn Ave NE
  206-523-1822
  Voted best bike shop in Seattle.

- **Ma Mo Jewelry Design** • 6317 Roosevelt Way NE
  206-525-4653
  Custom jewelry and services.
- **Trading Musician** • 5908 Roosevelt Way NE
  206-522-6707
  Good prices on great gear for musicians of all kinds.
- **Zenith Supplies** • 6300 Roosevelt Way NE
  206-525-7997
  Hippie emporium. In bulk!
- **zoëyogurt** • 6900 East Green Lake Way N
  206-829-8270
  Post Green Lake jog, replenish your calories with self-serve froyo.

Ravenna is a residential wasteland that lies just north of the U District. It is populated largely by grad students and young families. However, the densely green surroundings and the amazing woodland bubble of Ravenna Park lend a refreshing, non-suburban ambiance to the area.

## ○ Landmarks

- **Wedgwood Rock** • 28th Ave NE & NE 72nd St
  It's a bad sign when a neighborhood's major landmark is a rock.

---

##  Coffee

- **Cowen Park Grocery** • 1217 NE Ravenna Blvd
  206-525-1117
  Cafe attached to lovely Mom & Pop grocery with friendly baristas, Le Fournil pastries and Manny's on tap.
- **Diva Espresso** • 8014 Lake City Way NE
  206-525-5920
  Local chain with unpredictable service. I guess it's kind of like ordering coffee from a diva.
- **Espresso Express** • 6500 15th Ave NE
  206-524-6326
  Also food.
- **Herkimer Coffee** • 5611 University Way NE
  206-525-5070
  Roasting great coffee.
- **Muddy Waters Coffee Company** • 2258 NE 65th St
  206-729-7587
  Some places just get grandfathered in.
- **Rooster's** • 7809 Lake City Way NE
  206-632-6351
  Open early. Cock a doodle doo.

## ▼ Nightlife

- **Knarr Shipwreck Lounge** •
  5633 University Way NE
  206-525-3323
  Play pool and shuffleboard with grizzled Seattleites.
- **The Pub at Third Place** • 6504 20th Ave NE
  206-523-0217
  Board games and wood decor make you feel comfortably snowed in.
- **Ravenna Alehouse** • 2258 NE 65th St
  206-729-9083
  An innofensive neighborhood pub.

# Restaurants

- **Bagel Oasis** • 2112 NE 65th St
206-526-0525 • $
Boiled bagels! Just like Bubby used to make.
- **Cafe Kopi** • 8056 Lake City Way NE
206-523-6197 • $
Cuteing up Lake City with pastries and yummy rice bowls.
- **Chiang's Gourmet** • 7845 Lake City Way NE
206-527-8888 • $$
You don't have to be Chinese to eat here, but it sure helps.
- **Frank's Oyster House & Champagne Parlor** •
2616 NE 55th St
206-525-0220 • $$
Funky Montana meets the 80's decor.
- **Gaudi** • 3410 NE 55th St
206-527-3400 • $$$
Just like Spain (except the early closing time).
- **Harissa Mediterranean Cuisine** •
2255 NE 65th St
206-588-0650 • $$
- **Heidelberg Haus** • 2122 NE 65th St
206-466-5369 • $$$
The uber German experience.
- **Kidd Valley** • 5502 25th Ave NE
206-522-0890 • $
Hey, at least they have veggie burgers.
- **Mamma Melina** • 5101 25th Ave NE
206-632-2271 • $$
An Italian experience that will get you laid.
- **Mars** • 5247 University Way NE
206-632-5132 • $
There's nothing alien about this cozy late-night bistro.

- **Mr. Villa Mexican Restaurant** •
8064 Lake City Way NE
206-517-5660 • $$
As friendly and authentico as they come.
- **Pair** • 5501 30th Ave NE
206-526-7655 • $$$
Small, seasonal plates—you guessed it—"paired with wine. NFT approved.
- **Persepolis Grill** • 5517 University Way NE
206-524-3434 • $
Soups, stews and BBQ at ancient Persian prices.
- **Pizza Pi Vegan Pizzeria** • 5500 University Way NE
206-343-1415 • $
Who says vegans have to compromise? All vegan all the time.
- **Queen Mary Tea Room** • 2912 NE 55th St
206-527-2770 • $$$
Snack on proper British crumpets and tea. Don't forget to raise your pinky.
- **Tempero do Brasil** • 5628 University Way NE
206-523-6229 • $$$
A thrilling mix of cuisines is the remedy for "what to-try-next" syndrome.
- **Vios Café** • 6504 20th Ave NE
206-525-5701 • $
Beautiful Greek dishes. Wines for the adults, play area for the kiddies.
- **Wayward Vegan Café** • 5253 University Way NE
206-524-0204 • $$
Vegan comfort food with a punk vibe.
- **Zeek's Pizza** • 2108 NE 65th St
206-285-8646 • $$
Pizzas with pizzazz, like the Thai version with peanut sauce.
- **Zouave Restaurant** • 2615 NE 65th St
206-525-7747 • $$
Small but eclectic menu in an adorable hole-in-the-wall bistro.

Entertainment-wise, Ravenna isn't quite a destination. But if you live there and feel 'hoodbound, there are some options: board games and wood decor at **The Pub at Third Place** will make you feel snowed in at a ski lodge, **Ravenna Alehouse** is an inoffensive neighborhood pub and **Knarr** is a comfortable dive. The restaurant scene is looking good with the excellent **Pair** leading the way, along with **Gaudi**.

# Shopping

- **Cowen Park Grocery** • 1217 NE Ravenna Blvd
  206-525-1117
  Your friendly neighborhood mini mart. Fresh Korean tacos spring-summer!
- **Planet Happy** • 2914 NE 55th St
  206-729-0154
  See a baby hedgehog who lives in an old converted TV while you buy toys.
- **Ravenna Third Place Books** • 6504 20th Ave NE
  206-525-2347
  Revitalized neighborhood bookstore; bar downstairs.

- **Recess** • 5235 University Wy NE
  206-729-5099
  Designer casual hoodies, hats and sneakers for the urban man.
- **Rising Sun Farms & Produce** • 6329 15th Ave NE
  206-524-9741
  So cheap and delicious, you'll feel like you're scamming them.
- **Spotted Owl Berger Variety Shop** •
  5502 University Way NE
  206-632-1611
  Creative and original glasswear for, you know, your "coffee table."
- **Vegan Haven** • 5270 University Way NE
  206-523-9060
  Ethically-minded consumers shop at the only 100% vegan store in WA.

Like its NE counterpart, NW Seattle contains a blight (Aurora), a hidden corner of wanna-be elitists (Broadview), and a few funky neighborhoods that defy sensibilities of affordability. It isn't as dull as NE, but that's not saying much. It's slightly more developed and neighborhoody than the other side of I-5, but still nothing to get excited about.

##  Landmarks

- **Aurora Rents Elephant** • 8808 Aurora Ave N
  The fate of this elephant is still unknown, so see it while you can.
- **Granite Curling Club** • 1440 N 128th St
  206-362-2446
  Only dedicated curling rink on the West Coast. Need we say more?

## Coffee

- **Blue Saucer** • 9127 Roosevelt Way NE
  206-453-4955
  Seven Coffee Roasters brew and plenty of GF options make it a fine on-the-way stop.
- **Diva Espresso** • 14419 Greenwood Ave N
  206-417-1639
  Local chain with unpredictable service. I guess it's kind of like ordering coffee from a diva.
- **Gourmet Latté** • 8762 Holman Rd NW
  206-782-1535
  The most gourmet coffee available at this particular PetCo.
- **Holy Grounds Coffee** • 9000 Holman Rd NW
  206-783-1797
  Brewing Caffé Vita beans.
- **Sip & Ship** • 7511 Greenwood Ave N
  206-783-4299
  Like a home office with an espresso bar.

## Nightlife

- **Baranof** • 8549 Greenwood Ave N
  206-782-9260
  Classic dive bar with low hipster encroachment, sloppy burgers and daily karaoke.
- **Crosswalk** • 8556 Greenwood Ave N
  206-789-9691
  For serious drinkers only.
- **The House Sports Pub** • 8551 Greenwood Ave N
  206-403-1464
  For health-conscious sports enthusiasts who crave a brew and a salad.
- **Gainsbourg** • 8550 Greenwood Ave N
  206-783-4004
  Sip on absinthe and keep an eye out for Bob in the Black Lodge by the bathrooms.
- **Naked City Brewery & Taphouse** • 8564 Greenwood Ave N
  206-838-6299
  Balls-out beer selection and a killer food menu to boot.
- **The Ould Triangle** • 9736 Greenwood Ave N
  206-706-7798
  A solid Irish dive complete with heavy pours and Dropkick Murphys.
- **Rickshaw** • 322 N 105th St
  206-789-0120
  '70s karaoke paradise.
- **Yen Wor Garden** • 8580 Greenwood Ave N
  206-784-7422
  Nobody does karaoke like the North Seattle Chinese.

Map 5
28 29 30 31 32
23
24 25 26

# Restaurants

- **Ampersand Pantry & Cafe** • 424 N 85th St
206-257-5671 • $
Adorable gourmet foodstuffs shop with a dine-in option and the occasional wine tasting.
- **Baranof** • 8549 Greenwood Ave N
206-782-9260 • $
Classic dive bar with low hipster encroachment, sloppy burgers and daily karaoke.
- **Bick's Broadview Grill** • 10555 Greenwood Ave N
206-367-8481 • $$$
Fusion that's in your face.
- **Blue Saucer** • 9127 Roosevelt Way NE
206-453-4955 • $
Seven Coffee Roasters brew and plenty of GF options make it a fine on-the-way stop.
- **Burgermaster** • 9820 Aurora Ave N
206-522-2044 • $
Drive up, park, and let the old-school car-side service do all the work.
- **Burrito Loco** • 9211 Holman Rd NW
206-783-0719 • $$
The burritos here are loco good.
- **Dick's Drive-In** • 9208 Holman Rd NW
206-783-5233 • $
A local obsession, specializing in cheap burgers and shakes. Perfect at 1 am.

- **El Camion** • 11728 Aurora Ave N
206-367-2777 • $
Amazing truck tacos and tamales you can trust.
- **Fu Shen Chinese Seafood Restaurant** •
9019 Aurora Ave N
206-624-3888 • $$
Worth braving the dodgyness of Aurora for.
- **Kidd Valley** • 14303 Aurora Ave N
206-364-8493 • $
Hey, at least they have veggie burgers.
- **Lucy Ethiopian Restaurant and Lounge** •
10000 Aurora Ave N
206-402-3058 • $
Lucy's finally got her own club.
- **Mr. & Mrs. Wok** • 10000 Holman Rd NW
206-789-0558 • $
A marriage of deliciousness.
- **Patty's Eggnest** • 9749 Holman Rd NW
206-297-1545 • $
Fat omelets and fresh-squeezed OJ make this the best breakfast in town.
- **Saffron Grill** • 2132 N Northgate Wy
206-417-0707 • $$
Another offering from the Cedars empire dishing up bottomless chai.
- **Taqueria la Pasadita #2** • 2143 N Northgate Way
$
Calling these tacos some of Seattle's best is a serious claim. We're serious.

NW has a few pockets of commercial activity that contain life, most notably along 85th and north on Greenwood. The farther north you go, the more suburban the setting. Sticking to Aurora, you'll find an abundant selection of $2 beers, pull tabs, used cars and meth heads, with the occasional hooker waiting to reveal her "hidden neighborhood treasure."

# 🛍 Shopping

- **Ampersand Pantry & Cafe** • 424 N 85th St
  206-257-5671
  Not your mother's pantry (Unless your mother is a gourmet foodie and wino).
- **Childish Things** • 10002 Holman Rd NW
  206-789-1498
  Sell-me-downs and vintage maternity wear.

- **Lenny's Produce** •
  10410 Greenwood Ave N
  206-781-0619
  Cheaper cilantro, you'll never find.
- **Swansons Nursery** • 9701 15th Ave NW
  206-782-2543
  You don't have to live in Wenatchee to grow your own produce!
- **Value Village** • 8532 15th Ave NW
  206-783-4648
  Enormous second-hand store that sells everything from furniture to clothes.

Map 34

Like its NW counterpart, NE Seattle is a smattering of obscure neighborhoods and a horrid blight (Lake City Way). The neighborhood's defining monstrosity, Northgate Mall—the nation's first—should probably be avoided unless you're nostalgic for Forever 21. On the upside, the residential areas are quaint and hide a few gems. The libraries are good, the parks clean, and it's…um, a nice place to raise kids? If it's any consolation, it gets worse in Shoreline.

# Coffee

- **Bark! Espresso** • 11335 Roosevelt Way NE
  206-364-0185
  Great for those who don't enjoy leaving your dog tied up outside while they drink their coffee.
- **Bean City Coffee Company** •
  12547 Lake City Way NE
  206-650-5598
  The best quick-stop in the area, (unless you're one of those bikini espresso creeps).
- **Cloud City Coffee** • 8801 Roosevelt Way NE
  206-527-5552
  Great coffee and quiche. Better still, Darth Vader is nowhere in sight.
- **Kaffeeklatsch** • 12513 Lake City Way NE
  206-462-1059
  Bakery and coffee the German Hausfrau way.
- **Spotted Pony Espresso** • 12539 33rd Ave NE
  206-457-4187
  A little taste of Vashon in NE Seattle.
- **Treehouse Coffee Company** • 12303 15th Ave NE
  206-365-3224
  For those who prefer their treehouses heated, coffee-equipped and on the ground.

# Farmers Markets

- **Lake City Farmers Market** •
  28th Ave NE & NE 125th St
  Thursdays 3-7, early June to early October

# Nightlife

- **El Norte Lounge** • 13717 Lake City Way NE
  206-954-1349
  Mr. Villa's equally Mexican lounge.
- **Fiddler's Inn** • 9219 35th Ave NE
  206-525-0752
  When Wedgwoodies can find a babysitter.

# Restaurants

- **Dick's Drive-In** • 12325 30th Ave NE
  206-363-7777 • $
  A local obsession, specializing in cheap burgers and shakes. Perfect at 1 am.
- **Enat Ethiopian** • 11546
  15th Ave NE
  206-362-4901 • $
  Best Ethiopian restaurant in Seattle.
- **Five Guys** • 311 NE 103rd St
  206-729-5028 • $
  Chain burgers & fries that are actually good.
- **Judy Fu's Snappy Dragon** •
  8917 Roosevelt Way NE
  206-528-5575 • $
  Sopping-greasy Chinese—and still, mysteriously, a Seattle favorite.
- **Kaffeeklatsch** • 12513 Lake City Way NE
  206-462-1059 • $
  Bakery and coffee the German Hausfrau way.
- **Patty's Eggnest** • 1000 NE Northgate Way
  206-364-3463 • $
  Fat omelets and fresh-squeezed OJ make this the best breakfast in town.
- **Tengu Sushi** • 301 NE 103rd St
  206-525-9999 • $$
  Three words: Conveyor belt sushi!
- **Toyoda Sushi** • 12543 Lake City Way NE
  206-367-7972 • $$$
  Trend seekers go elsewhere: the sushi here is simple, fast, affordable.
- **Tub's Gourmet Subs** • 11064 Lake City Way NE
  206-361-1621 • $
  It ain't no Subway. Five stars for the "Hawaiian."

# Shopping

- **Fred Meyer** • 13000 Lake City Way NE
  206-440-2400
  Just like Target but with groceries too!
- **Northgate Mall** • 401 NE Northgate Way
  206-362-4778
  Large indoor shopping mall. Ugh.
- **Party @ Display & Costume** •
  11201 Roosevelt Way NE
  206-362-4810
  Go here if you are throwing a party or need a costume.
- **Silver Platters** • 9560 1st Ave NE
  206-524-3472
  No, it wasn't named after The Brady Bunch's band.

# Map 35 · **Alki / West Seattle / North Admiral**

Many Seattleites believe West Seattle is on the other side of the world. The monstrous West Seattle Freeway Bridge connects this area with the rest of the city. The California Avenue and Alaska Way intersection---known as The Junction---feels like a small, hip town of its own, littered with fabulous restaurants, shops, and historical landmarks. Similarly, west-facing Alki Avenue feels like a California beach town---with little sunshine, snow-capped mountains, and ferry boats.

37   38

## ○ Landmarks

- **Alki Beach Park** • Alki Ave SW & Bonair Dr SW
206-684-4075
The closest Seattle gets to SoCal for two months a year.
- **Birthplace of Seattle Monument** •
Alki Ave SW & 62nd Ave SW
Includes a piece of Plymouth Rock transported on the first cross-country road trip to Seattle.

- **Schmitz Preserve Park** •
5551 SW Admiral Way
206-684-4075
Old-growth forest paths wind along a creek.
- **Statue of Liberty** • Alki Ave SW & 61st Ave SW
In honor of the little New York that Alki never became.
- **Whale Tail Park** • SW Lander St & 58th Ave SW
Families come from all over Seattle to this little gem of a park. Close to the beach too!

Map 35

# Alki / West Seattle / North Admiral

## ☕ Coffee

- **Alki Juice & Java** • 1619 Harbor Ave SW
  206-938-0153
  Delicious organic smoothies and coffee. Why not get both enjoy the view?
- **Alki Mail and Dispatch** • 4701 SW Admiral Way
  206-932-2556
  Come for the fair trade espresso, stay for the notary.
- **C&P Coffee Company** • 5612 California Ave SW
  206-933-3125
  Lighthouse Roasters and wine tastings.
- **Cafe Osita** • 7349 35th Ave SW
  206-932-4299
  Coffee and Mike's Famous Chowdah. It's not as weird as it sounds.
- **Caffè Fiorè** • 2206 California Ave SW
  206-588-0708
  Makes the bold claim of being Seattle's first organic coffee.
- **Coffee to a Tea with Sugar** •
  4541 California Ave SW
  206-937-1495
  Brewing Vashon Coffee Company beans.
- **Cupcake Royale/Verite Coffee** •
  4556 California Ave SW
  206-883-7656
  Cupcakes and coffee go well together.
- **Easy Street Records & Cafe** •
  4559 California Ave SW
  206-938-3279
  Jacked up record shopping is a Seattle tradition.
- **Freshy's** • 2735 California Ave SW
  206-937-4316
  Plus beer, wine, food and arcade games.
- **Hotwire Online Coffeehouse** •
  4410 California Ave SW
  206-935-1510
  Small-batch roaster.
- **Pearl's Tea & Coffee** • 4800 Delridge Way SW
  206-937-6036
  THE place for boba and crepes in West Seattle.
- **Portside Coffee Company** •
  6720 W Marginal Way SW
  206-762-7509
  Coffee's not bad, though the quality matters less when it's served out of a big silver barge.
- **Red Cup Espresso** • 4451 California Ave SW
  206-913-0230
  Some of the best chai around and a convenient drive-thru.
- **Uptown Espresso** • 4301 SW Edmunds St
  206-935-3753
  Self-proclaimed "Home of the Velvet Foam", but the coffee underneath is just so-so.

Park free in lots around The Junction and start roaming. Get caffeinated before the in-store appearance at **Easy Street Records**. Stock up on potato guns, slingshots and other wholesome toys for the child in your life at **Max and Quinn's Atomic Boy's Shop-O-Rama**. Head downhill and west to **Alki Beach** for a Guinness at **The Celtic Swell** and explore what's referred to as the birthplace of Seattle.

## Farmers Markets

• **West Seattle Farmers Market** •
44th Ave SW & SW Alaska St
Sundays, 10-2, year-round

## Nightlife

• **Bamboo Bar & Grill** • 2806 Alki Ave SW
206-937-3023
The location and hours ('til 2 am) are the best thing they've got going.
• **Bang Bar Thai Restaurant & Lounge** •
4750 California Ave SW
206-935-8888
A little bit of Belltown in West Seattle.
• **The Benbow Room** • 4210 SW Admiral Way
206-922-3313
A secret pirate ship bar inside a family restaurant.
• **The Celtic Swell** • 2722 Alki Ave SW
206-932-7935
Children and fiddles welcome, just like Ye Olde Country.

• **Elliott Bay Brewery Pub** •
4720 California Ave SW
206-932-8695
Top-notch beers and organic local beef.
• **The Matador** • 4546 California Ave SW
206-932-9988
Loud. Dark. Fifty kinds of tequila.
• **OutWest Bar** • 5401 California Ave SW
206-937-1540
A cozy little bar for the gays who have gone west.
• **Poggie Tavern** • 4717 California Ave SW
206-937-2165
Not for the timid drinker.
• **West 5 Lounge & Restaurant** •
4539 California Ave SW
206-935-1966
Hip yet homey, but always crowded.
• **Yen Wor Village** • 2300 California Ave SW
206-932-1455
Known round the hood as the Young Whore. Karaoke seven nights a week.

## Map 35

# Alki / West Seattle / North Admiral

## Restaurants

- **Angelina's Trattoria** • 2311 California Ave SW
  206-932-4550 • $$
  Affordable, cozy, and consistently delicious Italian food.
- **Bakery Nouveau** • 4737 California Ave SW
  206-923-0534 • $
  World Cup-winning baker crafts inexplicably perfect croissants.
- **Cactus** • 2820 Alki Ave SW
  206-933-6000 • $$
  Pretend you're in SoCal, straight chillin' with a margarita by the beach.
- **Christo's on Alki** • 2508 Alki Ave SW
  206-923-2200 • $$
  Family friendly with Greek gusto.
- **Circa** • 2605 California Ave SW
  206-923-1102 • $$
  Exquisite food makes you forget the uncomfortable booths.
- **Duke's Chowder House** • 2516 Alki Ave SW
  206-937-6100 • $$
  The chowder truly is what it's cracked up to be.
- **Easy Street Records & Cafe** •
  4559 California Ave SW
  206-938-3279 • $
  Coffee, breakfast, and music. This place rocks.
- **El Chupacabra** • 2620 Alki Ave SW
  206-933-7344 • $$
  Frighteningly delicious Mexican munchies and margaritas.
- **Elliott Bay Brewery Pub** • 4720 California Ave SW
  206-932-8695 • $$
  Ice cream floats made with stout. C'mon, you know you wanna try it.
- **Heartland Cafe** • 4210 SW Admiral Way
  206-922-3313 • $$
  A little midwestern hospitality, doncha know.
- **Jak's Grill** • 4548 California Ave SW
  206-937-7809 • $$$$
  Both the food and atmosphere are upbeat.

- **La Rustica** • 4100 Beach Dr SW
  206-932-3020 • $$$$$
  Escape the beach buzz. Meat, seafood, and past in a seemingly remote setting.
- **Lee's Asian Restaurant** • 4510 California Ave SW
  206-932-8209 • $$
  The Seven-Flavor Beef will haunt your dreams.
- **Ma'ono Fried Chicken & Whisky** •
  4437 California Ave SW
  206-935-1075 • $$
  They sell other dishes, but the star attractions ar in the name.
- **Mashiko** • 4725 California Ave SW
  206-935-4339 • $$
  Sit back and let the chef choose for you. Good lu
- **Mission Tapas and Bar** • 2325 California Ave SW
  206-937-8220 • $$$
  Expensive and inviting atmosphere. Appetizers outdo the entrees.
- **Pagliacci Pizza** • 4449 California Ave SW
  206-726-1717 • $$
  Local favorite pizza chain makes crispy-chewy delights with seasonal ingredients.
- **Pailin Thai** • 2223 California Ave SW
  206-937-8807 • $$
  Gigantic fish tank and fresh food makes for peaceful dining.
- **Pegasus Pizza & Pasta** • 2770 Alki Ave SW
  206-932-4849 • $$
  Starved? Generous salads and loaded pizzas will do the trick.
- **Pepperdock's Restaurant** • 2618 Alki Ave SW
  206-935-1000 • $
  Tasty, cheap beach food.
- **Pho Than Brothers'** • 4822 California Ave SW
  206-937-6264 • $
  Cheap, fast, and filling, with a free cream puff to boot.
- **Pizzeria 22** • 4213 SW College St
  206-687-7701 • $
  Actual Neapolitan-style pizza forged in fire.
- **Shadowland** • 4458 California Ave SW
  206-420-3817 • $$
  Hearty.

# Alki / West Seattle / North Admiral

Map 35

Get the chef specials at **Mashiko**. Hit **Lee's Asian Restaurant** for its encyclopedic Asian cuisine; their Seven-Flavor Beef will haunt your dreams. Meanwhile, there is homemade ice cream to be had at the historic **Husky Deli**. If you get a jonesing for lubrication by fish and chips, **Spud** on Alki is classic. Dig on swine at **The Swinery**. And local chains **Pagliacci** and **Than Brothers**' serve up competent 'za and pho, respectively.

- **Shoofly Pie Company** • 4444 California Ave SW
  206-938-0680 • $
  Tons of sweet and several savory pies to please your pie hole.
- **Spud Fish & Chips** • 2666 Alki Ave SW
  206-938-0606 • $
  This place has been around for 75 years for a good reason.
- **Sunfish** • 2800 Alki Ave SW
  206-938-4112 • $$
  The best grilled halibut kabobs—batter not included.
- **The Swinery** • 3207 California Ave SW
  206-932-4211 • $$
  For those that dig on swine.
- **Tacos Guaymas** • 4719 California Ave SW
  206-935-8970 • $$
  Delicious tacos of all kinds including braaaaiiiins for your zombie friends.
- **Talarico's** • 4718 California Ave SW
  206-937-3463 • $
  Huge slices of pizza, but we miss the old New Luck Toy.
- **Zatz A Better Bagel** • 2348 California Ave SW
  206-933-8244 • $
  Super fresh.

## Shopping

- **Bin 41** • 4707 California Ave SW
  206-937-0411
  Great selection including many NW wines. Good tastings too.
- **Capers** • 4525 California Ave SW
  206-932-0371
  Classy, overpriced house wares that you really can't live without.
- **Click! Design That Fits** • 2210 California Ave SW
  206-328-9252
  Drool over cement-in-silver jewelry.
- **Coastal Surf Boutique** • 2532 Alki Ave SW
  206-933-5605
  Costly surf, brand names. Offers bike rental in summer.
- **Curious Kidstuff** •
  4740 California Ave SW
  206-937-8788
  Let your kids run wild while you buy them super-cool toys.
- **Easy Street Records & Cafe** •
  4559 California Ave SW
  206-938-3279
  You can't go to W. Seattle without stopping here for music.
- **Husky Deli** • 4721 California Ave SW
  206-937-2810
  Old-fashioned deli counter and homemade ice cream.
- **Max and Quinn's Atomic Boys Shop-O-Rama** •
  4311 SW Admiral Way
  206-938-3255
  The Archie McPhee's of West Seattle.
- **Metropolitan Market** • 2320 42nd Ave SW
  206-937-0551
  Fine grocery shopping.
- **Northwest Art & Frame** • 4733 California Ave SW
  206-937-5507
  Find an equal amount of useless gifts and art necessities.
- **PCC Natural Markets** • 2749 California Ave SW
  206-937-8481
  Organic to the core.
- **Seattle Fish Company** • 4435 California Ave SW
  206-938-7576
  Support the independents who don't sell farm-raised fish.
- **Small Clothes** • 3215 California Ave SW
  206-932-2222
  Upscale second-hand for the toddler set.
- **The Swinery** • 3207 California Ave SW
  206-932-4211
  For those that dig on swine.
- **West Seattle Farmers Market** •
  44th Ave SW & SW Alaska St
  May thru December.
- **Zamboanga** • 4531 California Ave SW
  206-933-6399
  Eclectic trinkets and flowy clothes.

# Map 36 · **North Delridge**

N

**1**    **2**

*Elliott Bay*

INDUSTRIAL DISTRICT

HARBOR ISLAND

NORTH DELRIDGE

West Seattle Golf Course

Camp Long

West Duwamish Waterway

East Duwamish Waterway

Duwamish Waterway

Seattle Frwy

SW Spokane Street Brdg

Seacrest Marina

Hamilton View Park

Belvedere Viewpoint Park

Hiawatha Plgd

Delridge Playfield

Puget Park

Fairmount Playground

South Seattle Community College

A

B

C

35

39

37

38

99

Alaskan Way S

Sunset Ave SW
California Ave SW
Fauntleroy Ave SW
Harbor Ave SW
Avalon Way SW
SW Admiral Way
E Marginal Way S
Delridge Way SW
23rd Ave SW
35th Ave SW
Fauntleroy Way SW

SW Massachusetts St
SW Holgate St
SW Hill St
SW Forest St
SW Stevens St
SW Hanford St
SW Hinds St
SW Manning St
SW Charlestown St
SW Bradford St
SW Andover St
SW Dakota St
SW Genesee St
SW Oregon St
SW Alaska St
SW Edmunds St
SW Hudson St
SW Dawson St
SW Brandon St
SW Findlay St
SW Juneau St
SW Raymond St
SW Graham St

1/2 mile    .5 km

Map 36

The charm of this part of town is that they seem to have one foot in the 1950s while the other foot steps bravely into the 21st century. A large elderly population thrives amongst a strong influx of young families seeking kid-friendly goods and services. Snap the ideal panoramic photograph of Seattle's skyline from Harbor Avenue or up steep Admiral Way. There's really nothing pretentious in this neck of the woods. A coffee stop at **Java Bean** in Luna Park is worth the detour.

## Landmarks
- **Seacrest Park** • 1660 Harbor Ave SW
  206-684-4075
  Scuba divers galore. Elliott Bay Water Taxi to downtown leaves from here.

## Coffee
- **Diva Espresso** • 4480 Fauntleroy Way SW
  206-937-5225
  Local chain with unpredictable service. I guess it's kind of like ordering coffee from a diva.
- **Java Bean** • 2920 SW Avalon Way
  206-938-5665
  Since 1989: organic, shade grown, fair trade.
- **Uptown Espresso** • 3845 Delridge Way SW
  206-933-9497
  Self-proclaimed "Home of the Velvet Foam," but the coffee underneath is just so-so.

## Nightlife
- **The Bridge** • 4439 35th Ave SW
  206-402-4606
  Attempts to bridge the gap between West Seattle and the rest of the world.
- **Skylark** • 3803 Delridge Way SW
  206-935-2111
  Real Seattle rock-n-roll happens here. No cover.
- **West Seattle Bowl** • 4505 39th Ave SW
  206-932-3731
  A dying breed.

## Restaurants
- **Beloved Mexico** • 4721 Fauntleroy Way SW
  206-478-0496 • $
  You'll be-like this healthy-ish taco truck. "Love" is a little strong.
- **Buddha Ruksa** • 3520 SW Genesee St
  206-937-7676 • $$
  Enlightenment attained.
- **Chaco Canyon Organic Café** • 3770 SW Alaska St
  206-937-8732 • $$
  A voyage into the Raw Food Universe.
- **Chelan Cafe** • 3527 Chelan Ave SW
  206-932-7383 • $
  Solid blue collar greasy spoon.
- **Luna Park Cafe** • 2918 SW Avalon Way
  206-935-7250 • $
  Plenty of fun for the kids; mimosas and piles of eggs for the adults.
- **Pho Aroma** • 5605 Delridge Way SW
  206-932-4343 • $
  Way better than the Tacoma Aroma.
- **Salty's on Alki Beach** • 1936 Harbor Ave SW
  206-937-1600 • $$$$
  The brunch is a must at least once in your lifetime.

# Map 37 • **Fauntleroy / Arbor Heights**

Fauntleroy Way, the street from which this area gets its name, is basically the "Gateway to Vashon," with its direct route to the ferry terminal through quaint, garden-lush, old neighborhoods bordering **Lincoln Park**. Arbor Heights and communities east of Fauntleroy, including White Center, reflect populations struggling to keep afloat as well as young families who can't afford to live closer to the water or in one of Seattle's pricier, more central neighborhoods.

## Landmarks

- **Lincoln Park** • 8011 Fauntleroy Way SW
  206-684-4075
  Bluff trails and a shoreline walk to salt-water filled Colman Public pool. Fun for the whole family.

## Coffee

- **Bird On A Wire Espresso** • 3509 SW Henderson St
  206-932-1143
  Also beer, wine and small plates.
- **Café Rozella** • 9434 Delridge Way SW
  206-762-7223
  Plus food.
- **Caffe Ladro** • 7011 California Ave SW
  206-938-8021
  Strong coffee for strong coffee drinkers.

## Nightlife

- **Beveridge Place Pub** • 6413 California Ave SW
  206-932-9906
  Grab a happy hour deal or sip a $75 brew.
- **Company Bar** • 9608 16th Ave SW
  206-257-1162
  White collar themed joint serves food and drink with soul.
- **Feedback Lounge** • 6451 California Ave SW
  206-453-3259
  A place for alcoholics who like music.
- **Roxbury Lanes** • 2823 SW Roxbury St
  206-935-7400
  Keeping bowling weird and sketchy.
- **Tug Inn** • 2216 SW Orchard St
  206-768-8852
  Mini pitchers, shag carpeting, duct taped furniture—dive in.

Map

37    38    41

# Restaurants

- **3.14 Bakery** • 9602 16th Ave SW
  206-420-4784 • $
  You don't have to be a math wiz to guess their specialty.
- **88 Restaurant** • 9418 Delridge Way SW
  206-768-9767 • $
  Your standard, ol' reliable pho/banh mi purveyor.
- **Café Rozella** • 9434 Delridge Way SW
  206-762-7223 •
  Plus coffee.
- **Eats Market Café** • 2600 SW Barton St
  206-933-1200 • $$
  A dual-purpose after-work pub and post-hangover breakfast spot.
- **Endolyne Joe's** • 9261 45th Ave SW
  206-937-5637 • $$
  American classics that are updated every season.
- **Locöl Barley & Vine** • 7902 35th Ave SW
  206-708-7725 • $$
  Comfort yourself with "a trio of beans" and a glass of wine.

- **Meander's Kitchen** • 9809 16th Ave SW
  206-491-8571 • $
  Otherwise ordinary diner wins with bourbon-battered challah French toast.
- **Proletariat Pizza** • 9622 16th Ave SW
  206-432-9765 • $
  Common pizza for the common people.
- **Salvadorean Bakery** • 1719 SW Roxbury St
  206-762-4064 • $
  Specialties from El Salvador: Stay for the sopa de pollo and the pupusas.
- **Tacos Guaymas** • 1622 SW Roxbury St
  206-767-4026 • $$
  Delicious tacos of all kinds including braaaaiiiins for your zombie friends.
- **Uncle Mike's BBQ** • 9640 16th Ave SW
  206-588-2713 • $
  A decent BBQ place with real vegetarian options
- **West Seattle Fish House** • 9005 35th Ave SW
  206-457-8643 • $
  It's a fish house in West Seattle. A damn good on too.
- **Zippy's Giant Burgers** • 1513 SW Holden St
  206-763-1347 • $
  How a quarter-pounder should be—chargrilled and served with a smile.

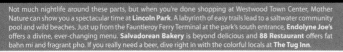

Map 3

Not much nightlife around these parts, but when you're done shopping at Westwood Town Center, Mother Nature can show you a spectacular time at **Lincoln Park**. A labyrinth of easy trails lead to a saltwater community pool and wild beaches. Just up from the Fauntleroy Ferry Terminal at the park's south entrance, **Endolyne Joe's** offers a divine, ever-changing menu. **Salvadorean Bakery** is beyond delicious and **88 Restaurant** offers fat bahn mi and fragrant pho. If you really need a beer, dive right in with the colorful locals at **The Tug Inn**.

## Shopping

• **Full Tilt Ice Cream** • 9629 16th Ave SW
206-767-4811
Ice cream in an arcade. It don't get no icier.

• **Sea Mart** • 1513 SW
Holden St
206-766-9669
Wide variety of international beers + lottery tickets.
• **West Seattle Thriftway** • 4201 SW Morgan St
206-937-0245
Locally owned and operated grocery store!

Map 38 • White Center, South Park, Beverly Park

1/2 mile     .5 km

Map 38

Where can you find two spacious, members-only country clubs poised over an industrial waterway area rivaling the worst of North Jersey and a town hub thick with ethnic markets and seedy tattoo parlors? Step right up folks—it's all here! Yup, life in White Center (a.k.a Rat City for reasons best left to urban legend) means never having to leave the 'hood for fun.

## Landmarks
- **Westcrest Park** • 9000 8th Ave SW
  206-684-4075
  Four-acre dog park has trails, balls, water dishes, and an obstacle course!

## Coffee
- **Caffè Delia** • 9622 16th Ave SW
  206-457-8860
  The darling of White Center, serving Velton's coffee and Macrina pastries out of Proletariat Pizza.
- **Dubsea Coffee** • 9910 8th Ave SW
  206-708-6806
  The Bohemian coffee house is alive and well.
- **Hecka Good Cafe** • 10801 Myers Way S
  206-453-5682
  Not bad. Not bad at all.
- **Java Express** • 11600 Des Moines Memorial Dr
  206-248-7933
  On way to or coming from SeaTac.

## Nightlife
- **Loretta's Northwesterner** • 8617 14th Ave S
  206-327-9649
  Wood paneling and classic beer signs from the 9 LB Hammer folks.

## Restaurants
- **Muy Macho** • 8515 14th Ave S
  206-763-3484 • $
  Good and cheap. Brain and tripe.

## Shopping
- **Pacific Industrial Supply Co.** • 1231 S Director St
  206-682-2100
  Industrial hardware junkie? Get your fix here.

# Map 39 • **SoDo / Beacon Hill / Georgetown**

This part of town is kind of like the one on the '90s sitcom, *Roseanne*; an industrial community that loves their burgers, BBQ, and Mexican food. Townies gather in dive bars after work for beer and conversation. They are so proudly blue-collar that their park houses beloved Sea-Town landmark, **Hat n' Boots**. This precious sculpture was rescued from an old Texico station and stands proudly next to a children's play structure. Ain't that America.

## Landmarks

- **Hat 'n' Boots** • 6430 Corson Ave S
Former roadside attraction now safely ensconced in Oxbow Park.
- **SoDo Freewall** • 2250 Occidental Ave S
Graffiti on a wall.
- **Starbucks Headquarters** • 2401 Utah Ave S
Still waiting for that giant mermaid to jump out and go Godzilla on downtown.

##  Coffee

- **All City Coffee** • 1205 S Vale St
206-767-7146
Where Georgetown caffeinates.
- **The Daily Coffee & Tea** • 5400 E Marginal Way S
206-486-6088
A nice little coffee oasis in a vast industrial dessert.
- **Espresso by Design** • 511 S Mead St
206-768-1061
Plus food.
- **The Station** • 2533 16th Ave S
206-453-4892
A nice Light Rail stop. Fill up on coffee before standing in the TSA line.
- **Victrola Coffee** • 3215 Beacon Ave S
206-860-7767
From a time before coffee was good.

## Nightlife

- **9lb. Hammer** • 6009 Airport Way S
206-762-3373
More fun than you can shake a hammer at. Plus free peanuts!
- **Aston Manor** • 2946 1st Ave S
206-382-7866
Just the place for folks who long for the exclusivity and superficiality of Vegas clubs.

- **Bogart's Airport Way** •
3924 Airport Way S
206-622-1119
Guitar Hero Tuesdays and karaoke with trannies.
- **Brass Tacks** • 6031 Airport Way S
206-397-3821
Perpetuating the bacchanalian celebration of meat and alcohol.
- **Georgetown Liquor Company** •
5501 Airport Way S
206-763-6764
Atari 2600 and beer. Can life get any better?
- **Hooverville Bar** • 1721 1st Ave S
206-264-2428
A bar for recovering corporate junkies.
- **Jules Maes Saloon** • 5919 Airport Way S
206-957-7766
Century-old tavern where punk meets country.
- **Marco Polo Bar & Grill** • 5613 4th Ave S
206-762-3964
Blue collar dive bar with all the fixins. You'll be happy you found it.
- **The Mix** • 6006 12th Ave S
206-767-0280
Another Georgetown gem from the overachiever of neighborhoods.
- **The Oak** • 3019 Beacon Ave S
206-535-7070
The folks from Redwood present a family-friendly pub for grownup hipsters.
- **Showbox SoDo** • 1700 1st Ave S
206-628-3151
Where the Showbox is concerned, bigger is NOT better.
- **Siren Tavern** • 3403 4th Ave S
206-223-9167
Both firemen and longshoremen answer the call of the Siren.
- **Studio Seven** • 110 S Horton St
206-286-1312
Jam to live music with grandma and your teenager.

Map 39

# SoDo / Beacon Hill / Georgetown

## Restaurants

- **American Pie** • 5633 Airport Way S
  206-708-7813 • $
  Sweet and savory pies and empanadas good for
  eating or boning.
- **Bar del Corso** • 3057 Beacon Ave S
  206-395-2069 • $$
  Wood-fired pizza and wine to share with your
  (adult) family.
- **Brass Tacks** • 6031 Airport Way S
  206-397-3821 • $$
  Perpetuating the bacchanalian celebration of meat
  and alcohol.
- **By's Drive-In** • 2901 4th Ave S
  206-622-9901 • $
  It's no Dick's, but it's better than the chains.
- **Calamity Jane's** • 5701 Airport Way S
  206-763-3040 • $$
  The vegetarian shepherd's pie is so much better
  than it sounds.
- **Dahlak Eritrean Cuisine** • 2007 S State St
  206-860-0400 • $$
  Complex and layered dishes that outshine most.
  Superfun with friends.
- **Denny's** • 2762 4th Ave S
  206-623-8375 • $
  Putting moons over Seattle's hammies once again.
- **El Sabroso** • 2524 16th Ave S
  206-551-1432 • $
  Best damn tortas in town.
- **The Essential Baking Company** • 5601 1st Ave S
  206-876-3746 • $
  Essentially delicious.
- **Fonda La Catrina** • 5905 Airport Way S
  206-767-2787 • $$
  Enjoy their small but solid menu in an adorable Dia
  de los Muertos shrine.
- **Gastropod** • 3201 1st Ave S
  206-403-1228 • $$
  The fancy pants snack bar inside Epic Ales' tasting
  room.
- **Georgetown Liquor Company** •
  5501 Airport Way S
  206-763-6764 • $
  Veggie sandwiches that Yoda would approve of.
- **Hudson** • 5000 E Marginal Way S
  206-767-4777 • $$
  Food good enough to die for, luckily located nex
  to a mortuary.
- **Katsu Burger** • 6538 4th Ave S
  206-762-0752 • $$
  Exactly what it sounds like, but way better than
  you might imagine.
- **Matt's Famous Chili Dogs** • 6615 E Marginal Wa
  206-768-0418 • $
  Midwestern folks affirm this is a true Chicago do
- **The Oak** • 3019 Beacon Ave S
  206-535-7070 • $$
  The folks from Redwood present a family-friendl
  pub for grownup hipsters.
- **Papa Bois** • 2401 Utah Ave S
  425-341-3657 • $
  The sandwiches that Caribbean/Asian Fusion
  dreams are made of.
- **Pecos Pit BBQ** • 2260 1st Ave S
  206-623-0629 • $
  Spicy sandwiches for hardworkin' tongues.
- **Philly Boys Cheesesteaks** • 3201 4th Ave S
  206-414-7707 • $
  Settles the cheese steak authenticity debate by
  having all the options.
- **Pho Cyclo** • 2414 1st Ave S
  206-382-9256 • $
  The fragrant pho ga really is chicken soup for the
  soul.
- **Pig Iron Bar-B-Q** • 5602 1st Ave S
  206-768-1009 • $$
  Southern-style eats and a tattooed ambiance.
- **The Sammich Truck** • 6100 4th Ave S
  206-992-6255 • $
  Simple American classics.
- **Slim's Last Chance** • 5606 1st Ave S
  206-762-7900 • $$
  Rockabilly chili.
- **Smarty Pants** • 6017 Airport Way S
  206-762-4777 • $$
  Covering all the bases from knockout veg grub t
  roasted pork. Smart!
- **SODO Deli** • 3228 1st Ave S
  206-467-0306 • $
  The food is Sodo-licious.

SoDo is great for pork lovers (**Pecos Pit BBQ**), those who worship at the temple of the mermaid (**Starbucks' corporate headquarters** is located here), and hardware store junkies. Georgetown is for the urban cowboy/girl. It contains a **9lb. Hammer** (a biker/punk hangout), a **Stellar** pizza joint, and a **Liquor Company**.

- **The Square Knot Diner** • 6015 Airport Way S
  206-915-5244 • $
  There's nothing square about this ice-cream laden 24-hour diner.
- **The Station** • 2533 16th Ave S
  206-453-4892 • $
  A nice Light Rail stop. Fill up on coffee before standing in the TSA line.
- **Stellar Pizza, Ale & Cocktails** • 5513 Airport Way S
  206-763-1660 • $
  Stellar. Really.
- **Viengthong** • 2820 Martin Luther King Jr Way S
  206-725-3884 • $
  Quality Thai-Laotian dishes that tend toward fire-engine spiciness.
- **Willie's Taste of Soul BBQ** • 3427 Rainier Ave S
  206-722-3229 • $
  Soul-satisfying baby backs and some insanely buttery yams.

# 🛍 Shopping

- **A Dog's Dream Natural Pet Supply** •
  5913 Airport Way S
  206-763-1546
  It's a good thing dogs don't have credit cards.
- **Borracchini's Bakery** • 2307 Rainier Ave S
  206-325-1550
  An adored local bakery with an emphasis on affordable.
- **Daniel Smith** • 4150 1st Ave S
  206-223-9599
  Mega mart art supplies. Make an artist happy.
- **Earthwise Architectural Salvage** • 3447 4th Ave S
  206-624-4510
  "Junk can be beautiful."
- **Epic Ales** • 3201 1st Ave S
  206-351-3637
  Seasonal microbrewery with a gourmet snack bar in their tasting room. Epic, indeed.
- **Esquin Wine Merchants** • 2700 4th Ave S
  206-682-7374
  Guess what they sell?

- **Georgetown Music Store** • 6111 13th Ave S
  206-767-2718
  Supplying the next generation of G-town artists with axes.
- **Georgetown Records / Fantagraphics** •
  1201 S Vale St
  206-762-5638
  Cool record store that now shares a space with the Fantagraphics flagship store.
- **Goodwill Outlet** • 1765 6th Ave S
  206-957-5516
  Paw thru bins of cast offs from the unwashed masses.
- **Grocery Outlet** • 1702 4th Ave S
  206-812-6622
  Why is the food so cheap? Don't ask, just buy.
- **JC Marble & Granite** • 2920 1st Ave S
  206-388-0909
  Stone good enough for Jesus Christ's tomb.
- **Maruta Shoten** • 1024 S Bailey St
  206-767-5002
  Ultra-authentic japanese grocery; like a tiny Uwajimaya without the foreign influence.
- **Northwest Shower Door** • 3223 1st Ave S
  206-264-1010
  Elegant doors for clean people.
- **Seattle Pottery Supply** • 35 S Hanford St
  206-587-0570
  When you want to recreate that scene from *Ghost*.
- **Second Use** • 3223 6th Ave S
  206-763-6929
  A (living) museum of old appliances.
- **Silver Platters** • 2930 1st Ave S
  206-283-3472
  No, it wasn't named after The Brady Bunch's band.
- **Visions Espresso Service** • 2737 1st Ave S
  206-623-6709
  The Wizard of Oz would be jealous of their coffee machine collection.

Map 40 • Mount Baker / Seward Park / Columbia City

Are your surroundings feeling a little homogeneous? Head south to the increasingly desirable Mount Baker, Seward Park, and Columbia City 'hoods. Orthodox Jews mingle with Vietnamese Presbyterians. Folks fishing from lake piers make way for Mount Baker's rowing crews. Potters, joggers, and picnickers frequent Seward Park. Warning: Seattle's answer to NASCAR, the Seafair Hydroplane and Blue Angel extravaganza takes over in early August. Locals exit (or turn their yards into parking lots) while 300,000+ party hearty.

## ○ Landmarks

- **Columbia City Farmers Market** •
  4801 Rainier Ave S
  Foodie heaven every Wednesday from May to October.
- **Martin Luther King Jr. Memorial Park** •
  2200 Martin Luther King Jr Way S
  206-684-4075
  A mountain of inspiration; words are inadequate.
- **Sicks Stadium Sign on Lowe's Hardware in Rainier Valley** • 2700 Rainier Ave S
  Once, men hit homers and grounded out here. Now they buy drill bits and caulk.
- **Tacos El Asadero** • 3513 Rainier Ave S
  206-722-9977
  The famous Taco Bus!

##  Coffee

- **Café Hope** • 3639 Martin Luther King Jr Way S
  206-805-8894
  All proceeds go to the Asian Counseling and Referral Service so your fix aids the greater good.
- **Caffe Vita** • 5028 Wilson Ave S
  206-721-0111
  The best of the local chains.
- **Empire Espresso** • 3829 S Edmunds St
  206-659-0588
  In case beer isn't enough to get you jacked up for the footie match.

## Farmers Markets

- **Columbia City Farmers Market** •
  4801 Rainier Ave S
  Wednesdays, 3-7, May through October

## Nightlife

- **AMF Imperial Lanes** • 2101 22nd Ave S
  206-325-2525
  Good clean fun. Which is rare for a bowing alley.
- **Billiard Hoang** • 3220 S Hudson St
  206-723-2054
  A couple regular tables, some of those weird pocketless ones and banh mi (!).
- **Lottie's Lounge** • 4900 Rainier Ave S
  206-725-0519
  Comfortable neighborhood joint with live music and full menu.
- **Rainier Billiards** • 5041 Rainier Ave S
  206-722-6508
  The World Pool-Billiard Association ain't sanctioning tournaments here any time soon, but it'll do.

**Map 40**

# Mount Baker / Seward Park / Columbia City

## 🍴 Restaurants

- **Bananas Grill** • 4556 Martin Luther King Jr Way S
  206-420-4839 • $
  Not your average gyrocery. There's always money in the banana grill.
- **Bent Burgers** • 5100 S Dawson St
  206-760-0291 • $
  Not as "bent" as they'd have you believe. But they'll do.
- **Cafe Ibex** • 3218 Martin Luther King Jr Way S
  206-721-7537 • $
  Decent Ethiopian open late.
- **Columbia City Ale House** • 4914 Rainier Ave S
  206-723-5123 • $$
  Not a chicken wing in sight: just catfish sandwiches, gumbo, fish tacos. Poor you.
- **Columbia City Bakery** • 4865 Rainier Ave S
  206-723-6023 • $
  Bread to make your grandmamma proud. Fabulous baguettes.
- **El Asadero Taco Truck** • 3517 Rainier Ave S
  $
  Mexi cola and carne asada for less than a latte.
- **Emerald City Fish and Chips** • 3756 Rainier Ave S
  206-760-3474 • $
  Local boys bring New Orleans flavor to their meticulous fish & chips experience.
- **Flying Squirrel Pizza Co** • 4920 S Genesee St
  206-721-7620 • $
  Imaginative pizzas made from local organic ingredients. So very Seatown.
- **Geraldine's Counter** • 4872 Rainier Ave S
  206-723-2080 • $$
  Diner fare that's far better than it needs to be.
- **Grilled Cheese Experience** • 5718 Rainier Ave S
  206-661-5225 • $$
  An experience you won't soon forget. Because cheese overdoses cause nightmares.

- **Island Soul** • 4869 Rainier Ave S
  206-329-1202 • $$
  Steel drums fuel the Caribbean favorites and ru cocktails.
- **Jones Barbeque** • 4417 Fauntleroy Way SW
  206-257-4946 • $
  The tenderest, juiciest dead cows one could imagine.
- **Jus Bar** • 4908 Rainier Ave S
  206-420-2535 • $
  They have pretty silly names, but these juices a serious business.
- **La Medusa** • 4857 Rainier Ave S
  206-723-2192 • $$$
  Sicilian food for the soul meets the neighborho farmer's market.
- **La Teranga** • 4903 Rainier Ave S
  206-725-1188 • $$
  Tiny portal to a Senegalese kitchen of delights.
- **Mioposto** • 3601 S McClellan St
  206-760-3400 • $$
  A splendid park view and light, family-friendly f from the Chow Foods crew.
- **Spice Room** • 4909 Rainier Ave S
  206-725-7090 • $$
  Thai-rific.
- **St. Dames** • 4525 Martin Luther King Jr Way S
  206-725-8879 • $$
  Vegetarian comfort food that's actually comforting.
- **Tutta Bella Neopolitan Pizzeria** •
  4918 Rainier Ave S
  206-721-3501 • $
  Their pizza has been certified by the Italian government. 'Nuff said.
- **Wabi-Sabi** • 4909 Rainier Ave S
  206-721-0212 • $$
  Solid sushi and pleasant ambiance.

Columbia City is a tiny triangular hub on Rainier Avenue between Orcas and Alaska, which has exploded in recent years with condos and adorable eateries. Our favorite cafe is **La Medusa**, where they serve edible miracles. It's **Columbia City Bakery** for artisanal fare, **Tutta Bella** for family dining, **Full Tilt** for dessert, and **Lottie's Lounge** for Beer-O'Clock.

## Shopping

- **Andaluz** • 4908 Rainier Ave S
  206-760-1900
  Gifts for girlie girls.
- **Bike Works!** • 3709 S Ferdinand St
  206-725-9408
  Non-profit bike shop that teaches maintainance to kids.
- **Bob's Quality Meats** • 4861 Rainier Ave S
  206-725-1221
  Seattle needs more old-school butchers like Bob.
- **Full Tilt Ice Cream** • 5041 Rainier Ave S
  206-226-2740
  Ice cream, beer & pinball. Sweet.
- **PCC Natural Markets** • 5041 Wilson Ave S
  206-723-2720
  Organic to the core.
- **Vientian Asian Grocery** • 6059 Martin Luther King Jr Way S
  206-723-3160
  This tiny Lao grocery and cafe packs a big punch.

You know real estate prices are insane when few can afford homes even in this predominantly low- to middle-income area. The exception is the recession-proof string of waterfront homeowners bordering Lake Washington. Kubota Gardens and the **Rainier Beach Library** are lovely and the public boat launch is handy. On the other hand, the crime rate here will make insurance more expensive than your car payment.

# Coffee

- **Jet Fuel Espresso** •
  11234 Tukwila International Blvd
  206-764-4944
  Drive thru.

# Restaurants

- **Cafe Vignole** • 9252 57th Ave S
  206-721-2267 • $$$
  Y'all ready to mangia?
- **Hong Kong Seafood Restaurant** •
  9400 Rainier Ave S
  206-723-1718 • $$
  Great Cantonese dim sum and noodles.
- **King Donut** • 9232 Rainier Ave S
  206-721-3103 • $
  Terrific trifecta of donuts, teriyaki, and laundromat.
  We kid you not.
- **Maya's Mexican Restaurant** • 9447 Rainier Ave S
  206-725-5510 • $
  Seafood is the speciality; wash it down with a
  fresh-queezed 'rita.
- **Pho Van** • 9150 Rainier Ave S
  206-725-2989 • $$
  Vietnamese soup. The perfect hangover cure!
- **Tammy's Bakery** •
  7101 Martin Luther King Jr Way S
  206-760-1172 • $
  Vietnamese baked goods and sandwiches (banh
  mi).
- **Taqueria Costa Alegre Taco Bus** •
  9000 Rainier Ave S
  206-725-0300 • $
  Board the awesome taco bus. Literally.

# Shopping

- **Van Asselt Beauty Salon** • 7136 Beacon Ave S
  206-725-2058
  They are committed to you looking fabulous.

Map 42

Once a mild-mannered dairy farm community, they soon turned that milk into gold and now Mercer Island is home to Seattle's rich and/or famous. This is the 'hood where Paul Allen sleeps, dreaming up new ways to show off his money. Regular folks are welcome too, as long as they know their place and enter around back.

# Coffee

• **The J Cafe** • 3801 East Mercer Way
206-232-7115
The place for nosh inside the Stroum Jewish Community Center.

# Restaurants

• **Bennett's** • 7650 SE 27th St
206-232-2759 • $$
Deli by day, fine dining by night.
• **Phobulous** • 3033 78th Ave SE
206-232-0828 • $
Pho and bubble tea on Mercer Island.
• **Pon Proem** • 3039 78th Ave SE
206-236-8424 • $$
They don't mess around with the chiles here.
• **Roanoke Inn** • 1825 72nd Ave SE
206-232-0800 • $$
Nuzzle up to the cozy fire in the company of millionaires.
• **Roberto's** • 7605 SE 27th St
206-232-7383 • $
A pizza place with salads that are actually tasty.
• **Seven Star** • 2775 78th Ave SE
206-230-8665 • $
More like two stars, but who's counting?

# Map 43 • Bellevue (Southwest)

Bellevue is home to a ton of smart teenagers—several high schools rank among the finest in the nation and it's safe to say that these Bellevue braniacs will probably be your boss one day. When not studying, you can find them hanging out at the food court in the Factoria Mall.

# Restaurants

- **Shanghai Café** • 12708 SE 38th St
  425-603-1689 • $$
  Homemade noodles keep 'em coming back.
- **Square Lotus** • 3540 Factoria Blvd SE
  425-679-0680 • $$
  Family-owned Vietnamese with substantial vegetarian menu.
- **Top Gun Seafood** • 12450 SE 38th St
  425-641-3386 • $$
  Take a ride into the dim-sum zone.

Map 44

As the third largest institution of higher education in Washington, Bellevue Community College sends more transfer students to four-year universities than any other community college in the state. At first glance the region appears to be quiet residential suburbs, but the proximity of I-90 and I-405 can make this area hell during rush hour.

# Coffee

- **148th Ave Coffee Shop** •
  2649 Landerholm Circle SE
  Spacious non-chain option.
- **BigFoot Java** • 5157 Lakemont Blvd SE
  425-391-1976
  Decent joe courtesy your favorite blurry hirsute pal.

- **Cafe Bella** • 106 148th Ave NE
  425-747-2781
  Roadside coffee with a nice personality.
- **Megan's Coffee Corner** • 15100 SE 38th St
  425-747-4410
  Beloved Bellevue coffee shack.
- **Sawdust Coffee Company** • 4055 Factoria Blvd SE
  425-643-2518
  They're selling themselves short. Their coffee is way better than sawdust.

# Map 45 • **Bellevue (West) / Medina**

As business continues to boom, construction cranes have become a permanent fixture amid shiny skyscrapers in downtown Bellevue. Bellevue Way becomes "Snowflake Lane" during the holiday season with nightly parades and Christmas lights on display. Upscale and strictly residential Medina is known for its homes right on Lake Washington's shoreline.

##  Landmarks

- **Bellevue Art Museum** • 510 Bellevue Way NE
  425-519-0770
  Across the street from Bellevue Square, exhibits arts and crafts from local artists.
- **Carillon Point** • 4100 Carillon Point
  425-822-1700
  Marina waterfront with carillons that ring every 30 minutes.
- **Meydenbauer Center** • 11100 NE 6th St
  425-637-1020
  Convention center featuring cultural, theater, and musical events.

## Coffee

- **Café Cesura** • 1015 108th Ave NE
  425-633-2362
  For those who like coffee, but think they should be paying more for it.
- **T'Latte** • 37 103rd Ave NE
  425-709-6868
  Bubble tea.

##  Nightlife

- **Black Bottle Postern** • 919 Bellevue Way NE
  425-223-5143
  This Belltown favorite brings the noise to Bellevue.
- **Lucky Strike Lanes** • 700 Bellevue Way NE
  425-453-5137
  Bowling gone upscale, with creative televisions and plasma cocktails.
- **Parlor Billiards & Spirits** • 700 Bellevue Way NE
  425-289-7000
  Upscale pool hall.

# 🍴 Restaurants

- **Bamboo Garden** • 202 106th Ave NE
  425-688-7991 • $
  Cheap, spicy Sichuan in a strip mall (adjacent to an adult entertainment store).
- **Bis on Main** • 10213 Main St
  425-455-2033 • $$$$
  Perfect for wining and dining—as long as you got the dough.
- **Cheesecake Factory** • 401 Bellevue Sq
  425-450-6000 • $$$
  Overpriced food straight from the assembly line.
- **Daniel's Broiler** • 10500 NE 8th St
  425-462-4662 • $$$$$
  Fancy folk (or those whose parents are paying) head here for decent steak.
- **Din Tai Fung** • 700 Bellevue Wy NE
  425-698-1095 • $$
  Seattle outpost of major dumpling multi-national.
- **Facing East Taiwanese Restaurant** •
  1075 Bellevue Way NE
  425-688-2986 • $
  Bet you never thought you'd the words oysters and pancakes together.
- **Ginza** • 103 102nd Ave SE
  425-709-7072 • $$$
  Specializing in Japanese barbecue—rare find (not literally).
- **John Howie Steak** • 11111 NE 8th St
  425-440-0880 • $$$$$$
  Highest-end steakhouse, no corners cut, priced accordingly.
- **Koral Bar & Kitchen** • 900 Bellevue Way NE
  425-623-1125 • $$
  A consolation for finding yourself at the Bellevue Hyatt Regency.
- **Mediterranean Kitchen** • 103 Bellevue Way NE
  425-462-9422 • $$$
  Garlicky Greek goodness.
- **The Melting Pot** • 302 108th Ave NE
  425-646-2744 • $$$$
  Gimmicky and retro, perhaps, but dipping thing in cheese can never be bad.
- **Pagliacci Pizza** • 563 Bellevue Sq
  425-726-1717 • $$
  Local favorite pizza chain makes crispy-chewy delights with seasonal ingredients.
- **Pasta & Co.** • 10218 NE 8th St
  425-453-8760 • $$
  One-stop gourmet chain has fresh bread, wine, and risotto cakes to go.
- **PF Chang's China Bistro** • 525 Bellevue Way SE
  425-637-3582 • $$$
  Shamelessly Americanized Chinese food.
- **PinkaBella Cupcakes** • 320 Bellevue Square
  425-453-2253 • $$
  Keeping the overpriced sugar bomb dream alive
- **Pogacha** • 119 106th Ave NE
  425-455-5670 • $$$
  Translation: yummy Croatian pizza.
- **Ruth's Chris Steak House** • 565 Bellevue Sq
  425-451-1550 • $$$$$
  Ubiquitous chain dishes out gargantuan portior of meat.
- **Seastar Restaurant and Raw Bar** •
  205 108th Ave NE
  425-456-0010 • $$$
  Known for the seafood and oysters.
- **Tap House Grill** • 550 106th Ave NE
  425-467-1730 • $$$
  160 beers on tap. We repeat: 160 beers. On tap.

Expect crowds and long waits at every nice restaurant within walking distance of Bellevue Square (or "Belle Square" if you're nasty). Skip the lines at **Lincoln Square Cinemas** by scoring tickets from kiosks sprinkled around Belle Square. If you've got the dough, the membership-only Bellevue Club is recognized for its vast athletic facilities, including an Olympic-size swimming pool and indoor track. **Carillon Point** is a perfect place to stroll and watch the sunset after dinner.

## Shopping

- **Bellevue Square** • NE 8th St & Bellevue Way NE
425-646-3660
Bellevue behemouth.
- **Element** • 575 Bellevue Way NE
425-453-3448
Looking cool in Bellevue can be hard to pull off.
- **Fireworks** • 196 Bellevue Sq
425-688-0933
Colorful gifts and home décor handmade by local artists.
- **Lincoln Square** • NE 8th St & Bellevue Way NE
425-646-3660
Just what Bellevue needed—an expansion of Bellevue Square.

- **Made In Washington** • 190 Bellevue Sq
425-454-6907
If you must give Northwest smoked salmon as a gift.
- **Oil & Vinegar** • 2086 Bellevue Square
425-454-8497
Olive oil on tap. Not to mention pestos, dips, mustards, sun-dried tomatoes…
- **Rudy's Barbershop** • 5 Bellevue Way NE
206-467-1462
Absolute best cheap haircut!
- **Sephora** • 141 Bellevue Sq
425-467-1337
All the make-up you can dream-up in one store.

The latest census reported Bellevue to have the highest percentage of non-white residents in the state, with the Chinese and Indian populations having increased twofold since 2000. Despite the materialistic air of the "SoCal of Puget Sound," Bellevue ranks consistently high in Money's "Best Places to Live." Have you noticed how much Western Washingtonians love their magazine list rankings?

## Landmarks

- **Bellevue Botanical Garden** • 12001 Main St
  425-452-2750
  Free guided tours on weekends through their 36 acres of gardens and woodlands.
- **Kelsey Creek Farm** • 410 130th Ave SE
  425-452-7688
  Ponies and farm animals for the kids.

## Coffee

- **Bellisimo Espresso** • 11909 NE 8th St
  425-451-7795
  Walk-up stand.
- **Boba Express** • 15600 NE 8th St
  425-641-1165
  Food court bubble tea and coffee. It is what it is.
- **Jitters Coffee** • 2200 148th Ave NE
  425-644-4645
  Go-to for Microsofties.

## Nightlife

- **Skate King** • 2301 140th Ave NE
  425-641-2047
  Bounce. Roll. Skate.

## Restaurants

- **Bai Tong Thai Restaurant** • 14804 NE 24th St
  425-747-8424 • $$$
  Thai with stylish decor and prices to match.
- **Blue Ginger Korean Grill and Sushi** •
  14045 NE 20th St
  425-746-1222 • $$
  BBQ up some Korean beef at your table.
- **Boba Express** • 15600 NE 8th St
  425-641-1165 • $
  Food court bubble tea and coffee.
- **Can-Am Pizza** • 15400 NE 20th St
  425-747-7777 • $
  Indian food on a pizza. Good news: Butter. Bad news: Bellevue.
- **Dixie's BBQ** • 11522 Northup Way
  425-828-2460 • $$
  Louisiana-style brisket slopped into styrofoam—it's so right.

- **I Love Sushi** • 11818 NE 8th St
  425-454-5706 • $$$
  We love I Love Sushi.
- **Malay Satay Hut** • 15230 NE 24th St
  425-564-0888 • $$
  Three cuisines unite under one roof, with delicious results.
- **Noble Court** • 1644 140th Ave NE
  425-641-6011 • $$
  Freakin' huge Hong Kong-style treats and dim sum. Gets packed.
- **Pho Hoa** • 15169 NE 24th St
  425-641-7898 • $
  Pho for an MSG fix.
- **Regent Bakery & Cafe** • 15159 NE 24th St
  425-378-1498 • $
  Family run Chinese bakery well known for their massive selection of cakes.
- **Saigon City** • 15045 Bel Red Rd
  425-401-0823 • $
  Mediocre pho, but cute menu adorned with family photos.
- **Seoul Hot Pot** • 2560 152nd Ave NE
  425-885-3355 • $$
  Korean convenient to Microsoft campus.
- **Sichuanese Cuisine** • 15005 NE 24th St
  425-562-1552 • $
  Greasy and spicy.
- **Szechuan Chef** • 15015 Main St
  425-746-9008 • $$
  Spicy red Szechuan hotpots with floating peppercorns are the trend.
- **Thai Kitchen** • 14115 NE 20th St
  425-641-9166 • $
  Curries and peppers will have you oohing and aahing in satisfaction.
- **Tosoni's** • 14320 NE 20th St
  425-644-1668 • $$$$$
  Loyal regulars hope the secret doesn't get out. Oops.
- **Zen Yai Noodles** • 15400 NE 20th St
  425-378-1100 • $$
  Better than hospital food.

## Shopping

- **Uwajimaya** • 699 120th Ave NE
  425-747-9012
  Awesome Asian superstore.

Map 47

Trees and scattered parks with numerous sports camps surround the quiet residential areas, keeping the moms and soccer vans busy. An ideal location for picnics and water sports, Idylwood Beach Park on Lake Sammamish is a popular hangout for teenagers eager (and longing) for the sun and warm weather. Rural farmland less than sixty years ago, Redmond is now a pricey city and home to a certain gazillion-dollar behemoth that goes by the unaccountably modest moniker of **Microsoft**.

## ○ Landmarks

• **Microsoft Corporate Headquarters** •
1 Microsoft Way
425-882-8080
Tiny software company named after that famous street in Redmond, Microsoft Way.

##  Restaurants

• **Firenze Ristorante Italiano** • 15600 NE 8th St
425-957-1077 • $$$
A go-to date place; the simplest dishes are the bestest.
• **New York Cupcakes** • 15600 NE 8th St
425-283-5445 • $
Mmmmm…Buttercream.

##  Shopping

• **Crossroads** • 15600 NE 8th St
425-644-1111
Less than glitzy shopping mall.

# Map 48 • Kirkland

With a landscape view of the Seattle skyline, apartments and condos here will eat your paycheck like it's a steak dinner. A waterfront and a quiet, romantic lifestyle attracts retirees. Kirkland's pedestrian-friendly (translation: major traffic), village-like character is maintained by the assortment of little consignment boutiques, art galleries, coffee shops, and restaurants. The home of the original headquarters of Costco (hence the Kirkland Signature brand), Kirkland is also the host of the Junior League Softball World Series, the Seattle Thunderbirds hockey team, and the Seattle Seahawks training facility.

## Landmarks

- **Kirkland Marina** • 25 Lake Shore Plaza
  Dig your toes into the sandy beach.
- **Kirkland Performance Center** • 350 Kirkland Ave
  425-893-9900
  400-seat theater hosting an array of performances.

##  Coffee

- **Artesano Espresso** • 1431 Market St
  Solid drive-thru coffee.
- **Caffe Ladro** • 104 Central Way
  425-827-5838
  Strong coffee for strong coffee drinkers.
- **Gourmet Latté** • 13270 100th Ave NE
  425-248-0663
  Gourmet is a relative term, but the coffee at this unassuming roadside shack is A-OK.
- **The Green Beanery** • 13039 NE 70th Pl
  425-893-9760
  A particularly eco-mindful coffee stand serving organic fair-trade, naturally.
- **Kitanda Açaí and Espresso** • 12700 NE 124th St
  425-820-4381
  The Brazilian coffee and pastries that you didn't know your life was missing.
- **Mercurys Coffee Co.** • 8506 122nd Ave NE
  425-406-8059
  Organic fair trade coffee that's good enough to forgive a missing apostrophe.
- **Rococo Coffee Roasting** • 136 Park Ln
  425-803-9081
  Their house-roasted coffee is good enough to make you forget you're in Kirkland.
- **St. James Espresso** • 355 Kirkland Ave
  425-896-8272
  Brewing Caffe D'arte beans.
- **Urban Coffee Lounge** • 9744 NE 119th Way
  425-820-7788
  Trying to approximate an actual urban coffee shop in Kirkland.
- **Zoka Coffee Roaster & Tea Company** •
  129 Central Way
  425-284-1830
  A true Seattle original. But in Kirkland.

Map
45 46 47

## Nightlife

- **TechCity Bowl** • 13033 NE 70th Pl
  425-827-0785
  32 lanes and a booming sound system.
- **Tiki Joe's Wet Bar** • 106 Kirkland Ave
  425-827-8300
  Cheap specials and rowdy karaoke for you and the
  frat boys.

## Restaurants

- **Anthony's** • 135 Lake St S
  425-822-0225 • $$$$
  Pacific Northwest fare with expansive view of La
  Washington.
- **Cactus** • 121 Park Ln
  425-893-9799 • $$$
  Outstanding mojitos and Mexican.
- **Café Juanita** • 9702 NE 120th Pl
  425-823-1505 • $$$$$
  Serenity exemplified, and stellar Italian. A must.
- **Hanuman Thai Cafe** • 115 Central Way
  425-605-2181 • $
  Too satisfying for words. You'll actually think you
  in Thailand.
- **Izumi** • 12539 116th Ave NE
  425-821-1959 • $$$
  An affordable Eastside alternative to Seattle's
  uberspendy sushi spots.
- **Lynn's Bistro** • 214 Central Way
  425-889-2808 • $$$$
  Bistro fare with an Asian flair.
- **The Original Pancake House** •
  130 Park Place Center
  425-827-7575 • $$
  Homemade batter! A dozen types of flapjacks! It
  breakfast heaven.
- **Padria Mediterranean Cafe** • 9708 NE 119th Wa
  425-814-1693 • $
  A challenge for the fast food generation…real
  food.

Your Sunday plans: grab a newspaper and a latté at **Caffe Ladro**, take a walk with your dog and feed the ducks at Marina Park, satisfy your stomach with a juicy burger at **The Slip**, catch a musical performance at the **Kirkland Performance Center**, then grab dinner at one of the many Thai restaurants. For the most authentic Japanese food on this side of the lake, it has to be **Izumi**, while **Anthony's** dishes out great seafood. If you must make a fool of yourself, there's karaoke at **Pegasus Pizza** and the "classy" **Tiki Joe's Wet Bar**.

- **Pegasus Pizza & Pasta** • 12669 NE 85th St
  425-822-7400 • $$
  Starved? Generous salads and loaded pizzas will do the trick.
- **Purple Café & Wine Bar** • 323 Park Place Center
  425-828-3772 • $$
  Tome-like wine list can be intimidating; food is upscale café fare.
- **Ristorante Paradiso** • 120 Park Ln
  425-889-8601 • $$$
  A little bit of Sardinia on the Eastside.
- **Santorini Greek Grill** • 106 Central Way
  425-822-0555 • $$
  Eastside local favorite is closer than a Greek island getaway.
- **Sarducci's Sub** • 955 6th St S
  425-827-8253 • $
  They claim to be the best in town. And it's no BS.
- **Shamiana** • 10724 NE 68th St
  425-827-4902 • $$$
  Generous buffet.
- **The Slip** • 80 Kirkland Ave
  425-739-0033 • $$
  Burgers so juicy they…slip.
- **Thai Kitchen** • 11701 124th Ave NE
  425-820-5630 • $
  Curries and peppers will have you oohing and aahing in spicy satisfaction.
- **Wing Dome** • 232 Central Way
  425-822-9464 • $
  Flamin' baskets of flavored chicken wings.

## Shopping

- **Champagne Taste** • 147 Park Ln
  425-828-4502
  Designer gown consignment store.
- **PCC Natural Markets** • 10718 NE 68th St
  425-828-4622
  Organic to the core.
- **Simplicity Décor** • 126 Park Ln
  425-803-0386
  Classy, simple Thai-style furniture.
- **Tim's Seafood** • 224 Park Ln
  425-827-0195
  Fresh, seasonal seafood for sale. They pack and ship for you.

# Map 49 • Redmond

Map 49

Easily accessible to and from the surrounding Eastside cities and Seattle, Redmond claims the title "Bicycle capital of the Northwest"—the eleven-mile Sammamish River Trail takes cyclists to the Burke Gilman Trail ending in Seattle. With what seems like hundreds of Starbucks (and counting) within a five-mile radius, the daily mocha will prevent you from dwelling on the drizzle. Picnic or catch a summer concert at **Marymoor Park**.

## Landmarks

- **Edge Skate Park** • NE 83rd St & 161st Ave NE
  Skateboard park and graffiti wall sponsored by the city. Cool.
- **Marymoor Park** •
  6046 W Lake Sammamish Pkwy NE
  206-205-3661
  640 acres for picnics, summer concerts, and chasing dogs.

## Coffee

- **Cascade Grind** • 8005 161st Ave NE
  206-881-2500
  Recognizing that you can get good coffee from attractive people who keep their clothes on.
- **Jitters Coffee** • 15010 NE 20th Pl
  425-747-8030
  Go-to for Microsofties.
- **Kitanda Açaí and Espresso** • 16349 NE 74th St
  206-556-7999
  The Brazilian coffee and pastries that you didn't know your life was missing.
- **Mercurys Coffee Co.** • 17980 Redmond Way
  425-881-0959
  Organic fair trade coffee that's good enough to forgive a missing apostrophe.
- **Peet's Coffee & Tea** • 17887 Redmond Way
  425-968-6125
  Bay Area interlopers.
- **Tapioca Express** • 15230 NE 24th St
  206-643-9406
  Espresso and bubble tea the Taiwanese way.
- **Victor's Celtic Coffee & Roasters** • 7993 Gilman St
  425-881-6451
  Own roasters plus wholesale.

## Farmers Markets

- **Redmond Saturday Market** • 7730 Leary Way NE
  425-556-0636
  Saturdays, 9am-3pm, May through October

## Nightlife

- **Celtic Bayou** • 7281 W Lake Sammamish Pkwy NE
  425-869-5933
  Irish/Cajun hybrid in case you need to fill that void.
- **The Matador** • 7824 Leary Way NE
  425-883-2855
  One of the few bar scenes in Redmond. Buffalo wings and stuff.

Map 49

Redmond

# 🍴 Restaurants

- **Family Pancake House** • 17621 Redmond Way
  425-883-0922 • $
  Chocolate chip pancakes that melt in your mouth.
- **Frankie's Pizza and Pasta** • 16630 Redmond Way
  425-883-8407 • $$
  Local favorite serving gourmet pizza and the usual Italian fare.
- **Marinepolis Sushi Land** • 8910 161st Ave NE
  425-284-2587 • $$
  Fun, cheap sushi.
- **Matt's Rotisserie & Oyster Lounge** •
  16651 NE 74th St
  425-376-0909 • $$
  Almost upscale, but tempered by kids and baseball caps.
- **Nara Japanese Restaurant** • 16564 Cleveland St
  425-885-0703 • $$
  Head for the sushi bar.
- **Ooba Tooba** • 15802 NE 83rd St
  425-702-1694 • $
  Flavorful, fresh Mexican.
- **Pomegranate Bistro** • 18005 NE 68th St
  425-556-5972 • $$
  Cute and tasty.
- **Sages Restaurant** • 15916 NE 83rd St
  425-881-5004 • $$$
  Intimate, rustic, mouthwatering Italian with candles and white tablecloths.
- **Spicy Talk Bistro** • 16650 Redmond Wy
  425-558-7858 • $$
  Authentic Szechuan in Redmond.
- **The Stone House** • 16244 Cleveland St
  425-558-5625 • $$$$
  Inventive cuisine in a charming setting.
- **Stone Korean Restaurant** • 16857 Redmond Wy
  425-497-0515 • $$$
  Especially the Korean fried chicken.
- **Thai Ginger** • 16480 NE 74th St
  425-558-4044 • $$$
  Try their trout salad.
- **Three Lions Pub** • 8115 161st Ave NE
  425-284-3399 • $$
  British cuisine? Yes, it's not always an oxymoron.
- **Yummy Teriyaki** • 17218 Redmond Way
  425-861-1010 • $
  Big portions of just that.

For most, the phrase, "Redmond Nightlife," is an oxymoron. Don't count on much being open after 10 p.m. With the exception of a few movie theaters and a few restaurants with decent happy hours, people head for downtown Seattle to get their kicks. Organic grocery chains **Whole Foods** and **PCC**, are decent shopping options. But you can simultaneously support local farmers and save some coin at the **Redmond Saturday Market**.

# Shopping

- **Bergman Luggage** • 16516 NE 74th St
  425-883-8400
  Serious stuff for serious travelers.
- **Half Price Books** • 7805 Leary Way NE
  425-702-2499
  New and used books at discounted prices.
- **PCC Natural Markets** • 11435 Avondale Rd NE
  425-285-1400
  Organic to the core.

- **Redmond Saturday Market** • 7730 Leary Way NE
  425-556-0636
  Eastside's oldest market—go early for the best pick in local fruits and vegetables.
- **Redmond Town Center** • 7525 166th Ave NE
  425-867-0808
  A mall. Outdoors.
- **REI** • 7500 166th Ave NE
  425-882-1158
  Heaven for wealthy weekend warriors.
- **Snapdoodle Toys** • 15752 Redmond Way
  425-869-9713
  Toys galore.

Gate Pass Rd NE
Gate Point Rd NE
Dolphin Dr
NE Dolphin Rd
Bloedel
Reserve
NE County Park Rd
NE Lafayette Ave
E Euclid Ave
NE Port Madison Rd
Springfield Rd NE
Manzanita Rd NE
Komedal Rd NE
NE Hidden Cove Rd
Hidden
Cove Park
NE Hidden Cove Rd
NE Torvanger Rd
Manzanita Rd NE
Manzanita
Park
Peterson Hill Rd NE
Miller Rd NE
NE Day Rd W
NE Day Rd E
N Madison Ave NE
Sunrise Dr NE
**305**
Battle
Point Dr
Ted Olson
Nature
Preserve
NE Battle Point Dr
Battle
Point
Park
Miller Rd NE
Meadowmeer
Golf & Country Club
NE Koura Rd
NE Valley Rd
NE Tolo Rd
NE Wardwell Rd
Manitou Beach Dr NE
NE Battle Point Dr
Strawberry
Hill Park
Island
Country
Inn
Sportsman Club Rd NE
Fletcher Bay Rd NE
NE High School Rd
Finch Rd NE
Grow Ave NE
Weaver Rd NE
Ericksen Ave NE
Madison Ave NE
Wyatt Way NE
Winslow Way W
Wing Point Golf
& Country Club
Bucklin Hill Rd
Ferry to Seattle
Blakely Ave NE
Eagle Harbor Dr NE
Eagledale
Park
Taylor Ave NE
Lynwood
Theater
Fort Ward
State Park

Grow Ave NW
Madison Ave
**305**
Cove Ave NE
Winslow Wy W
Churchmouse
Yarns and Teas
Madoka
Adam & Eve
Clothing Co
Winslow Wy W
Bainbridge
Arts & Crafts
Back of
Beyond
Canoe &
Kayak Rental
Eagle Harbor Books
Winslow Wy E
Ericksen Ave NE
Olympic Dr SE
Lovell Ave SW
Wood Ave SW
SW Parfitt Wy
Harbor
Public
House

## Overview

Over the centuries, Bainbridge has seen a little of everything—Native American battlefields, logging camps, strawberry farms, artist colonies, and more. Fort Ward and Battlepoint Park were two important military outposts. Battlepoint was the first place to receive the signal that Pearl Harbor had been bombed. No longer a sleepy little bohemian enclave, Bainbridge Island's recent growth has been tremendous, with condos sprouting like fungus and a highly affluent population flocking to live in them. Today, it's an upscale bedroom community, with the majority of its working citizens commuting across the Puget Sound to Seattle. And remember that old Pearl Jam song about the boy who played show and tell with a gun and his head? Yeah, he was a real kid from Bainbridge.

## Attractions

In addition to a nice main street, where an excellent Fourth of July parade happens every year, Bainbridge enjoys a lively arts scene. The Island Theater produces free play readings every two months and Bainbridge Arts and Crafts (bacart. org) features local artists in their gift shop (no crocheted toilet paper covers here!). Bainbridge Performing Arts (www. bainbridgeperformingarts.org) hosts theater, dance, and musical performances with a lower rate of Guffmanesque amateurism than most communities. The Lynwood Theatre (206-842-3080), with its tudor facade and Art Deco style marquee, is Bainbridge's arty movie house and has been continuously running since 1936. The Strawberry Farms are still around and deliver delectable fruit in the state, which can be sampled at the festival held every July. Stars are hard to come by on the mainland but Bainbridge can bring the skies back to you. Battle Point has a Hubble lens in its observatory tower that is open to the public.

The Bloedel Reserve (206-842-7631; www.bloedel reserve.org) is an immaculately kept wildlife and garden sanctuary. Reservations are necessary, so call ahead or reserve online. The waterfront park behind the main street offers tennis courts, a playground, and a dock for the nautically-minded. Canoes and kayaks can be rented seasonally from Back of Beyond Canoe and Kayak Rentals (206-842-9229).

## Shopping

Not exactly bargain territory, Bainbridge shops are upscale but casual. For the sewing crowd, Churchmouse Yarns and Teas (118 Madrone Ln; www.churchmouseyarns.com) carries the finest yarns available, and Esther's Fabrics (285 Winslow Wy E; www.esthersfabrics.com) stocks cloth that is expensive and worth every cent. With peaceful surroundings, frequent readings, and a fine selection, Eagle Harbor Books (157 Winslow Wy E; www.eagleharborbooks.com) is everything a bookstore should be.

## Restaurants

Oddly enough for an island, there aren't many restaurants with a water view. Worth noting, however, is the Harbor Public House (231 Parfitt Wy SW, 206-842-0969; www. harbourpub.com) with exceptional pub grub and a bar stocked with choice Washington State wines and beers. Café Nola (101 Winslow Wy E, 206-842-3822; www.cafenola.com) is a European style café with an excellent, reasonably priced menu. The upscale but overrated Four Swallows (481 Madison Ave, 206-842-3397; www.fourswallows.com) is a tourist trap which the locals steer clear of. For a casual breakfast or lunch, try Streamliner Diner (397 Winslow Wy E, 206-842-8595), or check out Pegasus Coffee (131 Parfitt Wy, 206-842-6725; www.pegasuscoffeehouse.org) for great java in a rustic, ivy-covered brick structure.

## Lodgings

The Island's two hotels, Best Western and Island Country Inn, which can be found next to the Safeway strip mall, both provide reasonably priced lodging. A better choice is selecting from one of the many bed-and-breakfast establishments on the Island, where all the amenities of home make an extended visit to Bainbridge a lot more inviting (find a comprehensive list at www.bainbridgelodging.com/list.html).

## How to Get There

### By Ferry

Washington State Ferries leave from Coleman Dock at Pier 52 on Alaskan Way every 50 minutes or so, but make sure to double check the schedule (www.wsdot.wa.gov/ferries). The round trip walk-on fare is $7.70 for adults. Youth ages 6-18 receive 20 percent discount with proof of age and children under 6 ride free. Cars are $13.25 or $16.40 depending on length of vehicle; each passenger is additional. There are buses that meet the boats during commuter hours; check Kitsap Transit (1-800-501-RIDE; www.kitsaptransit.org) for details.

### By Car

Driving to Bainbridge Island from Seattle without using the ferry is inconvenient, but not impossible. Take I-5 through Tacoma, then follow Highway 16 north through Bremerton. From there take Highway 3 to 305 and cross the Agate Pass Bridge. Depending on traffic, the whole trip takes about an hour and forty-five minutes and is recommended only for those desperate to get to or from the airport when the ferries aren't running.

## General Information

NFT Map        4
Address:       1635 11th Ave
               Seattle, WA 98102
Phone:         206-684-4075
Website:       www.seattle.gov/parks/Parkspaces/
               anderson.htm
Hours:         4 am–11:30 pm

## Overview

Cal Anderson Park, named after Washington's first openly gay state legislator, is located in the heart of Capitol Hill and includes the Lincoln Reservoir and the Bobby Morris Playfield. Formerly Lincoln Park, (no relation to Linkin Park) Cal Anderson has had numerous, and regrettably appropriate, nicknames over the years such, as "Hobo Park" and "Heroin Park." However, in 2005, Cal Anderson was the recipient of a major overhaul that transformed the strung-out little duckling into a beautiful countercultural swan.

Many doubted the renovations would do any good, but the success was undeniable when the park reopened on September 24th, 2005. The makeover included lush, manicured grass, new paths and benches, a wading pool, a reflecting pool, a fountain, a giant chess board, and a small playground.

Not a hint remains of its former desolate state. Cal Anderson is now a joyful, welcoming place. People from all walks of life come to relax and partake in their favorite outdoor activities, from dog-walking to sun-bathing, Live Action Role Playing to chillin' with their didgeridoo. It is a glimpse into a utopian society wherein hipsters, yuppies, and punks can all come together on a warm summer day and play kickball. Just be careful what you decide to smoke on a sunny day.

## Attractions

Between the wading pool, the reflecting pool, the fountain, and the reservoir, water features abound. And luckily, Cal Anderson is a park for the people, so none of these enticing fixtures are off limits. Adults climb to the top of the volcano-esque fountain. Kids splash each other in the reflecting pool or play on the jungle gym. It's also one of the best places to people-watch in Capitol Hill. Where else can you see a goth couple read under matching black parasols whilst a group of hippies fly their homemade kites several yards away?

The Shelterhouse is available to rent for small parties and gatherings. Call 206-684-4753 for more information.

## Sports

Bobby Morris Playfield is mostly used for soccer, baseball, tennis, and the occasional kickball practice. The Underdog Sports League also uses it for their amateur league games which include a dodgeball division. In other parts of the park, the word "sports" is used a bit more loosely. There are always joggers, skaters, and cyclists, but you can also find such alternative sports as lawn bowling, urban golf, Frisbee golf, kung-fu, tai chi, and hula hooping. Capitol Hillites are nothing if not creative about their means for exercise.

## General Information

NFT Map:    3
Address:    700 Seneca St
            Seattle, WA 98101
Website:    www.seattle.gov/parks/parkspaces/
            freewaypark.htm
Phone:      206-684-4075
Hours:      6 am–10:00 pm daily

## Overview

Freeway Park was an oh-so-lovely idea back in the day. In the '60s, city and state officials thought that a park spanning the recently-completed Seattle portion of I-5 would brighten up the area and add a little something green to downtown. They enlisted the genius of Lawrence Halprin, a prolific landscape architect, to make it extra-snazzy. And indeed, when unveiled in 1976, Freeway Park deftly combined elements of city and nature and was deemed a triumph of urban landscaping. That is, until people started getting stabbed and assaulted left and right. You see, Halprin's artistic stylings created a lot of maze-like and shadowy areas that seemed to call out to criminals, "Come! Do your evil deeds here!"

And so they did. An endless stream of seedy and downright scary events went down in Freeway's dark nooks and zigzagging pathways. The violent murder of a deaf and mute woman in 2002 finally got people talking about redesigning the park. A neighborhood group, the Freeway Park Neighborhood Association (FPNA), sprung up to lead the cause, advocating better lighting, increased security, and the removal of particularly obscuring shrubbery. The "New Vision for Freeway Park" seems to be working, with reported crime rates down. So go forth, enjoy the lovely fountains and water features (when they're operating), and pull up a newly sun-kissed spot to enjoy your take-out lunch. But you may still want to mosey on out before the sun goes down.

## Activities & Events

In light of the park's rather unsavory past, community leaders are trying to encourage community activities in the park (apparently, bingo is not only fun but also wards off the criminal element). For example, there's a walking group that meets at 10:30 am daily near the bathrooms. For your own walking pleasure, there are various trails and paths that wind through the park. But it is advisable to have a buddy along.

The summer months (July–August) usher in some fun Freeway events, like free lunchtime music concerts, public theater performances, and "inter-generational" activities that are geared towards children and seniors.

## What the Future Holds

Freeway Park is undergoing a definite makeover, although it has yet to be determined how that will actually pan out. Some ideas include a skating rink, a dog run, and a coffee stand. In the meantime, maintenance projects that are underway include the removal of trees to increase light exposure and the restoration of the park's four fountains, which never seem to be working.

## How to Get There

There are tons of Metro buses that will take you almost directly to the park. Routes 16, 255, and 358 are a few from downtown; it's advisable to check out Metro's website (metro.kingcounty.gov) for the best ones from your neighborhood. There is no designated parking lot for the park; you'll have to try your luck on the street or pay for a parking garage.

## General Information

NFT Map: 25
Address: 2101 N Northlake Wy
Seattle, WA 98103
Phone: 206-684-4075
Website: www.seattle.gov/parks/parkspaces/
gasworks.htm
Hours: 6 am–10:00 pm daily

## Overview

If ever you feel disenchanted with Seattle, head directly to Gas Works Park and stand at the top of the kite-flying hill. Even on a dreary day, the strange combination of water, sky, and rusted metal is dramatic, and the juxtaposition of natural beauty and urban architecture should be sufficient to remind you why you live here. The 20-acre park juts out into the north shore of Lake Union, creating a panoramic view of the downtown skyline framed by the hills of Queen Anne and Eastlake. On the water, seaplanes launch at regular intervals over a serene flotilla of kayaks, sailboats, and yachts. On a quiet afternoon, the proclamations of those dreadful Ride the Ducks tour guides are clearly audible from shore, but at least they don't wave at you from that distance.

The city first cleared this land in 1906 for use by the Seattle Gas Light Company. The Lake Station Plant, as it was then known, converted coal into methane gas until 1956, when natural gas became available via interstate pipeline. The City of Seattle purchased the gas works six years later and opened the public park in 1975. The gargantuan ruins of the plant have been left standing, now fenced off and scrubbed of decades of graffiti. Exhauster-compressor machinery has been converted into a children's play area. The former boiler house now houses picnic tables, barbecue grills, and a concession stand that operates sporadically during the summer months. The picnic area can be reserved by calling 206-684-4081, but keep in mind that this part of the park tends to double as a homeless shelter.

For some Seattle residents, the large quantities of benzene and other goodies left behind by the gasification plant raise the question, "Will picnicking at Gas Works shave precious years off of my life?" According to the Washington State Department of Ecology—no. The site underwent a massive, $3-million cleanup project in 2001 to remove contaminants from the soil, and chemical levels remain under constant observation. Nevertheless, visitors are still advised not to eat the dirt. Swimming, wading, and fishing are prohibited.

## Sports

Conveniently located along the Burke-Gilman Trail, Gas Works Park receives its share of bicycle traffic, though trails within the park are relatively few. The park's abundance of concrete and freestanding metal is a draw for skate boarders, and the city is considering building a skate park there. Yoga and tai chi classes are also known to congregate on the lawns. However, the most numerous enthusiasts at the park seem to be the kite flyers that flock to the landscaped hill, faces tilted to the sky, fists holding tight to the strings of their kites.

## Festivals & Events

Gas Works Park leads Seattle in events for naked people. The annual Solstice Parade, featuring the famous (and fabulous) naked cyclists, pedals its way from Fremont to Gas Works where the pageant continues into the evening. The park has also served as the starting point of Seattle's World Naked Bike Ride, an event that protests oil dependency and suggests better living through nudity.

The Independence Day festivities at Gas Works are an all-day affair, complete with food vendors, a beer garden, and loud music. Though the fireworks over Lake Union are spectacular, sitting in the squalor beneath a giant inflatable Statue of Liberty head is likely to make you feel like a huddled mass.

## How to Get There

**By Car**
From I-5, take the 45th Street exit and go west on NE 45th Street. Turn left on Meridian Avenue N and continue to the end of the street. Turn right on N Northlake Way and turn into the parking lot. Parking lot hours: 6 am–9 pm.

**By Bus**
Take Metro bus 26 and get off at 35th and Wallingford. It's only a two block walk south until you're relaxing and flying your kite at Gas Works.

## General Information

NFT Map:   33
Address:   8498 Seaview Pl NW
           Seattle, WA 98117
Website:   www.seattle.gov/parks/parkspaces/
           golden.htm
Hours:     6 am–11:30 pm

## Overview

Originally designed as a destination at the end of an electric car line for folks to escape hectic city life, Golden Gardens is just that, minus the electric car line.

Hidden from (or hiding) the city behind immense bluffs, Golden Gardens is Puget Sound at its finest and then some—romantic vistas of the Olympics, tranquil waters, barking sea lions locked in a floating cage, an occasional thundering train, and heaps of hippies drumming randomly around bonfires. On any given day you'll find a black-tie wedding, a Mexican barbeque, Chinese karaoke, beach volleyball, the ubiquitous drum circle, a pick-up soccer game, and young lovers smooching in the tall grass.

The park is divided by train tracks into lower and upper sections. The lower section features sandy beaches, picnic areas, fire pits, restored wetlands, a renovated bathhouse for rent (206-684-7254), beached logs, and lots and lots of bonfires. The upper portion is a maze of trails zigzagging up the bluffs, a 2.2 acre off-leash dog area, and tons of blackberry bushes.

The park has overcome "problems" of the past—namely, excessive drinking, loud music, and out-of-control bonfires. The city took efforts to get things under control (you'd think that people would know not to burn things like futons and wooden crates, but alas the police had to intervene to reinforce that rule). Now sentries are present on the summer weekends to make sure you're burning firewood and that you don't have any alcohol (try keeping a straight face when you say "no," and they'll try to believe you).

Long gone are the days when you could cavort with friends around a toasty fire late into the evening. Park officials promptly come by at 10:30 pm and without saying a word, douse all bonfires with a large bucket of water. At 11:30 pm the park closes and the gates are locked.

## How to Get There

**By Car**
Take Market Street through Ballard and beyond the locks, where it turns into Shilshole Avenue. Another mile past the marina sits the entrance to the park; a public boat launch is at the south end (next to Coney's, a generic burger/shake/fish joint), and the first of several parking lots. The road turns right and winds up the bluffs to 85th Street. There is parking at the south end of the park, in the middle of the park, and just across under the railroad tracks.

**By Bus**
Take the 46 bus from the U District or take the 18 from downtown.

**By Bike**
Golden Gardens should be the natural end of the Burke-Gilman Trail, though planners haven't yet put those pieces together.

Shilshole Bay

W Sheridan St
W Cramer St
W Sheridan St

Salmon B
Waterwa

Daybreak Star
Cultural-Education
Center

Picnic
Area

Picnic
Area

Picnic Area

W Commodore Way

Army Reserve
(No Trespassing)

Picnic
Area

Wolf Tree Nature

Lawtonwood Rd

Illinois St

Kansas Ave

Loop Trail

Coast Guard
Lighthouse

North Beach

West Point
Wastewater Treatment
Facility

Hidden Valley Trail

South Beach

W Utah St

Military Housing
(No Trespassing)

Stables

Utah St

Military Housing
(No Trespassing)

Teamster's
Quarters

Guardhouse

Band House

Post Exchange

Headquarters

Vermont Ave

Authorized
Vehicles Only

Fort Lawton Ceme

Washington Ave

NIKE
Warehouse

Visitors
Center

W Go
Pie

South Beach Trail

Loop Trail

Military Housing
(No Trespassing)

Discovery Park
Environmental
Learning Center

Ter
Co

Iowa St

Chapel

Picnic Area

Oregon Ave

Carolina St

W Emerson St

Playgro

Maintenan
Facili

Puget Sound

W Texas Ln W

Parkins Ln W

45th Ave W

43rd Ave W

Magnolia Blvd W

41st Ave W

Arapahoe Pl W

40th Ave W

39th Ave W

38th Ave W

W Ruffner St

W Viewmont Way W

W Way W

W Bertona St

W Prosper St

W Dravus St

MAP
11

## General Information

NFT Map:  11
Address:  3801 W Government Wy
          Seattle, WA 98199
Phone:    206-386-4236
Website:  www.seattle.gov/parks/environment/
          discovery.htm
Hours:    6 am–11 pm

## Overview

Discovery Park is by far Seattle's largest park, covering over 530 acres. Located on the Magnolia bluffs, the park occupies most of the former Fort Lawton military base. Discovery offers the most extensive hiking trails within the city, just under 12 miles worth of trails, making it the perfect destination for those times when you've just had enough of the city, but don't want to go too far away.

You will find that Discovery has an amazing amount of natural diversity. On a single trail you will encounter open meadows, breathtaking sea cliffs (don't get too close!), forested areas, thickets, streams, and even an active sand dune. There is a short hike down to two miles of protected tidal beaches with tree houses along the way for scenic views of the Puget Sound and a resting place for the brutal hike back. All of the trails are well marked, but be sure to remember which parking lot you left your car in, because it's easy to get lost. You can print out a map of the trails from the Discovery Park website.

The views you'll find at Discovery are phenomenal. You can see Puget Sound spread out before you, framed by the majestic Olympic Mountains. On a clear day, there is also the opportunity to gaze upon Mt Rainier, which true Seattleites never get sick of seeing. Stroll by the Coast Guard Lighthouse or look for the enormous West Point Treatment Facility located just next to Discovery Park.

## Park History

Discovery's history is an interesting one. The city of Seattle originally donated this land to the Federal Government to use as a military base. In 1938 the US Army offered to give all of Fort Lawton back to Seattle for the bargain price of one dollar. The city actually refused this sweet deal because they weren't sure they could afford the upkeep. Then in 1964, the US Secretary of Defense decided that 85% of Fort Lawton was to be surplus and Seattle would have to cough up 50% of fair market value (whoops). Luckily, in 1965, legislation was passed that said Seattle could have it for free because it was given as a donation in the first place (phew). Then the United Indians of All Tribes jumped into the mix in 1970, claiming that all lands might be declared surplus, so they were allowed to lease 17 acres. You can now find the Daybreak Star Cultural-Education Center on those 17 acres.

## How to Get There—Driving

Discovery is huge, and if you stray from the main path, it is easy to get lost in the maze of homes surrounding the park. When all else fails, just keep heading west. However, if you follow these directions, you can't miss it.

From I-5 take the 45th Street exit and head west. 45th Street becomes 46th Street then turns into Market Street. From Market, turn left onto 15th Avenue NW and take the first right after the bridge onto Emerson Street. Turn right onto West Gilman, which becomes West Government Way. Follow that until you come to the east entrance of the park. Go straight and you will find the Visitor Center to your left.

## Parking

Once you get to the east entrance of the park from West Government Way, you can go straight to find several parking lots or turn left and head towards the south parking lot.

## How to Get There—Mass Transit

If you don't mind a long bus ride, the 33, 24, and 994 will take you to Discovery Park.

Green Lake Dr N

N 80th St

N 79th St

N 78th St

N 77th St

**MAP 30**

N 76th St

Winona Ave N

N 75th St

E Green Lake Dr N

West Beach

Bathhouse Theatre

**P**

Tennis Courts

**P**

Commu & Evans

East Beach

Aurora Ave N

**Green Lake**

E Green Lake Way N

N 65th St

N 64th St

N 63rd St

N 63rd St

N 62nd St

**MAP 31**

N 60th St

W Green Lake Way N

N 59th St

N 58th St

Aurora Ave N

Green Lake Way N

N 57th St

N 56th St

5

## General Information

NFT Map:      31
Address:      7201 E Green Lake Dr N
              Seattle, WA 98103
Phone:        206-684-4075
Website:      www.seattle.gov/parks/parkspaces/
              greenlak.htm
Hours:        Open 24 hours a day

## Overview

For over a century, Seattleites have enjoyed the cool tranquility of Green Lake Park, a popular destination for joggers, dog walkers, bikers, roller skaters, and what have you. This is one of Seattle's loveliest parks, which guarantees crowds on pleasant weekends, but the calming vibe of the water and the woods tends to ease everyone's need for personal space. A paved 2.8-mile trail circles the lake, providing two separate tracks for those on foot and those on wheels, and another unpaved trail for joggers meanders a bit longer at 3.2 miles. A stroll around Green Lake is a painless way to grab some exercise in the city without an overdose of auto exhaust or having to dodge panhandlers.

As for wildlife, waterfowl abound, from ducks to Canadian Geese to majestic herons, and they're not only unafraid of the constant human traffic, they're nearly confrontational about it. Don't feed these birds, no matter how adorable they seem—it's not allowed. New visitors to Green Lake will remark on the robust rabbit population, the result of certain short-sighted folks letting their domesticated pet bunnies free in the foliage by the water. Many generations hence, great fat rabbits infest the area, breeding and burrowing and wreaking havoc on native plant life. As with the waterfowl, do not feed these cuddly-yet-feral beasts.

## Activities

The lake's moniker stems from its susceptibility to algae blooms, a picturesque affliction that the city has fought often during the park's history, leading to a number of beach closures throughout the years. While some brazen water-worshippers insist that Green Lake is the best swimming hole in Seattle, the city's official website warns of the possibility of contracting swimmer's itch. Consider dipping instead into the chlorine-fueled Evans Pool, a large indoor swimming facility on the lakeshore, or take the kids to the outdoor wading pool, which writhes every summer with the kinetic energy of splashing toddlers.

Green Lake's Small Craft Center offers classes for young and old alike in the arts of kayaking, canoeing, sweep rowing, and sculling (don't forget to pass your "float test" first—it's required). For private paddleboat rentals, the Green Lake Boat Rental company is at your service, and there's no nicer way to share the lake with someone special. Three annual rowing regattas invade the lake each year for exhibition-style water sports, sponsored by the local Rowing Advisory Council.

Or you could ignore the water altogether. Work out on one of the park's tennis courts, try a few holes of mild golfing at the Green Lake Pitch & Putt, or just laze beneath a shady pine and take in some people-watching. The park draws groups of tai chi and martial arts devotees, novice tightrope walkers, and even medieval faire types practicing their swordplay in full costume. The strains of bagpipes and plaintive guitar strummers float among the Frisbee tossers and sunbathers, and if you're lucky you'll see the guy who walks around the lake with "Spanish Lessons" emblazoned on his shirt (it's no gag—he'll tutor you on the spot).

## How to Get There

**By Bus**

The 48 rolls past Green Lake on an average of every fifteen minutes during the day, servicing the University District, Montlake, Greenwood, and Loyal Heights among other neighborhoods. The 16 stops about every twenty minutes and will cart you up from downtown or down from the Northgate Mall. The 26 is slightly less frequent and a longer ride, starting off downtown, threading up through Fremont and Wallingford until reaching the end of the line on Green Lake Way.

**By Car**

If coming by Aurora Avenue, take the Green Lake Way exit and follow it until you're circling the lake.

If coming by I-5 southbound, take exit 171 toward NE 71st Street/NE 65th Street, merge onto 6th Avenue NE, turn right on NE 71st Street and follow it to East Green Lake Drive N.

If coming by I-5 northbound, take exit 170 toward NE 65th Street, merge onto NE Ravenna Boulevard and follow it to E Green Lake Drive N.

Pontiac Bay

National Oceanic & Atmospheric Administration

NE 77th St

NE 75th St

Main Entrance

NE 74th St

The Brig

Dog Run

Magnuson Park Fields

Tennis Courts

Playground

Magnuson Community Center

Sand Point Fields

Sand Point Way NE

MAP 27

Boat Launch

NE 65th St

65th Ave NE

NE 64th St

Sand Point Way NE

Lake Washington

NE 61st St

Windermere Rd

## General Information

NFT Maps: 27
Address: 7400 Sand Point Wy NE
Seattle, WA 98115
Website: www.seattle.gov/magnusongarden
Phone: 206-684-4946
Hours: May 1 to Labor Day: 4 am–11:30 pm
Labor Day to April 30: 4 am–10 pm

## Overview

There are parks, and then there are parks. With 350 acres on the shores of Lake Washington, Seattle's second largest park is a recreational wonderland. It wasn't always so. The park was purchased by the government at the turn of the century and given to the federal government to turn into a naval base. Over the years, parts of the park were relinquished to the public and became Warren G. Magnuson Park, so named for the community-friendly senator who advocated for public use of the land, in lieu of a noisy airfield. The Navy continued to use part of the park all the way until 1990, when it was officially closed for military purposes and handed over to the city.

The park is crammed full of things to do. The historic Art Deco and Colonial Revival buildings are now home to a variety of non-profit community groups, ranging from sailing enthusiasts to an organization dedicated to protecting bats (nocturnal, not wooden). There's a boat launch, playground, basketball courts, tennis courts, picnic facilities, trails, windsurfing areas, and a huge off-leash dog park. Then there's the public art. And the community garden. And the butterfly garden. And…well, a million other things. It doesn't end there—even more features and renovations are being planned.

If you've exhausted all the possibilities of the park's resident features, there are a multitude of events throughout the year, like the Fall Wild Mushroom Show (www.psms.org) and an antiques market. Check out the Seattle Parks website for an updated events calendar.

**Magnuson Community Center**
*7110 62nd Ave NE, 206-684-7026*
The Community Center has always been a recreational hub and meeting ground, even during its military years, during which there was a library, swimming pool, and a bowling alley, all integral to Navy training exercises. Nowadays, one may find amenities no less entertaining, such as a 560-seat auditorium, gymnasium, racquetball court, and meeting room. Still, bringing back the bowling alley would be pretty cool.

**The Brig**
*6344 NE 74th St, 206-684-7026*
The Brig is another community center that's had a colorful past, from its original purpose as a jail for holding military prisoners and its more recent use as a set for several episodes of the X-Files. It's adjacent to the community garden and has been renovated with large, wood-floored activity spaces and meeting rooms.

**Warren G. Magnuson Off-Leash Dog Area**
*7400 Sand Point Wy NE, 206-684-4946;*
*www.seattle.gov/parks/magnuson/ola.htm*
This is absolute dog heaven, stretching for nine acres and including several varied environments such as dirt hills, flat gravel for fetch, tall brush, and a mud pit. The highlight is the accessible shoreline on Lake Washington—dogs go crazy for it, and Magnuson boasts the only dog park with water access within city limits. To get to the shore, there's a winding fenced-in trail so you can get some walking in while Rover is permitted to roam and

sniff off-leash alongside. Small and shy dogs will appreciate their own separate and spacious pen. As always, be sure your pooch is properly vaccinated and that you clean up after him.

**Magnuson Community Garden**
*7400 Sand Point Wy NE, 206-684-4946;*
*www.cityofseattle.net/magnusongarden/*
This former parking lot has been converted into a thriving garden with the purpose of serving the community of Seattle. There's the outdoor amphitheatre, which hosts various performances and events during the year, a garden tailored to gardeners with disabilities, and orchards and P-patches growing food for local food banks. It's a nice little oasis that just warms your heart.

**NOAA Art Walk and Sound Garden**
*7400 Sand Point Wy NE, 206-526-6163 (NOAA facility manager);*
*www.seattle.gov/parks/magnuson/art.htm*
Right in the park's backyard is a bunch of outdoor art installations made by some pretty well-known artists (at least in the outdoor art installation crowd). The National Oceanic and Atmospheric Administration (NOAA) campus is located at the northern end of the Sand Point Peninsula. Though it's not technically included in the park, its close proximity invites a lot of park visitors to come check out the half-mile trail that passes by six outdoor artworks. The most popular is the Sound Garden, from which a certain Seattle grunge band lifted its own moniker. Per its self-descriptive name, the installation is composed of pipes that generate different tones that vary with the changing wind. Apparently even artwork is not immune from the security scares generated by 9/11; the facility was put on threat level Yellow (no weekends; no cars; backpack searches). Whatever.

**Sail Sand Point**
*7777 62nd Ave NE #107, 206-525-8782; www.sailsandpoint.org*
Sail Sand Point is Seattle's new community sailing center. It's located on the north shore of the park on Lake Washington. There are programs and classes for both youth and adults.

## How to Get There

**By Bus**
Metro bus routes 74 and 75 serve the park along Sand Point Way NE. Connections are in the University District (Routes 74 and 75) and Northgate (Route 75).

**By Bike**
The Burke-Gilman Trail is approximately 1/4 mile west of Warren G. Magnuson Park. With a traffic signal and crosswalks, the NE 65th Street crossing is the safest point to enter the park. Once on the east side of Sand Point Way NE bicyclists can continue either east along NE 65th Street, or north along 62nd Avenue NE. Note that bicycle riding is limited to paved surfaces within Warren G. Magnuson Park. There are no designated bike trails in the park.

**By Car**
From I-5 you can exit at either NE 45th Street (Exit 169) or NE 65th Street (Exit 171). From the NE 45th Street exit, go east on 45th, past the UW campus, and down the 45th Street ramp. Continue east past University Village Shopping Center. Bear left and continue about 2 miles. From the I-5 NE 65th Street exit, head east approximately four miles on 65th (stay on the arterial!) until you have crossed Sand Point Way NE into the NE 65th Street entrance.

## Parking

Parking is free and ample. There are two lots—one on 65th with parallel parking, and a larger lot on 77th.

## Overview

Plopped between Puget Sound and Lake Washington, Lake Union is the baby bear of the Seattle waterways. On the east, it has a watery arm that stretches to Lake Washington—Portage Bay—and another to the west that connects it to Puget Sound.

Lake Union itself is riddled with marinas and a vibrant, eclectic houseboat community (eclectic in this instance means high-end homes as well as scows). The area around the lake was fairly neglected and somewhat industrial until recently. It's got a rapidly growing biotechnology corridor along the east side; the south side is undergoing rapid development (www.discoverslu.com) which will include the usual stuff—condos, coffee shops, spas, and lots of cash for the developers. The north side has Gas Works Park, an old gas manufacturing plant that has a playground, trails and well, gas works. The Seattle Streetcar is now open, connecting South Lake Union to downtown (www.seattlestreetcar.org). But the most exciting addition in decades is the new Lake Union Park. Its 12 acres reconnect the lake to the surrounding (and booming) neighborhood.

## Attractions

As you'd expect for a lake, most of the attractions have at least something to do with water. At the south end of Lake Union, located at Valley Street and Fairview Avenue North, is the Center for Wooden Boats (www.cwb.org). There is a small museum, of sorts, and you can rent both sailboats and rowboats. Moving up the west side of the lake, on aptly named Westlake Avenue N, catch a scenic tour of Seattle in a seaplane for $99 with Kenmore Air. (866-435-9524; www.kenmoreair.com) It's also possible to fly to Vancouver, Victoria, or the San Juan Islands from here.

## Shopping

Unless you're in the market for a yacht, there's not much shopping around the lake. REI's flagship store (222 Yale Ave N, 206-223-1944; www.rei.com), is the exception. For all your outdoor needs, which, in Seattle, are considerable.

## Restaurants

What Lake Union does have plenty of, other than water, is restaurants. There's Daniel's Broiler, a steak house with a view (809 Fairview N, 206-621-8262). Nearby is Chandler's Crabhouse and Fish Market (901 Fairview N, 206-223-2722). As the name implies they rely heavily on fresh fish dishes. While we're on fresh fish, there's I Love Sushi (1001 Fairview N, 206-625-9604). Try to overlook the silly name; it's a great sushi place with more spectacular views. For great happy hour hooch and hot, hand-made soft pretzels with dipping sauces perfect for soaking up the drink, head to the Brave Horse Tavern (310 Terry Ave N), owned by superstar chef and restaurateur Tom Douglas. If you want to spend big money (and here you actually do get what you pay for), try Canlis (2576 Aurora Ave N, 206-283-3313). It features the absolute best of Northwest cuisine.

## Lodging

**Silver Cloud Inn**
www.silvercloud.com
1150  Fairview N, 206-447-9500

**Residence Inn**
800 Fairview N, 206-624-6000

**Marriott Courtyard**
925 Westlake Ave N, 206-213-0100

## How to Get There—Driving

Lake Union is immediately off I-5 at exit 167. Turn right off the exit onto Fairview Avenue N, then left on Valley Street.  Lake Union is bound by Valley Street on the south, Westlake Avenue N on the west, N Northlake Way on the north, and on the east is Eastlake and Fairview Avenue N. You can pretty much circumnavigate it in roughly 20 minutes. On a good traffic day. With no construction anywhere. This, of course, never happens.

## How to Get There—Mass Transit

Metro bus routes 70, 71, 72, and 73 will all deliver you to the south end of the lake. The 25, 66, and 74 all run up the east side.

## General Information

NFT Map:    1
Website:    www.seattleartmuseum.org/visit/osp
Entry:      Free

## Overview

Seattle Art Museum's 8.5-acre waterfront sculpture park opened in January 2007. The sculpture includes a massive piece by Richard Serra, *Wake*, as well as pieces by Claes Oldenburg, Alexander Calder, and Louise Bourgeois. There's also a *Vivarium* by Mark Dion featuring a nurse log and its attendant nurslings—in all, 22 pieces of phenomenal sculpture.

If you like a little controversy with your art, check out *Father and Son*. A popular target for those whose mantra is 'Think of the children!', it depicts a man and a boy, both nude, facing each other with arms outstretched as water from a fountain rises and falls around them.

Art is only part of the attraction. As well as monumental sculpture, the park has meadows, forests, and stunning views. The other reason to visit the park is the setting. Walking on the z-path from the Pavilion, as you come through a recreated Northwest native trees forest, the view is, well, ok, breathtaking…an unobstructed view of the Olympics and Puget Sound. Seattle's chronic rainfall can't mess with that. Even if you hate museums, maybe especially if you hate museums, this place will afford you an entirely different experience of art—art like it's s'posed to be.

## How to Get There—Driving

The park occupies 8.5 acres between Western Avenue and Elliott Avenue at Eagle and Broad Streets. Take exit 167 at Mercer Street, turn right on Fairview, left on Valley. Valley becomes Broad Street. (The Space Needle should appear on your right.) Turn right on Western Avenue. There is parking under the Pavilion at the park.

## How to Get There—Mass Transit

Metro routes 1, 2, 13, 15, 18, and 19 heading north from downtown.

**MAP 3**

Victor Steinbru... Park

LaSalle

Post Alley

Western Ave

**Main Arcade, North Arcade, DownUnder & Western Ave**

Economy Market

Pike Place

Triangle

Post Alley

**Corner Market, Sanitary Market & Post Alley**

1st Avenue

Pike Street

Pine Street

Stewart Street

**Stewart House & Soames-Dunn Building**

Post Alley

**Pine to Stewart Block**

**1st Avenue Buildings**

## Economy Market & LaSalle Buildings

**SHOPS**
Art Stall Gallery
Ed Newbold Wildlife Artist
Studio Solstone
J&J Gifts & Sportswear
Pike Place Outfitters
Best Flowers
First & Pike News
Raven's Nest Treasures
Rings 'n Things
Tenzing Momo
The Great Wind Up

**RESTAURANTS & TAKE-OUT**
Alibi Room
Belle Epicurean
Crepe de France
Danny's Wonder Freeze
Il Bistro
La Vaca Burrito Express
Maximilien Bistro
Place Pigalle

**SERVICES & ENTERTAINMENT**
Chapel of Sts. Martha & Mary
Market Foundation
Pike Place Dental
Pike Place Market Merchants Assoc.
Pike Place Market Preservation & Development Authority
Ticket Ticket
Top of the Market
Unexpected Productions/Market Theater
Washington Wine Commission

**SPECIALTY FOOD & BEVERAGE**
Bottega Italiana
Daily Dozen Donuts
DeLaurenti Specialty Food & Wine
Don & Joe's Meats
Market Cellar Winery
MarketSpice
Pike Place Fish
Simply the Best

## Main Arcade, North Arcade, DownUnder & Western Ave

**SHOPS**
Antique Touch
Charlotte's Web
Golden Age Collectables
Grandma's Attic
Miniature Car Dealer
Old Friends Antiques
Old Seattle Paperworks
Pen & Ink Drawings by Patrick T. Kerr
Pike's Asian Art
Portraits by Nick Elizar
Twilight Artist Collective
Two Angels Antiques & Interiors
Yesterdaze
Afghani Crafts
Cibola
Marakesh Leathers
Mobeta Shoes
Yazdi Imports
All Things Lavender
Animal Gifts & Collectibles
At Random Productions
Baja Bath Salts
Benavi's
Big Boys Toys
Black Creek Botanicals
BLMF Books
Candy Store
CINTLI Fine Mexican Imports
F & J Great Western Trading Co.
Gem Heaven

Hands of the World
Holy Cow
House of Jade
House of Silver & Gold
Lionheart Books
Market Coins
Market Magic & Novelty Shop
Mastercraft Leather
Moon Valley Honey
Outback Opal
Pharaoh's Treasures
Pike Discount Camera and Electronics
Pike Place Bags
Pike Place Gifts
Pike Place Nutrition
Pipe Palace
Polish Pottery Place
Ruby's Seattle Gifts
Sunshine Jewelry
Swanberg Gifts
Sweeties Candy
Taj Mahal
The Bead Zone
The Giving Tree
Women's Hall of Fame

**RESTAURANTS & TAKE-OUT**
Athenian Inn
Lowell's Restaurant
Market Grill
Pike Place Chinese Cuisine
Soundview Café

**SERVICES**
Balcony Barber Shop
Christopher's Lamp
Downtown Food Bank
Heritage Center
Heritage House
Madame Lazonga Tattoo
Pike Market Childcare & Preschool
Public Market Parking Garage

**SPECIALTY FOOD & BEVERAGE**
Catanzaro & Sons
Chicken Valley
Chukar Cherries
City Fish
Manzo Bros. Produce
Mick's Peppourri
Pike Place Bakery
Pure Food Fish
Rotary Grocery
Sosio's Produce
Uli's Famous Sausage
Woodring Orchards

## Corner Market, Sanitary Market, Post Alley & Triangle Buidlings

**SHOPS**
Milagros Mexican Folk Art
Earth, Wind & Fire
Etruscan Design
Old Duffers Stuff
African Treasures
Dar Salaam
Dog Alley
Dragon's Toy Box
House of Woks
Kitchen Basics
Lamplight Used Books
Left Bank Books
Made in Washington
Metsker Maps
Pike Place Flowers

**RESTAURANTS & TAKE-OUT**
Café Mimosa
Café Yarmarka
Chez Shea
Copacabana Restaurant
Falafel King
Jasmine
La Buona Tavola Truffle Café & Specialty Foods
Lee's Corner
Lo Priore Brothers
Matt's in the Market
Mee Sum Pastries
Mr. D's Greek Deli
Pan Africa Café & Market
Pike Place Bagel Bakery
Pike Place Bar & Grill
Pike Place Chowder
Shea's Lounge
Sisters Café
Three Girls Bakery

**SERVICES**
Bohemia Therapeutic Massage
Matchmaker in the Market
New Mark Tailor
Paul Souders World Foto
Pike Place Barber
Pike Place Naturopathic
Rummage Hall
Tony Puma
US Bank

**SPECIALTY FOOD & BEVERAGE**
Choice Produce
Cinnamon Works
Corner Produce
Confectional Cheesecakes
Crumpet Shop
El Mercado Latino
Fero's Meat Market

Frank's Quality Produce
Jack's Fish Spot
Oriental Mart
Pike Place Market Creamery
Quality Cheese
Seattle's Best Coffee
Shy Giant Frozen Yogurt
Sotto Voce
Stewart's Meats
The Juice Emporium

## Pine to Stewart Block

**SHOPS**
Orca Bay Gallery
Fini
Sur La Table
Watson Kennedy Fine Living

**RESTAURANTS & TAKE-OUT**
Bacco
Campagne
Café Campagne

**LODGING**
Inn at the Market

**SERVICES**
Arne Bystrom, Architect
New London Salon

**SPECIALTY FOOD & BEVERAGE**
Beecher's Handmade Cheese

## Stewart House & Soames-Dunn Building

**SHOPS**
Lisa Harris Gallery
Little Shanghai
Lungu Gifts
Market Tobacco Patch
Paper Moon
Seattle Cutlery
The Soap Box

**RESTAURANTS & TAKE-OUT**
Emmett Watson's Oyster Bar
Japanese Gourmet
Michou
Piroshky-Piroshky
Sabra Mediterranean
Saigon Restaurant
The Pink Door

**SERVICES**
Market Optical
Sergio's Barbershop
Wagner Architects
Wanderers Mail Service

**SPECIALTY FOOD & BEVERA...**
Bavarian Meats
Chocolate & Ice Cream Delig...
Le Panier
Mexican Grocery
Starbucks Coffee
The Souk
Totem Smokehouse

## 1st Avenue Buildings

**SHOPS**
Antiques at Pike Place
Market Graphics
Boston St. Children's
Isadora's Antique Clothing
Maggie's Shoes
Zebra Club

**LODGING**
Pensione Nichols

**RESTAURANTS & TAKE-OUT**
Caffe Lieto
Kell's Irish Restaurant & Pub
Le Pichet
94 Stewart
Sonya's
Starlite Lounge
Taxi Dogs
Turkish Delight
Virginia Inn

**SERVICES**
American Institute of Architect...
Coupe Rokei
Pike Market Medical Clinic
Pike Market Senior Center
Site Workshop

**SPECIALTY FOOD & BEVERA...**
Perennial Tea Room
Pike and Western Wine
Pike Place Grocery & Deli
Rose's Chocolate Treasures
The Tasting Room/ Wines of Washington
White Horse Trading Co

## General Information

| | |
|---|---|
| NFT Map: | 3 |
| Manager: | Pike Place Market Preservation & Development Authority |
| Address: | 85 Pike St, Rm 500 |
| | Seattle, WA 98101 |
| Phone: | 206-682-7453 |
| Website: | www.pikeplacemarket.org |
| Hours: | 10 am–6 pm daily; many fish and produce stands open by 8 am or earlier; some store and restaurant hours may vary so make sure to call ahead; closed Thanksgiving, Christmas, and New Year's |

## Overview

While it doesn't share the Space Needle's phallic elegance, Pike Place Market matches the monument's importance as a symbol of Seattle. The oldest farmers market in the country has experienced myriad changes over its past century of operation, but still exists primarily for the purpose of bringing farmers and consumers together without the sticky fingers of the middleman.

Early on a weekday morning is the best time to hit the Market if sustenance-shopping is the goal. Perusing the bounty of ripe fruit, crisp root vegetables, and tender greens while contending with the bovine rush of tourists isn't always an attractive option for the average city dweller. But sometimes the Pike Place Market is worth a little hassle—supporting local farmers is easy when the produce is this fresh and priced better than the average supermarket. The organic Wednesday market takes place from June to October and is especially worth checking out.

In 2008, Seattle voters gave the market a huge gift in the form of a $75 million property tax levy to renovate Pike Place's aging innards. In spring of 2012, all of the major construction was completed and the market is now better, and safer, than ever.

## Fresh Fish

A Seattle-centric trope as strong as coffee, rain, and dot-coms, the flashy flying fish of the imaginatively-named **Pike Place Fish** pack in gawking yokels from around the world every day with their zany antics. A crew of handsome (but smelly) fishmongers engage their shoppers in boisterous banter and throw fish corpses to each other (and potential buyers) all day long, usually with uncanny accuracy. Other fishmongers at the market feel obliged to compete with such flamboyance, so you'll find most white-smocked fin-handlers at **Pure Food Fish** and **City Fish** to be fairly gregarious, handing out samples, and glad-handing their prey. But **Jack's Fish Spot** isn't trying to impress anybody, so choose them to buy fresh flounder, live crabs, or grab a quick snack of fried salmon at Pike Place Market without all the jive.

## Fresh Meat

The old-school butcher shop is quickly disappearing in Seattle (and everywhere else for that matter). Even at Pike Place there used to be dozens of great little meat markets back in the day. Luckily, there are still a few high quality shops left. **Don & Joe's** prides itself on good quality and personal service. Don't see it? They'll order it for you. For your next Oktoberfest party, head to **Bavarian Meats** for all kinds of brats and wursts. And for the best sausage in Seattle, **Uli's Famous Sausage** will hook you up.

## Unique Shops

The lower levels and hidden corners of the market hold plenty of weird little shops that vary from straight-up tourist fleecing joints to truly eccentric stands that couldn't exist anywhere else. Choose **Market Magic** when shopping for the professional magician, clown, or ventriloquist in your life—card tricks, collapsible canes, juggling clubs, and vintage magic ephemera. The **Polish Pottery Place** sells very pretty, traditionally patterned tableware and kitchenware, sourced from an artisan pottery collective in Poland. You can spend hours at the toy shop, **The Great Wind-Up**, testing out the menagerie of hopping, spinning, and punching wind-ups or choosing just the right gag gift. A handful of shops offer upscale kitchen equipment, with **Sur La Table** being the most ostentatious, and there's a plethora of unique boutiques dedicated to eclectic fashions for all.

One could spend hours sifting through the vintage posters, advertisements, and postcards available at **Old Seattle Paperworks**. Readers can peruse used books at **Lamplight Books** or **BLMF Books**, grab specialty magazines at **First and Pike News**, or study rabble-rousing political screeds from **Left Bank Books**. Imported art, clothing, and products from Africa, Mexico, China, and other exotic climes can also be had. And if you just happen to need a haircut, head straight to **Sergio's Barber Shop** in the Stewart House.

## Restaurants & Bars

Pike Place is an eating and drinking wonderland. Hungry shoppers can grab a quick snack of French pastries from **Le Panier**, Italian gelato at **Bottega Italiana**, Russian fare at **Piroshky-Piroshky**, piping hot dunkers at **Daily Dozen Donuts**, free cheese samples at **Beecher's**, Greek food from **Mr. D's**, and almost anything else you can think of. If you have more time, grab a seat at **Matt's in the Market**, **Le Pichet**, or **Japanese Gourmet**. Gluttons for punishment are welcome to visit the purported site of the "first" **Starbucks** store—actually the beast was born on Western Avenue in 1971 and didn't relocate to the market until 1976, but whatever.

Say, who needs a drink? **Lowell's** is a homely three-floor operation that still looks as scruffy as it probably did when it opened in 1957. But the food is cheap and plentiful, and you'll get a fine eyeful of the Puget Sound. **The Athenian Inn** is the requisite old-school hang-out complete with great views and colorful locals. Head there for the latest Market gossip. If the **Alibi Room** is too cool for school, head to **Zig Zag** for a classic drink or to **Copacabana** for a Bolivian beer on the deck to check out the real scenery at the market—the people.

## Arts & Crafts

Buskers can apply for a performer's badge, which allows them to entertain the shopping throng for up to an hour at a time at one of twelve designated points. A variety of music flows forth as a result, from ham-fingered folk strummers to electrifying doo-wop vocalists. Remember the Spoonman of Soundgarden fame? He's there too. It's not just music—puppeteers, dancers, and sleight-of-hand artists pass the hat at Pike Place Market, as well as the "cat guy" who wears modified cat suits and brings his feline pets along as visual aids as he solicits funds for a local animal shelter.

Most of the art hawked on the upper level of the market falls into the tie-dyed, air-brushed, pastel-colored variety, of interest only to those who feel compelled to buy something to commemorate their dream vacation in Seattle. Want a generic pink or teal souvenir t-shirt festooned with a cartoon salmon or the Space Needle? You got it, along with wind chimes, dream catchers, belt buckles, incense burners, and "specialty pipes." But if you look hard and long enough, you'll find some good and interesting art hidden amongst the kitsch. Plenty of Mother Nature's art is on hand too, in the form of gorgeous fresh floral bouquets available for very reasonable prices every few steps, so take your time when picking out that perfect arrangement.

## How to Get There—Driving

**Pike Place Market Parking Garage Address:** *1531 Western Ave*
Parking at Pike Place Market can be a big 'ol pain in the butt. People expect to drive right down the ever packed Pike Place and find a spot right next to Rachel the Pig. It's not gonna happen. And if it does, you'll probably get a ticket. Try your luck on the metered spots downtown or head to the main parking garage on Western Avenue for the best deals.

**From I-5 northbound**, take exit #165, turn left on Madison Street and follow to Western Avenue. Turn right on Western, follow for five blocks to the parking garage

**From I-5 southbound**, take exit #166 toward Stewart Street, follow to 1st Avenue and turn right. After two blocks turn left onto Lenora Street, then left onto Western Avenue, follow three blocks to the parking garage.

## How To Get There—Bus

Many Metro bus lines go right past Pike Place Market. The 1 starts at 5th Avenue S and passes the market on its way to Queen Anne. The 10 originates downtown and goes on up to Capitol Hill. The 15 and 18 both pass by the market on their way to the northern part of Seattle. The 21, 22, and 36 come from way down south and land you right on 1st and Pike.

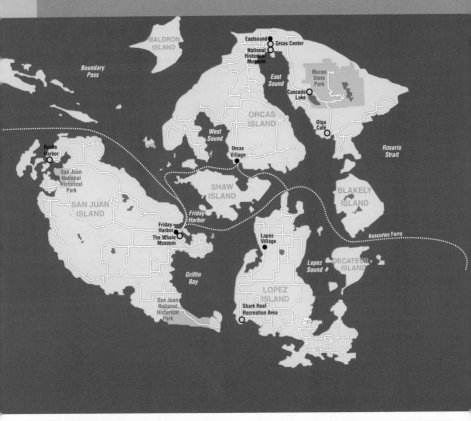

## Overview

The San Juan Islands provide an idyllic escape from the city and a memorable excursion into pristine wilderness, with abundant whale-watching opportunities to boot. Situated in the San Juan Channel between the Strait of Juan de Fuca and the Georgia Strait, there are more than 700 islands in the archipelago; of those, 450 have been named, and most are uninhabited. Only 80 miles northwest of Seattle, the San Juans are an excellent weekend getaway to relax and have fun in the outdoors.

## Lopez Island

City slickers might find themselves questioning whether they've got long lost relatives here, as nearly every person who passes waves at visitors. It's a bit like the "Twilight Zone" until one realizes that inhabitants of this small, exceedingly friendly island are just genuinely nice.

### Lopez Village

This street is the meeting place for island folk, filled with cafés, antique shops, a bookstore, and small grocery store. Take a stroll along the nearby hiking trail on a weekend morning, and don't miss the summer farmers market.

### Shark Reef Recreation Area

A popular hiking spot noted for its beautiful bluff, Shark Reef will delight any nature enthusiast.

## Orcas Island

The largest of the islands, Orcas Island maintains a tranquil balance of creature comforts and natural outdoor adventures. You know you're entering someplace special as you cruise the winding streets beneath Calder mobiles hanging from the lush trees.

### Eastsound

The epitome of quaint, Eastsound is a place to lose yourself in the many restaurants, spa services, and bookstores bordering the water. Stock up on essentials at the natural food store or the larger supermarket, or catch a performance at Orcas Center (917 Mt. Baker Rd, Eastsound, 360-376-2281; www.orcascenter.org) Don't miss the Orcas Island Historical Museum (181 N Beach Rd, Eastsound, 360-376-4849; www.orcasmuseum.org for a recreated glimpse into the island's past.

## Olga

Cafe Olga (11 Point Lawrence Rd, Olga, 360-376-5098) is a homey place with good food and a local art gallery. The last commercial business in the bend in the road which is the tiny town of Olga, the café is located within an old strawberry packing plant. It's definitely worth the drive and the perfect place for a quiet dinner away from the more populous Eastsound and Orcas Village. Be cautious when driving its winding roads, especially at night, since many deer graze close to the roadsides.

## Orcas Village

This tourist trap is the central hub of activity as passengers load and depart the ferries at the harbor. The elegant Orcas Hotel (888-672-2792; www.orcashotel.com), overlooking the waterfront, is a nice place for a relaxing beverage on the wrap-around porch while waiting for the ferry.

## Cascade Lake

Family fun abounds at this wilderness lake, located between Eastsound and Olga. Swimming, paddle boats, a nature trail, and a wooded picnic area are just some of the ways to enjoy this day use area situated at the base of Mt. Moran.

# Moran State Park/Mt. Constitution

*www.parks.wa.gov/parks/?selectedpark=Moran&subject=all*
Moran State Park is a nature lover's dream, with camping and 30 miles of hiking trails. Those who challenge themselves to climb from base to summit of Mt. Constitution, the highest point in the San Juan Islands, should come well-equipped with a compass, plenty of water, good hiking shoes, and a cell phone for emergencies. Look across to distant Vancouver, BC from atop the stone observation tower at the peak of the mountain.

# San Juan Island

San Juan Island is the most commercial and the second-largest of all the islands. It was originally inhabited by Native Americans before sailors arrived in the 1850s and transformed the area into a busy seaport by the end of the century.

## Friday Harbor

The only incorporated town in the islands, Friday Harbor has something for everyone, especially the shopping-inclined. Enjoy the Whale Museum (62 First St N, Friday Harbor, 360-378-4710) for an education about the area's native underwater inhabitants. Or, spend an afternoon browsing the local art galleries, cafés, and a multitude of specialty shops.

## Roche Harbor

This resort and marina on the northwest tip of the island provides a quiet retreat from the bustling tourism of Friday Harbor. Explore the nearby English Camp on West Valley Road, part of the San Juan Island National Historical Park (360-378-2902; www.nps.gov/sajh).

# Shaw Island

If Shaw Island had a motto, it would be, fittingly, "Not For Tourists." The least-welcoming of the four ferry-accessible islands, its residents prefer their remote isolation and have chosen to avoid the commercialism of their island sisters. Expect to find a primitive campsite and not much else.

# Island Activities

There's a plethora of things to do and see in the San Juans, and more businesses that provide sightseeing excursions, vehicle rentals, and adventure packages than there's room to print. Here's a sample:

## Bicycling

**Island Bicycles**
380 Argyle Ave
Friday Harbor, WA 98250
360-378-4941
www.islandbicycles.com

**Wildlife Cycles**
350 North Beach Rd
Orcas Island, WA 98245
360-376-4708
www.wildlifecycles.com

**Lopez Bicycle Works**
2847 Fisherman Bay Rd
Lopez Island, WA 98261
360-468-2847
www.lopezbicycleworks.com

## Camping

**San Juan Island County Parks**
www.co.san-juan.wa.us/parks/

**Moran State Park Camping**
www.parks.wa.gov/parks/?selectedpark=Moran&subject=camping

## Kayaking

**Lopez Island Sea Kayak**
2845 Fisherman Bay Rd
Lopez Island, WA 98261
360-468-2847
www.lopezkayaks.com

**Outdoor Odysseys Inc.**
86 Cedar St
Friday Harbor, WA 98250
800-647-4621
360-378-3533
www.outdoorodysseys.com

**Orcas Outdoors Inc.**
P.O. Box 284
Orcas Island, WA 98280
360-376-4611
www.orcasoutdoors.com

## Lodging

www.guidetosanjuans.com
www.orcasisland.org
www.orcasisle.com
www.orcas-lodging.com

www.san-juan-island.net
www.sanjuanweb.com
www.sanjuansites.com
www.visitsanjuans.com

# Ferries

The islands are only accessible by air and water. By far the most popular way to travel to them, for those without private planes and boats, is via the Washington State Ferry system (www.wsdot.wa.gov/ferries). Plan to arrive in Anacortes extra early in the summer, at least two hours before your scheduled ferry departs. Bring books, playing cards, or other amusements, as a minimum of three-hour-long waits are not unusual during the busy season.

Two ways to avoid the long lines is to walk on or bring a bike rather than a car onto the ferry; there are peak and off-season parking rates if you choose to leave your car behind. Ferries from Anacortes travel to the four largest and most populated islands: Lopez, Orcas, San Juan, and Shaw.

Fares vary depending on the island destinations. During the peak season, be prepared to pay an average of $40 per vehicle and driver, and an additional $12 per passenger. Discounted rates are available for seniors and children. Bicycle surcharge rates are only $4 during the peak season.

Directions to Anacortes Ferry Terminal: Anacortes is about two hours north of Seattle. Take I-5 North for approximately 85 miles to SR 20. Take exit 230, turn left at the light and follow the signs into downtown Anacortes. Turn left on 12th Street and follow the signs to the terminal.

1 South Court Secured Parking
2 Northwest Rooms
3 Northwest Craft Center
4 Seattle Repertory Theater
5 Color Craft Building
6 Cornish Playhouse
7 Founder's Court
8 SIFF Film Center
9 Sculpture Garden
10 Pacific Science Center / IMAX
11 Mural Amphitheater
12 Children's Garden
13 Nate McMillian Basketball Court

14 Pottery Northwest
15 Blue Spruce
16 Park Place
17 Seattle Sonics / Storm Team Shop
18 Experience Music Project / Sci-Fi Museum
19 Frontier Galllery
20 Seattle Center Monorail
21 Seattle Center House / The Children's Museum
22 Seattle Center Pavilion

## General Information

NFT Map:     15
Address:     305 Harrison St
             Seattle, WA 98109
Phone:       206-684-7202
Website:     www.seattlecenter.com

## Overview

Seattle Center is the hub of tourism in the city, but it also provides a number of interesting pursuits for the locals. While the out-of-towners flock to the Space Needle, Monorail, and EMP (or board those damned Ducks across the street), Seattleites attend concerts or sporting events at the Key Arena, see a play at one of several theaters, or hang out at Bumbershoot, Folklife, or Beerfest. Each year on New Year's Eve, the Space Needle is lit up by an impressive fireworks display.

But Seattle Center isn't just about partying and tourism. It's also about getting your learn on. The Children's Museum and the Pacific Science Center have interactive exhibits year-round. The IMAX Theater provides the typical educational fare as well as some new releases in 3D. And of course, each weekend you can rock out to your favorite psychedelic band at the Laser Dome.

There have been a few news-making events at Seattle Center. After his suicide in 1994, Nirvana fans came out in droves for a candlelight vigil memorializing Kurt Cobain. It has also been the site of several protests. In 2006, the annual Gay Pride Parade was moved from Broadway in Capitol Hill to the Seattle Center.

## Space Needle

The Space Needle (800-937-9582; www.spaceneedle.com) is categorically the most overrated and over-photographed landmark in Seattle. The view might be impressive, but it's not the best one in the city, and it's certainly not worth the price of admission. There may be a modicum of charm in eating a meal in a rotating restaurant, but it's rarely a recipe for a quality meal.

## Experience Music Project

Seattleites widely regard the EMP (877-367-5483; www.emplive.org) as an eyesore. Furthermore, no one but designer Frank Gehry and owner Paul Allen think it looks like a smashed guitar (the phrase "psychedelic clown poop" comes to mind). But if you're a music fan, you're in for a treat. That is, if you're *really* into Jimi Hendrix and looking at famous sweaters. In short, visiting the EMP is like paying $20 to go to the Hard Rock Café.

## Monorail

Like the Space Needle, the Monorail (206-448-3481; www.seattlemonorail.com) is a novelty that was built for the World's Fair. It runs about a mile from the Seattle Center to Westlake Center Mall. Round-trip fare for adults is $4.50 and $2 for children 5–12. 65+ are $2 and kids 4 and under are free. If this sounds like a rip-off for a two-minute trip, you aren't wrong.

No Seattle resident has ever used the Monorail as public transportation. Don't let any film or TV show set in Seattle convince you otherwise. It is nothing but a tourist trap. And lately, it has also been a bit of a death trap. In recent years, collisions, de-railings, and fires have repeatedly put the Monorail out of commission. But it sure does look cool on camera!

## Children's Museum

Located on the first floor of the Center House, the Children's Museum (206-441-1768; www.thechildrensmuseum.org) features several child-sized environments designed for education, including a mountain forest, a global village, a mini-Seattle neighborhood, and Cog City. They also offer the typical gambit of youth programs and workshops. Admission is $8.25 for adults and children and $7.25 for grandparents. Children under 1 are free.

## Cornish Playhouse

Housed in a World's Fair-era building, the Cornish Playhouse has a 476-seat main theater and a separate black-box theater. The space was formerly the Intiman Theatre, which won a Tony Award in 2006 for outstanding regional theater. Unfortunately, it wasn't enough to keep them in the black as debts mounted, and the theater was forced to fire its entire staff and abruptly cancel a portion of its 2011 season. Subsequently, the space formerly occupied by Intiman was taken over by Cornish College and renamed The Cornish Playhouse. Since its precipitous fall, the Intiman has been reconceived as a yearly summer festival in its former home at the Seattle Center.

## Center House Stage

Located on the first floor of the Center House, it encompasses the administrative offices of the Seattle Shakespeare Company and the Book-It Repertory Theatre (206-684-7200). Zounds!

## Seattle Children's Theatre

Comprised of the Charlotte Martin Theatre and the Eve Alvord Theatre, the Seattle Children's Theatre (206-441-3322; www.sct.org) naturally offers a season of family-oriented plays as well as classes, workshops, and even birthday parties.

## Seattle Repertory Theatre

The Seattle Rep (206-443-2222; www.seattlerep.org) includes the Bagley Wright Theatre, the Leo Kreielsheimer Theatre, and the PONCHO Forum. They perform classic and contemporary plays as well as original works and adaptations of novels.

## Center House

The Center House is occupied by the Children's Museum and their very own theater. They also have various exhibits, dance exhibitions, and choral concerts throughout the year. Looking for an alternative to expensive fair food and Honey Buckets during Bumbershoot? Duck into the food court for a more reasonable meal and an actual restroom.

## McCaw Hall

The $127 million McCaw Hall (206-684-7200) is home to the Pacific Northwest Ballet, the Seattle Opera, and the SIFF Cinema. A lecture hall and an array of meeting rooms are available for rent for your next grandiose function.

## Key Arena

Since its ugly divorce with the SuperSonics in 2007, the Key Arena (206-684-7200) has had a hard time picking up the pieces. Fortunately, they will always be available to accommodate the concert overflow from the CLink Events Center. They also have the lovely ladies of the Seattle Storm basketball team and the Rat City Rollergirls to help keep the $6 Bud Light flowing.

## Pacific Science Center/IMAX

The Pacific Science Center (206-443-2001; www.pacificsciencecenter.org) houses a very good collection of science-related entertainment. From the dinosaur exhibit to the Butterfly House, the Insect Playground to the interactive Science Playground, adults and children alike owe it to themselves to explore the grounds at least once. Don't miss the Planetarium. In addition to the usual documentaries and nature films at the IMAX, they also present the odd theatrical release (such as Harry Potter and Superman Returns) in giant wrap-around screen splendor, and, occasionally 3D. And, of course, there's always Laser Floyd.

## SIFF Film Center

The SIFF Film Center (206-464-5830; www.siff.net) is Seattle's Chinese Democracy. They have been talking about building it for years, all but begging for money every year during their flagship event, the Seattle International Film Festival. Apparently, they finally filled up their donation box because the Film Center opened in July, 2011. The word is still out on whether or not it was worth the wait. But it certainly can't be any worse than "Shackler's Revenge."

## Chihuly Garden and Glass

After the Fun Forest (the endearingly rickety amusement park) met its demise in 2011, there was much debate about what to build in its stead. The Seattle Center owners agreed to consider proposals (such as a KEXP music stage or a park) but they never intended to do anything other than collect a big old paycheck from Dale Chihuly and his glassblowing empire. The museum opened in May 2012 and has been raking in the dough ever since, so I'm sure the Powers That Be do not regret their decision. Still, how cool would that KEXP stage have been?

## The Armory

What was once the saddest food court this side of the Cascades is now a wonderland of Seattle cuisine and is now a destination in and of itself. From the sweet or savory mini pies of Pie to the upscale comfort food at Skillet, ordering lunch is at once exhilarating and overwhelming. Bean Sprouts offers healthy, kid-friendly plates for that post-Children's Museum snack. The surprisingly cheap, freshly fired mini pizzas at MOD are worth the line and the vegan burgers at Plum would make even the most staunch carnivore reconsider their dietary stance. The lone holdover from the Dark Ages is a Subway, but with all this competition, their days are surely numbered.

## Art & Fountains

As you stroll through the Seattle Center, you will notice a multitude of abstract sculptures and unusual fountains. Many of them, such as the whale-esque Neototem Series, and the can't-miss-because-it's-a-giant-ball-in-the-center-of-the-grounds International Fountain, double as jungle gyms for the kids. The Olympic Iliad, a series of orange tubes intertwined, sits on the lawn of the Pacific Science Center. The Reeds, a row of 30-foot, well, reeds, divide the walkway and parking lot outside of the EMP. The Vortex Fountain aptly swirls between the INTIMAN Theatre and McCaw Hall.

## How to Get There

**By Car**
From I-5, take the Mercer Street/Seattle Center Exit #167. At the first light, turn right onto Fairview and follow the flow of traffic to the left, turning onto Broad Street. Take a right onto Fifth Avenue and a left onto Roy Street. From there you can find on-street parking, or use one of the lots or garages.

**By Bus**
From Downtown, catch routes 1, 2, 3, 4, 8, 13, 15, 16, 18, 19, 24, or 33.
From Queen Anne, catch the 1, 2, 3, 4, 8, or 13.
From First Hill, catch the 2, 3, or 4.
From Capitol Hill, catch the 8.
From Wallingford/Northgate, catch the 16.
From Ballard, catch the 15 or 18.
From Magnolia, catch the 19, 24, 33 or 45.
From the Fremont/U-District, catch the 74.

**By Monorail**
Don't be a chump. Take the bus.

## General Information

NFT Map: 3
Address: 1000 Fourth Ave
Seattle, WA 98104
Phone: 206-386-4636
Website: www.spl.org
Hours: Mon-Thurs: 10 am–8 pm, Fri-Sat: 10 am–6 pm, Sun: 12 pm–6 pm

## Overview

Opened to the public in May 2004 to much fanfare, the Seattle Central Library has helped to rescue the city from its growing reputation as an architectural vacuum. The stunning, avant-garde glass and steel structure designed by Dutch architect Rem Koolhaas is the third incarnation of the Central Library, with over 160,000 more square footage of program space than its dingy 1960s predecessor. The new building's diamond-grid "glass skin" makes the most of Seattle's scarcest resource—sunlight—filling the library's vast open spaces with light and framing 360-degree views of the surrounding buildings. The interior combines striking, modern decor with more serene touches. Polished steel surfaces abut scrap wood floors; fluorescent yellow escalators lead to grass-patterned carpeting. Particularly eccentric are the blood red hallways of the Meeting Level on the fourth floor. The place is downright trippy. But unlike other experimental buildings around town (sorry EMP), this architectural gem actually lives up to the hype.

True to Seattle ideals, the building is energy efficient, earthquake safe, and unbelievably high-tech, with self-checkout terminals, an automated book-sorting system, and wireless communication devices for staff members. The library's nonfiction stacks are housed in an innovative "books spiral," which, much like the Guggenheim Museum in New York, allows uninterrupted progress through the collection. Other highlights include the 400-seat Betty Jane Narver Reading Room featuring views of Elliott Bay, a wall of audio booths for language study, several video art installations, and the 275-seat Microsoft Auditorium where free author events are a regular occurrence.

## Internet

The Central Library, housing nearly 400 public computers, was designed with access to technology in mind. A valid library card or a temporary guest pass is required for internet use on a library PC. Free Wi-Fi access is available throughout the building. Most seating in reading rooms and in the stacks is equipped with electrical outlets for laptops.

## For the Kids

Kid-sized bookshelves and a toddler play area can be found in the cheerfully rubberized Faye G. Allen Children's Center on Level 1. The Anne Marie Gault Story Hour Room hosts children's activities almost every day of the week. On Level 3, discernable by its bright orange flooring, is the Starbucks Teen Center, complete with young adult books and graphic novels, a special teen reference desk, and computers and workstations exclusively for teen use.

## Food and Gifts

The FriendShop on Level 3 near the Fifth Avenue entrance sells an assortment of trendy gift items and is one of the better places to buy a greeting card downtown. You can purchase espresso, pastries and sandwiches in the adjacent Fare Start Café. You must consume snacks in the cafe area, but feel free to roam the stacks with your lidded latte.

## How to Get There—Driving

From the north take I-5 exit 165B at Union Street. Follow Union three blocks west to Fifth Avenue, then turn left and go south three blocks to Spring Street.

From the south, take I-5 exit 165 at Seneca Street. Follow Seneca one block west. Turn left on Fifth Avenue and go south one block to Spring Street.

From the east, drive to the end of I-90 and take the ramp toward northbound I-5. Take the second exit at Madison Street. Turn left on Madison Street and go west two blocks to Fifth Avenue.

## Parking

Underground parking is accessible on Spring Street between Fourth and Fifth Avenues. The first 20 minutes are free; 20 to 40 minutes cost $3; 40 to 60 minutes, $7; then gradually increasing for each additional hour. The Sunday rate is $6 for up to four hours and $2 for each additional hour. Bike racks are located at all major entrances and inside the parking garage.

## How to Get There—Mass Transit

Most downtown buses stop within walking distance of the Central Library.

Andrews Bay

Lake Washington S

S Orcas St

Seward Park Ave S

**MAP
40**

S Juneau St

S Upland Rd

S Hawthorn Rd

Lake Shore Dr S

Seward Park Ave S

Lake Washington Blvd S

Bath House &
Art Studio

Picnic
Shelter

Environmental
Education Center

Picnic Shelter

Picnic
Shelter

Amphitheater

Picnic
Shelters

Lake Washington

Tennis
Courts

## General Information

NFT Map: 40
Address: 5920 Lake Washington Blvd S
Seattle, WA 98118
Park Hours: 6 am–11 pm
Phone: Environmental Learning Center
206-684-4396;
Art Studio 206-722-6342
Seattle City Park Website:
www.seattle.gov/parks/parkspaces/
sewardpark.htm
Friends of Seward Park:
www.sewardpark.org

## Overview

Seward Park was purchased by the city in 1910 for $322,020, less than today's price for a tiny home in south Seattle's nearby neighborhoods. It is a gigantic 300-acre thumb of land jutting into the (relatively) fresh water of Lake Washington, and much of the acreage encompasses old growth forest. Thanks to the ongoing work of Friends of Seward Park and city staff weeding out invasive non-indigenous plants, the park retains much of its splendid original habitat and native flora and fauna. On a clear day, walking around the peninsula's 2.4-mile lakefront loop allows views of Mount Rainier to the south, the Cascade Mountain range to the east, Mount Baker to the north, and a glimpse of the Olympic Mountain range to the west. You won't find a better walking trail in Seattle for a 360-degree vista of the glories of the Pacific Northwest, but the park does attract some unsavory characters—don't leave valuables in your car or send your children into the restrooms alone. Located amid the ethnically and income diverse neighborhoods of Mount Baker, Leschi, Seward Park, and Rainier Beach, you are as likely to see joggers in spandex pushing high-tech baby strollers as men in yarmulkes walking arm in arm or Muslim women cloaked in traditional garb. The park hosts many community events, from running and bicycle races to charity pet walks—check the park calendar for the schedule of evening hayrides, concerts in the spacious outdoor amphitheater, and the listing of classes offered by park naturalists.

## How to Get There

Car, bike, bus, boat, or kayak will all get you there from here. Parking lots are plentiful and usually only crowded on summer weekends and sunny days. Driving south along Lake Washington Boulevard is scenic—if the route is open. From May to September, the stretch of road along the lakeshore from Mount Baker to Seward Park is closed two days a month for bicycle use on weekends. When the road is open to car traffic, you may be tempted to cut in front of the hordes of cyclists, but bear in mind that bicycles have the right of way. If you can't beat 'em, hop on an expensive Klein racing bike or a beat up Schwinn, and join 'em. Metro Bus Routes 34 and 39 stop at Seward Park Avenue S and S Juneau Street.

## Activities

This 300-acre park packs a wallop. Stay all day and you'll see the sun rise over Mount Rainier and set over downtown Seattle's Columbia Tower. In between, fish off the dock, swim in the lake, study lichens and mushrooms, add diving ducks to your life list of birds, use the Art Studio to fire your pottery, overhear a half dozen different languages, and glaze over watching a tai chi class on the beach. Your Aunt Mildred (or Jonathan Franzen if you happen to be entertaining famous authors for the weekend) can focus her binoculars on the bald eagle nests in the old growth forest, while your nephews play tennis on the waterfront courts. After catching his day's quota of fish, Dad can relax with a cool one in the picnic shelters overlooking the lake and he'll enjoy the same views as Lake Washington's multi-millionaire waterfront homeowners. There is anchorage for your uncle's yacht in protected Andrews Bay; in the summer he can row ashore to buy a hotdog and a sno-cone from the park's snack truck. If your family includes canine members, they are welcome, but keep them on a leash—if your rambunctious Airedale runs off you can (and will) be ticketed by park rangers intent on keeping the grebes, herons, and cormorants in the lake and the dogs out. There are hiking trails through the woods, grassy playfields for Frisbee tossing, and a small but well-used playground for the kids. Best of all, you can paddle off from the whole fam-damily in your kayak without anyone knowing you've slipped away.

## Seward Park Environmental & Audubon Center

After years of planning, fundraising, and community input, the Seward Park Environmental & Audubon Center opened its doors in 2008. The multi-million dollar project, a joint venture of Audubon Washington and Seattle Parks & Recreation, included the renovation of the old Tudor-style brick building at the entrance to the park. The building was transformed into an environmental education center complete with an extensive library, a laboratory, and a gift shop.
Some neighbors fear that the already heavily used park will become even more crowded now that the education center is open (although birding isn't quite as popular with Americans as, say, football), but most welcome the opportunity to teach Seattle's next generation of REI shoppers why they need to leave no tracks behind when they trek off into Washington's wilderness.

# Parks & Places · **University of Washington**

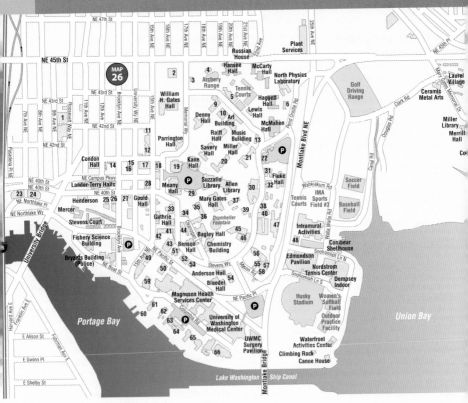

1. UWMC Roosevelt
2. Burke Memorial Museum
3. Theodor Jacobsen Observatory
4. Hughes Penthouse Theatre
5. Hutchinson Hall
6. Cyclotron Shop
7. NorthWest Horticultural Society Hall
8. Issacson Hall
9. Balmer Hall
10. Mackenzie Hall
11. Eagleson Hall
12. Social Work/Speech and Hearing Sciences Building
13. Clark Hall
14. Brooklyn Building
15. Playhouse Theater
16. Staff HR Center
17. Schmitz Hall
18. Henry Art Gallery
19. Odegaard Undergrad Library
20. Smith & Gowen Halls
21. Thomson Hall/Communications Building
22. Padelford Hall
23. Research & Technology Building

24. Publications Services Building
25. Child Care Center
26. Ethnic Cultural Center
27. Instructional Center/Theater
28. Commodore-Duchess Apartments
29. Gerberding Hall
30. Student Union Building (HUB)
31. Hall Health Center
32. The University of Washington Club
33. Architecture Hall
34. Cunningham Hall
35. Johnson Hall
36. Atmospheric Sciences-Geophysics
37. Sieg Hall
38. Engineering Library
39. Kirsten Aeronautical Lab
40. Loew Hall
41. Physics/Astronomy Building
42. Physics/Astronomy Tower
43. Physics/Astronomy Auditorium
44. Chemistry Library Building
45. Electrical Engineering Building
46. Paul G. Allen Center for Computer Science & Engineering

47. Power Plant
48. Graves Hall
49. W.H. Foege Bioengineer & Genome Sciences Buil
50. Hitchcock Hall
51. Kincaid Hall
52. Botany Greenhouse
53. Plant Lab
54. Winkenwerder Forest La
55. Roberts Hall
56. More Hall
57. Wilcox Hall
58. Wilson Ceramic Lab
59. Ocean Sciences Buildin
60. Marine Sciences Buildin
61. Oceanography Teaching
62. Harris Hydraulics Lab
63. South Campus Center
64. Oceanography Building
65. Fisheries Center
66. Experimental Education

## General Information

NFT Map:   26
Address:   1410 NE Campus Pkwy
           Seattle, WA 98105
Phone:     206-543-2100
Website:   www.washington.edu

## Overview

Founded November 4, 1861, the University of Washington, or UW (pronounced U-Dub) is the oldest university on the west coast and the largest in the Pacific Northwest. There are three campuses—Tacoma, Bothell, and Seattle—Seattle being the main one and largest of the three. It is a public research school of over 40,000 students with many of its programs ranked in the top ten in the country, including its medical and nursing schools. It doesn't hurt that UW gets a great deal of funding from—yeah, those guys again—Microsoft masterminds Paul Allen and Bill Gates. It also boasts one of the most beautiful campuses in the country, with dramatic views of Mt. Rainier. It's well worth a stroll, even if you're not the studious type.

The 643-acre Seattle campus is home to 218 buildings and contains a courtyard full of cherry trees that are in the shape of a W when viewed from the sky. Unfortunately, they always seem to be in bloom when school is out of session for spring break. Although UW is best known for its medical programs, the Creative Writing Department received $15 million in 2006 from the S. Wilson and Grace M. Pollock Foundation, the largest donation ever made to the College of Arts and Sciences.

## Tuition

For the 2013–2014 academic school year, tuition and fees for the University of Washington is $12,397 for residents and $31,971 for non-residents. On campus room and board will run you $10,752; for books and supplies you will need to get about $1,200 together.

## Sports

Students and Seattle citizens are extremely proud of their Huskies and flock to the football games at Husky Stadium. You'll find die hard fans tailgating on their boats on Lake Washington during games, even in miserable weather. The Huskies participate in the NCAA Division I-A and the PAC 10. The football team may not be setting the world on fire like the old days, but the girl's volleyball team definitely is, recently becoming NCAA Division 1 national champions. Men's basketball is nothing to sniff at either thanks

to a resurgence under head coach Lorenzo Romar, who frequently leads them to the NCAA tournament. Rowing is where the Huskies really shine. Men's Crew has won eleven national titles and 15 Olympic gold medals, while the women have won ten national titles and two gold medals. The Marching Band of UW is also well known, using a traditional high step, one of very few marching bands left to use this strategy of hyping up the already excited crowds.

## Culture on Campus

The University of Washington's Seattle campus has culture up the wazoo. If you're into museums, try the Burke, which is the state museum of natural and cultural history. There is also the Henry Art Gallery, the first public art museum in the state of Washington, which features contemporary art (including the trippy *Skyspace* by James Turrell). Meany Hall is the place for performing arts and is home to the performances of UW's School of Drama, often ranked as one of the top theater programs in the country. They put on at least seven shows per year, but you can also catch performances from the Schools of Dance, Music, Digital Arts, and Experimental Media Program. If you're more into the outdoors, head over to the Botanic Gardens, otherwise known as the arboretum. You will run out of time and energy before you run out of land to explore. The university also runs the RainyDawg Radio, a student run internet radio station and UWTV which is broadcast state-wide and is available to cable television viewers.

## Departments

Undergraduate Admissions .......................206-543-9686
College of Arts and Sciences ....................206-543-5340
Business School.........................................206-543-4750
School of Dentistry....................................206-543-5982
College of Education ................................206-616-4805
College of Engineering .............................206-543-0340
College of Forest Resources......................206-685-1928
The Graduate School.................................206-543-5900
Information School.....................................206-685-9937
School of Law.............................................206-543-4550
School of Medicine ...................................206-543-2100
School of Nursing......................................206-543-8736
College of Ocean and Fishery Sciences ....206-543-6605
School of Pharmacy...................................206-543-2030
Daniel J Evans School of Public Affairs......206-543-4900
Henry M Jackson School of .......................206-543-4370
  International Studies
School of Public Health and .....................206-543-1144
  Community Medicine
School of Social Work................................206-543-5640

Ferry to Southworth

Ferry to Fauntleroy

SW 120th St

Wingluhu King County Park

Vashon Hwy SW

Culman Rd

SW Cedarhurst Rd

Vashon Heights Rd

AYH Ranch Hostel

Vashon Municipal Airport

Agren Park

Rock Island Pub & Pizza
Bob's Bakery
Cafe Luna
Bishop's

The Hardware Store

Westside Hwy SW

**Colvos Passage**

**Puget Sound**

Vashon Hwy SW

SW 204th St

Green Valley Creek

Paradise Ridge Park

11th Ave SW

Judd Creek

**Tramp Harbor**

SW 220th St

SW Quartermaster Dr.

Jael Creek

103rd Ave SW

SW Point Robinson Rd

SW Luana Beach Rd

Dockton Rd SW

Burton Acres Park

SW 240th St

Wax Orchard Rd SW

Vashon Island Golf and Country Club

**Paradise Cove**

**Quarter-Master Harbor**

Dockton Rd SW

Dockton Park

SW Dock St

99th Ave SW

Vashon Hwy SW

**East Passage**

Spring Beach Park

Tahlequah Creek

SW 304th St

Point Defiance

Tahlequah

## Overview

Vashon Island plays the role of that forgotten, odd-ball, self-isolated community populated with eccentric characters and legendary landmarks only locals can appreciate (a bike in a tree, a strawberry festival without strawberries, and so on). Vashon is less a destination than Bainbridge or the San Juans. In fact, with no hotels, only a dozen-ish B&Bs, and virtually no camping allowed anywhere on the island, Vashon doesn't exactly encourage tourism.

Roughly the same size as Seattle, but with only 10,000 inhabitants, Vashon is rural and decentralized—perfect for the organic farmers and radical GOP-hating liberals who call it home (These guys make Seattleites look like Bill O'Reilly). Vashon is great for a short visit, especially if you have friends on the island.

Lacking any stoplights, "Downtown Vashon" at Vashon Highway and Bank Road lies two miles from the ferry. There you'll find independent cafés, bookshops, art galleries, and restaurants. Bishop's is *the* center of nightlife (and that's not a snotty, emphatic "the," but a singular "the" as in "only place"). The locals go to Thriftway to hobnob and gossip. The Hardware Store was just that for over 100 years until 2005, when it was turned into a happening eatery.

## Art Night

The rural, getaway nature of Vashon has attracted a flock of artists and galleries. A few of them have banded together for the First Friday Gallery Cruise. Also, twice a year (May, December) over 40 artists open their studios to the public. Information on both can be found at www.vashonalliedarts.org.

## Strawberries?

The famed Vashon Island Strawberry Festival happens every July. It's much like small town fairs all over the country—elephant ears, nauseating rides, creepy carnies—but oddly, no strawberries. To the lament of the island's hippies, it occurs the same weekend as the venerated Oregon Country Fair. A highlight for car enthusiasts is the classic car parade which attracts gear heads from all over the state to show off their retro beauties that spend the rest of the year hiding under tarps.

## Earth Island

The Vashon Earth Island Fair happens every August and features a variety of alterna-activities, focusing on speakers and workshops on sustainability, renewable energy, healing arts, and healthy living, as well as musicians and legalized camping.

## Where to Eat and Drink

**The Hardware Store**, 17601 Vashon Hwy SW, 206-463-1800. Serving lunch and dinner, plus breakfast on Sundays, the menu features straightforward café fare that includes buttermilk fried chicken and a nice selection of salads. Don't miss the bar area, a perfect perch for watching the ferry traffic stream into town while you sip some good vino from their wine list.

**Rock Island Pub & Pizza**, 23319 Vashon Hwy SW, 206-463-6814. A good range of pies and pastas. Take it outside to the patio with a pitcher of beer on a nice day or sidle up to the stone fireplace in the winter.

**Bob's Bakery**, 17506 Vashon Hwy SW, 206-463-1441. Bob bakes up a great selection of breads and sweet things, chief among them a slab of a maple bar that's not to be missed

**Café Luna**, 9924 SW Bank Rd, 206-463-0777. Serves up the best mocha on the island and offers a range of teas, baked goods, and grilled paninis.

**Red Bicycle Bistro & Sushi**, 17618 Vashon Hwy SW, 206-463-5959. The local restaurant/bar that frequently has live music on the weekends.

## How to Get There

**By Car**

Take I-5 south to the West Seattle Bridge, keep to your left toward Alaska Junction to Fauntleroy and follow the signs to the ferry.

Ferries leave from the Fauntleroy terminal in West Seattle seven days a week. On weekdays, you can take a passenger-only ferry from Pier 50 in Seattle. Bus 54 will take you directly to the Fauntleroy ferry terminal from downtown. Bus 560 will take you there from the airport. To get to Fauntleroy by car, take I-5 to exit 163 to the West Seattle bridge to Fauntleroy Way SW. Follow Fauntleroy Way SW to the end, and look for signs for the ferry.

## Where to Stay

Sadly, Vashon's hostel closed in 2013 and its future remains undecided. The Vashon Island Chamber of Commerce website lists the island's other lodging options (vashonislandchamber.chambermaster.com/list/ql/lodging-travel-24).

## General Information

NFT Map:   17 & 20
Address:   1247 15th Ave E
           Seattle, WA 98112
Phone:     206-684-4555
Website:   www.seattle.gov/parks/parkspaces/
           volpark.htm
Hours:     6 am–1 pm daily

## Overview

By day, Volunteer Park is another jewel in Seattle's crown of gorgeous public spaces. This 48.3-acre park features a museum, a conservatory, and many fine public art pieces. However, locals whisper that at night, Volunteer Park becomes a seedier place, where the randier citizens of Seattle lurk in the underbrush in search of anonymous partnerships. NFT cannot confirm or deny this rumor, only assist in spreading it. What is sure is that Volunteer Park (so named in 1901 to honor Spanish-American War recruits) suffers not a whit from these purported nocturnal dalliances—it's still a peaceful place to stroll away from the city with assorted trails and paths that allow one to gently meander or stretch the legs in a vigorous jog. A children's wading pool draws countless tykes all summer long, a quartet of tennis courts welcomes the net set, and the band stand provides a stage for regular outdoor music performances.

## Seattle Asian Art Museum & Volunteer Park Conservatory

Volunteer Park has long been a popular destination for lovers of art and botany. Abstract sculptures and statues honoring local pioneers, military heroes, and public servants distinguish the grounds. The park is also home to the Seattle Asian Art Museum, an extensive collection of historical and modern art with ever-changing exhibits. The nearby Volunteer Park Conservatory has been here since 1912, featuring five different habitats for a wild assortment of exotic plants from around the world.

## The Water Tower

The water tower on the south side of Volunteer Park is a popular landmark for those planning to meet up for a little Frisbee golf or friendly dog-walking. If you can handle 106 steps, you can visit the tower's observation deck, which automatically puts you at the highest point of Capitol Hill and affords a beautiful view. While there, take the time to peruse the historical exhibit that celebrates the Olmsted brothers, early-20th-century pioneers in establishing the park system in Seattle, including Volunteer Park.

## Lake View Cemetery

Volunteer Park borders the Lake View Cemetery, a historical spot filled with graves of the many founding fathers and mothers of Seattle. Those who know names like Denny, Mercer, and Yesler only from street signs will come face to face with the resting places of the fabled men themselves. Lake View also boasts the graves of the mighty Bruce Lee and his son Brandon, both charismatic martial arts action heroes who died mysteriously. Sorry Mr. Mercer, but being in the eternal presence of Kato and the Crow is a bigger thrill, even if you did clear the trees to make way for the University of Washington.

## How to Get There—Bus

The 10 hits Volunteer Park nearly every fifteen minutes with service from downtown.

## How to Get There—Driving

From I-5 northbound, take exit 166 and turn right on E Olive Way, following until it merges with E John Street. Turn left on 15th Avenue E, then enter Volunteer Park after 3/4 mile.

From I-5 southbound, take exit 168A and turn left on E Roanoke Street. Turn right at 10th Avenue E, turn left onto E Boston Street until it becomes 15th Avenue E. Volunteer Park will be on the left.

## General Information

NFT Map:    22 & 19
Address:    2300 Arboretum Dr E
            Seattle, WA 98122
Phone:      206-543-8800
Website:    depts.washington.edu/uwbg/gardens/
            wpa.shtml

## Overview

The Washington Park Arboretum is 230 acres of sprawling beauty that contains more than 5,000 different plant species. You will find a large collection of sorbus and maple as well as an abundance of wildlife. The Arboretum is huge. It is difficult to see it all in one day, but definitely fun to try. There are many meandering trails with few hills, so it's perfect for jogging (just look out for people taking pictures!). You will find a strange combination of the beauty and serenity in the view in front of you and the constant din of traffic from the nearby freeway. However, once you push that out of your head, it is a wonderful place to get away from it all. And speaking of traffic, it can be pretty bad surrounding the park, so give yourself extra time to navigate it. Once there, take a stroll to Foster Island, where the floating bridges provide extra fun when boats go by and create a wake. Here especially, keep your eye out for birds and turtles. But don't go too quickly! The fragile earth under your feet wishes you to walk not run. If you really love the plants and desperately want to take them home with you, seedlings are available for purchase. Your only shot is on Tuesday's 10 am–12 pm at the Pat Calvert Greenhouse located just south of the Graham Visitor Center.

## Japanese Gardens

Address:    1075 Lake Washington Blvd E
            Seattle, WA 98122
Phone:      206-684-4725
Website:    www.seattle.gov/tour/gardens.htm
Hours:      March–Apr: Tues-Sun 10 am–6 pm
            May–Aug 28th: Daily 10 am–8 pm
            Aug 29th–Sep 30th: Daily 10 am–7 pm
            Oct 1st–Oct 28th: Tues–Sun 10 am–6 pm
            Oct 29th–Nov 30th: Tues–Sun 10 am–4 pm
Admission:  18-64 $6; youths 6-17, seniors 65+, college
            students with ID, and disabled $4; children
            0-5 free.

This 3.5-acre, formal garden was dreamed up by world-renowned Japanese garden designer Juki Iiada in 1960. He oversaw all construction of this garden, which includes a koi pond and a traditional tea house. The Garden is exceptionally beautiful and unique as it incorporates both plants traditionally found in a Japanese garden and plants native to the Northwest. It can be a welcome sanctuary from busy city life and well worth the admission fee. Try to catch a tea ceremony, which is periodically offered in the tea house.

## Guided Tours

To better appreciate the diversity of the different plant species at the arboretum, take a free guided tour on the 1st and 3rd Sunday of each month. Guides will expertly highlight the plant collections, different seasonal displays of beauty, and the history of the arboretum in 60–90 minutes. Tours start at the Graham Visitor Center, and it's best to call ahead to ensure availability.

Scheduled guided tours are offered for groups of ten or more. These, however, are not free. Choose between whatever seasonal tour is being offered, the Foster Island Ecology tour, or the Native Plants and Ethnobotany tour. These tours require three weeks advance notice.

Address:    Graham Visitor Center
            2300 Arboretum Drive E
            Seattle, WA 98122
Phone:      free tours 206-543-8800;
            guided tours 206-543-8801
Website:    depts.washington.edu/uwbg/visit/
            tours.shtml

## Boating

The arboretum now includes three public, non-motorized boat-launching sites and is a part of the Lakes to Locks Water Trail which starts in Lake Sammamish and ends at Puget Sound. Since it used to be illegal to land your boat at a public park, it's a welcome addition. If you don't own a boat or kayak, you can rent one from the Washington Activities Center (206-543-9433; H2ofront@u.washington.edu) just across the lake from the park. Once you're on the water, paddle around the water lilies and under the famous "ramp to nowhere" as you head over to Foster Island to explore its watery corridors. You will be treated to excellent bird watching, and the chance to see otters, turtles, or perhaps even a beaver dam. Once again, you'll come face to face with a thriving eco-system next to a busy freeway, giving you renewed hope for the future of planet Earth.

## How to Get There—Driving

**From Downtown**: Go east on Madison Street to Lake Washington Boulevard E then turn left into the arboretum.

**From I-5:** Take exit 168 onto highway 520. Take the first exit to Lake Washington Boulevard E and follow it into the arboretum.

## How to Get There—Bus

The 11, 43, and 48 will get you close to the park.

Deception Pass
State Park ○

Ala
Spit ○

*Skagiit
Bay*

20

Ault Field Rd

Oak Harbor ●

Fort Nugent Rd

*Crescent
Harbor*

West Beach Rd

Ebey's
Landing ○

*Penn Cove*

Coupeville ●

Fort Ebey
State Park

Engle Rd

20

Wannamaker Rd

525

*Admiralty
Bay*

Port Townsend - Keystone Ferry

Greenbank
Farm ○

Greenbank ●

S Smugglers Cove Rd

Saratoga Rd

SE Harbor Rd

Langley ●

525

Cultus Bay Rd

Clinton - Mukilteo Ferry

Double Bluff
Beach ○

Clinton ●

*Useless
Bay*

## General Information

Phone:     888-747-7777 x 22
Website:   www.whidbeycamanoislands.com

## Overview

One of Seattle's biggest perks is its proximity to an endless variety of retreats and getaways. Just miles from the hustle and bustle lay idyllic islands that can wipe away any memory of hellish downtown traffic. One of the prettiest and closest of these is Whidbey Island, known for its scenic shores, quaint island communities, and increasingly-precious real estate.

As with most of the territory in North America, Whidbey was once occupied by several local Native American tribes until those pesky Europeans came over. A guy named Joseph Whidbey came along and circumnavigated the whole island, which apparently was impressive enough for it to be named after him. Full colonization of the island took its sweet time, though. The first permanent arrival was murdered and beheaded by some unhappy natives, and understandably there was a bit of healthy skepticism on the part of would-be immigrants. Nowadays Whidbey is a thriving agricultural community as well as home to a naval station, a healthy tourism industry, and the most visited state park in Washington. Despite all that Whidbey's got goin' on, it's an extremely laid-back kind of place.

## Activities

Though the island's motto of "Do Nothing Here" might imply a lazy sort of attitude on the part of Whidbey residents, that's certainly not the case. If you feel compelled to do more than skipping rocks on the bay or snuggling in your cottage (both more-than-acceptable activities), the island teems with things to do for all tastes and energy levels. There are no fewer than ten public beaches on the island where you can go clamming, watch gray whales in season, or, if you're brave, go swimming. A few favorites include Ala Spit (popular with birdwatchers) and Double Bluff (with an off-leash area for your pup).

Adults can check out the different wineries and pubs, like the Whidbey Island Winery (www.whidbeyislandwinery.com), or go treasure-hunting at the scores of antique shops. There are also several farmers markets during the peak of the season where you can buy local loganberries and homemade ice cream. And if you *really* want to do something instead of nothing, there are sites for almost every type of outdoorsy activity, from hiking to fishing to kayaking. Basically, Whidbey's got it all.

## Towns

One of the biggest draws is the quaint postcard towns scattered across the island. Visitors and residents alike enjoy spending an entire day strolling and soaking up the charm. Towards the south and only a few miles from the Clinton ferry dock is Langley, an artists' village with the highest concentration of boutique lodgings in the state. Further north, historic Coupeville is situated on Penn Cove (home to the famously delectable mussels of the same name) and is the second oldest town in the entire state. It's loved for its charming shops and B&Bs, the Historical Society Museum, and the town ice cream parlor (yum).

## Tours

The Whidbey Island Garden Tour (www.wigt.org) is an extremely popular once-yearly event. Tickets are limited, so reserve well in advance in early summer. Also fun, is the annual Whidbey Island Farm Tour, held in September (www.whidbeyfarmtour.com), when you can explore the island's Crops and critters for free!

## Deception Pass State Park

*360-675-9438; www.parks.wa.gov/parks/?selectedpark=Deception %20Pass*
Deception Pass State Park is a 4,134-acre marine and camping park just north of Oak Harbor with amazing stretches of saltwater shoreline, as well as freshwater shoreline on three lakes. The park is the most popular in the state, and for good reason. There are breath-taking views, rugged cliffs, old-growth forests, and abundant wildlife. The park is open year-round for camping and day use, although select campgrounds are closed during the winter.

## How to Get There—Driving

There's only one way to go if you're choosing to drive all the way to Whidbey—the breathtaking entrance to the north end of the island otherwise known as Deception Pass Bridge. Take the Anacortes exit off I-5, just north of Mt. Vernon. There are pull-outs and several points along the way where you can get out and take it all in. Trust us, it's stunning.

## How to Get There—Ferry

Ferries are probably the most popular way to get to the island and the easiest from Seattle. The Mukilteo-Clinton ferry departs every 30 minutes from Mukilteo. Take I-5 north from Seattle and follow the Mukilteo/Whidbey Island exit (#189), which will take you straight to the ferry dock. At peak times there can be a significant wait, so check the current wait times before you go (www.wsdot.wa.gov/ferries). The ride takes about 20 minutes and will take you to the town of Clinton on the southern end of the island.

The Pt. Townsend-Keystone ferry also takes about 30 minutes and connects the Olympic Peninsula to Keystone Landing in Ebey's National Historical Reserve on the island. From the Peninsula, head east on Highway 101 and take the SR20 East exit. The highway will turn into Sims Way and then Water Street, which will take you to the ferry dock.

## How to Get There—Plane

Seaplanes are a fun and incredibly scenic way to go, departing from Lake Union. If you want to bypass the whole ferry trip (which, on a bad day, can take hours), Kenmore Air (www.kenmoreair.com) will fly you for $29-$49 each way.

## How to Get There—Bus

If you're up further north, the Island Transit system will take you between Mt. Vernon and the island for absolutely nothing. Check out the schedules at www.islandtransit.org.

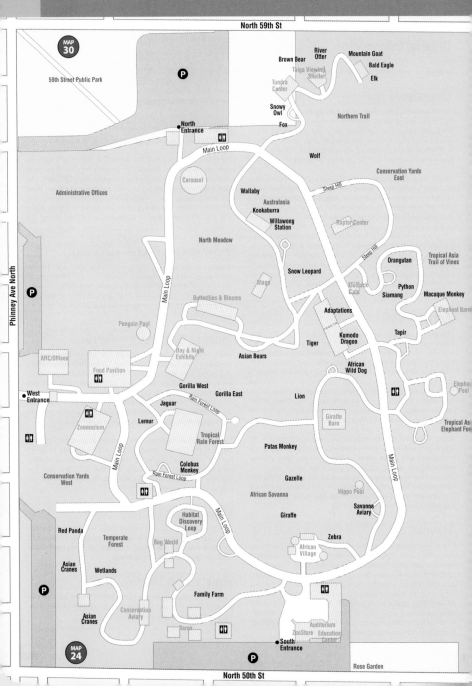

North 59th St

MAP 30

59th Street Public Park

P

Brown Bear
River Otter
Mountain Goat
Bald Eagle
Elk

Taiga Viewing Shelter

Tundra Center

Snowy Owl
Fox

Northern Trail

Wolf

North Entrance

Main Loop

Carousel

Wallaby
Australasia
Kookaburra
Willawong Station

Conservation Yards East

Steep Hill

Raptor Center

Administrative Offices

North Meadow

Snow Leopard

Steep Hill

Orangutan
Tropical Asia
Trail of Vines

Python
Siamang
Macaque Monkey
Elephant Barn

Main Loop

Stage

Outback Café

Butterflies & Blooms

Phinney Ave North

P

Penguin Pool

Adaptations

Komodo Dragon

Tiger

Tapir

Elephant Pool

ARC/Offices

Day & Night Exhibits

Asian Bears

African Wild Dog

Food Pavilion

West Entrance

Gorilla West
Gorilla East

Lion

Tropical Asia
Elephant Fore

P

Jaguar

Rain Forest Loop

Lemur

Zoomazium

Tropical Rain Forest

Giraffe Barn

Main Loop

Colobus Monkey

Patas Monkey

Rain Forest Loop

Conservation Yards West

Gazelle

Hippo Pool

African Savanna

Savanna Aviary

Habitat Discovery Loop

Giraffe

Main Loop

Red Panda

Temperate Forest

Bug World

Zebra

African Village

Asian Cranes

Wetlands

Family Farm

P

Conservation Aviary

Asian Cranes

Barns

Auditorium
ZooStore
Education Center

MAP 24

South Entrance

Rose Garden

P

North 50th St

# Parks & Places • **Woodland Park Zoo**

## General Information

NFT Map: 24 & 30
Address: 5500 Phinney Ave N
Seattle, WA 98103
Phone: 206-684-4800
Website: www.zoo.org
Hours: Open everyday of the year, except
Dec. 25;
Oct 1–April 30: 9:30 am–4 pm;
May 1–Sep 30: 9:30 am–6 pm
Admission: Oct 1–April 30 $12.75 adults (13-
64), $8.75 kids (3-12); May 1–Sep
30 $18.75 adults, $11.75 kids. $2
discount off regular admission prices
for Seniors (65+) and disabled. Kids
0-2 are free.

## Overview

It may not be the biggest, it may not have the rarest
animals, but what the Woodlawn Park Zoo lacks in
size, it makes up for in style. There is a strong focus
on education and conservation and the exhibits
themselves will not leave you feeling depressed
like some other zoos can. It's easy to tell why this
zoo is world-renowned for its animal exhibits and
education programs.

## Zoomazium

Geared to kids eight and younger, this all-weather
facility is the coolest indoor playground ever. You
will find a stage, a project place, and an active
space where parents let their kids loose to tire them
out before the drive home. It's a great place for kids
to learn as they play. There is a 20-foot tree to climb,
caves to explore, and a watering hole that reflects
an animal face when you look into it.

## Jaguar Cove

The zoo's Jaguar Cove exhibit contains a large
pool and waterfall as jaguars are the only large
cat willing to get their tootsies wet. Even more
impressive, this is the only zoo to boast a cross-
section for underwater viewing of an enormous
hungry jaguar coming right at you.

## Other Interesting Zoo Offerings

As if their exhibits weren't amazing enough, here
are some other highlights:

**Rose Garden:** This is technically located outside
of the zoo, but admission is free, so don't miss a
quick stroll through the 2.5-acre garden. This is a
popular and affordable spot for weddings, making
the photographer's job a no brainer. There are 280
varieties of roses and over 5,000 individual plants. It
is one of only 24 All American Rose Selections Test
Gardens in the US. You can smell it before you even
walk in.
**ZooTunes:** Summer concerts at the zoo!
**Zoo Overnight Adventure:** If you just can't
get enough of the zoo, you can stay there
overnight. Small groups can reserve overnight
accommodations that include private tours and
breakfast. Approximately $39 per person.

## Eating at the Zoo

When you get hungry like the wolf:

**Naturally Untamed Grill:** Burgers and fries,
vegetarian friendly.
**Cucina Rosso:** Fast Italian food.
**Bamboo Hut:** Asian fare.
**Rain Forest Deli:** Soups and sandwiches.
**Dreyers Ice Cream:** Just what it sounds like.
**Rain Forest Express:** Hot dogs, nachos, and other
deliciously guilty pleasures.
**Jungle Java:** When you just can't make it to the
jaguar without your java.
**Tortilla Express:** Mexican food.
**Outback Café:** BBQ, hotdogs, and "bear
necessities."

Picnic tables are also available for food brought
from home.

## How to Get There

**By Car:** From I-5 take the 50th Street exit (#169)
west for 1.3 miles to the south gate located on N
50th Street and Fremont Avenue N.
**By Bus:** From downtown take the MT 5 from 3rd
Avenue and Pine Street to the west gate at N 55th
Street & Phinney Avenue N.
**Parking:** $5, but try for free street parking first.

# Sports • **Biking**

Come the weekend, Seattleites don't mess around with their bicycle recreation. This usually means snapping their expensive Trek mountain bike to their Subaru and hitting the nearby offroading trails. But for a growing number of city slickers, Saturday means grabbing their bike out of their living room and hitting the urban trails. The granddaddy of them all is the The Burke-Gilman Trail, a 27-mile route along a former railway corridor that stretches from Redmond all the way to Ballard. Other car-free escapes include Green Lake Trail, Ship Canal Trail, and Alki Beach Trail in West Seattle. Wherever you ride, you can't miss the hills. But luckily, they work both ways. They can be a pain in the butt to climb (especially early in the morning on your way to a coffee shop), but for those willing to conquer them, you are rewarded with picture perfect views usually reserved for postcards. Unless of course it's raining. Again. And if you're traveling really far and wide, check out King County's excellent interactive bike map feature: www.kingcounty.gov/transportation/kcdot/Roads/Bicycling.aspx

Bicycle Sundays is becoming an annual tradition when sections of Lake Washington Boulevard are completely shut down to vehicle traffic on select weekends in the spring and summer from Mount Baker Beach to Seward Park. Cruise along this beautiful stretch of Seattle without the stress of a giant SUV racing to cut you off. If only biking in Seattle was like this everyday. Check out the website for more information and specific dates: www.seattle.gov/transportation/bikesatsun.htm

There's still a lot of work to be done to eclipse Northwest rival and biking utopia Portland. If you find yourself frustrated with the Emerald City's progress, sign up for the annual Seattle to Portland Classic. Over 10,000 riders join in this summer tradition (sponsored by the Cascade Bicycle Alliance) for a 200-mile journey by bike to Puddletown (sorry, Portland). While you're there, cruise around America's most bike-friendly city and hope that Seattle can follow in their impressive bikesteps.

## Burke-Gilman Trail

Seattle's been heralding its crown jewel of bike trails, the Burke-Gilman, for nearly 20 years. Starting from Lake Sammamish on the Eastside (with extensions to Issaquah), the trail runs 25 miles around the north of Lake Washington to the University of Washington. But beware! Even the official bike map warns about neglected stretches along the north Seattle section. From the UW, the BGT traces the ship canal and Lake Union through Wallingford and Fremont to the edge of Ballard, where it mysteriously disintegrates into a gravel-strewn truck route.

Many commuters from north Seattle cross the Fremont Bridge onto Dexter, the unofficial bike highway that two miles further, um, ends abruptly at Denny. It's not difficult to cut across to Second Avenue, a one-way south-bound artery with bike lanes, but don't look for such luxury returning north. The city is currently debating how to solve that issue.

## Elliott Bay Trail

This is another nice, yet incomplete, trail. Starting from Golden Gardens, a short trail leads you to the Ballard Locks. After walking across the locks (or paying the $25 fine for riding), you can either follow the truck lane to the left or go straight uphill on the dead-end street to one hell of a suspension bridge. Take the bridge across some railroad tracks before turning onto a proper bike lane on Government Way/Gilman Avenue. The lane turns into a bike trail that cuts right through the rail yard, with some harrowing and extremely narrow sections, before blossoming into the **Elliott Bay Trail**. The trail empties into downtown, where it is sprinkled with tourists under the Alaska Way Viaduct. Ostensibly, this is a designated bike route that leads to the West Seattle Bridge, but the potholes and trucks flooding in from the port make it an unpleasant journey. If you can make it to the West Seattle Bridge, things get much better, quieter, and easier to navigate. Turn north for the **Alki Trail** or south on yet another missing link before reaching the **Duwamish Trail** to South Park. From there, a spotty connection of side roads connects you to W Marginal Way S before smoothing out to the **Green River Trail**, which takes you all the way to Kent.

## Lake Washington Loop

You can also use a combination of the Burke-Gilman to make a less frustrating trip circling Lake Washington. Depart the BGT at Montlake, cross the Montlake Bridge, and wind through the Arboretum (a nice ride, even with all the cars). From there, a route leads to Lake Washington Boulevard, one of Seattle's more pleasant and peaceful rides that continues all the way to Renton. A series of other trails bring you up the east side of the lake. Neither of southeast Seattle's main arteries, Rainier Avenue or Martin Luther King Way, are known for being bike-friendly.

Coming to/from the Eastside, the I-90 Trail makes for an interesting ride along side eight lanes of traffic. Luckily, the trail has its own tunnel and connects to downtown.

Face it. In a city where it's fashionable to commute to work by kayak, Seattle's traffic problems aren't isolated to the Mercer mess; they spill over into the area's multiple salt and fresh waterways. Everyone and their sister owns some sort of boat in Seattle, and many Seattleites have more boats than kids. After all, you need different kinds of boats for salmon fishing, river kayaking, sculling, cruising the San Juans, racing Vic-Maui, or rounding the buoys on a Wednesday night Duck Dodge. Plus, you gotta have a Zodiac or a dinghy to row into shore when your yacht is anchored out in Andrews Bay during Seafair. And of course it takes a little Boston Whaler to buzz over from Portage Bay on a summer night to have a beer and a bowl of steamed clams in a waterfront joint on Lake Union.

In Elliott Bay, Seattle's main harbor, tugboats, barges, container ships, fishing vessels, ferries, sailboats, powerboats, and cruise ships as big as football fields all vie for the same waterway space. Floating homes with deepwater boat moorage on Lake Union are more highly coveted than a landlubber's three-car garage, and if you have room to tie up your float plane, so much the better.

Seattle's boating scene can be as silly as it can be serious—more than one yacht club has a tavern as its clubhouse, but Seattle has produced world class rowers, some of the America Cup's best crews, and Olympic-class kayakers.

Of course, there are rivalries between the "stinkpotters" and vessels powered by sails, oars, or paddles. Hydroplanes? Love 'em or get out of town the first weekend of August, when the gas guzzling, engine whining hydros churn up Lake Washington at Seafair, Seattle's answer to NASCAR, and the lake fills up with log booms of yachts, festooned with bikini clad women and beer guzzling men intent on partying hearty. All of this is in stark contrast to Lake Washington's typical bucolic scene of rowers and scullers practicing for the next regatta. Many local universities, private schools, city parks, non-profit rowing clubs, and kayaking organizations teach water skills and advocate to preserve Seattle's precious waterways for future generations.

Like the human body, Seattle is made up primarily of water. So find your boat of choice and get out there. You'll have lots of company.

| Small Boats Centers | Address | Phone |
|---|---|---|
| The Center for Wooden Boats | 1010 Valley St | 206-382-2628 |
| Green Lake Boat Rental | 7351 E Green Lake Dr N | 206-527-0171 |
| Moss Bay Rowing, Kayaking, and Sailing Center | 1001 Fairview Ave N | 206-682-2031 |
| Waterfront Activities Center | Behind Husky Stadium at the University of Washington | 206-543-9433 |

| Yacht and Cruising Clubs | Address | Phone |
|---|---|---|
| Corinthian Yacht Club - Shilshole | 7755 Seaview Ave NW | 206-789-1919 |
| Corinthian Yacht Club - Leschi | 106 Lakeside Ave | 206-322-7877 |
| Hidden Harbor Yacht Club - Seattle | 319 Nickerson St | 206-284-1047 |
| Meydenbauer Yacht Club - Bellevue | 9927 Meydenbauer Wy SE, Bellevue | 425-454-8880 |
| Puget Sound Yacht Club - Lake Union | 2321 North Northlake Wy | 206-634-3733 |
| Queen City Yacht Club - Portage Bay | 2608 Boyer Ave E | 206-709-2000 |
| Rainier Yacht Club - Lake Washington | 9094 Seward Park Ave S | 206-722-9576 |
| Seattle Yacht Club - Montlake | 1807 E Hamlin St | 206-325-1000 |
| Sloop Tavern Yacht Club - Ballard | 2830 NW Market St | 206-782-3330 |
| Tyee Yacht Club - Lake Union | 3229 Fairview Ave E | 206-324-0200 |
| University of Washington Yacht Club - Campus Boat Club | University of Washington Activities Center | |

| Rowing Clubs and Centers | Address | Phone |
|---|---|---|
| Lake Washington Rowing Club | 910 N Northlake Wy | 206-547-1583 |
| Green Lake Crew | 5900 W Greenlake Wy N | 206-684-4074 |
| Green Lake Small Craft Center | 5900 W Greenlake Wy N | 206-684-4074 |
| Lake Union Crew | 11 E Allison St | 206-860-4199 |
| Mount Baker Rowing and Sailing Center | 3800 Lake Washington Blvd S | 206-386-1913 |
| Pocock Rowing Center | 3320 Fuhrman Ave E | 206-328-7272 |

| Kayaking Clubs and Centers | Address | Phone |
|---|---|---|
| Kayak Academy | 11801 188th Ave SE, Issaquah | 206-527-1825 |
| Mountaineers Club | 300 Third Ave W | 206-284-6310 |
| Northwest Outdoor Center | 2100 Westlake Ave N | 206-281-9694 |
| Seattle Canoe and Kayak Club | 5900 W Greenlake Wy N | 206-684-4074 |
| University of Sea Kayaking | PO Box 12249, Mill Creek | 425-741-0960 |
| Washington Water Trails Association | 4649 Sunnyside Ave N #305 | 206-545-9161 |

Bowling alleys have not quite gone the way of the drive-in theater yet, but sophisticated, urbane Seattle seems to have little use for them. Over the years bowling spots have declined in the heart of the city, leaving downtown-bound hipsters dry, but on Capitol Hill a billiards hall called the **Garage (Map 4)** filled the gap in 2003 by adding fourteen swanky lanes for metrosexual pin pals. By contrast **Imperial Lanes (Map 40)** is old-school bowling at its finest. The popular Underdog Sports League (www.underdogseattle.com) holds their team competitions here while locals hang out at the no-frills bar. Aside from that, Seattle bowlers are forced to seek their sport in outlying townships and unfashionable parts of the city proper.

**ACME Bowling, Billiards, and Events** houses the newest, shiniest lanes in the greater Seattle area, adjacent to the Southcenter Mall in Tukwila and decked out in a sleek faux-retro fashion. This is the bowling alley for people who are afraid to go to bowling alleys. It's an open, well-lit place that serves gourmet pizzas and portobello mushroom sandwiches directly to your lane. Private bowling with cool blue neon lighting and projection screens is available, the perfect spot for bachelorette parties or an ironic evening out with co-workers.

For those after a more traditional bowling experience, South Seattle can satisfy. The **Skyway Park Bowl** tore out their indoor miniature golf course to expand the casino, but retained its warmth and old-school appeal. **Magic Lanes (Map 37)** is open 24 hours a day and looks a little tired, but there's a great bar and TV sets next to the scoring screens. The nearby **Roxbury (Map 37)** advertises "saloon and casino" in the same breath as "family-friendly" and that's about the size of it—expect exuberant children on the lanes and enthusiastic drinkers in the bar.

**West Seattle Bowl (Map 36)** strikes a nice compromise between the sterility of ACME and the earthier tones of the older bowling alleys, with a Chinese restaurant on site, comfy booths on the lanes, and a video bowling game if you really are that lazy. And to the north, **Lynnwood Bowl & Skate** brings pins and wheels together for all-ages action, or check out **Spin Alley** in Shoreline, which opened in 1997 as a smoke-free bowling emporium (a fine sentiment rendered moot by Initiative 901, which banned smoking in public places statewide eight years later). For information on tournaments and other bowling-related news, check out the Greater Seattle Bowling Association (www.seattlebowling.org).

| Bowling | Address | | Phone | Map | Fees |
|---|---|---|---|---|---|
| Garage Billiards & Bowl | 1130 Broadway | Seattle | 206-322-2296 | 4 | $14.00/hr, $3.00/shoes. |
| West Seattle Bowl | 4505 39th Ave SW | Seattle | 206-932-3731 | 36 | $3.67/game, $2.50/shoes. |
| Magic Lanes | 10612 15th SW | Seattle | 206-244-5060 | 37 | $3.50/game, $2.50/shoes. |
| Roxbury | 2823 Roxbury St | Seattle | 206-935-7400 | 37 | $3.95/game, $3.50/shoes. |
| Imperial Lanes | 2101 22nd Ave S | Seattle | 206-325-2525 | 40 | $4/game, $3.25 for shoes. |
| AMF Sun Villa Lanes | 3080 148th SE | Bellevue | 425-455-8155 | 44 | $5.25/game, $4.50/shoes. |
| Lucky Strike Lanes | 700 Bellevue Wy NE | Bellevue | 425-453-5137 | 45 | |
| TechCity Bowl | 13033 NE 70th Pl | Kirkland | 425-827-0785 | 48 | $5.60/game, $3.75/shoes. |
| ACME Bowling | 100 Andover Park W | Tukwila | 206-340-2263 | n/a | $5.50/game. $3 for shoes. |
| Adventure Bowling Center | 3740 Railroad Ave SE | Snoqualmie | 425-888-1377 | n/a | $4.50/game, $2.50/shoes. |
| Brunswick Majestic Lanes | 1222 164th SW | Lynnwood | 425-743-4422 | n/a | $4.39/game, $3.69/shoes. |
| Chalet Bowl | 3806 N 26th St | Tacoma | 253-752-5200 | n/a | $4.00/game, $3.25/shoes. |
| Daffodil Entertainment Center | 1624 E Main | Puyallup | 253-845-9166 | n/a | $4.00/game, $3.00/shoes. |
| Evergreen Lanes | 5111 Claremont Wy | Everett | 425-259-7206 | n/a | $2.35/game, $2.25/shoes. |
| Glacier Lanes | 9630 Evergreen Wy | Everett | 425-353-8292 | n/a | $3.25/game, $2.25/shoes. |
| Hi-Line Lanes | 15733 Ambaum Blvd SW | Burien | 206-244-2272 | n/a | $4.25/game, $3.25/shoes. |
| Kenmore 50 Lanes & Casino | 7638 NE Bothell Wy | Bothell | 425-486-5555 | n/a | $2.50/game, $2.50/shoes. |
| Kent Bowl | 1234 Central N | Kent | 253-852-3550 | n/a | $4.25.game, $3.00/shoes. |
| Lynnwood Bowl and Skate | 6210 200th St SW | Lynnwood | 425-778-3133 | n/a | $4.50/game, $3 for shoes. |
| Pacific Lanes | 7015 S D St | Tacoma | 253-474-0594 | n/a | $2.75/game, $2.50/shoes. |
| Paradise Bowl | 12505 Pacific Ave S | Tacoma | 253-537-6012 | n/a | $3.50/game, $3.00/shoes. |
| Rocket Alley Bar and Grill | 420 N Olympic Ave | Arlington | 360-435-8600 | n/a | $15.00/hr, $1.00/shoes. |
| Secoma Lanes | 34500 Pacific Hwy S | Federal Way | 253-927-0611 | n/a | $3.50/game, $2.50/shoes. |
| Skyway Park Bowl Casino | 11819 Renton Ave S | Seattle | 206-772-1220 | n/a | $3.50/game, $2.99/shoes. |
| Spin Alley Bowling Center | 1430 NW Richmond Beach Rd | Shoreline | 206-533-2345 | n/a | $3.50/game, $2.50/shoes. |
| Strawberry Lanes | 1067 Columbia Ave | Marysville | 360-659-7641 | n/a | $3.25/game, $2.00/shoes. |
| Tower Inn & Lanes | 6323 6th Ave | Tacoma | 253-564-8853 | n/a | $2.50/game, $3.00/shoes. |
| Twin City Lanes | 27120 92nd Ave NW | Stanwood | 360-629-3001 | n/a | $3.00/game, $1.50/shoes. |

| Golf | Address | Phone | Map | Fees | Par, Holes |
|---|---|---|---|---|---|
| Interbay Golf Center | 2501 15th Ave W | 206-285-2200 | 12 | Mon-Fri$13, Sat-Sun $15 | Par-28, 9 holes |
| Green Lake Pitch & Putt | 5701 E Green Lake Wy N | 206-632-2280 | 30 | | |
| Battle Creek Golf Course | 6006 Meridian Ave N | 360-659-7931 | 31 | Mon-Fri $25, Sat-Sun $32 | Par-73, 18 holes |
| Jackson Park Golf Course | 1000 NE 135 St | 206-363-4747 | 34 | Mon-Fri $28, Sat-Sun $33 | Par-71, 18 holes |
| Jefferson Park Golf Course | 4101 Beacon Ave S | 206-762-4513 | 34 | Mon-Fri $28, Sat-Sun $33 | Par-70, 18 holes |
| West Seattle Golf Course | 4470 35th Ave SW | 206-935-5187 | 36 | Mon-Fri $28, Sat-Sun $33 | Par-72, 18 holes |
| Bellevue Municipal Golf Course | 5500 140th Ave NE | 425-452-7250 | 46 | Mon-Thurs $27, Fri-Sun $31 | Par-71,18 holes |
| Foster Golf Links | 13500 Interurban Ave S | 206-242-4221 | n/a | Mon-Fri $21, Sat-Sun $23 | Par-69, 18 holes |

## Tennis

| Tennis | Address | Phone | Map | |
|---|---|---|---|---|
| Bobby Morris PF | 1635 11th Ave | 206-684-4062 | 4 | 2 courts, Lighted |
| Garfield PF | 23rd Ave & E Cherry St | 206-684-4062 | 5 | 3 courts, Lighted |
| Madrona Playfield | 34th Ave E & E Spring St | 206-684-4062 | 6 | 2 courts, Lighted |
| I-90 Lid/Sam Smith | 1400 Martin Luther King Jr Wy S | 206-684-4062 | 10 | 2 courts |
| Leschi Park | 201 Lakeside Ave S | 206-684-4062 | 10 | 1 court |
| Discovery Park | 3801 W Government Wy | 206-684-4062 | 11 | 2 courts |
| Magnolia Park | 1461 Magnolia Blvd W | 206-684-4062 | 11 | 2 courts |
| Magnolia PF | 2518 34th Ave W | 206-684-4062 | 11 | 4 courts |
| David Rodgers Park | 2800 1st Ave W | 206-684-4062 | 13 | 3 courts, Backboard |
| Kinnear Park | 899 W Olympic Pl | 206-684-4062 | 14 | 1 court |
| Miller PF | 400 19th Ave E | 206-684-4062 | 18 | 2 courts, Lighted |
| Volunteer Park | 1247 15th Ave E | 206-684-4075 | 18 | 4 court, Lighted, Backboard |
| Rogers PG | Eastlake Ave E & E Roanoke St | 206-684-4062 | 20 | 3 courts |
| Madison Park | 2300 43rd Ave E | 206-684-4062 | 22 | 2 courts, Lighted |
| Gilman PG | 923 NW 54th St | 206-684-4062 | 24 | 2 courts |
| Woodland Park (Lower) | 5851 West Green Lake Wy N | 206-684-4062 | 24 | 10 courts |
| Woodland Park (Upper) | Midvale Ave N & N 50th St | 206-684-4062 | 24 | 4 courts |
| Wallingford PF | 4219 Wallingford Ave N | 206-684-4062 | 25 | 2 courts |
| University PG | 9th Ave NE & NE 50th St | 206-684-4062 | 26 | 2 courts, Backboard |
| Bryant PG | 4103 NE 65th St | 206-684-4062 | 27 | 2 courts |
| Laurelhurst PF | 4544 NE 41st St | 206-684-4062 | 27 | 4 courts, Lighted, Backboard |
| Magnuson Park | 6500 Sand Point Wy NE | 206-684-4062 | 27 | 6 courts |
| Froula PG | 7200 12th Ave NE | 206-684-4062 | 31 | 2 courts |
| Green Lake Park | 7201 E Green Lake Dr N | 206-684-4062 | 31 | 5 courts |
| Cowen Park | 5849 15th Ave NE | 206-684-4062 | 32 | 3 courts |
| Ravenna Park | 5520 Ravenna Ave NE | 206-684-4062 | 32 | 2 courts, Backboard |
| Ravenna-Eckstein | 6535 Ravenna Ave NE | 206-684-4062 | 32 | 1 court |
| Bitter Lake PF | 13030 N Park Ave N | 206-684-4062 | 33 | 4 courts, Lighted |
| Soundview PF | 1590 NW 90th St | 206-684-4062 | 33 | 2 courts |
| Meadowbrook PF | 10533 35th Ave NE | 206-684-4062 | 34 | 6 courts, Lighted |
| Victory Heights PG | 1737 NE 106th St | 206-684-4062 | 34 | 1 court |
| Alki PG | 5817 SW Lander St | 206-684-4062 | 35 | 1 court, Lighted |
| Hiawatha PF | 2700 California Ave SW | 206-684-4062 | 35 | 3 courts, Lighted, Backboard |
| Delridge PF | 4458 Delridge Wy SW | 206-684-4062 | 36 | 2 courts |
| Jefferson Park | 4165 16th Ave SW | 206-684-4062 | 36 | 2 courts, Lighted |
| High Point PF | 6920 34th Ave SW | 206-684-4062 | 37 | 2 courts |
| Lowman Beach Park | 7017 Beach Dr SW | 206-684-4062 | 37 | 1 court |
| Solstice Park | 8603 Fauntleroy Wy SW | 206-684-4062 | 37 | 6 courts, Lighted, Backboard |
| Highland Park PG | 1100 SW Cloverdale St | 206-684-4062 | 38 | 1 court |
| Riverview PF | 7226 12th Ave SW | 206-684-4062 | 38 | 2 courts |
| South Park PG | 738 S Sullivan St | 206-684-4062 | 38 | 2 courts |
| Beacon Hill PG | 1902 13th Ave S | 206-684-4062 | 39 | 2 courts, Backboard |
| Cleveland High | 5511 15th Ave S | 206-684-4062 | 39 | 2 courts |
| Georgetown PF | 750 S Homer St | 206-684-4062 | 39 | 1 court |
| Amy Yee Tennis Center | 2000 Martin Luther King Jr Wy S | 206-684-4764 | 40 | 4 courts |
| Beer Shiva Park | 55th Ave S | 206-684-4062 | 40 | 1 court |
| Brighton PF | 6000 39th Ave S | 206-684-4062 | 40 | 2 courts |
| Dearborn Park | 2919 S Brandon St | 206-684-4062 | 40 | 2 courts |
| Mount Baker Park | 2521 Lake Park Dr S | 206-684-4062 | 40 | 2 courts, Lighted |
| Rainier PF | 3700 S Alaska St | 206-684-4062 | 40 | 4 courts, Lighted |
| Seward Park | 5902 Lake Washington Blvd S | 206-684-4062 | 40 | 1 court |
| Hutchinson PG | S Norfolk St & 59th Ave S | 206-684-4062 | 41 | 2 courts |
| Rainier Beach PF | 8802 Rainier Ave S | 206-684-4062 | 41 | 4 courts, Lighted |
| Homestead Park | 82nd Ave SE & SE 40th St | 206-236-3545 | 42 | 4 courts |
| Luther Burbank Park | 2040 84th Ave SE | 206-236-3545 | 42 | 3 courts |
| Park on the Lid | I-90 & W Mercer Wy | 206-236-3545 | 42 | 4 courts |
| Robinswood Tennis Center | 2400 151st Pl SE | 425-452-7690 | 44 | 6 indoor, 2 outdoor |
| Everest Park | 500 8th Ave S | 425-587-3347 | 48 | 1 outdoor |
| Heritage Park | 111 Waverly Wy | 425-587-3342 | 48 | 2 outdoor |
| Juanita Beach Park | 9703 NE Juanita Dr | 425-587-3340 | 48 | 2 outdoor |
| Peter Kirk Park | 202 3rd St | 425-587-3342 | 48 | 2 outdoor |
| Grass Lawn Park | 7031 148th Ave NE | 425-556-2311 | 49 | 2 outdoor |

# Sports • Hiking

## Overview

The Northwest is famous for its mountainous terrain, so finding a trail to hike in these parts is not difficult. But if you don't have a car, or don't feel like venturing outside of King Country, there are plenty of urban hikes to keep your Nalgene bottle dust-free.

The Burke-Gilman is the most popular urban trail. Parks like Carkeek, Lincoln, and Magnuson have trails along the waterfront as well as beautiful vistas that will make you forget you're a stone's throw from civilization. If it's communing with nature you're after, visit the Arboretum or the Schmitz Park Reserve. If you crave a real endorphin-kicker, you still need only drive a few minutes east to the switchbacks of Tiger Mountain. Since none of the parks are very expansive, it's difficult to lose your way. But if you're the type to get lost in your own museum, never fear. All of these parks have kiosks with trail maps.

If most of your friends consider lifting pint glasses exercise, you can meet other hiking enthusiasts by means of the Seattle Mountaineers (www.mountaineers.org). They offer regularly scheduled hikes as well as other outdoor activities.

## Carkeek Park

*950 NW Carkeek Park Rd • 6 miles • Easy • Map 29-30*
Carkeek is most famous for the salmon preserve in Pipers Creek. In the late fall, you can follow the Piper's Creek trail to catch a glimpse of the fish-filled waters. Year-round, North Bluff Trail provides fantastic views of the Olympic Mountains and Puget Sound. The Wetland Trail leads you down to the beach.

## Mt. Si

*North Bend • 4 miles • Moderate-Difficult*
Another great day hike just a short drive out of the city, Mt. Si, rewards your workout with amazing views of the Snoqualmie Valley and Puget Sound. Everyone in Seattle seems to know about this hike, which is reflected in the lack of parking spaces on a sunny Saturday. The trail gains 3,100 feet over the four miles and will really get the heart rate up. If you get a late start and are looking for a shorter walk, you'll come to the first vista about one mile in. This also serves as a good place to turn around.

## Burke-Gilman Trail

*60th Place NE and Bothell Wy to 8th NW • 14 miles • Easy-Moderate • Map 23-27, 34*
This multi-purpose trail covers over 14 miles from 11th Ave NW to Tracy Owen Station in Kenmore. It allows bikers and joggers as well as hikers, so it can sometimes be a bit too crowded for a contemplative, woodsy walk. But it is the longest urban trail around, so no matter what neighborhood you live in, there is most likely an access point near you. Among the many entrances to the trail are Ballard, Fremont, Sand Point, and Matthews Beach Park. The trail also runs through the University of Washington campus. They are constantly renovating it and adding new trail segments. For a complete map of the trail please visit www.seattle.gov.

## Lincoln Park

*8011 Fauntleroy Wy SW • 5 miles • Easy-Moderate • Map 37*
If you're after a mostly water vista for your hike, Lincoln Park is the place for you. The 100-foot high Bluff Loop trail provides a stunning view of Puget Sound. The South Beach trail borders Fauntleroy Cove. Those trails are fantastic in the warm weather, but the wind can make them unpleasant during the off-season. The North Beach Trail is slightly more shielded by trees, so it is ideal for a hike on those blustery winter days. In the summer, you can conclude your hike by taking a dip in the heated saltwater Colman Pool.

## Schmitz Park Preserve

*5551 SW Admiral Wy • 2 miles • Easy • Map 35*
One of the few urban areas to boast old growth forest, the Schmitz Park Preserve (www.seattle.gov/parks/park_detail.asp?ID=465) is a great place to stroll in quiet contemplation amidst the majesty of nature. Despite its diminutive size (a mere 53 acres), it isn't difficult to feel secluded as you stroll along the often-empty figure 8 trail that curves through the area. Be on the lookout for foxes, bats, and coyotes.

## Seward Park

*5900 Lake Washington Blvd • 3 miles • Easy • Map 40*
Like Schmitz Park, Seward Park possesses the splendor of old growth forest: 250 acres of impressively ancient Douglas Firs and Western Red Cedars. The perimeter path, popular with joggers and bikers, runs along the beach and presents views of the Seattle skyline, Lake Washington, Mercer Island, and Mount Rainier. The interior path, which breaks off into several shorter trails, runs through the thick of the forest. Despite being surrounded by urban sprawl, the area is often dead quiet, particularly in the winter.

## Discovery Park

*3801 W Government Wy • 7 Miles • Easy-Moderate • Map 11*
The city's largest public park was built on an old Army base. This urban oasis is a veritable checklist of habitats including forest, meadow, saltwater beach, and sand dunes. Aptly named, Discovery Park is a versatile dominion in which you can take a quick 30-minute jaunt or play "Blair Witch" and get lost in the wilderness. The grounds are rife with fruit during blackberry season, providing a delectable mid-hike snack. The main trail is the 3-mile Loop Trail, which meanders through many of the aforementioned habitats and past the abandoned army barracks. Several steep trails will take you down to the beach and to the West Point lighthouse, which was built in 1881. Off of West Point, you can sometimes spot sea lions, seals, orcas, or porpoises. While the water is never quite warm enough to swim in, people often sunbathe on the beaches during those scorching 75-degree summer days. Some of the less-modest park visitors have deemed the beach clothing-optional. The South Bluff Trail will lead you to spectacular views of Mount Rainier and the city skyline. For a short but interesting jaunt, the half-mile Wolf Tree nature trail brings you through the dwellings of coyotes, river otters, muskrats, and bobcats. Additionally, 253 species of birds dwell within the park.

## Washington Park Arboretum

*2300 Arboretum Dr E • 4 miles • Easy • Map 22*
Stroll through the 250 acres of one of the Northwest's largest collections of plants and trees, numbering upwards of 5,500 species. The Arboretum Waterfront Trail starts at the parking lot and leads to Marsh and Foster Islands. In the warm seasons, this trail is ideal for bird watching. From Foster Island, you can hike to the north tip and enjoy a stunning view across Union Bay. Azalea Way is an easy-going ¾-mile walk through the—you guessed it—azaleas. To get there from downtown Seattle, drive east on Madison Street to Lake Washington Boulevard and turn left into the Arboretum.

## Sand Point Magnuson Park

*7400 Sandpoint Wy NE • 4 miles • Easy • Map 27*
Magnuson Park is a 350-acre area located in the middle of a former Navy facility. Parts of it are paved and crowded, but you can also find secluded grass and wetland habitats to wander through. The trailhead to the Cross-Park Trail, located next to the playground, will take you through the grasslands. Promontory Point meanders through a restored wildlife habitat. You can find that trail at the south end of the park.

## Tiger Mountain

*Issaquah • Moderate*
If the above-mentioned urban hikes aren't extreme enough for your lifestyle, but you still don't want to travel far from the city, Tiger Mountain affords the perfect temporary wilderness retreat. It's also a good alternative for hardcore hikers who can't get their cars over the snowy passes in the wintertime. The West Tiger 3 provides a 2,000-foot elevation stretched over five miles. Its switchback-heavy path will definitely make you feel worthy of your fleece. For a less-strenuous wander through the woods, try the Around The Lake Tradition Trail. The Tradition Plateau and Bus Trail are moderate hikes. Look for the skeleton of an abandoned Greyhound bus that gives the latter trail its name. To get there, take exit 20 off I-90 East and follow the signs.

## General Information

NFT Map:     26
Address:     University of Washington, 315 Hec Edmundson Pavilion, Seattle, WA 98195
Tickets:     206-543-2200
Website:     www.gohuskies.com

## Overview

Husky Stadium, home to the University of Washington Huskies, is recognized as one of the nation's most scenic football stadiums. From the upper deck on the stadium's north side, fans have views of downtown Seattle, the Olympic Mountains, and Mt. Rainier (when it's clear, that is). Built in 1920, the stadium seats 72,500 fans—more than 70 percent between the end zones—and ranks among the nation's loudest venues. Game days have turned into ten-hour events, thanks to the pre- and post-game tailgating, which takes place in automobiles, RVs, and boats that dock in special moorings. 1991 saw the peak of Husky football glory with its second National Championship (the other was way back in 1960). In 2001 the Huskies won the Rose Bowl, and things were looking good for the future. Tickets were almost impossible to come by, and Husky pride was near an all time high. But in the coming years, former head coach Rick Neuheisel became embroiled in a seemingly harmless NCAA betting scandal that took down the athletic director and signaled a downward spiral in the team's fortunes. Despite a few coaching changes, the Huskies have been floundering near the bottom of the Pac-10 ever since. A word of advice: Unless you are on foot, bike or Segway, get a copy of the Husky schedule and avoid the U-District at all costs during game times lest it quadruple your travel time.

## How to Get Tickets

Individual game tickets can be purchased from the Huskies' website, by calling 206-543-2200, or in person at the ticket office (3910 Montlake Blvd, Graves Building 101). The office is open Monday through Friday from 8:30 am–5 pm.

## How to Get There—Driving

From I-5 north or south, take the Highway 520 exit toward Bellevue-Kirkland, then exit on Montlake Boulevard. Turn left and cross the bridge. Husky Stadium is on the right. From Highway 405 north or south, take Highway 520 exit toward Seattle and cross the Evergreen Point Floating Bridge heading west. Exit on Montlake Boulevard. Turn left and cross the bridge. Husky Stadium is on the right.

## Parking

Parking in adjoining neighborhoods is prohibited. Public parking lots on the east side of the UW campus generally fill 30–60 minutes before kick-off. Parking is on a first-come, first-served basis.

## How to Get There—By Bus

The UW offers all ticket holders free bus rides to and from games when they present their game ticket to the driver. Seattle Metro buses offer dozens of routes from throughout the Puget Sound region.

## General Information

NFT Map:         15
Address:         305 Harrison St, Seattle, WA 98109
Tickets:         206-283-DUNK
Seattle Storm
 website:        www.wnba.com/storm
Arena Website:   www.keyarena.com

## Overview

Since Clay Bennett stole away the Sonics to Oklahoma in 2007, the 17,000-seat stadium has been taken over by the ladies. The two-time world champion Seattle Storm of the WNBA and the bad-ass babes of the Rat City Rollergirls both call Key Arena home. It also hosts circuses, ice skating exhibitions, professional wrestling, NCAA basketball and any musical acts who don't have the fan base for the much large CenturyLink Events Center. Located in Seattle Center under the Space Needle, the arena opened in 1962 and has served as the host of Seattle's professional sports championships—the 1979 Sonics and the 2004 and 2010 Storm. In 1995 the arena received a $75-million renovation, leaving the exterior as is, but dropping the playing court 22 feet underground to provide 3,000 additional seats. A 15-year naming rights deal with a bank has provided TV announcers endless pun opportunities such as "the Key to tonight's game" and "the defense is really Keyed in right now." The Rat City Roller Girls roller derby season runs February to October. Throw on your Sockit Wenches or Grave Danger team jersey and get ready for some hair pulling and spectacular wipeouts. Ah, but we do miss our SuperSonics. Perhaps they'll return one day. A city can dream.

## How to Get Tickets

If you want to save on service charge fees, you can buy individual tickets in person at the Key Arena box office (Mon-Sat, 10 am–6 pm) located near the team shop at West Plaza off 1st Ave. You can also get tickets by calling 1-800-745-3000 or by buying them online via Ticketmaster.com. If you're feeling brave, scalpers are known to wander the grounds of Seattle Center looking to unload tickets before a game. For the Rat City Roller Girl bouts you can also purchase tickets via www.ratcityrollergirls.com.

## How to Get There—Driving

From the north or south on I-5, take the Mercer Street exit and follow the signs to Seattle Center. Key Arena is on the northwest corner of the Seattle Center grounds, with street access along First Avenue North and cross streets Thomas and Republican.

## Parking

Public lot, meter, and street parking are available along First Avenue and Fifth Avenue North, Mercer Street, and throughout the lower Queen Anne neighborhood.

## How to Get There—By Ferry

Boats arrive hourly at Colman Dock on the waterfront. Key Arena is about 1-1/2 miles north of the ferry terminal, best reached by Seattle Metro busses.

## How to Get There—By Bus

Seattle Metro buses offer dozens of routes from throughout the Puget Sound region. For routes and schedules, visit metro.kingcounty.gov.

## How to Get There—By Monorail

Even if the 'ol heap of tourist metal is actually running, it's still not worth the $4 roundtrip ticket price.

## General Information

| | |
|---|---|
| NFT Map: | 7 |
| Address: | 800 Occidental Ave. S |
| | Seattle, WA 98134 |
| Mariners Office Phone: | 206-346-4000 |
| Tickets: | 888-635-4295 |
| Football Website: | www.seahawks.com |
| Soccer Website: | www.soundersfc.com |
| Stadium Website: | www.centurylinkfield.com |

## Overview

After years of sweating inside the dark and dingy (but beloved) Kingdome, the Seattle Seahawks finally moved to a place where they could play football as it was meant to be played: outside in the elements. At the start of the 2002 season, Seattle's favorite underdogs abandoned the Kingdome for the newfangled Seahawks Stadium, as it was then called. Thanks to corporate interest, the stadium was soon re-named, Qwest Field. In 2011, CenturyLink bought Qwest and changed the stadium's name again. Suddenly, we were asked to start calling it, "CenturyLink Field". Not ones to fall in line easily, Seattleites immediately dubbed it "the CLink". And that's how it shall be known until the next corporate merger.

With more than 67,000 seats and a sloping roof design that covers 70 percent of the seating area, the CLink is both comfortable and loud. Fans enjoy wide seats that, in the front rows, are only 40-50 feet from the playing field. If you're up for it, grab a metal bleacher seat in the Hawk's Nest on the north side of the field and bond with the die-hards.

This joyful atmosphere has provided the Seahawks with one of the NFL's top home field advantages, one that helped lead the team, to its first (but so far, only) Super Bowl in 2006.

The CLink also hosts the other kind of football, Seattle's well-adored MLS soccer team, the Sounders. But good luck getting a ticket. They sold 22,000 season tickets the first year. Attendance continues to soar, with nearly every game selling out. Did I mention they were popular? Apparently, Footie is the perfect sport for cloud-covered cities. It helps that these guys aren't half bad. We're not sore losers in Seattle, but it's also nice to win sometimes.

## How to Get Tickets

Tickets sell out fast, so buy them early from the Seahawks website, by calling 888-635-4295, or in person at the CenturyLink box office when they go on sale. Tickets are required for children ages 2 and up. For Sounders games, get tickets thru Ticketmaster or at the stadium box office (weeks in advance if you actually want to get in).

## How to Get There

From the north and south, exit I-5 at James Street, Fourth Avenue or Airport Way. From the east, exit I-90 where it ends at Fourth Avenue and turn right. Then turn right at Royal Brougham Way.

## Parking

For Sunday afternoon games, street parking can be had for free if you get there at least three hours early to snag a space. It can be found in Pioneer Square, SoDo, and the International District. Three parking lots near the stadium open three hours prior to game time, however many of these spaces are sold in advance so be aware of limited status. Private lots are available on First and Fourth Avenues surrounding the stadium.

## How to Get There—By Ferry

Boats arrive hourly at Colman Dock on the waterfront, just a 10-minute walk from the stadium. Walk east on Occidental Avenue and turn right.

## How to Get There—By Bus

Most Seattle Metro buses swing through downtown close to the stadium.

## How to Get There—By Light Rail

Sound Transit runs special trains on Sundays from Tacoma and Everett when the Seahawks are playing. Check the website for details (www.soundtransit.org).

## General Information

NFT Map: 7
Address: 1250 First Ave S,
Seattle, WA 98134
Mariners Office Phone: 206-346-4000
Tickets: 206-622-HITS
Website: seattle.mariners.mlb.com

## Overview

Mariners fans like to revel in the glory days of 1995, when the team played in the Kingdome and almost (yeah, almost) made it to the World Series. But baseball purists point to the opening of Safeco Field on July 16, 1999, as the real crowning achievement for the Mariners. Finally, Seattle fans had a real ballpark with real grass, real sky, and real natural light. Since then, Safeco Field has become the city's summer cathedral, a gathering place for families, friends, couples, and singles to watch baseball, nosh on fancy baseball fare, and socialize in the ballpark's many congregation areas—all of which offer unobstructed views of the field. And in case the rain clouds come rushing in, a mechanical roof can cover the ballpark in just 12 minutes to keep the faithful dry. More than 3 million people jammed into Safeco annually during the early 2000s, especially during the Mariners' record-setting 116-win season in 2001. But thanks to the traitor trifecta (Ken Griffey, Randy Johnson, and Alex Rodriguez) and clueless ownership, a million or so have been whittled from that attendance figure. The M's were smart enough to sign Ichiro Suzuki in 2001 and fans flocked to right field to watch him work his magic until 2012 when he was taken away by those damn Yankees. But if you're a true baseball fan, you will never stop appreciating Ichiro's game. The crowd is one of the most polite in baseball (except when Pay-Rod is in town) which makes for a fun-for-the-whole-family type of environment. If you like your games a little rowdier, head for the beer garden in center field. They have a bunch of micro brews on tap to ensure an eventful and entertaining evening, even if the Mariners' bullpen gives up the lead in the eighth inning again. Accompany your overpriced beer (last call is at the first pitch of 8th inning) with a basket of their inexplicably delicious nachos. Damn, those things are tasty.

## How to Get Tickets

Individual game tickets can be purchased from the Mariners' website by calling 206-822-HITS, or in person at Mariners Team Stores at Safeco Field and downtown Seattle. You can also buy tickets at the Safeco Field Box Office, open on non-game days from 10 a.m.–6 p.m. and on game days from 10 a.m. until the end of the game. You can also try your luck with a variety of scalpers that troll Occidental Avenue before the games. Bargains can be had, but beware of scams. Tickets are required for children older than two.

## How to Get There—Driving

Seattle is notorious for its freeway traffic, so travel with care and patience on the way to weeknight games. From the south, exit I-5 at Spokane Street and turn right on First Avenue. From the north, exit I-5 at James Street, and turn left on First Avenue. From the east, exit I-90 where it ends at Fourth Avenue and turn right. Then turn right at Royal Brougham Way.

## Parking

Street parking can be found in Pioneer Square, SoDo, and the International District. The Mariners operate a parking garage across Edgar Martinez Way. In addition, dozens of parking lots within ten blocks of Safeco Field provide game day parking for anywhere from $10 to $40, depending on convenience and location.

## How to Get There—By Ferry

Ferryboats arrive hourly at Colman Dock on the waterfront, just a 10-15 minute walk from the ballpark. Walk two blocks east to First Avenue and turn right.

## How to Get There—By Bus

Any bus that goes downtown will get you close, since Safeco is only a 10-minute walk from downtown. Seattle Metro buses 15 and 18 stop closest to Safeco Field but can get packed on game days.

## General Information

Directions and hours for beaches, pools, and parks: www.seattle.gov

## Overview

Since there are only 1-2 months out of the year when the water in Seattle becomes warm enough to swim in without the threat of hypothermia, there are not a great deal of favorable options for swimming. Even when it's been hot for a while, the water rarely heats up enough to entice most people, particularly in the open water areas. Still, on any given sunny day, many Seattleites adorn their ashen bodies with bathing suits and take to the beaches and pools. Options may be slightly deficient, but they are numerous nonetheless.

## Beaches

The water in Lake Washington remains frigid year round, but that can feel pretty good on those rare stiflingly hot summer days. Of course, everyone in town has the same idea, so most of the beaches get crowded fast. **Magnuson Park (Map 27)** and **Madison Park (Map 22)** are by far the most popular, followed by **Madrona (Map 6)** and **Mount Baker (Map 40) Parks**. They are more for waders and sunbathers. **Matthews Beach Park (Map 34)**, **Seward Park (Map 40),** and **Prichard Island Beach (Map 41)** tend to be less crowded and a bit more pleasant overall. All of the beach parks have rafts, diving boards, picnic areas, and lifeguards on duty. If you are looking for open water swimming, you can find it off the beaten path at Matthews and Seward. Matthews Beach is a welcome end to a hike along the Burke-Gilman Trail.

**Golden Gardens (Map 33),** which overlooks the Puget Sound, is by far the most beautiful swimming location. Unfortunately, the water is almost always unbearably cold, but the nice sandy beach is good for sunbathing, strolling, and BBQs.

The water in Green Lake is notoriously filthy (swimmer's itch, anyone?), but that doesn't appear to deter people on a hot day. There are two beaches on Green Lake, **East Beach (Map 31)** and **West Beach (Map 30)**. They both have rafts, diving boards, and lifeguards.

## Pools

If you want to swim in clean water that isn't just warmed by the urine of children, Coleman and Mounger pools are another option. They both heat their water to 85 degrees. **Coleman (Map 37)** is an Olympic-sized pool which overlooks the beach and is filled with saltwater. It also boasts a giant tube slide. **Mounger (Map 11)** has a large pool with a corkscrew slide and a smaller pool for wading and children's swimming lessons. Both of these outdoor pools are only open during the summer.

If you are dying for a dip in the off-season, you can always pay a visit to one of Seattle's warm-water indoor pools which offer lap swimming and water aerobics. There are nominal admission fees.

## Wading Pools & Water Features

If you just want to cool off your feet, there are numerous shallow wading pools in parks and playfields around the city. They are, of course, usually crawling with children. Wading pools are drained in the off-season.

For that invigorating, running-through-the-sprinklers sensation, check out the water features at **Judkins Park (Map 9)** and **Pratt Park (Map 9)**. **The International Fountain (Map 15)** (the giant, water-spewing ball) in Seattle Center is usually full of tourists, but if you find yourself sweltering at the Bite, Folklife, or Bumbershoot, it can be welcome refreshment. It's also great fun to play in the volcano fountain at **Cal Anderson Park (Map 3)**.

## Beaches

| Beaches | Address | Phone | Map |
|---|---|---|---|
| Madrona Park Beach | 853 Lake Washington Blvd | 206-684-4075 | 6 |
| Madison Park Beach | E Madison St & E Howe St | 206-684-4075 | 22 |
| Warren G Magnuson Park Beach | 7400 Sand Point Wy NE | 206-684-4075 | 27 |
| Green Lake Park West Beach | 7312 West Green Lake Dr N | 206-684-4075 | 30 |
| Green Lake Park East Beach | 7201 East Green Lake Dr N | 206-684-4075 | 31 |
| Golden Gardens | 8498 Seaview Pl NW | 206-684-4075 | 33 |
| Matthews Beach Park | 49th Ave NE & NE 93rd St | 206-684-4075 | 34 |
| Mount Baker Park Beach | 2521 Lake Park Dr S | 206-684-4075 | 40 |
| Seward Park Beach | 5898 Lake Washington Blvd S | 206-684-4075 | 40 |
| Prichard Island Beach | 8400 55th Ave S | 206-684-4075 | 41 |
| Calkins Landing | SE 28th St & 60th Ave SE | 206-236-3545 | 42 |
| Clarke Beach | 7700 E Mercer Wy | 206-236-3546 | 42 |
| Groveland Beach | 80th Ave SE & SE 58th St | 206-236-3547 | 42 |
| Luther Burbank Park | 2040 84th Ave SE | 206-236-3548 | 42 |
| Enatai Beach Park | 3519 108th Ave SE | 425-452-6914 | 43 |
| Newcastle Beach Park | 4400 Lake Washington Blvd SE | 425-452-6914 | 43 |
| Chesterfield Beach Park | 2501 100th Ave SE | 425-452-4445 | 45 |
| Chism Beach Park | 1175 96th Ave SE | 425-452-6914 | 45 |
| Clyde Beach Park | 2 92nd Ave NE | 425-452-6914 | 45 |
| Medina Beach Park | 501 Evergreen Pt Rd | 425-233-6400 | 45 |
| Meydenbauer Beach Park | 419 98th Ave NE | 425-452-6914 | 45 |

## Pools

| Pools | Address | Phone | Map | | Fees |
|---|---|---|---|---|---|
| Medgar Evers Pool | 500 23rd Ave | 206-684-4766 | 5 | Indoor | Ages 1–17 & over 64: $2.75, 18–64: $3.75 |
| Mounger Pool | 2535 32nd Ave W | 206-684-4708 | 11 | Outdoor | Ages 1–17 & over 64: $2.75, 18–64: $3.75 |
| Queen Anne Pool | 1920 1st Ave W | 206-386-4282 | 13 | Indoor | Ages 1–17 & over 64: $2.75, 18–64: $3.75 |
| Ballard Pool | 1471 NW 67th St | 206-684-4094 | 29 | Indoor | Ages 1–17 & over 64: $2.75, 18–64: $3.75 |
| Evans Pool | 7201 E Green Lake Dr N | 206-684-4961 | 31 | Indoor | Ages 1–17 & over 64: $2.75, 18–64: $3.75 |
| Madison Pool | 13401 Meridian Ave N | 206-684-4979 | 33 | Indoor | Ages 1–17 & over 64: $2.75, 18–64: $3.75 |
| Meadowbrook Pool | 10515 35th Ave NE | 206-684-4989 | 34 | Indoor | Ages 1–17 & over 64: $2.75, 18–64: $3.75 |
| Coleman Pool | 8603 Fauntleroy Wy SW | 206-684-7494 | 37 | Outdoor | Ages 1–17 & over 64: $2.75, 18–64: $3.75 |
| Southwest Pool | 2801 SW Thistle St | 206-684-7440 | 37 | Indoor | Ages 1–17 & over 64: $2.75, 18–64: $3.75 |
| Rainier Beach Pool | 8825 Rainier Ave S | 206-386-1944 | 41 | Indoor | Ages 1–17 & over 64: $2.75, 18–64: $3.75 |
| Bellevue Aquatic Center | 601 143rd Ave NE | 425-452-4444 | 46 | Indoor | Adults: $4.75, under 12: $3.75 |
| Redmond Pool | 17535 NE 104 St | 425-233-3031 | 49 | Indoor | $3.50, Seniors $3.25 |

## Wading and Sprinklers

| Wading and Sprinklers | Address | Phone | Map | Type |
|---|---|---|---|---|
| Cal Anderson Park | 1635 1st Ave | 206-684-7796 | 3 | Wading |
| Judkins Park | 2150 S Norman St | 206-684-7796 | 9 | Wading, Sprinkler |
| Pratt Park | 1800 S Mainv St | 206-684-7796 | 9 | Sprinkler |
| Peppi's Playground | 3233 E Spruce St | 206-684-7796 | 10 | Wading |
| Powell Barnett Park | 352 Martin Luther King Jr Wy | 206-684-7796 | 10 | Wading |
| E Queen Anne Playfield | 160 Howe St | 206-684-7796 | 13 | Wading |
| International Fountain | 305 Harrison St | 206-684-7200 | 15 | Sprinkler |
| Miller Playfield | 330 19th Ave E | 206-684-7796 | 18 | Wading |
| Volunteer Park | 1247 15th Ave E | 206-684-7796 | 18 | Wading |
| Ballard Commons Park | 5701 22nd Ave NW | 206-684-7796 | 23 | Sprinkler |
| Gilman Playground | 923 NW 54th St | 206-684-7796 | 23 | Wading |
| Wallingford Playfield | 4219 Wallingford Ave N | 206-684-7796 | 25 | Wading |
| View Ridge Playfield | 4408 NE 70th St | 206-684-7796 | 27 | Wading |
| Warren G Magnuson Park | 7400 Sand Pointt Wy NE | 206-684-7796 | 27 | Wading |
| Green Lake Park | N 73rd St & W Green Lake Dr N | 206-684-7796 | 31 | Wading |
| Dahl Playfield | 7700 25th Ave NE | 206-684-7796 | 32 | Wading |
| Ravenna Park | 5520 Ravenna Ave NE | 206-684-7796 | 32 | Wading |
| Bitter Lake | 13035 Linden Ave N | 206-684-7796 | 33 | Wading |
| Sandel Playground | 9053 1st Ave NW | 206-684-7796 | 33 | Wading |
| Soundview Playfield | 1590 NW 90 St | 206-684-7796 | 33 | Wading |
| Northacres Park | 12800 1st Ave NE | 206-684-7796 | 34 | Wading |
| Hiawatha Playfield | 2700 California Ave SW | 206-684-7796 | 35 | Wading |
| Delridge Playfield | 4501 Delridge Wy SW | 206-684-7796 | 36 | Wading |
| EC Hughes Playground | 2805 SW Holden St | 206-684-7796 | 37 | Wading |
| Lincoln Park | 8011 Fauntleroy Wy SW | 206-684-7796 | 37 | Wading |
| Highland Park Playfield | 1100 SW Cloverdale St | 206-684-7796 | 38 | Wading |
| South Park Playground | 8319 8th Ave S | 206-684-7796 | 38 | Wading |
| Beacon Hill Playfield | 1820 13th Ave S | 206-684-7796 | 39 | Wading |
| Georgetown Playfield | 750 S Homer St | 206-684-7796 | 39 | Wading |
| Van Asselt Playground | 2820 S Myrtle St | 206-684-7796 | 41 | Wading |

## Information

| | |
|---|---|
| Am... ...ervations: | 1-800-USA-RAIL (872-7245) |
| Amtrak Website: | www.amtrak.com |
| King Street Station Address: | 303 S Jackson St 98104 |
| King Street Station Phone: | 206-382-4125 |
| Hours: | 6 am–10:30 pm daily |

## Overview

Some travelers hate to fly. Others just hate the airlines. And don't even mention Greyhound. When the fear and anger become too profound, there's always Amtrak. Amtrak is hardly a perfect substitute—because of geographic and commercial concerns, train routes can't match the flexibility of flying, and the bureaucracy can get just as snarled and inefficient as any airline. However, there's a sweet Zen to the experience of sitting still for hours as the train chugs towards its destination, with nothing to do but read or stare out the windows as America flies by.

Located in Pioneer Square on the cusp of the International District, King Street Station services Seattle Amtrak traffic. It's a handsome rust brick building complete with a clock tower; it was the city's tallest structure when erected in 1906. Clueless mid-century renovations dulled the station's luster, and travelers dwindled over the years, leading to a certain defeated quality in the air as one waits for a train. While a renovation project is finally underway to restore King Street Station's original stateliness, progress has been sluggish, so don't get there too early.

## Fares

Amtrak prices tend to fluctuate wildly, so like airlines, it's best to book your trip early. Bargain hunters with sufficient lead time can find promotional discounts. Last minute types may find themselves paying near airline prices for a trip that takes ten times as long. Student and senior discounts are available, so consider lying about your age. Amtrak coach seats are very comfortable, and many passengers elect to sleep sitting up (or hunched over) on red-eye trips. But it's a rare voyager who can take that kind of punishment more than one night in a row, so contemplate a sleeping car for marathon train sessions. It's not cheap—a private car can easily double the price of a ticket, and they're hardly deluxe accommodations (imagine a closet with bunk beds). But lying prone behind a locked door is a dream shared by every coach passenger after the first 24 hours of travel.

## Service

Amtrak doesn't own the tracks their trains roll on, giving freight trains the right of way. This can occasionally lead to frustrating delays. If you need to get there fast, it is advisable to find alternate means. Rail travel is as much about the journey as the destination. Speaking of which, alcohol is available in the club car at airport bar prices. Luckily, they don't have that 3oz rule, so sneaking your own adult beverages on board is a piece of delicious cake.

Carry a stash of food along, adjusting quantities to suit the length of the trip. Even if you spring for expensive meals in the dinner car, the food can be lousy and there isn't enough of it. The prices of snacks in the club car are inflated as a courtesy to Amtrak's captive clientele, so bring your own pretzels.

## Going to Portland

Stumptown is a fun place to visit, and the Amtrak Cascades takes you there in style. The Spanish-designed Talgo trains provide comfy seats with big windows for great views of Puget Sound. They thankfully discourage the use of cell phones on board, and they even offer a free film (just make sure to bring your own headphones). And once you dig into some Ivar's clam chowder and sip on a Black Butte Porter in the dining car, you'll never take Greyhound to Portland again.

## Going to Vancouver, BC

The Amtrak Cascades departs Seattle every morning for a four hour trip to "the poor man's Amsterdam." Be advised that Vancouver, British Columbia is located in the sovereign nation of Canada—make sure to bring your passport and remember that all Amtrak trains are subject to random searches by border officials. It's a beautiful journey up along the coast, but pesky freight train traffic will inevitably cause delays. For a fun Friday night getaway, Amtrak also offers a very un-Greyhound like bus from King Street Station for a good price.

## Going to Los Angeles

The Coast Starlight leaves Seattle every morning headed south and makes Los Angeles in about 35 hours. Prices for a one-way fare range between $89 and $180, depending on what time of year and how far in advance you are buying your tickets. Popular stops along the way include Portland, OR (although take the Cascades if you can) and Emeryville, CA (about 23 hours of travel, and only an hour's bus ride from San Francisco).

## Going to Chicago

The Empire Builder leaves Seattle daily and reaches the Windy City in a mere 45 hours for a one-way fare between $134 and $294. That's a long ride with two guaranteed nights sleeping upright in coach and not bathing, but such asceticism can sometimes lead to spiritual fulfillment. So think of it as time to get to know yourself. Among the cities the Empire Builder services are Whitefish, MT, Fargo, ND, Minneapolis, MN, and Milwaukee, WI. Plus, there's no better way to appreciate the scenery of the heartland than through the window of a train.

## General Information

| | |
|---|---|
| Address: | 811 Stewart St |
| | Seattle, WA 98101 |
| Main Phone: | 206-628-5526 |
| Baggage: | 206-628-5555 |
| Greyhound | |
| Package Express: | 206-628-5555 |
| Customer Service: | 206-628-5561 |
| Greyhound Charter: | 800-454-2487 |
| Greyhound Website: | www.greyhound.com |
| Hours: | 6:00 am–11:30 am daily |
| Greyhound | |
| Package Express: | 6:00 am–11:30 am daily |
| Ticketing: | 6:00 am–11:30 pm daily |
| Food Service: | Monday–Sunday: 6 am–9 pm |
| | Holiday: 6 am–9 pm |

## Overview

Nothing epitomizes a "long day's journey into night" like traveling on a bus full of folks bridging the many miles between Los Angeles and Vancouver. Sure, Amtrak is cleaner, faster, and more scenic, but where else can you experience traveling in close quarters amongst more parolees than voting-eligible citizens? Ah, the smells, the stories, the uniquely gritty perspective you get only from traveling Greyhound. Of course it's dirt cheap, considering current eye-gouging gas prices. What could be better than a weekend jaunt to Oly and a show at Capitol Theater for only $22 round-trip, or check out some of Tacoma's up-and-coming talent at Hell's Kitchen for only $12 (round-trip from Seattle).

## Station

Seattle's Greyhound station is not the most awe-inspiring public space in town. In fact, it makes King Street Station look downright Grand Central-esque. It's located in one of the last truly sketchy parts of downtown at 811 Stewart Street (at 8th Ave). It's a short walk east from the Westlake Center shopping nucleus, where many cross-city Metro buses travel. Or take the 66 or 545 to be deposited closer to the Greyhound terminal.

## Tickets

Tickets may be purchased in person at the terminal, online at www.greyhound.com, or over the phone at 1-800-231-2222. The first option is the least convenient due to the long and disorderly lines at the Seattle station; advance reservations are not necessary.

## Fares

The Greyhound website offers special e-fares, including eSavers, Companion Fares, and Go Anywhere Fares. Discounted fares are also available for students, seniors, children, and military personnel.

## Baggage

Passengers are allowed two pieces of checked baggage and two carry-on items per person. An additional fee will be charged for baggage over the 50 pound weight limit. Baggage insurance is available, but as with any type of travel (especially Greyhound), it's wise to keep your most valuable items on your person or leave them at home.

## Other Services

Greyhound Package Xpress is available for fast shipping on oversized or overweight items, or as a shipping alternative to USPS, FedEx, and UPS. They offer door-to-door and online service. For more information about Package Xpress call 1-800-739-5020.

## General Information

Cascade Bicycle Club: www.cascade.org
Bicycle Alliance of
  Washington: www.bicyclealliance.org
City of Seattle Bicycle
  Program: www.seattle.gov/transportation/
bikeprogram.htm
Seattle Bike Blog: www.seattlebikeblog.com

## Commuting

Environmentally conscious Seattle is finally starting to bloom as a true bike-friendly city. There's a growing system of bike lanes and routes connecting neighborhoods, including over 40 miles of off-street lanes. You can find over 2,000 bike racks scattered throughout the city. Heck, even the current mayor gets to work on a two-wheeler with a six-mile ride from Greenwood each morning. To plan your route from the comfort of your own living room on the nearest bike trails and on-street lanes, check out the city's bike map, available online via the Seattle Department of Transportation website: www.seattle.gov/transportation

But before you hop on your brand new Schwinn and take off down Capitol Hill, just remember it's not a biking paradise just yet. Trails can end abruptly in the middle of nowhere, paths and routes can be poorly marked, and many major arteries have no bike lanes. Plus, you'll have to come back up that hill after a long day at the office. And it will probably be raining, so pack a breathable coat and waterproof pants if you want to look respectable at your next destination.

Drivers are aware and cautious for the most part, but most of the infrastructure is still set up for cars. Case in point: sometimes the light won't change until a vehicle rolls up. Look for a t-shaped symbol on the ground to plant your front wheel. Hopefully, this will change the light and get you moving again. Other cyclist-friendly features include green bike boxes, so bikes can pull up ahead of vehicles, and bike dots on the pavement with arrows to show the path of a bike route without having to look up. Plus, there's even serious talk of bike share launching in the next few years. Watch your back, Portland…

## Safety and the Law

Part of biking is riding responsibly, so to that end, obey traffic laws. And by "obey traffic laws," we don't mean running red lights, riding against traffic and generally giving non-bicyclists any reason to carp. Ride defensively: avoid blind spots, pass on the left, keep three feet away from parked cars (even the word "dooring" sounds violent), and use hand signals (yes, even if they seem lame). Unlike other cities, in Seattle bicyclists are permitted use the sidewalk, but bikes must yield the right-of-way to pedestrians. Helmets are required in Seattle. Cyclists may ride two abreast on streets but not more than that. Reflectors and lights at night are mandatory. A single arrow on the road indicates

a dedicated bike lane, while the double chevron "sharrow" is used to indicate a shared lane. When a portion of a bike lane is painted green, it means that cars are permitted to cross into the lane.

## Bikes on Mass Transit

If you really don't want to bike back up the hill, had a few too many at happy hour with your coworkers, or are just feeling plain lazy, you're in luck. Metro and Sound Transit both have bike racks on the front of buses to make it a breeze to get around town with your two wheels in tow. Just alert the driver first, then place your bike in one of the two racks. The rails are even easier to use. Bicycles are allowed on Sounder commuter lines, Link light rail, and the Seattle Streetcar. Just look for the doors marked with a bike symbol and make sure to always have your bike securely in hand while in motion, so it doesn't smack a fellow passenger in the leg. Light rail stations even offer bike lockers for rent at a rate of $50/month.

## Independent/Underground Biking

Who's that fit dude or lady with a scrape on their knee, hip shoulder bag, coffee cup tattoo, and cool fixie? Probably one of the hundreds of bike messengers that roll all over town. A lot of them play bike polo (www.seattlebikepolo.com) when they're not hanging out at Monorail Espresso or Shorty's. The 2013 North American Cycling Courier Championships were even held in Seattle giving an insight into the street cred of the city's underground scene. If you're not quite tough enough to be a messenger, but still want in on some indie biking action, there's always Critical Mass. The group meets every last Friday of the month at Westlake Center to ride through the streets of Seattle at their own will, much to the chagrin of commuters and cops--who are, ironically, probably on bike themselves.

## A Few Bike Shops

**Bike Works** · 3709 S Ferdinand St · 206-725-9408 · www.bikeworks.org

**Coastal Surf Boutique** · 2532 Alki Ave SW · 206-933-5605 · www.coastalseattle.com

**Electric Vehicles Northwest** · 4810 17th Ave NW · 206-547-4621 · www.electricvehiclesnw.com

**Gregg's** · 7007 Woodlawn Ave NE · 206-523-1822 · www.greggscycles.com

**Montlake Bicycle Shop** · 2223 24th Ave E · 206-329-7333 · www.montlakebike.com

**Recycled Cycles** · 1007 NE Boat St · 206-547-4491 · www.recycledcycles.com

**REI** · 7500 166th Ave NE · 425-882-1158 · www.rei.com

## Taxis

For its size, Seattle has much fewer taxis than some might expect. It seems that most of the residents here simply prefer hoofing, biking, or bussing it around town (if they're not cruising in their hybrids). Thus, hailing a cab can be a bit dicey, and it's dang near impossible to find one outside downtown. Your best bet is to call ahead—Puget Sound Dispatch will quickly hook you up with either a Yellow (206-622-6500) or a Redtop cab (206-789-4949). Normally, you won't be kept waiting much longer than 10–15 minutes. If you're cabbing it home after a night at the bars, try to leave before last call or you'll be waiting at least an hour for a ride home.

If you're milling about downtown, there are a couple designated taxi stands. There's one outside the Westin Hotel (on 5th Ave) and another at the Washington State Convention & Trade Center (on Pike St). If cabs are cruising at all, hotels are a good place to spot one. The standard drop rate for two is $2.50 plus $2.70 per mile and $.50 per extra passenger. And with our fun and fluctuating oil market, some cab companies might hit you with an additional $1.00 gas surcharge—but make *sure* this is posted clearly on the dash before going anywhere. And on top of that, a 10–15% tip is expected. If you don't happen to have wads of cash on you to pay for all that, most cabs do come equipped with credit card devices, although some driver get pretty surly if you use plastic for a short trip.

Should you be heading to Sea-Tac, the Central Link light rail (www.soundtransit.org) will take you there for a mere $2.75 from downtown Seattle. But should you be toting an obscene amount of baggage or are extremely averse to the idea of traffic-free public transit, taxis will chauffeur you gladly for a flat rate of $40 from downtown. Coming back to Seattle from the airport is a whole 'nother ballgame, as there is no flat rate from Sea-Tac. There appears to be no satisfying explanation for this. Just take the light rail.

| | |
|---|---|
| **Yellow Cab** | 206-622-6500 |
| **Redtop** | 206-789-4949 |
| **Farwest Taxi** | 206-622-1717 |
| **Orange Cab** | 206-522-8800 |

## Car Service

After years of unreliable service from our local cab companies (i.e. showing up late or not at all and getting lost with the meter running) San Francisco-based car services arrived on the scene to make everything better. You can do it all from your smartphone, from ordering a car to paying for it and you can rate your drivers, too (cab dispatchers balk at customer service complaints). Best of all, you can track your car via GPS so you know exactly where it is and when it will arrive. Uber (www.uber.com) is the classy one, Lyft, with their giant pink car mustaches and fist-bump greetings, (www.lyft.me) is the fun one, and Side Car (www.side.cr) is the thrifty one.

## General Information

Seattle is a walkable city with fairly adequate public transportation, so it's feasible for denizens to live comfortably without owning a car. In fact, the freedom that comes with removing that albatross from around the neck can be quite exhilarating. Farewell to high insurance and fuel costs, the travails of big city parking, and the constant threat of mechanical breakdown—hello to the smug satisfaction of reducing one's ecological impact on the tender earth. Still, schlepping laundry, groceries, and children around the city on the bus isn't always ideal, and sooner or later, a private conveyance becomes temporarily necessary. Hence the concept of "car sharing" catching on in nearly fifty American cities, including Seattle.

## Zipcar

Zipcar Website:       www.zipcar.com
Zipcar Phone:         866-4ZIPCAR

Zipcar provides customers with access to a fleet of autos parked in dozens of convenient parking spots throughout the area. For an annual subscription fee, users can reserve a vehicle up to fifteen minutes in advance (via website or Zipcar app) and drive for $8–9.50 an hour. A membership card and a PIN unlocks the car, which is programmed to start only for the particular subscriber holding the reservation. Frequent drivers can choose various monthly packages that include pre-paid road time and reduced hourly rates. Zipcar covers gas, insurance and maintenance costs, and well over 100 cars, trucks, SUVs and hybrids are available— even a few sporty convertibles for a spontaneous joy ride.

Zipcar took over Flex Car, a Seattle-based company with a similar business plan, which was partly funded by the King County government. Flex Car suffered some growing pains which caused grief to its customers in the early days. Of course there were customer complaints about Zipcar at first as well. How many Seattleites does it take to change a light bulb? Five: One to change it and four to complain about how the old one was better. Nonetheless, most citizens of the Emerald City agree that car sharing is an excellent idea in light of current affairs.

## Car2go

Car2go Website:       seattle.car2go.com
Car2go Phone:         877-488-4224

Car2go, from Germany by way of Austin is a cross between ZipCar and bike share. The super-tiny green Smart Fortwo cars are parked in any City of Seattle metered or time-limited on-street parking space in the "Home Area." Users pick up and return cars to any spot within this area--bordered to the north by 130th Street, to the south by Michigan Street/Orcas Street in Georgetown/Beacon Hill, Lake Washington to the east, and Puget Sound to the west. The home area includes parts of West Seattle, but does not include certain areas like the University District and Discovery Park. It costs $35 to register with car2go, but unlike Zipcar, there are no monthly fees or charges. Trips are 38 cents a minute up to $13.99 per hour and $72.99 per day. Charges are billed to your credit card. Cars include parking, fuel, insurance, GPS, and roadside assistance.

# Transit · **Driving**

## General Information

**City of Seattle Department of Transportation (DOT)**

Address:     PO Box 34996
                Seattle, Wa 98124
Phone:       206-684-ROAD (7623)
Website:     www.seattle.gov/transportation
Webcams:   www.seattle.gov/trafficcams/

## Orientation

The bad news is, Seattle is not an easy city to drive in without getting lost or frustrated. There are tons of one-way streets, dead ends, windy roads, and many bridges. Sometimes a street will disappear for awhile, then reappear blocks later. In fact, it was listed by Sterling as one of the top-ten most difficult cities to navigate, clocking in at number eight. On top of all that, traffic, especially on I-5, is absolutely horrendous, with no cure on the horizon. This is all due to the fact that Seattle keeps growing at a furious pace and is split between large bodies of water and I-5, making it nearly impossible to get from point A to point B via a straight line. The good news is, once you do figure out how to get around, there are many alternative routes to take to avoid traffic. Just get out there, strap on your seatbelt, and force yourself to learn the roads. Once you get a route down, try changing it up. Sometimes it can be as simple as going one street over to avoid traffic. Generally, only streets that run more or less east-west are called "streets." Only streets that run for the most part north-south are called "avenues." However, roads, boulevards, and ways can go any direction they please. In other words, good luck. Also, Seattle is full of bold cyclists, but if you just keep reminding yourself that they mean one less car on the road, you'll find your patience for them will increase.

## Bridges

Seattle is surrounded by water, so get used to dealing with lots of bridges. Drawbridges are enemy number one for the hurried driver. There is no way to know when a bridge is going to go up, unless you are in a really big hurry. Then it's guaranteed. Drawbridge hijinks include the Ballard, University District, and Montlake bridges. And that's when someone hasn't decided to make stopping traffic their final act, by leaping off of it. The other drawbridges you will have to deal with are the Ballard, University District, and Montlake Bridges. If you get stuck when a bridge is going up, all you can do is turn off your engine (idling cars are bad for the environment) and wait it out. Another notable bridge that serves I-90 and connects Seattle to Mercer Island is the Lacey V. Murrow Memorial Bridge—the second longest floating bridge in the world. If you're keen to experience the longest floating bridge in the world, you're in luck—the Evergreen Point Floating Bridge (a.k.a. Bridge 520) is just a few miles north. Both of these get you to I-405, and one is usually busier than the other, so be sure to check traffic status on the WSDOT (Washington State Department of Transit) website before you make your choice. Either way, you will be treated

to a beautiful view on your way across. Also important to water-body navigation are the West Seattle Bridge and the George Washington Memorial Bridge (a.k.a. the Aurora Bridge).

## Dealing with Highway 99

Highway 99, the original superhighway of Seattle, runs parallel to I-5. It can be a useful route when I-5 is congested (which is almost always). However, it can be difficult to navigate. You may find yourself heading north on the stretch from Greenlake Avenue N to Denny and you need to be going south or vice versa. Well, that's too bad. Sometimes you just have to stick it out until you find an exit or risk turning off into the black hole that is Queen Anne Hill. Also, the Alaskan Way Viaduct Replacement Program (the viaduct, part of Highway 99, has been torn down and is being replaced by an underground car tunnel) is underway and is expected to be finished (fingers crossed) in late 2015. Until then, check WSDOT for traffic closures and updates on Seattle's version of the Big Dig.

## Major Expressways

I-5, Seattle's main freeway, running north/south, is almost always congested. From I-5 you can access either I-90 or SR520 running east/west parallel to each other. One is often busier than the other, so pay attention to traffic reports. Running parallel to I-5 is Highway 99, which will go no farther than five miles west of it, and I-405 running on the other side of Lake Washington. I-5 has expressways in the center of the freeway that anyone can access, but be careful because exits are limited and you may end up going farther than you would have liked. The city provides real-time traffic and web cameras at their website listed above.

## DMVs

Visits to the Seattle DMV are relatively painless, especially if you go on a weekday morning. If you must go on a Saturday, be prepared to wait. However, try saving yourself a trip by visiting their website at www.dol.wa.gov or visiting www.dmv.org to find out what can be done online.

| Seattle DMVs | Address | Phone |
|---|---|---|
| Greenwood | 320 N 85th St Seattle, WA 98103 | 206-706-4269 |
| Seattle-North | 907 N 135th St Seattle, WA 98133 | 206-368-7261 |
| Seattle-Downtown Limited Service Office | 380 Union St Seattle, WA 98101 | 206-464-6845 |
| Seattle-East | 5811 Rainier Ave S Seattle, WA 98118 | 206-721-4560 |
| Seattle-West | 8830 25th Ave SW Seattle, WA 98106 | 206-764-4143 |

## General Information

Parking Ticket Payments

In Person:   600 5th Ave
             Seattle, Wa 98104
Phone:       206-233-7000
Website:     www.seattle.gov/courts/ticket/
             ticketinformation.htm

## Parking Meters

Seattle has installed green computerized meters throughout the city that accept credit cards. You simply pick the amount of time you want, slide your credit card, and a sticker will be printed for you to place on the inside of the window closest to the sidewalk. This is truly amazing for those striving for a cashless society. It's also handy because the sticker is valid at any location, so any unused time can be used somewhere else. Unfortunately, if the machine is not accepting your credit card or is broken, you can't park there! The city, of course, apologizes for the inconvenience, but who is going to apologize to your boss? Curiously, the machines also accept change but not bills.

## Residential Parking Zone Program

Many Seattle neighborhoods (usually those near commercial strips) participate in a permit program. It is meant to discourage long-term parking by non-residents. Look for the green and white signs which limit you to two hour parking except by permit. Permits cost $65 and are good for two years. Permits can only be issued to residents who live on a block with signs installed or within the boundaries of the RPZ. In order to apply, you must have proof of residency and current Washington State vehicle registration. One permit is issued per vehicle and one guest permit can be issued per household. Temporary permits may be issued for up to sixty days for construction, out of state, new, and student vehicles. You may obtain a permit by mail or in person. Call 206-684-5086 Monday through Friday 8 am to 4:30 pm for more information.

Mail requests to:

Seattle Department of Transportation
Traffic Permits
PO Box 34996
Seattle, WA 98124-4996

## Curbs

It is important to understand Seattle's curb color system. After searching for a parking spot on Capitol Hill for two hours, you finally find the perfect one right in front of your apartment. Too good to be true, right?

Well, it probably is. If the curb is painted white, it is either a three-minute loading zone or police and fire department parking. If the curb is yellow, it is a thirty-minute loading zone. Red means no parking anytime and they mean it. You will get towed so fast it'll make your head spin. Alternating yellow and red makes it a bus zone, so don't even think about parking there.

## Parking Tickets and Impound

Parking tickets issued by the Seattle Police Department are handled by the Seattle Municipal Court. You can pay them online at www.seattle.gov or over the phone at 206-684-5600. If you fail to pay your ticket within 15 days, the fine will automatically double. Unpaid parking tickets will result in a hold on your vehicle registration tabs.

To contest a parking ticket, you can request a hearing before a Municipal Court Magistrate to gently explain why they should shove their fines where the sun doesn't shine. You can contact them at 206-684-5600.

If your car gets towed, call the Seattle Police Department (206-682-2869), although it may take a few hours for it to show up in their system. Towed cars are taken to one of three impound lots in Seattle, ABC Towing (206-682-2869), E T Towing (206-622-9188), or Lincoln Towing (206-364-2000). In order to get your vehicle free, you will be required to pay the fine to the impound lot immediately, and the registered owner must be present with appropriate documentation. Under special circumstances, arrangements can be made for someone other than the registered owner to retrieve the vehicle. Vehicles in storage for over 21 days may be put up for auction and/or shipped to Albania.

## Extra Parking Tips:

It is legal to park facing any direction on either side of the street. Well, within reason of course; you can't veer across three lanes into oncoming traffic to catch that that perfect spot on the other side of the street.

There are signs all over that say No Parking north/south/east/west of here. It just means, don't park past that sign, so keep an eye out for those sneaky little things.

Street parking is free after 6 pm, and on Sundays and holidays.

It is illegal to park a car in the same spot for more than 72 hours. Failure to move your car around the block for no good reason will result in a ticket or towing. It is also illegal to let your car bumper hang even a millimeter over the driveway (including your own) into the sidewalk. If a traffic cop is bored, they will slap you with a $38 fine with no apologies

## General Information

| | |
|---|---|
| Mailing Address: | 201 S Jackson St |
| | KSC-TR-0415 |
| | Seattle, WA 98104 |
| | |
| Website: | metro.kingcounty.gov |
| Main Phone: | 206-553-3000 |
| Customer Service: | 206-553-3060 |
| Lost and Found: | 206-553-3090 |

## Overview

Anyone who isn't convinced that Seattle is a colorful town of eccentrics and madmen needs to ride the bus. This could be true about many American cities, but Seattle's lost souls take to public transportation in a major way. A Seattle transplant will have a "Bus Nut" story within a week of moving here. This is not to dissuade the timid rider, but one should always expect the unexpected when facing so much humanity within an enclosed space.

Many city dwellers who lack wheels for ideological or financial reasons find getting around Seattle on Metro buses a necessity. Service is extensive, reaching throughout the city, but the quality and comfort of the ride varies from one line to the next. Buses between Capitol Hill and the University District run reliably every ten minutes or so for most of the day. You can also count on regular bus service connecting downtown with the northern hoods like Wedgwood and Ravenna. The express buses that rocket passengers to outlying suburbs are always on time. However, like any modern urban transit system, the city faces unique geographical challenges (in this case hills, water, and bridges) that can lead to trouble. Some Metro routes are chronically late, crowded with standing passengers, or peppered with anti-social types, and woe be to the rider who depends on such a bus to get to work every day. Check Metro's website for alternate (if inconvenient) itineraries.

In 2012, Seattle Metro ended its downtown area Ride Free Zone which included the confusing pay upon boarding/pay while exiting system. Now, all riders pay upon boarding the bus. On RapidRide lines with stations that have ORCA readers, and on Sound Transit Light Rail and Sounder, riders may enter through any door. Standard adult fare is $2.25 off peak, but during peak hours (weekdays 6 to 9 am and 3 to 6 pm) it's $2.50 for one zone and $3 for two zones. It's exact change only and drivers and riders alike are impatient to people fiddling in their pockets, so make sure you have your money and pass ready when you step on board. The price rises depending on how far out of the city limits the ride takes you. Discounts for students, seniors, and the disabled cut the cost, and buses are fully equipped

to handle those with mobility challenges. Transfers allow re-boarding for up to two hours on most lines. To make it easier for regular riders, Metro has created the ORCA (One Regional Card for All). They issue the first card for free to all Seattle residents. You can fund your ORCA at many locations downtown including the Metro office and kiosks located in the bus tunnel. You can also do it online or create an "e-purse," which will automatically re-fund your ORCA from your credit card or bank whenever the balance dips below the lowest possible fare. If you lose your card, they will issue you a new one for $5. See the ORCA website (www.orcacard.com) for more details about how to receive and fund a card of your very own.

Bicyclists can stash their machines on racks attached to the front of the bus (metro.kingcounty.gov/tops/bike/bike.html). Car owners can leave their vehicles at a number of Park & Ride locations available through King County, so those with longer commutes can avoid the snarl of inner-city traffic.

Seattle loves to waste money on useless public transportation. The adorable George Benson Line Waterfront Streetcar is no longer running, but you can bike or stroll along the tracks and check it out whenever you like.

In 2008, the downtown bus tunnel re-opened after undergoing retrofitting for Light Rail. The tunnel whisks express buses underneath downtown Seattle while suckers in cars sit motionless above ground.

Speaking of Light Rail, they finally completed the Central Link, meaning Seattle now has a viable means of cheap public transportation to the airport! Next, they're tackling the University and Capitol Hill Links so that folks don't have to schlep their luggage to Westlake on the bus first. It's possible that by 2016, we may have something resembling a rapid transit system. Aw, Seattle. You're getting to be such a big girl! Yes, you are!

PS: A charming custom in Seattle is the bus rider's habit of thanking the driver as he/she disembarks. Most Metro drivers deserve this simple courtesy. It must be a stressful, monotonous task battling traffic to haul sullen strangers to their jobs every day. So don't forget to give your driver a verbal tip for a job well done.

Light Rail

Westlake Station
University Street Station
Pioneer Square Station
International District/
Chinatown Station
Stadium Station
Beacon Hill
Station
SODO
Station
Mount
Baker
Station
Columbia City Station
Othello Station
Rainier
Beach
Station
Tukwila
International Boulevard
Station
SeaTac/Airport Station

## General Information

Sound Transit Address:   401 S Jackson St
                         Seattle, WA 98104
Phone:                   888-889-6368
Website:                 www.soundtransit.org
Email:                   main@soundtransit.org

## Light Rail Overview

Sound Transit was created by the Washington State Legislature to build a mass transit system that connects King, Pierce, and Snohomish Counties. The organization has the Central Puget Sound region covered with a broad range of bus, light rail, and commuter rail services.

In addition to operating Link light rail, Sound Transit operates express buses and commuter rail, called Sounder, around the region, connecting major employment centers such as Everett, Bellevue, and Renton. Though many of the buses operate on weekends, Sounder is strictly a weekday affair. If you're lucky enough to live near one of the stations in Everett or Edmonds, commuting into Seattle via the cushy, wi-fi-equipped Sounder as it winds its way along Puget Sound's breathtaking shoreline, is one of the nicest ways to start your day. Sounder and Express Bus stations outside of Seattle city limits often do have free parking, though the lots are often fully by 8 a.m.

## Light Rail History

Seattle's Link Light Rail--which opened in 2009--was a long time in the making.

Underground transit had been proposed in Seattle as far back as 1912, but wasn't until 1968 that the idea really took off.  These were the heady, messy days of "urban renewal" in America's cities, and Seattle had been on the list for a federally-financed rapid transit system like the one being built in Washington DC.  Senator Warren G. Magnuson secured a $900M earmark (an eye-popping $6 billion in 2013 dollars) to pay for the majority of the system, which would have consisted of two lines crossing the city in an X shape.  Seattle voters, however, earning their reputation for fickleness, said "thanks, but no thanks" and didn't give the ballot measure the 60% supermajority it needed to pass. The money instead went to finance Atlanta's MARTA.

In the 1990s, talk of rail transit heated up again, with basically the same X-shaped system that had been outlined in 1968. Not coincidentally, this is around the time of Cameron Crowe's 1992 film *Singles*, in which the main character tries unsuccessfully to convince the city of the value of building a "super train." (He does, however, succeed in finding love, so there's that.) After failing on the first three votes, the Central Puget Sound Regional Transportation Authority (now known as "Sound Transit") was approved in November of 1996, just two days before the release of the documentary *Hype!* chronicling the rise and fall of Seattle's grunge scene.

The plan was for a 21-mile line connecting Sea-Tac airport and Northgate Mall, roughly along the I-5 corridor. Sound Transit ran into trouble, though, when the costs spiraled and years of delays mounted. Frustrated, Seattle voters approved a monorail along the western half of the city. After buying land and spending hundreds of millions of taxpayer dollars, the monorail plan, too, went over budget and was eventually killed by another popular vote.

Sound Transit survived, however, thanks to support from the local political establishment. A shortened, 14-mile line between Downtown Seattle and Tukwila, known as Central Link, finally opened in 2009. A short extension to SeaTac Airport followed in 2010. Extensions are being built to Capitol Hill and UW (opening in 2016), Northgate (2021), and finally Bellevue, Redmond, and Lynwood (2023).

## Light Rail Operating Hours

Central Link operates from 5 p.m. to 1 a.m. Monday through Saturday, and 6 a.m. to midnight on Sunday. As of 2013 it carries an average of 26,000 passengers per day. Trains operate every 7.5 minutes during rush hour and every 10-15 minutes in the evenings.

## Light Rail Fares

Fares on the system are distance-based, ranging from $2.00 to $2.75 for adults depending on how far you're traveling. You pay your fare using the same ORCA card system described in the King County Metro section above (though built by Sound Transit, Link is operated by Metro). You can buy tickets from a machine at any station.

When it comes time to board, however, Seattle's true nature shines. Since we're nice, honest folk, Link stations don't have the turnstiles or gates you might find in a crowded East Coast subway station. No sir. Like the Europeans, whose traditions of soccer and espresso we so adore, Link uses "proof-of-payment," which means you tap your card on a mechanical reader when you get on, and again when you get off. It's all very civilized. Of course, that doesn't mean you can ride for free. As in Europe, fare enforcement officers board the trains from time to time to ensure that riders have paid.

Civilized as it might be, proof-of-payment is a bit confusing in action, especially in the downtown bus tunnel. If you're riding Link, you should tap your ORCA on one of the yellow card readers when you get on and when you get off (because the fares are based on distance travelled). If you're riding a bus, however, you tap your card once you get on the bus.

## Light Rail Stations & Destinations

Downtown, the stations can be a bit hard to find. Look for the blue Sound Transit "T" to enter the bus tunnel, which is shared by buses and Link (at least for the next few years). One entrance to Westlake Station, for example, is inside the downtown Nordstrom, while an entrance at University Street is tucked into Benaroya Hall.

The SeaTac Airport station is accessible via a five-minute walk from the terminal. Follow the signs for Link, which will take you through the parking garage and to the Link station on the other side.

While many tourists use Link from the Airport to downtown, locals know there are many interesting destinations along the route, including Pioneer Square, the sports stadia, the International District, Beacon Hill and the Rainier Valley. Some of the best Vietnamese food and some of the freshest, cheapest produce in the city can be found along the route. And there are great views of the city to be had from the elevated portions.

## Light Rail Parking

Unlike the 1960s-era systems in DC, Atlanta, and San Francisco, Link stations aren't surrounded by oceans of parking. Only Tukwila station, outside of the Seattle limits, has free parking (and it's almost always full). Paid parking is available near several Rainier Valley stations including Mt. Baker. If you're not within walking distance of a station, your best bet is to get there via bus, bicycle (see below), or a car share service like Car2Go.

## Bicycles

Taking the bike to the train is encouraged. There are bike lockers at several of the stations and bike areas inside the train cars. Keep in mind you might find yourself in a passive-aggressive Seattle-style standoff with a tourist using the bike storage area for his or her giant wheeled luggage. Proceed with caution.

**The Sounder**

Everett Station

Edmonds Station

FARE ZONE

King St Station

FARE ZONE

Tukwila Station

Kent Station

Auburn Station

FARE ZONE

Tacoma Dome Station

Puyallup Station

Summer Station

## ST Express

The Sound Transit Regional Bus line connects Seattle, Bellevue, Everett, and Tacoma with the largest urban centers in the region. Transit centers, park-and-ride lots, and HOV access projects throughout the region have improved transit service for all bus riders and provide some help to the daily commute. The line connects more than 30,000 people each day throughout the three counties

Fares: Adults ages 19-64 pay $2.50 for one zone and $3.50 across multiple zones. Youths ages 6-18 pay $1.25 and $2.50. Senior citizens and the disabled pay $0.75 and $1.50. Children under 6 ride free with a paying passenger.

## The Sounder

Sounder commuter trains run 75 miles every weekday (Monday to Friday only) between Everett and Tacoma. The Sounder North train connects Everett with Seattle (with stops in Edmonds and Mukilteo). The Sounder South train runs from Tacoma to Puyallup, Sumner, Auburn, Kent, Tukwila, and downtown Seattle. The Sounder also runs special trains for Seahawk home games and for select Mariners games. Check the website for more details.

Fares: Ranges from $1.50 to $5.25, depending on how far you travel.

## Tacoma Link Light Rail

The Tacoma Link light rail line began operating in August 2003 and quickly became a major factor in the renaissance of downtown Tacoma. The 1.6-mile route connects downtown Tacoma with the Tacoma Dome Station, where connections can be made to ST Express regional bus and Sounder commuter rail.

Fares: At the outset, the cost of collecting fares outweighed the income derived from fares, meaning that the Tacoma Link light rail was free. Although it took ten years to get to the point where it literally paid to collect fares, it appears that an adult fare in the $1-2 range will soon be implemented on the line.

## Seattle Streetcar

| | |
|---|---|
| NFT Maps: | 2 & 16 |
| Address: | Seattle Department |
| | of Transportation |
| | P.O. Box 34996 |
| | Seattle, WA 98124 |
| Phone: | 206-553-3000 |
| Lost and Found: | 206-553-3090 |
| Route and Schedule | |
| Information: | 206-553-3000 |
| Other Inquiries: | 206-684-ROAD |
| Website: | www.seattlestreetcar.org |

## Seattle Streetcar Overview

If the Metro bus is the faithful plain Jane of Seattle's public transportation system, then the streetcar is her much more glamorous yet vapid younger sister. Ah, but the lil' sister is growing up--or out. The South Lake Union Streetcar comprises eleven stops scattered along a 2.6-mile loop around the Denny Triangle and South Lake Union neighborhoods, and its pretty purple streetcars zoom by every fifteen minutes. With construction underway on the First Hill Streetcar, and plans for the Broadway Extension and a Center City Connector being hashed out, the streetcar is becoming more than just eye candy. Honesty rules since riders hop on and off without anyone checking their fares, although supposedly you may be asked at anytime to present your proof of payment. ORCA and bus transfers are accepted or you can purchase tickets from machines located at the stations and on the streetcar itself. Strangely, the station ticketing machines don't accept bills but those on the cars do. Bicyclists can store their wheels in the open center section of the streetcars. The streetcar was originally named the South Lake Union Trolley (the SLUT) until city officials realized the unfortunate acronym this creates. Though the moniker was changed, Seattleites still delight in saying "Yeah, I rode the SLUT." We are easy to please here in the Emerald City.

**....** Auto/Passenger
**....** Passenger Only

KINGSTON

EDMONDS

BAINBRIDGE
ISLAND

SEATTLE

BREMERTON

SOUTHWORTH

FAUNTLEROY

VASHON
ISLAND

## General Information

Website:     www.wsdot.wa.gov/ferries
Phone:       206-464-6400

## Overview

The largest ferry system in the country, Washington State Ferries can actually make commuting pleasurable—once you're on the boat. The ferry system encompasses a total of ten routes and twenty terminals, so be sure you know where you want to go. The boats running to Bainbridge, Bremerton, and a passenger-only boat to Vashon Island are located at Colman Dock at Alaskan Way and Marian Street. The most popular route, from Seattle to Bainbridge, sails every 50 minutes or so during peak hours and approximately every hour at other times until 2 am. Check the website for exact schedules, and note that there is a slight variation at the end of the day on weekends and holidays. The ferries run in all weather, but the Port Townsend and Vashon runs are occasionally limited by extreme low tides. The website will have current information as well as real-time web cams on the docks. Bikes and motorcycles load through the auto gates and are given preference over cars at loading time. Colman Dock has recently added several food and coffee vendors as well as a small wine bar. (Commuter Comforts is the best of the lot.) There is food, beer, and wine available on the boats (hooray!) until about 8 pm, but don't get too excited since the food is abysmal and everything is overpriced. Once you're actually on the boat, settle in and enjoy the ride. There's an open deck upstairs for viewing. The scenery on a good day is awe-inspiring—the Cascades to the east, Mt. Rainier to the south, the Olympic mountain range to the west, and Puget Sound is, obviously, everywhere. It's a good guess that there are frequent proposals (of one kind or another) on the ferries.

## Parking

Parking? Oh please. Your choices are to drive your car on (expensive and time-consuming—during peak hours, you can sometimes wait through several boat departures), or find a parking spot near the terminal. There are a number of them sprinkled on Western Avenue between Yesler Way and Spring Street. There are also buses that stop in front of Coleman Dock. Check Metro's website (metro.kingcounty.gov) for details.

## Fares

Fares can vary depending on where and when you'll be going, so make sure to check the website before heading out. Of course, bringing a car always drives up the price and in the peak season (May 1 to the second Saturday in October) you'll have to pay more. Thankfully, the ferry system accepts all major credit cards, so you won't have to abandon your car and make a run for an ATM. Round trip fare for passengers from Seattle to Bainbridge/Bremerton and from Edmonds to Kingston is now $7.70 for adults and $6.20 for children. $3.85 for seniors and disabled. Car and driver is $16.40 (peak). Fauntleroy to Vashon is $5.00 for adults, $4.05 for children and $2.50 for seniors/disabled. Car and driver is $20.90. When possible, leave the car at home and pay an extra buck to bring your bicycle aboard. Your wallet and body will thank you. Finally, for those who ride the boats often, commuter books are available and will save you a bunch of dough.

| Airline | Phone | Terminal | Airline | Phone | Terminal |
|---|---|---|---|---|---|
| Air Canada | 800 247-2262 | Concourse A | Hainan Airlines | 888 688-8813 | South Satellite |
| All Nippon Airways | 800-235-9262 | South Satellite | Hawaiian Airlines | 800 367-5320 | South Satellite |
| Alaska Airlines | 800 426-0333 | ConcourseC,D, North Satellite | Icelandair | 800-223-5500 | South Satellite |
| | | | JetBlue Airways | 800-JETBLUE | Concourse D |
| American Airlines | 800 433-7300 | Concourse D | Korean Air | 800-438-5000 | South Satellite |
| Asiana Airlines | 800 227-4262 | South Satellite | Lufthansa Airlines | 800 399-LUFT | South Satellite |
| British Airways | 800 247-9297 | South Satellite | Southwest Airlines | 800 435-9792 | Concourse B |
| Condor | 866-960-7915 | South Satellite | Sun Country | 800 359-6786 | Concourse A |
| Delta Air Lines | 800 221-1212 | South Satellite | United Airlines | 800 241-6522 | Concourse A |
| EVA Air | 800 695-1188 | South Satellite | United Express | 800 241-6522 | Concourse A |
| Emirates | 800-777-3999 | South Satellite | US Airways | 800 428-4322 | Concourse A |
| Frontier Airlines | 800 432-1359 | Concourse B | Virgin America | 877 359-8474 | Concourse B |

## General Information

| | |
|---|---|
| Address: | 17801 International Blvd Seattle, WA 98158 |
| Phone: | 206-433-5388 |
| Websites: | www.portseattle.org/Sea-Tac/ Pages/default.aspx |
| Airport Police: | 206-431-3490 |
| Ground Transportation: | Various providers. Please check website. |
| Lost & Found: | 206-443-5312 |
| Customer Service: | 800-508-1705 |

## Overview

Prior to 1944, Boeing Field was Seattle's main passenger airport. When the U.S. Military took it over for use in World War II, we needed a new commercial airport. Thus, Sea-Tac International Airport was born.

Though in the top 30 of the world's busiest airports, Sea-Tac isn't a terribly harrowing travel experience. It consists of a main terminal with four concourses and two satellite terminals, which are connected to the main terminal via an underground tram. Trains run every 5–10 minutes, so it never takes long to get from one terminal to another. Overall, Sea-Tac is a well-run and organized airport, which is impressive when you consider that it catered to over 33 million passengers in 2012.

As with most airports these days, it is advisable to either check in online or at a self check-in station. However, our TSA agents seem to have a handle on security checks, as the line moves fairly quickly most of the time. Of course, in terms of airport travel, it is always advisable not to temp fate.

The one area in which Sea-Tac needs improvement is baggage handling. Even before the ban on liquids forced everyone to check their bags, it took forever for a flight to bring the luggage back to their owners. It is not unheard of for travelers to wait over an hour to collects their bags from a direct and on-time flight.

If you find yourself with some time, you can grab a bite to eat in the food court or take your chances with the inevitable Starbucks or gift shops in your terminal. For a decent sit-down meal, Anthony's in the Central Terminal is your best bet for quality. Beecher's Handmade Cheese, in Concourse C, serves

up great Mac and Cheese and Caffe Vita coffee and espresso. For a cocktail, glass wine, or pint of microbrew, there are several choices, none of which stand out as great. Anyone out there want to take up the challenge of opening a classic airport lounge?

## How to Get There—Driving

From the north or south, take I-5 to Exit 154 B and drive west on State Route 518 to the Sea-Tac Airport Exit. Heading east, take I-405, which turns into State Route 518, to the Sea-Tac Airport Exit. Signs are clearly marked from that point on.

## Parking

With cost-effective alternatives available, choosing to drive to Sea-Tac is akin to burning money, but there are many options for those willing to lighten their wallet. The top four floors of the garage offer hourly parking ($4 for the first and up to $35 a day). Long-term parking is also available for $28 a day with a "special weekly rate" of $130. Don't forget to bring your parking ticket with you for use in the exitxpress pay stations.

If you've managed to bribe a friend into picking you up, they can wait for you in the Cell Phone Waiting Lot. To get there, take the 170th/Air Cargo exit from the Airport Expressway. Turn right and take an immediate left into the clearly marked lot. To get to Baggage Claim from the lot, take a right out of the lot and then an immediate left at the To Terminal sign. Follow the signs to Arrivals.

## How to Get There—Mass Transit

Dreams do come true! You can now take the Light Rail straight to the airport from downtown in about 35 minutes. It's cheap, clean, and easy. It's a little bit of a hike to the terminals, but we don't mind after waiting years for the Light Rail to open. If you want to take the bus, look for route numbers 194 (about 30 minutes) or 174 (about 45 mintutes) to and from downtown Seattle. You can also take route numbers 140 and 560 to Burien and West Seattle and route number 574 to Lakewood. Metro also has route 180 to service Auburn, Kent, and Burien. If you are traveling during rush hour, you'll be trapped for a few hours in cramped quarters with surly Seattleites. You'll get enough of that on the airplane. For Metro schedules and trip planning, visit metro.kingcounty.gov.

## How to Get There—Shuttle

For shared rides, Shuttle Express (800-487-7433) services areas within a 30 mile radius. Pick-up and drop-off is on the third floor of the Airport Garage. The check-in for scheduled Airporter services is on the Baggage Claim level. Airporter Shuttle (866-235-5247) serves Western Washington. Capital Aerporter serves Seattle (253-838-7431), Olympia (360-754-7113), Tacoma (253-927-6179), and outside of Western Washington (800-962-3579). Gray Line Downtown Airporter (800-426-7532) departs twice an hour until 11 pm to major downtown Seattle hotels. Check the website for Airport Express schedules and other service areas.

## Car Rentals

Sea-Tac has a single car rental location from which all car rental companies do business from. A 24 hour, free shuttle takes customers to the location. Exit the baggage claim area at either carousel #1 or #15 and walk to the two designated pickup areas.

| | |
|---|---|
| Advantage | 800-777-5500 |
| Alamo | 800-462-5266 |
| Avis | 800-331-1212 |
| Budget | 800-527-7000 |
| Dollar | 206-433-5825 |
| Enterprise | 206-248-9013 |
| EZ Rent-A-Car | 800-277-5171 |
| Fox Rent-A-Car | 800-225-4369 |
| Hertz | 800-654-3131 |
| National | 800-328-4567 |
| Payless | 800-729-5377 |
| Sixt Rent A Car | 888-749-8227 |
| Thrifty | 206-246-7566 |

## January

**Martin Luther King Jr. Day**
March for peace, equality, or both—it's your choice. www.mlkseattle.org
**Seattle Asian American Film Festival**
Specialty showcase for Asian-American filmmakers nationwide. seattleaaff.org
**Children's Film Festival Seattle**
Films for kids and their families from all over the world. childrensfilmfestivalseattle.nwfilmforum.org

## February

**Mardis Gras**
Head to Pioneer Square, if that's your scene.
**Northwest Flower & Garden Show**
Annual flora fest bringing together green thumbs of all abilities since 1989. www.gardenshow.com

## March

**Seattle Moisture Festival**
A twisted cabaret with the scope of vaudeville. www.moisturefestival.com
**The Seattle Center Irish Festival**
Celebrating true Irish heritage, not simple stereotypes of shamrocks and whiskey.
**Seattle Erotic Art Festival**
Promotes freedom of sexuality, speech, and creativity. www.seattleerotic.org
**Emerald City Comicon**
Geek out at the largest gathering of comic book and pop culture fans in the Pacific NW. www.emeraldcitycomicon.com

## April

**Seattle Cherry Blossom & Japanese Cultural Festival**
Martial arts, kites, and tea at Seattle Center.
**Seattle Restaurant Week - Spring Edition**
Foodies short on cash can partake in 3-course prix fixe menus all over the city. seattletimes.com/seattlerestaurantweek
**Ballard Jazz Festival**
4 days, 15 venues, internationally renowned jazz musicians, and a Swedish pancake jazz brunch.
ballardjazzfestival.com

## May

**U District Street Fair**
First of the big summer festivals, crowded with art and dripping with funnel cake grease. udistrictstreetfair.org
**Folklife Festival**
Keeping traditional art and music alive. www.folklife.org
**Seattle International Film Festival**
Largest film fest in the US. Really. www.siff.net
**Seattle Beer Week**
Breweries, brewmasters, beery bearded dudes, and beer swigging babes unite! www.seattlebeerweek.com

## June

**Fremont Solstice Parade**
The wildest art party in the city. And yes, lots of naked people, for better or worse. www.fremontfair.com
**Seattle Pride**
Gay pride, that is. www.seattlepride.org
**Juneteenth**
A celebration of freedom from slavery in Pratt Park. scacc2108.org
**Ballard Locks Summer Concerts and Events**
Picnic every Saturday and Sunday at this free event, June through Labor Day. Just don't eat the migrating salmon.

## July

**Seafair**
A month-long tribute to Seattle's nautical heritage, with loud fighter jets and boat races. Beware of grown men dressed like pirates roaming the streets. www.seafair.com
**Bite of Seattle**
A showcase for local culinary excellence. www.biteofseattle.com

## July–continued

**Capitol Hill Block Party**
Who's who of Cap Hill rock culture. If you pay to get in, you're not really "in." www.capitolhillblockparty.com

**Ballard Seafood Fest**
Who knew fishermen still live in Ballard? www.seafoodfest.org

**Wooden Boat Festival**
Take a boat ride on Lake Union. www.cwb.org

**Seafair Summer Forth**
Fireworks over Lake Union. Who needs Chase bank anyway. www.seafair.com/AnEvent.aspx?ID=24&SecID=1018

**International District Dragon Fest**
Pan-Asian American party at Hing-Hay Park. Here be dragons. www.cidbia.org/events

**Seattle International Beerfest**
Brauereien, Braumeister, beery bärtigen Jungs und Bier saufenden Babes vereinigt euch! Thanks Google Translate!
www.seattlebeerfest.com

## August

**Sunset Supper**
Chow down and drink up at Pike Place Market for a good cause. www.pikeplacemarketfoundation.org

**Hempfest**
Rick-Steves-approved pro-legalization really, but who can think about politics after a few of those brownies?
www.hempfest.org

**Arab Festival**
Authentic Arabic food and strong coffee! arabcenterwa.org

**Central Area Festival & Parade**
Fostering community pride and cultural diversity. www.cacf.com

## September

**Bumbershoot**
The granddaddy of all Seattle festivals, with big stars and long lines. www.bumbershoot.org

**Do the Puyallup!**
Two words: mutton bustin'. www.thefair.com

**Fremont Oktoberfest**
Squeeze two weeks of beer tasting into one bleary-eyed weekend. www.fremontoktoberfest.com

**St. Demetrios Greek Festival**
Going strong since 1960. Eat, drink, and summon your inner Zorba in Montlake. www.seattlegreekfestival.com

## October

**Earshot Jazz Festival**
Bringing top jazzers to the Emerald City since 1989. www.earshot.org

**Seattle Restaurant Week - Fall Edition**
Foodies short on cash can partake in 3-course prix fixe menus all over the city. seattletimes.com/seattlerestaurantweek

**Turkfest**
Indulge your senses with a strong dose of Turksih culture. www.turkfest.org

## November

**Seattle Marathon**
Burn off some of the previous year's holiday gorging. www.seattlemarathon.org

## December

**Christmas Ship Festival**
Big boats in bright lights, and vice-versa. www.argosycruises.com/dining-cruises/christmas-ship-festival

**Pacific Northwest Ballet's Nutcracker**
Tchaikovsky's score with Maurice Sendak's scenic and costume design. Wild!
www.pnb.org/AboutPNB/Repertory/Nutcracker.aspx

**ACT A Christmas Carol**
Bah humbug to you if you don't go see this classic Seattle holiday show!
www.acttheatre.org/Tickets/OnStage/AChristmasCarol

## General Information

Website: www.seattle.gov/parks/parkspaces/
yodogs.htm

## Overview

Seattleites aren't just tree-huggers; they're dog lovers, too. Animals are dear to their hearts (if the plentitude of vegetarians/vegans is any indication) and dogs both abound and are bound here. And with the gorgeous backdrop that is the Emerald City, Seattle's dog parks are a far cry from most of the drab, chain-link gravel pits you'll find in other large cities. The eleven dog areas in Seattle are usually well-maintained, spacious, and just as much fun for man as it is for his best friend. Of course, there are a few obvious rules to follow. Keep your dog on a leash outside of the off-leash area (duh), make sure he or she has had all of the proper shots and licensing, and please, for heaven's sake, scoop the dang poop. The Citizens for Off-Leash Areas (COLA) is a community of dog owners committed to everything dog-park, so check out their site (www.coladog.org) for all you need to know. If you're not a good little doggie owner, beware—you could be slapped with a fine up to $150. Now, that's ruff! (Sorry.)

## Off-Leash Areas

### Genesee Park (Map 40)
4316 S Genesee St
Genesee Park and Playfield is a broad, rough meadow stretching for about five blocks north from Genesee Street to Stan Sayres Memorial Park on Lake Washington Boulevard. There is a separate fully-fenced off-leash area, complete with a doggie drinking fountain (aw!). It's gravelly and not all that interesting, but is flat and open—perfect for playing fetch.

### Golden Gardens (Map 33)
8498 Seaview Pl NW
This waterfront park is huge, running alongside Puget Sound. There are hiking trails for a nice little walk, restored wetlands, sandy beaches, fishing, boating, picnic tables—you name it, Golden's got it. The icing on the cake is the stunning view of the Olympics along the rugged coastline. Uphill to the east is a moderately-sized off-leash area for your doggie. Just be sure to bring your galoshes if there's a hint of rain, as it can get extremely mucky.

### I-5 Colonnade (Map 20)
Beneath I-5, south of E Howe St b/w Lakeview Blvd & Franklin Ave E
This is a weird, creepy park underneath roaring I-5 on Capitol Hill. It's a huge, maze-like gravel pit with lots of chain-link fence, no open areas, and concrete blocks everywhere, their function mysterious. Not the best for fancy-free frolicking with your dog, but if you're just taking Fido out to do his business, it works. There is however a cool mountain bike course under construction and an art installation by John Roloff.

### Magnuson Park (Map 27)
7400 Sand Point Wy NE
The absolute crème de la crème of dog parks in Seattle. The park itself is 40 acres, with a whopping *nine* of them dedicated to an off-leash pooch area. It's a veritable Disneyland for dogs, with several different scenic areas (dirt hills, grassy brush, mud pit), an exclusive shy/older dog pen, and a flat gravel area for fetch. The highlight is a long winding trail leading down to the shores of Lake Washington—Magnuson is the only dog park within city limits with water access. It's also a great park for socializing with other owners.

### Northacres Park (Map 34)
12718 1st Ave NE
Tucked away next to some athletic fields, this park is small but lots of fun. It's an intimate maze-like affair with lots of short trails through dense, well-kept foliage. Small open areas spring up along the way with benches for a quick rest while your dog bounds through the brush.

### Blue Dog Pond (Map 9)
Martin Luther King Jr Wy S & S Massachusetts

### Dr. Jose Rizal Park (Map 8)
1008 12th Ave S

### Plymouth Pillars Park (Map 3)
Boren Ave b/w Pike St & Pine St

### Regrade Park (Map 1)
2251 3rd Ave

### Westcrest Park (Map 38)
8806 8th Ave SW

### Woodland Park (Map 31)
W Greenlake Wy N

## Best Rainy Day Activities

Here are a several places to help you and your kids battle cabin fever and keep your sanity during those long, rainy months of winter.

**International District:** Yes, honey, those ducks are for eating.

**Waterfront/Piers:** Fish n' chips! Seagulls! An arcade! Pirates!

**Pacific Science Center:** Giant insects.

**Seattle Central Library:** Holy cow, this place is huge!!!

**Ballard Library:** The roof is alive and growing!

**Experience Music Project:** Mommy, what's that man doing to his guitar?

**Burke Museum:** Dinosaurs!

**Museum of History and Industry (MOHAI):** Learn about Seattle from its humble beginnings to its dotcom boasting present-day. Speculate about its future in the excellent Compass Café.

**Seattle Center:** A big, urban park with museums, food courts, and a huge fountain.

**PlayDate SEA:** This 8,500 square foot indoor playground is custom made for free-range children and the coffee-addicted parents who love them.

**Seattle Children's Museum:** Kid-centered museum.

**Seattle Aquarium:** Pretty fish.

**Woodlawn Park Zoo:** Yes, it's mostly outside, but those animals sure are cool.

## The Best of the Best

### Rock on, Dude

The Vera Project is a long-time all-ages music venue and teen-centered non-profit recently relocated to the Seattle Center's Snoqualmie Room. Kids rock out to Seattle bands big and small while parents go to the opera. They also have volunteer projects for kids and host a variety of classes including breakdancing and punk rock.

### Feed the Seagulls

Take your kids to Ivar's on the pier, munch on fish and chips while watching the ferries come and go, then fend off the seagulls with those crusty, hard leftover bits at the bottom.

### Ice Cream Cruise

Yeah, kids like ice cream. But what's better than ice cream? Ice cream on a boat! Sip on a classic root beer float and enjoy the scenery. Departs hourly 11 am to 5 pm, every Sunday from under the Aurora Bridge (801 N Northlake Wy, 206 713-8446; www.seattleferryservice.com)

### Learn to Build a Bike

At Bike Works, kids can learn how to build a bike. And after working eight hours, that bike is theirs to take home.

### Give Them Gas

The giant iron wrought structures of Gasworks Park make this a great kid-friendly destination. Fly a kite at the top of the hill, watch the seaplanes land on Lake Union, or look for unrefined oil ooze out of the ground (and if you find some, please contact the authorities).

### Ferries

Did you see that? Was that a Whale? They say 90 orcas (once known by the killer nickname, killer whales) live in Puget Sound, so if you take a ferry ride you should see one, right? Wait! What's that? Is that a whale? Maybe it's a shark? Or a sturgeon? Can you see sturgeons from the ferries? Ride the ferries and find out.

### Culture: Seattle Style

Quirky Fremont is a kid-like, permanently silly place. Start the tour off at 36th and Fremont Place at the Lenin Statue, and ponder the future of communism in Seattle. Head across the street towards the water a block to The Rocket, which traveled to the moon thirty-five times before retiring in 1986. From there, take a left to the other end of the block and you'll be standing at the actual Center of the Universe. Pretty cool, huh? But don't stand too long or you'll cause an imbalance. Next, cross the street and head downhill until you see those people Waiting for the Interurban. They've been waiting so long, they've turned to stone. Head under the Aurora Bridge to find the infamous Fremont Troll. This troll wandered the thick forests of north Seattle, mercilessly devouring all those who dared to cross the water, until a group of kids turned him to stone in a grueling 22-day battle in 1950. Unfortunately, the troll destroyed their VW Bug in the process.

### Let's Go Sledding

It rarely snows in Seattle—bummer, eh? But when it does, boy is it fun. The entire city shuts down with the thought of three inches of snow—businesses cut their hours, downtown office workers play hooky, buses take alternate routes, and best of all, schools close. Actually, that's second best. The best part about snow in Seattle is that all these huge hills turn into giant, carless sledding runs. Grab a cardboard box, wrap yourself in cellophane, and hit the slopes! Be sure to supervise the kids and have hot chocolate ready upon the return to home. If you don't want to wait for Mother Nature to get freaky, hop on I-90 to the relatively snowy Summit at Snoqualmie, where they rent tubes every winter.

### Shopping Essentials

**Magic Mouse Toys** • 603 1st Ave • 206-682-8097 • We think it's run by elves.

**Archie McPhee** • 1300 N 45th St • 206-297-0240 • All the greatest pleasures in life—rubber lizards, fake spiders-in-ice, and boxing nun puppets.

**Top Ten Toys** • 104 N 85th St • 206-782-0098 • Educational toys for kids of all ages.

**Math N Stuff** • 8926 Roosevelt Wy NE • 206-522-8891 • Fun Math?! No Way?!

**Elliott Bay Books** • Elliott Bay Book Company • 1521 Tenth Ave • 206-624-6600 • Great kids section and children's storytime every Saturday.

**Schmancy** • 1932 2nd Ave • 206-728-8008 • Super quirky "toy shop," more for the childish adult or the mature minded child.

**Blue Highway Games** • 2203 Queen Anne Ave N • 206-282-0540 • Old school and very cool. Board games, brainteasers, card games, jigsaw puzzles. Free instore game nights every Saturday.

**Greenwood Space Travel Supply** • 8414 Greenwood Ave N • 206-725-2625 • For budding astronauts and freeze-dried dessert aficionados.

## Emergency Rooms

| | Address | Phone | Map |
|---|---|---|---|
| Children's Hospital and Regional Medical Center | 4800 Sand Point Wy NE | 206-987-2000 | 27 |
| Evergreen Hospital Medical Center | 12040 NE 128th St | 425-899-1000 | 48 |
| Evergreen Urgent Care | 8301 161st Ave NE | 425-883-3333 | 49 |
| Harborview Medical Center | 325 9th Ave | 206-731-3000 | 8 |
| Northwest Hospital and Medical Center | 1550 N 115th St | 206-364-0500 | 33 |
| Overlake Hospital | 1035 116th Ave NE | 425-688-5325 | 46 |
| Swedish Medical Center / Ballard | 5300 Tallman Ave NW | 206-782-2700 | 23 |
| Swedish Medical Center - First Hill | 747 Broadway | 206-386-6000 | 4 |
| Swedish Medical Center - Providence | 500 17th Ave | 206-320-2000 | 5 |
| University of Washington Medical Center | 1959 NE Pacific St | 206-598-3300 | 26 |
| Virginia Mason Medical Center | 1100 9th Ave | 206-223-6600 | 4 |

## Other Hospitals

| | Address | Phone | Map |
|---|---|---|---|
| City of Hope | 1309 114th Ave SE | 425-646-9530 | 43 |
| Fairfax Psychiatric Hospital | 10200 NE 132nd St | 425-821-2000 | 48 |
| Group Health Capitol Hill Campus | 201 16th Ave E | 206-326-3000 | 18 |
| Kindred Hospital | 10631 8th Ave NE | 206-364-2050 | 34 |
| The Polyclinic First Hill | 1145 Broadway | 206-329-1760 | 4 |

# General Information · **Hotels**

Sometimes you need a hotel room that's a step up from Aurora Avenue. Maybe you'd like to offer your visiting Aunt Mildred something more comfy than your futon. Maybe it's late and your condo on the Eastside seems intolerably far away. Maybe there are things you need to do in this hotel that you can't do at home. Whatever your business, here are the options.

## Obscenely Expensive

Ranking as the only AAA five-diamond hotel in the Pacific Northwest, the **Fairmont Olympic (Map 3)** is in a class by itself, with single rooms starting around $300. The terrifying grandeur of the lobby is worth a peek, even if you have neither means nor motive to stay there. Or, for an Italianate flair, try the **Sorrento Hotel (Map 4)**, a bit more out of the way on First Hill. Starting at $215, you can stay at **The Edgewater (Map 1)**, a sort of the posh Chelsea Hotel steeping with rock history involving the Beatles, Led Zeppelin and fish. **Hotel Max (Map 2)** doubles as an art gallery, running $215-250. **The Arctic Club (Map 3)** was a private retreat for those who struck it rich in Alaska's Gold Rush. In 2008, Doubletree bought it but it retains the vintage hotel vibe. **Hotel 1000 (Map 3)** is perhaps so called because rooms go for around a grand (but at least they throw in free champagne at check-in). Kimpton Hotels are quirky and fun, great for treating yourself without feeling like a sell-out. In descending rate order: **Hotel Monaco (Map 3)**, **The Alexis Hotel (Map 3)** and **Hotel Vintage Park (Map 3)**. **The Inn at the Market (Map 3)** is an extremely popular boutique hotel located right in tourist central that averages $300 a night. If you're staying in Kirkland but want to feel like you're somewhere better, you can plunk down $200 at **The Heathman (Map 48)**.

## Indulgent, but Not Ostentatious

Downtown Seattle is glutted with boutique hotels who make their names on style and service. **The Inn at El Gaucho (Map 1)** evokes a retro, boys' club glamour. Take a voyage of discovery to the **Mayflower Park Hotel (Map 3)**, a vintage boutique with a cool bar to match. If you like a more hands-on accommodation, **Pensione Nichols (Map 3)** provides the tenuous experience that's synonymous with B&Bs.

## Avoid the Indignities of Motel 6

A fine choice north of Lake Union is the **Watertown Hotel (Map 26)** in the U District. In addition to providing a nice clean place at a reasonable price, they sweeten the deal with free lobby cupcakes. If a glamorous hotel experience just isn't in the cards, your first choice should be Belltown's **Ace Hotel (Map 1)**. Though the cheapest rates require a shared bathroom, that bathroom is the height of modern design. The **Moore Hotel (Map 3)** offers immaculate, no-frills accommodation in a great location for downtown entertainment. The **University Inn (Map 26)** goes for $100 a night for an experience that is perfectly adequate. The B&B experience at **9 Cranes Inn (Map 30)** starts at $139 and they don't slack in either B department. **The College Inn (Map 26)** flirts with hostel territory, but if you don't mind sharing a bathroom, you can have your very own bed and wash basin for around $75. The **Georgetown Inn (Map 39)** is a decent option within walking distance one of Seattle's hippest strips. At around $140, the **Gaslight Inn (Map 4)** and **11th Avenue Inn (Map 17)** are an economical and exceedingly pleasant way to experience Capitol Hill. Lest we leave out our backpacking friends, the best bunks are at the friendly and inauspicious **Green Tortoise Hostel (Map 3)** and go for about $35.

## Map 1 · Belltown

| | Address | Phone | Nightly Rate $ |
|---|---|---|---|
| Ace Hotel | 2423 1st Ave | 206-448-4721 | 99 |
| Belltown Inn | 2301 3rd Ave | 206-529-3700 | 150 |
| The Edgewater Hotel | 2411 Alaskan Wy | 206-728-7000 | 215 |
| Hotel Andra | 2000 4th Ave | 206-448-8600 | 200 |
| Hotel Five | 2200 5th Ave | 206-866-7977 | 150 |
| Inn At El Gaucho | 2505 1st Ave | 206-728-1133 | 175 |
| King's Inn | 2106 5th Ave | 206-441-8833 | 57 |
| Ramada Seattle Downtown | 2200 5th Ave | 206-441-9785 | 100 |
| Vermont Inn | 2721 4th Ave | 206-441-0101 | 75 |
| Warwick Seattle Hotel | 401 Lenora St | 206-443-4300 | 170 |
| The Westin Seattle | 1900 5th Ave | 206-728-1000 | 189 |

## Map 2 · South Lake Union

| | Address | Phone | Nightly Rate $ |
|---|---|---|---|
| Best Western Loyal Inn | 2301 8th Ave | 206-682-0200 | 144 |
| Days Inn Town Center | 2205 7th Ave | 206-448-3434 | 100 |
| Holiday Inn | 211 Dexter Ave N | 206-728-8123 | 130 |
| Holiday Inn Exp City Center | 226 Aurora Ave N | 206-441-7222 | 160 |

| | | | |
|---|---|---|---|
| Hotel Max | 620 Stewart St | 206-728-6299 | 215 |
| La Quinta Inn & Suites Seattle Downtown | 2224 8th Ave | 206-624-6820 | 160 |
| Pan Pacific Hotel Seattle | 2125 Terry Ave | 206-264-8111 | 275 |
| Seattle Pacific Hotel | 325 Aurora Ave N | 206-441-0400 | 139 |
| Sixth Avenue Inn | 2000 6th Ave | 206-441-8300 | 75 |
| SpringHill Suites Seattle Downtown/ South Lake Union | 1800 Yale Ave | 206-254-0500 | 119 |

## Map 3 · Downtown

| | | | |
|---|---|---|---|
| Alexis Hotel | 1007 1st Ave | 206-624-4844 | 300 |
| Arctic Club Hotel | 700 3rd Ave | 206-340-0340 | 199 |
| Crowne Plaza Downtown | 1113 6th Ave | 206-464-1980 | 189 |
| Doubletree Arctic Club Hotel | 700 3rd Ave | 206-340-0340 | 345 |
| Executive Hotel Pacific | 400 Spring St | 206-623-3900 | 189 |
| Fairmont Olympic Hotel | 411 University St | 206-621-1700 | 300 |
| Four Seasons Hotel | 99 Union St | 206-749-7000 | 375 |
| Grand Hyatt | 721 Pine St | 206-774-1234 | 245 |
| Green Tortoise Hostel | 105 Pike St | 206-340-1222 | 35 |
| Hilton Seattle | 1301 6th Ave | 206-624-0500 | 192 |
| Hotel 1000 | 1000 1st Ave | 206-957-1000 | 1000 |
| Hotel Monaco | 1101 4th Ave | 206-621-1770 | 389 |
| Hotel Seattle | 315 Seneca St | 206-623-5110 | 110 |
| Hyatt at Olive 8 | 1635 8th Ave | 206-695-1234 | 150 |
| Inn at Harbor Steps | 1221 1st Ave | 206-748-0973 | 175 |
| The Inn at the Market | 86 Pine St | 206-443-3600 | 300 |
| Mayflower Park Hotel | 405 Olive Wy | 206-623-8700 | 159 |
| Moore Hotel | 1926 2nd Ave | 206-448-4851 | 85 |
| Pacific Plaza Hotel | 400 Spring St | 206-623-3900 | 100 |
| The Paramount Hotel | 724 Pine St | 206-292-9500 | 169 |
| Pensione Nichols | 1923 1st Ave | 206-441-7125 | 99 |
| Red Lion Hotel On Fifth Avenue | 1415 5th Ave | 206-971-8000 | 165 |
| Renaissance Seattle Hotel | 515 Madison St | 206-583-0300 | 210 |
| The Roosevelt Hotel | 1531 7th Ave | 206-621-1200 | 125 |
| Seattle Waterfront Marriott | 2100 Alaskan Wy | 206-443-5000 | 270 |
| Sheraton Seattle Hotel | 1400 6th Ave | 206-621-9000 | 200 |
| Vintage Park Hotel | 1100 5th Ave | 206-624-8000 | 270 |
| W Seattle | 1112 4th Ave | 206-264-6000 | 330 |

## Map 4 · First Hill / Pike / Pine

| | | | |
|---|---|---|---|
| The Baroness Hotel | 1005 Spring St | 206-624-0787 | 127 |
| Gaslight Inn | 1727 15th Ave | 206-325-3654 | 130 |
| Homewood Suites by Hilton | 1011 Pike St | 206-682-8282 | 180 |
| Inn at Virginia Mason | 1006 Spring St | 206-583-6453 | 149 |
| Seattle Suites | 1400 Hubbell Pl | 206-232-2799 | 130 |
| Silver Cloud Inn - Seattle Broadway | 1100 Broadway | 206-325-1400 | 200 |
| Sorrento Hotel | 900 Madison St | 206-622-6400 | 270 |

## Map 5 · Central District (North)

| | | | |
|---|---|---|---|
| Sleeping Bulldog Bed & Breakfast | 816 19th Ave S | 206-325-0202 | 200 |

## Map 7 · Pioneer Square / SoDo

| | | | |
|---|---|---|---|
| Best Western Pioneer Square Hotel | 77 Yesler Wy | 206-340-1234 | 160 |

## Map 8 · International District

| | | | |
|---|---|---|---|
| Panama Hotel | 605 S Main St | 206-223-9242 | 85 |

## Map 14 · Queen Anne (West)

| | | | |
|---|---|---|---|
| Homewood Suites Seattle | 206 Western Ave W | 206-281-9393 | 150 |

## Map 15 · Lower Queen Anne / Seattle Center

| | | | |
|---|---|---|---|
| Best Western Executive Inn | 200 Taylor Ave N | 206-448-9444 | 140 |
| Comfort Suites | 601 Roy St | 206-282-2600 | 150 |
| Hampton Inn & Suites Downtown/ Seattle Center | 700 5th Ave N | 206-282-7700 | 170 |
| Inn At Queen Anne | 505 1st Ave N | 206-282-7357 | 100 |
| MarQueen Hotel | 600 Queen Anne Ave N | 206-282-7407 | 130 |
| Mediterranean Inn | 425 Queen Anne Ave N | 206-428-4700 | 100 |
| Quality Inn & Suites Seattle Center | 618 John St | 206-728-7666 | 75 |
| Travelodge By The Space Needle | 200 6th Ave N | 206-441-7878 | 130 |

## Map 16 · Westlake / South Lake Union

| | | | |
|---|---|---|---|
| Courtyard Seattle Downtown/Lake Union | 925 Westlake Ave N | 206-213-0100 | 170 |
| Residence Inn Downtown Lake Union | 800 Fairview Ave N | 206-624-6000 | 170 |
| Silver Cloud Inn - Seattle Lake Union | 1150 Fairview Ave N | 206-447-9500 | 180 |

## Map 17 · Capitol Hill (West)

| | | | |
|---|---|---|---|
| 11th Avenue Inn | 121 11th Ave E | 206-720-7161 | 79 |
| Bacon Mansion Bed and Breakfast | 959 Broadway E | 800-240-1864 | 150 |
| Shafer Baillie Mansion Bed and Breakfast | 907 14th Ave E | 206-322-4654 | 150 |

## Map 18 · Capitol Hill (East) / Madison Valley

| | | | |
|---|---|---|---|
| Mildred's Bed and Breakfast | 1202 15th Ave E | 206-325-6072 | 125 |
| Salisbury House Bed and Breakfast | 750 16th Ave E | 206-328-8682 | 150 |

## Map 20 · Eastlake / Montlake / Portage Bay

| | | | |
|---|---|---|---|
| Eastlake Inn | 2215 Eastlake Ave E | 206-322-7726 | 65 |

## Map 23 · Ballard

| | | | |
|---|---|---|---|
| Starlight Hotel | 5300 Ballard Ave NW | 206-784-8304 | 109 |

## Map 24 · Fremont

| | | | |
|---|---|---|---|
| Chelsea Station On The Park | 4915 Linden Ave N | 206-547-6077 | 110 |
| Marco Polo Motel | 4114 Aurora Ave N | 206-633-4090 | 65 |
| Park Plaza Motel | 4401 Aurora Ave N | 206-632-2101 | 45 |

## Map 26 · U District

| | | | |
|---|---|---|---|
| Best Western University Tower Hotel | 4507 Brooklyn Ave NE | 206-634-2000 | 170 |
| Chambered Nautilus Bed Breakfast Inn | 5005 22nd Ave NE | 206-522-2536 | 120 |
| College Inn | 4000 University Wy NE | 206-633-4441 | 40 |
| Silver Cloud Inn - Seattle University | 5036 25th Ave NE | 206-526-5200 | 200 |
| Travelodge Seattle University | 4725 25th Ave NE | 206-525-4612 | 145 |
| University Motel Suites | 4731 12th Ave Ne | 206-522-4724 | 70 |
| University Inn | 4140 Roosevelt Wy NE | 206-632-5055 | 99 |
| Watertown Hotel | 4242 Roosevelt Wy NE | 206-826-4242 | 213 |

## Map 30 · Greenwood / Phinney Ridge

| | | | |
|---|---|---|---|
| Sun Hill Motel | 8517 Aurora Ave N | 206-525-1205 | 55 |
| Travelodge Seattle North of Downtown | 8512 Aurora Ave N | 206-522-5000 | 90 |

## Map 33 · Northwest Seattle

| | | | |
|---|---|---|---|
| Ambassador Motel | 12059 Aurora Ave N | 206-362-6000 | 49 |
| Aurora Nites Inn | 11746 Aurora Ave N | 206-365-3216 | 50 |
| Columbus Motor Inn | 9613 Aurora Ave N | 206-524-8880 | 55 |
| Days Inn | 9100 Aurora Ave N | 206-524-3600 | 65 |
| Georgian Motel | 8801 Aurora Ave N | 206-524-1004 | 50 |
| Green Lake Motel | 8900 Aurora Ave N | 206-523-4703 | 41 |
| Holiday Inn Exp Ste Northgate | 14115 Aurora Ave N | 206-365-7777 | 110 |
| Hotel Nexus | 2140 N Northgate Wy | 866-578-9512 | 100 |
| Klose in Motel | 9309 Aurora Ave N | 206-527-0330 | 40 |
| Orion Motel | 12045 Aurora Ave N | 206-364-6095 | 45 |

## Map 36 · North Delridge

| | | | |
|---|---|---|---|
| Seattle West Inn | 3512 SW Alaska St | 206-937-9920 | 80 |

## Map 37 · Fauntleroy / Arbor Heights

| | | | |
|---|---|---|---|
| Wildwood Bed & Breakfast | 4518 SW Wildwood Pl | 206-819-9075 | 80 |

## Map 38 · Delridge / White Center

| | | | |
|---|---|---|---|
| Munson Motel | 7060 E Marginal Wy S | 206-762-6684 | 50 |

## Map 39 · SoDo / Beacon Hill / Georgetown

| | | | |
|---|---|---|---|
| Georgetown Inn | 6100 Corson Ave S | 206-762-2233 | 70 |
| La Hacienda Motel | 5414 1st Ave S | 206-762-2460 | 50 |

## Map 44 · Bellevue (South)

| | | | |
|---|---|---|---|
| Days Inn Bellevue | 3241 156th Ave SE | 425-643-6644 | 90 |
| Embassy Suites Hotel Seattle-Bellevue | 3225 158th Ave SE | 425-644-2500 | 130 |
| Silver Cloud Inn - Bellevue Eastgate | 14632 SE Eastgate Wy | 425-957-9100 | 180 |

## Map 45 · Bellevue (West) / Medina

| | | | |
|---|---|---|---|
| Courtyard Seattle Bellevue Downtown | 11010 NE 8th St | 425-454-5888 | 140 |
| Hilton Bellevue | 300 112th Ave SE | 425-455-1300 | 129 |
| Hyatt Regency Bellevue | 900 Bellevue Wy NE | 425-462-1234 | 150 |
| La Quinta Inn Seattle Bellevue | 10530 Northup Wy | 425-828-6585 | 100 |
| La Residence Suite Hotel | 475 100th Ave Ne | 425-455-1475 | 135 |
| Paragon Hotel Bellevue | 818 112th Ave NE | 425-455-1515 | 100 |
| Red Lion Hotel Bellevue | 11211 Main St | 425-455-5240 | 200 |
| Silver Cloud Inn - Bellevue 12th St | 10621 NE 12th St | 425-637-7000 | 180 |
| The Westin Bellevue | 600 Bellevue Way NE | 425-638-1000 | 279 |
| The Woodmark Hotel on Lake Washington | 1200 Carillon Point | 425-822-3700 | 260 |

## Map 46 · Bellevue (Central)

| | | | |
|---|---|---|---|
| Coast Bellevue Hotel | 625 116th Ave NE | 425-455-9444 | 100 |
| Courtyard Seattle Bellevue Redmond | 14615 NE 29th Pl | 425-869-5300 | 120 |
| Residence Inn Seattle Bellevue Downtown | 605 114th Ave SE | 425-637-5800 | 149 |
| Silver Cloud Inns - Redmond | 2122 152nd Ave NE | 425-746-8200 | 180 |

## Map 48 · Kirkland

| | | | |
|---|---|---|---|
| Baymont Inn & Suites | 12223 NE 116th St | 425-822-2300 | 100 |
| Clarion Inn At Totem Lake | 12233 NE Totem Lake Wy | 425-821-2202 | 165 |
| Comfort Inn Kirkland | 12204 NE 124th St | 425-821-8300 | 100 |
| The Heathman Hotel | 220 Kirkland Ave | 425-284-5800 | 200 |
| Motel 6 | 12010 120th Pl NE | 425-821-5618 | 60 |

## Map 49 · Redmond

| | | | |
|---|---|---|---|
| Redmond Inn | 17601 Redmond Wy | 425-883-4900 | 85 |

Seattle is a city of few monuments and has little in the way of epic architecture (the **Central Library (Map 3)** notwithstanding). When other American cities were stockpiling marble and granite, Seattle was still a muddy outpost with wooden sidewalks. Today, post-boom, there remains an unfinished feeling to the landscape. Our most iconic landmark, The **Space Needle (Map 15)**, is largely ignored and sometimes reviled by Seattleites. Same goes for that useless hunk-o-metal better known as the **Monorail (Map 15)**. On the other hand, Seattle possesses no shortage of humorous, weird, usually misguided displays of civic pride and identity.

## Historic Seattle

An obvious place to start is the 100-plus-year-old **Pike Place Market (Map 3)**. Beset though it is by tourists determined to see airborne fish, the market still has a lot to offer local residents. **Smith Tower (Map 7)** was the tallest building west of the Mississippi for nearly 50 years. Both the **Paramount Theatre (Map 3)** and **5th Avenue Theatre (Map 3)** take visitors back to vaudeville days. The **Seattle Asian Art Museum (Map 17)** is a 1933 Art Deco wonder in the middle of Volunteer Park. To go back even further, the **Birthplace of Seattle Monument (Map 35)**, an obelisk on Alki Point, marks the arrival of the first white folk in 1851.

## Open Spaces

Though there have been a few missteps in the parks department—consider the scary, concrete wonderland of **Freeway Park (Map 3)**—the out-of-doors is what Seattle does best. From the untouched to the intricately landscaped, you are never far away from a patch of green in the Emerald City. For complete respite from the urban din, **Discovery Park (Map 11)** is the largest, and perhaps wildest, park within city limits. If it's botany you're after, **Washington Arboretum (Map 22)** on Union Bay contains an herbarium, horticulture center, the **Japanese Garden (Map 19)**, and it's accessible by kayak. The gardens at **Woodland Park (Map 30)** and the **Hiram M. Chittenden Locks (Map 28)** (a.k.a. the Ballard Locks) are gorgeous in season. Both **Gas Works Park (Map 24)** and **Kerry Park (Map 14)** afford postcard-worthy views of the skyline. Finally, **Volunteer Park (Map 18)** on the Hill is Seattle's ultimate urban oasis.

## Public Art

Despite Seattle's reputation for lefty-leaning political attitudes, the existence of a mammoth statue of **Vladimir Lenin (Map 24)** in the heart of the Fremont neighborhood strikes most spectators as puzzling. Built in Slovakia and transported to the Emerald City after the fall of communism, this handsome piece now stands among Mexican restaurants, fashionable clothing boutiques, and other bastions of capitalism. Other public sculptures make for easier contextualization, such as Pioneer Square's life-size bronze **Fallen Firefighters' Memorial (Map 7)**, Fremont's six cast-aluminum **Waiting for the Interurban (Map 24)**, and the **Jimi Hendrix Statue (Map 4)** on Capitol Hill. The alluring **Bettie Page Mural (Map 31)** makes commuting interesting for those stuck on I-5, while the **Martin Luther King Jr. Mural (Map 5)** inspires contemplation and reflection each time you stroll by.

## Lowbrow Landmarks

With esoterica such as the mammoth, hippy-hating **Fremont Troll (Map 24)**, Seattle's oddball landmarks expose the real character of the city. Not even Wikipedia can explain the existence of Post Alley's **Gum Wall (Map 3)** or the **Wall of Death (Map 26)**, a sculpture that pays homage to, of all things, a motorcycle stunt. The pink pachyderms of the **Elephant Carwash (Map 2)** offer a comment on the historic value of neon. The **Spooky Coke Machine (Map 17)** is a thirst-quenching mystery. Georgetown's **Hat 'n' Boots (Map 39)** is pure Americana—a roadside wonder built for a gas station now ensconced in a local park. As funky bars go, none is so well-steeped in grime and history as the **Blue Moon Tavern (Map 25)**, a former haunt of beat poets and other counterculture figures.

Shortly after Stonewall's major breakthrough in 1969, Seattle's queer culture began to rally for its rights. Students of the University of Washington united to claim their existence and formed organizations. Political activists set up shop in Pioneer Square to protest discrimination. In 1973, the Seattle City Council passed the Fair Employment Practice Ordinance which protected gays and lesbians in the workforce. Eventually, 1977 gave birth to Gay Pride Week which paraded the streets of downtown and traveled up Capitol Hill's slope, where LGBT culture currently reigns. Throughout years of struggles and victories, the women and men of sexual diversities built a strong community for one another. And to this day their efforts thrive in every proud, queer Seattleite.

Seattle's rainy streets are willing and able to compassionately support you in many ways. Local newspapers and guides post listings of entertainment, organized groups, health centers, and gay friendly synagogues. Community publications are distributed to coffee bars, restaurants, clubs, bookstores, and well, just about anywhere dry. Flip through pages and pages of gay adventures for any night or day (both if you get lucky). You can find dykes to dance with and cowboys to ride. Whatever floats your boat, plenty of information can easily be found.

For the most part you can feel safe to publicly express gay affection. Not too many straight citizens express hatred when men grasp hands and women passionately embrace. Also, if your gaydar is finely tuned (or you're just obvious), then it's almost certain to acknowledge family anywhere in the city. Even though the rainy city is a bit introverted, Seattle queers are not too shy to engage in friendly chats. Yes indeed, it's a quaint little home for any ol' chap or dyke. In fact, many queer southerners venture north to saddle up here.

## Publications/Media

**Greater Seattle Business Association (GSBA)** • Directory of businesses and community organizations that are owned, operated, and allies of LGBT.

**Seattle Gay News** • 1605 12th Ave, #31 • 206-324-4297 • www.sgn.org • Local newspaper featuring LGBT everything a gay community needs.

**Seattle Treatment Education Project (STEP)** • 206- 328-8979 • www.thebody.com/content/art1792.html • E-zine resource distributed to people affected by HIV/AIDS, case managers, front line workers, and other health professionals.

**Capitol Hill Times** • www.capitolhilltimes.com • Local newspaper covering Capitol Hill and First Hill news.

**GO!** • www.gomag.com • Woman loving women zine featuring national news, events, art, and culture.

## Arts and Culture

**Rainbow City Band** • 12144 Shorewood Dr SW • 206- 431-9484 • www.rainbowcityband.com

**Seattle Men's Chorus/ Seattle Women's Chorus** • 319 12th Ave • 206- 323-0750 x212 • Both can be found at www.flyinghouse.org

## Sports and Recreation

**Different Spokes Bicycling Club** • www.differentspokes.org

**Emerald City Softball Association (Open Division)** • 3828 Beach Dr SW Ste 202 • 206-938-7402 • www.seattlegaysoftball.com

**Orca Swim Team** • 1122 E Pike, PMB #869 • www.orcaswimteam.org

**Seattle Frontrunners** • www.seattlefrontrunners.org

**Seattle Tennis Alliance** • www.seattletennisalliance.org

**Team Seattle Gay Sports Network** • 206- 367-4064 • www.teamseattle.org

## Social Groups / Organizations

**BinNet Seattle** · 206-728-4533 ·
www.binetseattle.org

**Border Riders Motorcycle Club** · 206-686-4176 ·
www.borderriders.com

**Cookboys Potluck** · 206-860-6969 · event for all ages

**Ethyl Forever Car Club** · 206-995-8833 ·
ethylforever@hotmail.com

**Gay Fathers' Association of Seattle** ·
www.gfas.org

**Mature Friends** · 206-781-7724 ·
www.maturefriends.org

**Northwest Bears** · 206-903-9288 ·
www.nwbears.com

**Puddletown Dancers** · 425-487-0219 ·
www.puddletowndancers.org

**Queer Ladies Stitch & Bitch** ·
queerladiesstichnbitch@yahoo.com

**Queer Teen Ensemble Theatre (QUTET)** · 608
19th Ave E · www.washingtonensemble.org

**Seattle Bisexual Women's Network** ·
www.sbwn.net

**Seattle Gay Couples** · www.seattlegaycouples.com

**Seattle Men in Leather** ·
www.seattlemeninleather.org

**Seattle Prime Timers** · 206-329-0793 ·
www.seattleprimetimers.org

**Trikone-Northwest: South Asian Queer
Community** · 1122 E Pike St, #1174 ·
425-985-4376 · www.trikone-nw.org

## Political Groups/Activism

**Equal Rights Washington** · PO Box 12216 ·
206-324-2570 · www.equalrightswashington.org

**Greater Seattle Business Association (GBSA)** ·
2150 N 107th St, Ste 205 · 206-363-9188 ·
www.thegsba.org

**Greater Seattle Chamber of Commerce** ·
1301 15th Ave, #250 · 206-389-7215

**National Gay and Lesbian Chamber of
Commerce** · 202-419-0440 · www.nglcc.org

**National Gay & Lesbian Task Force** ·
202-393-5177 · www.thetaskforce.org

**Pride Foundation** · 1122 E Pike St, PMB 1001 ·
206-323-3318 · www.pridefoundation.org

**Seattle Out and Proud (Seattle Pride)** ·
1605 12th Ave, Ste 2 · 206-322-9561 ·
www.seattlepride.org

## Religious/ Spiritual Services

**All Pilgrims Christian Church** · 55 Broadway E ·
206-322-0488 · www.allpilgrims.org

**Broadview Community United Church of Christ** ·
325 N 125th St · 206-363-8060 ·
www.broadviewucc.org

**Central Lutheran Church** · 1710 11th Ave ·
206-322-7500 · www.loveiscentral.org

**Dharma Buddies/Seattle Gay Buddhist
Fellowship** · 303 17th Ave E · 206-329-4164 ·
www.dharmabuddies.org

**Dignity/Seattle** · 206-325-7314 ·
www.dignityseattle.org

**Directions NW/Evangelicals Concerned** ·
206-781-6754 · www.ecwr.org

**Findlay St. Christian Church
(Disciples of Christ)** · 4620 S Findlay St ·
206-725-5067 · www.findlaystchurch.org

**Metropolitan Community Church** · 1122 E Pike St
PMB 930 · 206-325-2421 · www.mccseattle.org

**Plymouth Congregational Church** · 1217 6th Ave ·
206-622-4865 · www.plymouthchurchseattle.org

**Temple De Hirschi Sinai** · 1511 E Pike St ·
206-315-7392 · www.tdhs-nw.org

**University Congregational United Church of
Christ** · 4515 16th Ave NE · 206-524-2322 ·
www.universityucc.org

**University Unitarian Church** · 6556 35th Ave NE ·
206-525-8400 · www.uuchurch.org

**Wallingford United Methodist Church** ·
2115 N 42nd · 206-547-6945 ·
www.wallingfordumc.org

## Health Centers and Support Organizations

**Northwest Network** · 206-568-7777 · 206-517-9670 (tty) · www.nwnetwork.org · Voice support & advocacy for bisexual, trans, lesbian & gay survivors of abuse & dating violence.

**Seattle Area Support Groups and Community Center (SASG)** · 206-322-2437 · sasgcc.org

**Gay City** · 206-869-6969 · www.gaycity.org · Organizes events and activities for Gay and Bi men & offers anonymous and confidential HIV/STD testing.

**GLBT National Help Center** · 1-888-843-4564 www.glnh.org · Non-profit, peer counseling, information, and local resources.

**HIV/AIDS Program, Seattle/King County Dept of Public Health** · 206-296-4600 · www.kingcounty. gov/healthservices/health/communicable/ hiv.aspx · Provides confidential/anonymous information about and testing for HIV/AIDS.

**Ingersoll Gender Center** · 206-329-6651· www.ingersollcenter.org · A service agency for the Transsexual, Transvestite, & Transgender community offering support groups, referrals to therapists, publications, and trainings.

**Lifelong AIDS Alliance** · 206-328-8979 · www.lifelongaidsalliance.org

**PFLAG** · 206-325-7724 · 1122 E Pike St PMB 620 · www.seattle-pflag.org · Seattle Parents/Families/ Friends of Lesbians and Gays

**Project Neon** · 511 E Pike · 206-323-1768 · www.projectneon.org · Speed, sex, and sanity— information group about crystal meth and the gay community.

**Seattle Counseling Service for LGBT** · 206-323-1768 · www.seattlecounseling.org/Services.htm Mental Health counseling for the LGBT community.

## Bars/Clubs

**C.C. Attle's** · 1501 E Madison

**Changes** · 2103 N 45th St · 206-545-8363

**Crescent Lounge** · 1413 E Olive Wy · 206-726-1774

**Cuff Complex** · 1533 13th Ave · 206-323-1525

**Elite Tavern** · 1520 E Olive Wy · 206-324-4470

**Madison Pub** · 1315 E Madison St · 206-325-6537

**Neighbours Nightclub** · 1509 Broadway · 206-324-5358

**PURR Cocktail Lounge** · 1518 11th Avenue · 206-325-3112

**RPlace** · 19 E Pine St · 206-322-8828

**The Seattle Eagle** · 314 E Pike St · 206-621-7591

**Wildrose** · 1021 E Pike St · 206-324-9210

## Youth & Families

**American Friends Service Committee-GLBT Youth Program** · 814 NE 40th St · 206- 632-0500 x13 · www.afsc.org

**CampTen Trees** · 1122 E Pike St #1488 · 206- 985-2864 · www.camptentrees.org

**Diverse Harmony** · 1111 Harvard Ave, #762 · www.diverseharmony.org

**Family Works- Family Resource Center** · 206- 694-6727 · www.familyworksseattle.org

**Seattle Young People's Project** · 2820 Cherry · 206- 860-9606 · www.sypp.org

If you still associate the library with rubber date stamps and dusty card catalogs, you haven't made use of the Seattle Public Library lately. In keeping with our digital culture, the two-million-item catalog and hold system are easily accessed online (www.spl.org). From the safety of your home computer you can have books, CDs, and DVDs delivered to your local branch. (Think of it as Netflix for really patient people.) The website also gives library card holders access to a collection of databases including periodical searches, phone and postal directories, and otherwise pricey reference sources such as the Oxford English Dictionary. Patrons can download digital media online and subscribe to library-related podcasts. Many of the 26 branches offer free Wi-Fi, and internet access is available on library PCs with a limit of 90 minutes per patron per day. Audio books and large print editions can be found in most branches, but for a wider selection visit the **Washington Talking Book and Braille Library (Map 2)**.

| Libraries | Address | Phone | Map |
|---|---|---|---|
| Washington Talking Book & Braille Library | 2021 9th Ave | 206-615-0400 | 2 |
| Central Library | 1000 4th Ave | 206-386-4636 | 3 |
| Madrona-Sally Goldmark Branch | 1134 33rd Ave | 206-684-4705 | 6 |
| International District / Chinatown Branch | 713 8th Ave S | 206-386-1300 | 8 |
| Douglass-Truth Branch | 2300 E Yesler Wy | 206-684-4704 | 9 |
| Magnolia Branch | 2801 34th Ave W | 206-386-4225 | 11 |
| Queen Anne Branch | 400 W Garfield St | 206-386-4227 | 14 |
| Capitol Hill Branch | 425 Harvard Ave E | 206-684-4715 | 17 |
| Montlake Branch | 2401 24th Ave E | 206-684-4720 | 21 |
| Ballard Branch | 5614 22nd Ave NW | 206-684-4089 | 23 |
| Fremont Branch | 731 N 35th St | 206-684-4084 | 24 |
| Wallingford Branch | 1501 N 45th St | 206-684-4088 | 25 |
| University Branch | 5009 Roosevelt Wy NE | 206-684-4063 | 26 |
| Northeast Branch | 6801 35th Ave NE | 206-684-7539 | 27 |
| Greenwood Branch | 8016 Greenwood Ave N | 206-684-4086 | 30 |
| Green Lake Branch | 7364 E Green Lake Dr N | 206-684-7547 | 31 |
| Broadview Branch | 12755 Greenwood Ave N | 206-684-7519 | 33 |
| Lake City Branch | 12501 28th Ave NE | 206-684-7518 | 34 |
| Northgate Branch | 10548 5th Ave NE | 206-386-1980 | 34 |
| West Seattle Branch | 2306 42nd Ave SW | 206-684-7444 | 35 |
| Delridge Branch | 5423 Delridge Wy SW | 206-733-9125 | 36 |
| High Point Branch | 3411 SW Raymond St | 206-684-7454 | 37 |
| Southwest Branch | 9010 35th Ave S | 206-684-7455 | 37 |
| Beacon Hill Branch | 2821 Beacon Ave S | 206-684-4711 | 39 |
| Columbia Branch | 4721 Rainier Ave S | 206-386-1908 | 40 |
| NewHolly Branch | 7058 32nd Ave S | 206-386-1905 | 40 |
| Rainier Beach Branch | 9125 Rainier Ave S | 206-386-1906 | 41 |
| Mercer Island Library | 4400 88th Ave SE | 206-236-3537 | 42 |
| Lake Hills Library | 15228 Lake Hills Blvd | 425-747-3350 | 44 |
| Newport Way Library | 14250 SE Newport Wy | 425-747-2390 | 44 |
| Belluvue Library | 1111 110th Ave NE | 425-450-1765 | 45 |
| Kirkland Library | 308 Kirkland Ave | 425-822-2459 | 48 |
| Redmond Library | 15990 NE 85th St | 425-885-1861 | 49 |

## Television

| | | | | |
|---|---|---|---|---|
| 4 (ABC) **KOMO** | www.komonews.com | | 9 (PBS) **KCTS** | kcts9.org |
| 5 (NBC) **KING** | www.king5.com | | 11 (CW) **KSTW** | cwseattle.cbslocal.com |
| 7 (CBS) **KIRO** | www.kirotv.com | | 13 (FOX) **KCPQ** | q13fox.com |

## AM Stations

| | |
|---|---|
| **570 KVI** | Talk |
| **630 KCIS** | Christian Talk |
| **710 KIRO** | Sports Talk |
| **770 KTTH** | Talk |
| **820 KGNW** | Christian Talk |
| **880 KIXI** | Oldies |
| **950 KJR** | Sports Talk |
| **1000 KOMO** | Talk |
| **1050 KBLE** | Catholic Talk |
| **1090 KPTK** | Progressive Talk |
| **1150 KKNW** | Alternative Talk |
| **1250 KKDZ** | Radio Disney |
| **1300 KOL** | Talk |
| **1360 KKMO** | Spanish Language Programming |
| **1420 KRIZ** | Oldies |
| **1560 KZIZ** | Gospel |
| **1590 KLFE** | Christian Talk |
| **1620 KYIZ** | Urban |

## FM Stations

| | |
|---|---|
| **88.5 KPLU NPR** | Don't forget to pledge. |
| **89.5 KNHC** | Top 40 • Operated by Nathan Hale High School students. |
| **89.9 KGRG** | Rock |
| **90.3 KEXP** | Eclectic Hipster Fare • Best station… well, ever |
| **91.3 KBCS** | KBCS Bellevue Community College |
| **92.5 KLSY** | Top 40 |
| **93.3 KUBE** | R&B/Hip-Hop • Beyonce, Snoop Dogg, and Parliament unite. |
| **94.1 KMPS** | Country/Western |
| **94.9 KUOW NPR** | Mandatory blue state listening. |
| **95.7 KJAQ** | Playing whatever the hell they want, apparently. |
| **96.5 KRQI** | Adult contemporary |
| **97.3 KBSG** | Talk |
| **98.1 KING** | Classical |
| **98.9 KWJZ** | Smooth Jazz • Yes, Kenny G is from Seattle. |
| **99.9 KISW** | Rock |
| **100.7 KQBZ** | Talk |
| **101.5 KPLZ** | Rock |
| **102.5 KZOK** | Classic Rock • Sometimes you need to get the Led out. |
| **103.7 KMTT** | Rock |
| **105.3 KCMS** | Christian Music |
| **106.1 KBKS** | Top 40 |
| **106.9 KRWM** | Soft Favorites • Perfect dental office soundtrack. |
| **107.7 KNDD** | Alternative • Where Grunge has become the oldies. |

## Print Media

**Capitol Hill Times**

**City Arts Magazine**
425 N 85th St
206-443-0445
Monthly all-encompassing art rag.

**Kirkland Reporter**
www.kirklandreporter.com
Formerly the Kirkland Courier. Around since 1978.

**Madison Park Times**

**Magnolia News**

**Pacific Publishing Company**
4000 Aurora Ave N, Ste 100
206-461-1300
Publishes free neighborhood-specific newspapers.

**Pike Place Market News**
93 Pike St, #312
206-251-2588
Monthly news and gossip from the market.

**Queen Anne News**

**Real Change**
2129 2nd Ave
206-441-3247
Raising awareness about local homeless issues.

**Seattle City Living**
www.citylivingseattle.com
Mid-monthly mag for North Seattle.

**Seattle Daily Journal of Commerce**
83 Columbia St
206-622-8272 • www.djc.com
Daily business news.

**Seattle Gay News**
1605 12th Ave, Ste 31
206-324-4297
Free LGBT weekly.

**Seattle Magazine**
1505 Western Ave, Ste 500
206-284-1750 • www.seattlemag.com
Monthly lifestyle magazine.

**RIP: Seattle Post-Intelligencer**
www.seattlepi.com
Voice of the Northwest since 1863.

**Seattle Sound**
1201 1st Ave S, Ste 309
206-382-9220
Monthly local music and arts magazine.

**Seattle Times**
1120 John St
206-464-2111 • www.seattletimes.com
City's biggest daily. Happy 111th birthday.

**Seattle Weekly**
1008 Western Ave, Ste 300
206-623-0500 • www.seattleweekly.com
Free alternative weekly going strong for over three decades.

**The Stranger**
1535 11th Ave, 3rd Floor
206-323-7101 • www.thestranger.com
Seattle's best rag with entertaining political and arts news.

**Where Magazine**
1904 3rd Ave, Ste 623
206-826-2665
For tourists.

| Police | Address | Phone | Map |
|---|---|---|---|
| West Precinct | 810 Virginia St | 206-684-8917 | 2 |
| Seattle Police Headquarters | 610 5th Ave | 206-625-5011 | 3 |
| East Precinct | 1519 12th Ave | 206-684-4300 | 4 |
| North Precinct | 10049 College Wy N | 206-684-0850 | 33 |
| Southwest Precinct | 2300 SW Webster St | 206-733-9800 | 37 |
| South Precinct | 3001 S Myrtle | 206-386-1850 | 41 |
| Mercer Island Police Dept | 9611 SE 36th St | 206-275-7610 | 42 |
| Bellevue Police Dept | 450 110th Ave NE | 425-452-6917 | 45 |
| Clyde Hill Police Dept | 9605 NE 24th St | 425-454-7187 | 45 |
| Medina Police Dept | 501 Evergreen Point Rd | 425-233-6420 | 45 |
| Kirkland Police Dept | 123 5th Ave | 425-587-3400 | 48 |
| Redmond Police Dept | 8701 160th Ave NE | 425-556-2500 | 49 |

## Post Offices

| Post Offices | Address | Phone | Map |
|---|---|---|---|
| CPU Harbor Heights 111 | 2512 5th Ave | 206-448-9287 | 1 |
| Columbia Center | 701 5th Ave, Ste 306 | 206-625-2293 | 3 |
| Federal | 909 1st Ave, Ste 100 | 206-625-2293 | 3 |
| Midtown | 301 Union St | 206-748-5417 | 3 |
| Seafirst | 1001 4th Ave | 206-682-3958 | 3 |
| East Union | 1110 23rd Ave | 206-328-9712 | 5 |
| Pioneer Square | 91 S Jackson St | 206-625-2293 | 7 |
| International | 414 6th Ave S | 206-625-2293 | 8 |
| Magnolia | 3211 W Mcgraw St | 206-284-5958 | 11 |
| Queen Anne | 415 1st Ave N | 206-378-2506 | 15 |
| Broadway | 101 Broadway E | 206-324-5474 | 17 |
| Ballard | 5706 17th Ave NW | 206-781-4656 | 23 |
| Wallingford | 1329 N 47th St | 206-547-1406 | 24 |
| University | 4244 University Wy NE | 206-675-8114 | 26 |
| Wedgwood | 7724 35th Ave NE | 206-527-8896 | 27 |
| Greenwood | 8306 Greenwood Ave N | 206-547-1406 | 30 |
| Bitter Lake | 929 N 145th St | 206-364-0663 | 33 |
| Lake City | 3019 NE 127th St | 206-364-0608 | 34 |
| Northgate | 11036 8th Ave NE | 206-364-0546 | 34 |
| West Seattle | 4412 California Ave SW | 206-923-0485 | 35 |
| Westwood | 2721 SW Trenton St | 206-938-7769 | 37 |
| Georgetown | 620 S Orcas St | 206-764-9565 | 39 |
| Terminal Finance Station | 2420 4th Ave S | 206-652-2467 | 39 |
| Columbia | 3727 S Alaska St | 206-721-2368 | 40 |
| Mercer Island | 3040 78th Ave SE | 206-232-8834 | 42 |
| CPU Factoria | 4020 Factoria Sq Mall SE | 425-957-0640 | 43 |
| Bellevue | 1171 Bellevue Wy NE | 425-453-5655 | 45 |
| Medina | 816 Evergreen Point Rd | 425-656-8111 | 45 |
| Midlakes | 11405 NE 2nd Pl | 425-462-7508 | 46 |
| Crossroads | 15731 NE 8th St | 425-401-0892 | 47 |
| CPU Totem Lake | 12556 120th Ave NE | 425-821-9755 | 48 |
| Kirkland | 721 4th Ave | 4255-739-6727 | 48 |
| Redmond | 16135 NE 85th St | 425-885-1057 | 49 |
| Redmond Carrier Annex | 7241 185th Ave NE | 425-885-0207 | 49 |

## Useful Phone Numbers

| | |
|---|---|
| Emergencies: | 911 |
| Police Department: | 206-625-5011 |
| Fire Department: | 206-386-1400 |
| King County Medic One: | 206-296-8550 |
| Seattle Mayor's Office: | 206-684-4000 |
| Animal Control: | 206-386-PETS (7387) |

## Websites

**www.historylink.org** · Seattle history and more.

**www.seattlepi.com** ·
The Voice of the Northwest Since 1863.

**www.seattletimes.com** · The largest daily newspaper in Washington State.

**seattle.curbed.com** · Seattle nabe and real estate blog.

**seattle.eater.com** · Indepth Seattle food and drink.

**www.seattle.gov** · Official website of the City of Seattle.

**www.seattle.gov/parks** · Seattle Parks and Recreation.

**seattle.craigslist.org** · Find a job, join a band, buy a second-hand car, or fall in love.

**www.spl.org** · Seattle public library's website.

**www.thestranger.com** · Seattle's sharpest (and narrowest) alternative newsweekly.

**www.supersonicsoul.com** · The ultimate Sonic fansite.

**www.sevennites.com** · Search for happy hours in Seattle and drink all week.

**www.seattle.net** · Info on restaurants, shopping, hotels, and events (if NFT just ain't enough).

**www.seattlefoodtruck.com** · Hungry? Find any of our 100+ food trucks by neighborhood, day or cuisine.

**www.threeimaginarygirls.com** · Seattle's sparkly indie-pop press. Local music news, reviews and commentary.

**metro.kingcounty.gov** · Seattle public transit website.

**www.urbanspoon.com/c/1/Seattle-restaurants.html** · Restaurant ratings and reviews.

## Essential Seattle Movies

*Tugboat Annie* (1933)
*It Happened At The World's Fair* (1967)
*Five Easy Pieces* (1970)
*Cinderella Liberty* (1973)
*McQ* (1974)
*WarGames* (1983)
*Streetwise* (1984)
*Trouble in Mind* (1985)
*Say Anything* (1989)
*My Own Private Idaho* (1991)
*The Hand That Rocks The Cradle* (1992)
*Singles* (1992)
*Sleepless in Seattle* (1993)
*Hype!* (1996)
*10 Things I Hate About You* (1999)
*The Ring* (2002)
*Police Beat* (2005)
*Battle in Seattle* (2007)
*Zoo* (2007)
*Humpday* (2009)
*Grassroots* (2012)
*Safety Not Guaranteed* (2012)

## We're Number One!!!

- Seattleites buy more sunglasses per capita than any other American metropolis, because it's totally sunny here all the time.
- The Washington State Ferry system is the largest in the USA.
- The term "skid row" originated in Seattle, derived from the "skid road" that 19th-century loggers used to transport lumber through Pioneer Square—the area hit financial ruin during the Depression and the phrase became shorthand for any destitute neighborhood.
- Bertha Landes became the first female mayor of a large American city when she won the Seattle mayoral race in 1926.
- The world's first gas station opened in Seattle in 1907.
- The first publicized report of a flying saucer occurred in Lake City in 1947.
- The first radio station in America to play a Beatles song was in Seattle.
- Seattle is considered the nation's most literate city, and boasts the highest percentage of library card holders and college graduates in the country.

## Essential Seattle Songs

"Seattle the Peerless City" — Official Song since 1909
"Seattle Ain't Bullshitting" — Sir Mix-A-Lot
"Posse on Broadway" — Sir Mix-A-Lot
"Seattle" — Public Image, Ltd.
"Seattle" — The Wailers
"Seattle" — Cop Shoot Cop
"Seattle" (from the Screen Gems TV Program Here Come the Brides) — Bobby Goldsboro, Perry Como, Connie Smith and others
"Seattle, WA" — Western Keys
"Seattle Hunch" — Jelly Roll Morton
"Seattle Was a Riot" — Anti-Flag
"Seattle Town" — Flatt & Scruggs
"Seattle Sonics Do It" — Luther Rabb
"Chief Seattle" — Gene Parsons
"Seattle Twist" — Rod McKuen
"Flight to Seattle" — DJ Magic Mike
"Seattle Shuffle" — Damo Suzuki's Network
"Seattle to Chicago" — Woody Guthrie
"The Day Seattle Died" — Cold
"Frances Farmer Will Have Her Revenge on Seattle" — Nirvana
"The Last One To Leave Seattle" — Waylon Jennings
"Sub Pop Rock City" — Soundgarden
"Viva! Sea-Tac" — Robyn Hitchcock
"Stranger" — The Presidents of the United States of America
"Nuke Seattle" — Quincy Punx

## Essential Seattle Books

*Sons of the Profit*, by William Speidel. Entertaining and honest look at Seattle's early history.

*Buddy Does Seattle*, by Peter Bagge. Classic slacker comics.

*Eccentric Seattle: Pillars and Pariahs Who Made the City Not Such a Boring Place After All*, by J. Kingston Pierce. The mavericks and misfits who shaped our city.

*Never Mind Nirvana: A Novel*, by Mark Lindquist. Former grunge rocker turns lawyer and experiences angst.

*Loser: The Real Seattle Music Story*, by Clark Humphrey. Indispensable guide to the city's rich rock and roll heritage.

*The Kid: What Happened After My Boyfriend and I Decided to Go Get Pregnant*, by Dan Savage. Openly gay Stranger editor/sex advice columnist adopts a young boy, then writes about it.

*J.P. Patches, Northwest Icon*, by Julius Pierpont Patches and Bryan Johnston. The story behind this beloved local kid's TV star.

*Skid Road: An Informal Portrait of Seattle*, by Murray Morgan. History of Seattle's rough-and-tumble frontier days.

*Waxwings: A Novel*, by Jonathon Raban. British-born UW prof finds his life falling apart in Seattle.

*Madison House*, by Peter Donahue. Novel about Seattle at the dawn of the 20th century.

*Selling Seattle*, by James Lyons. Academic exploration of Seattle's impact on American culture.

*I Sing the Body Electronic: A Year With Microsoft on the Multimedia Frontier*, by Fred Moody. A freelance writer goes inside the machine and lives to tell the tale.

*The World of Chief Seattle: How Can One Sell the Air?* by Warren Jefferson. All about the Suquamish tribe and the treaties that changed everything.

*Rat City*, by Curt Colbert. Mystery novel set in post-WWII Seattle.

*Screaming Life*, by Charles Peterson. This is what Seattle rock looks like.

*21 Dog Years: Doing Time @ Amazon.com*, by Mike Daisy. Hilarious account of Amazon culture during the boom years.

## Seattle Timeline

1805: Lewis and Clark explore the Pacific Northwest, including the future state of Washington.
1851: Midwestern settlers led by David and Arthur Denny arrive and begin populating the area that will one day become Seattle.
1869: City of Seattle is incorporated.
1872: Earthquake measuring 7.4 on the Richter scale shakes Seattle.
1878: Seattle's first telephone service established.
1889: Great Seattle Fire destroys downtown.
1890: Bon Marche opens in Seattle as a dry goods store.
1891: Seattle University established.
1893: Transcontinental train line reaches Seattle.
1917: Boeing Airplane Company incorporated, and the Seattle Metropolitans hockey team wins Stanley Cup.
1919: Seattle General Strike begins; the first city-wide strike in the nation.
1928: Inventor/entrepreneur Don Ibsen spends the summer on Lake Washington trying to perfect water skis.
1933: Seattle Art Museum established.
1934: The Muzak corporation established.
1936: University of Washington rowing crew wins Olympic gold.
1938: World's first pressurized airliner, the Boeing Model 307 Stratoliner, is launched.
1940: World's first floating bridge opens on Lake Washington.
1942: Jimi Hendrix born in Seattle.
1949: Seattle-Tacoma International Airport established. Also an earthquake measuring 7.1 on the Richter scale shakes Seattle.
1954: Dick's Drive-In serves its first hamburger.
1959: First documented sample of HIV-infected blood collected by University of Washington geneticist Dr. Arno Motulsky while working in the Congo.
1962: Seattle hosts the World's Fair. Science Center, Space Needle, and Monorail are erected for the celebration. Elvis Presley shoots *It Happened at the World's Fair* on location.
1965: Earthquake measuring 6.5 on the Richter scale shakes Seattle.

1970: Abortion legalized by state voters.
1979: Seattle SuperSonics win NBA Championship. Also, future indie-rock label Sub Pop is launched as a fanzine in nearby Olympia.
1980: Mount St. Helens erupts.
1983: Thirteen dead in the Wah Mee massacre in the International District.
1986: Microsoft goes public.
1991: Nirvana releases *Nevermind*, cementing Seattle's growing reputation as Rock City USA.
1995: Mariners almost make it to the World Series. Amazon.com founded.
1994: Nirvana's Kurt Cobain commits suicide, and major record companies start looking for "the next Seattle."
1998: The US Government sues Microsoft for antitrust violations.
1999: The World Trade Organization holds conferences in Seattle, leading to clashes between protesters and policemen downtown.
2000: Kingdome imploded.
2001: Boeing moves corporate offices to Chicago. Earthquake hits measuring 6.8 on the Richter scale.
2003: Green River Killer pleads guilty to 48 murders.
2004: New Seattle Central Library opens to global fanfare. Storm win WNBA championship. Ichiro sets record for most hits in a season (262).
2005: Citywide monorail plan falls apart (again), and Seattleites resigned to riding the bus for the next 2,000 years.
2007: The ultimate urban bible is published (NFT Seattle).
2008: Ballard's historic Sunset Bowl closes, hipster hearts irreparable.
2009: Airport light rail opens. No joke!
2009: Seattle Sounders FC begins play and immediately blows away MLS attendance records.
2010: Lusty lady closes, changing downtown forever.
2013: Sounders get US Men's Soccer captain Clint Dempsey from Tottenham for MLS record $9 million transfer fee.
2013: Washington becomes the first (or second, if you ask Colorado) state to legalize marijuana for recreational use.

**A Contemporary Theatre (ACT) (Map 3)** provides some of Seattle's best drama, with two stages to host new plays from nationally recognized playwrights as well as the occasional revival. The Intiman Theatre won a Tony Award in 2006. Unfortunately, it wasn't enough to keep them in the black as they were forced to cancel their 2011 season. Subsequently, the institution has been reconceived as a yearly summer festival and its space has been taken over by Cornish College and renamed **The Cornish Playhouse at Seattle Center (Map 15)**. Another big player in Seattle performance arts is **On the Boards (Map 15)**, a risk-taking organization that specializes in artist development, particularly through their 12 Minute Max series, which offers brief glimpses of new and in-progress works from up-and-coming performers

and writers. On the Boards also hosts local alt-weekly The Stranger's annual amateur porn film festival, thus, er, firming up the link between porn and art.

Seattle's live theater scene is also robust enough to support a slew of small stages where aficionados can catch the latest experimental performances, new works from local playwrights, or revivals of much-loved classics. **Theater Schmeater (Map 4)**, **Bathhouse Theatre (Map 31)**, **Eclectic Theater Company (Map 3)**, and others toil tirelessly in often cramped conditions and stumble as often as they soar, but that's how great theater is made. Check out seattleperforms.com for the latest theatrical happenings in the Emerald City.

| Theaters | Address | Phone | Map |
|---|---|---|---|
| 5th Avenue Theatre | 1308 5th Ave | 206-625-1900 | 3 |
| ACT Theatre | 700 Union St | 206-292-7676 | 3 |
| ArtsWest Theatre | 4711 California Ave SW | 206-938-0339 | 35 |
| Bathhouse Theater | 7312 W Green Lake Dr N | 206-524-1300 | 30 |
| Benaroya Hall | 200 University St | 206-215-4800 | 3 |
| Capitol Hill Arts | 1621 12th Ave | 206-388-0569 | 4 |
| Center House Theatre | 305 Harrison St | 206-216-0833 | 15 |
| Historic University Theater | 5510 University Wy NE | 206-781-3879 | 32 |
| Intiman Theatre | 201 Mercer St | 206-269-1900 | 15 |
| Kirkland Performance Center | 350 Kirkland Ave | 425-893-9900 | 48 |
| Langston Hughes Permorning Arts Center | 104 17th Ave S | 206-684-4657 | 9 |
| The Little Theatre | 608 19th Ave E | 206-675-2055 | 18 |
| Magnuson Community Center Auditorium | 7400 Sand Point Wy NE, Bldg 47 | n/a | 27 |
| Market Theater | 1428 Post Aly | 206-587-2414 | 3 |
| McCaw Hall | 321 Mercer St | 206-733-9725 | 15 |
| Meany Hall for the Performing Arts | 4001 University Wy NE | 206-543-4880 | 26 |
| Meydenbauer Center | 11100 NE 6th St | 425-637-1020 | 45 |
| Moore Theatre | 1932 2nd Ave | 206-467-5510 | 3 |
| Northwest Puppet Center | 9123 15th Ave NE | 206-523-2579 | 34 |
| Odd Duck Studio | 1214 10th Ave | 206-375-8945 | 4 |
| On The Boards | 100 W Roy ST | 206-217-9886 | 15 |
| Open Circle Theater | 429 Boren Ave N | 206-382-4250 | 2 |
| Paramount Theatre | 911 Pine St | 206-682-1414 | 3 |
| R.E.D. Performance Loft | 89 Yesler Wy | 206-331-6673 | 7 |
| Richard Hugo House | 1634 11th Ave | n/a | 4 |
| Seattle Children's Theatre at Seattle Center | 201 Thomas St | 206-441-3322 | 15 |
| Seattle Repertory Theatre - Bagley Wright Theatre | 155 Mercer St | 206-443-2222 | 15 |
| Second Story Repertory | 16587 NE 74th St | 425-881-6777 | 49 |
| Spectrum Dance Theater | 800 Lake Washington Blvd | 206-325-4161 | 6 |
| Taproot Theatre | 204 N 85 St | 206-781-9707 | 30 |
| Teatro Zinzanni | 222 Mercer St | 206-802-0015 | 15 |
| Theater Schmeater | 1500 Summit Ave | 206-324-5801 | 4 |

## Overview

The city's art gallery epicenter has revolved around the architecturally traditional and not-so-funky Pioneer Square for many years. Perhaps it is the history of the place, the old cobblestones, and faded brick facades that make the neighborhood a natural backdrop for art. But lately the scene has been shifting to new neighborhoods, and Seattle's art scene is now spread out across the city. Make sure to get out and explore beyond Pioneer Square.

Although many neighborhood business associations offer monthly art walks, you'll have vastly differing experiences depending on which locale you choose. Head to Pioneer Square for more traditional art, such as abstract and still life paintings in oils and acrylics, paired with cheap wine and respectful crowds. In the summer months, Occidental Square is abuzz with tents of artists and crafts vendors selling unique jewelry, photography, and smaller works in the street until dark. Wander to Belltown for kitschy, lowbrow art at the nationally esteemed **Roq la Rue (Map 7)**. Ballard has a great art walk the second Saturday of each month. For an alternative to the refined gallery set, check out the personal studios at the **Tashiro-Kaplan Building** (115 Prefontaine Pl S) during public events.

The Georgetown Second Saturday Art Attack showcases the talents of the neighborhood's funky artist community. Most of the art walk takes place along Airport Way South and hits up thirty different galleries, cafes, and shops.

## Glass Art

Thanks to the international fame and regional influence of local glass artist/corporation Dale Chihuly, Seattle goes wild for anything fragile and hand-blown. Along with area galleries like **William Traver (Map 3)** and **Foster/White (Map 3, 7)** that carry the famed Chihuly pieces, there are numerous galleries specializing in glass art from less-famous names, such as **Avalon Glassworks (Map 36)** or the **Seattle Glassblowing Studio (Map 1)**. Smaller local boutiques carry knockoffs that only the trained eye might be able to distinguish from so-called "fine art" pieces (or so we assume), proving the popularity of glass art among Seattle's hoi polloi as well as dot-com millionaires and other arbiters of taste.

## Off the Beaten Path

The non-profit Jack Straw Productions, founded in 1962, supports local audio arts first and foremost, providing recording studio assistance and performance space for its members. However, with the organization's **New Media Gallery (Map 26)**, the Straw extends the art of noise through combination with various disciplines, creating installations that are as visually arresting as they sound. Locally based alternative comics press Fantagraphics recently opened a flagship store as well at **Georgetown Records (Map 39)**, not only to hawk its wares, but also to host showings of original artwork from renowned cartoonists.

## Map 1 • Belltown

| | Address | Phone |
| --- | --- | --- |
| AT.31 Gallery | 109 W Denny Wy | 206-283-5253 |
| McLoed Residence | 2209 2nd Ave | 206-441-3314 |
| Roq La Rue Gallery | 2312 2nd Ave | 206-374-8977 |
| Seattle Glassblowing Studio | 2227 5th Ave | 206-448-2181 |
| Suyama Space | 2324 2nd Ave | 206-256-0809 |

## Map 2 • South Lake Union

| | | |
| --- | --- | --- |
| Art Not Terminal Gallery | 2045 Westlake Ave | 206-233-0680 |
| Patricia Cameron Fine Art | 234 Dexter Ave N | 206-343-9647 |
| Winston Wachter Fine Art | 203 Dexter Ave N | 206-652-5855 |
| Woodside/Braseth Gallery | 2101 9th Ave | 206-622-7243 |

## Map 3 • Downtown

| | | |
| --- | --- | --- |
| Benham Gallery | 1216 1st Ave | 206-622-2480 |
| Carolyn Staley Fine Japanese Prints | 2001 Western Ave | 206-621-1888 |
| Facere Jewelry Art Gallery | 1420 5th Ave | 206-624-6768 |
| Friesen Gallery | 1210 2nd Ave | 206-628-9501 |
| Gallery Mack | 2100 Western Ave | 206-448-1616 |
| Jeffrey Moose Gallery | 1333 5th Ave | 206-467-6951 |
| Kim Drew Studio and Gallery | 1311 Post Aly | 206-343-4101 |
| The Legacy Ltd | 1003 1st Ave | 206-624-6350 |
| Lisa Harris Gallery | 1922 Pike Pl | 206-443-3315 |
| Milagros Mexican Folk Art | 1530 Post Aly | 206-464-0490 |
| Patricia Rovzar Gallery | 118 Central Wy | 425-889-4627 |
| Phoenix Rising Gallery | 2030 Western Ave | 206-728-2332 |
| Vetri International Glass | 1404 1st Ave | 206-667-9608 |
| William Traver Gallery | 110 Union St | 206-587-6501 |

## Map 4 • First Hill / Pike / Pine

| | | |
|---|---|---|
| Bluebottle Art Gallery | 415 E Pine St | 206-325-1592 |
| Martin-Zambito Fine Art | 721 E Pike St | 206-726-9509 |
| Photographic Center Northwest | 900 12th Ave | 206-720-7222 |
| Warren Knapp Gallery | 1530 Melrose Ave | 206-381-3335 |

## Map 7 • Pioneer Square / SoDo

| | | |
|---|---|---|
| Artforte Gallery | 307 Occidental Ave S | 206-748-0187 |
| Azuma Gallery | 530 1st Ave S | 206-622-5599 |
| Davidson Contemporary | 313 Occidental Ave S | 206-624-7684 |
| Flury & Company Gallery | 322 1st Ave S | 206-587-0260 |
| Foster/White Gallery | 220 3rd Ave S | 206-622-2833 |
| G Gibson Gallery | 300 S Washington St | 206-587-4033 |
| Gallery 110 | 110 S Washington St | 206-624-9336 |
| Gallery 4 Culture | 101 Prefontaine Pl S | 206-296-8674 |
| Glasshouse Studio | 311 Occidental Ave S | 206-682-9939 |
| Greg Kucera Gallery | 212 3rd Ave S | 206-624-0770 |
| Grover/Thurston Gallery | 309 Occidental Ave S | 206-223-0816 |
| Howard House Contemporary Art | 604 2nd Ave | 206-256-6399 |
| James Harris Gallery | 206-587-4033 | 206-903-6220 |
| Kagedo Japanese Art | 520 1st Ave S | 206-467-9077 |
| Kibo Galerie | 323 Occidental Ave S | 206-442-2100 |
| La Familia Gallery | 117 Prefontaine Pl S | 206-291-4608 |
| Linda Hodges Gallery | 316 1st Ave S | 206-624-3034 |
| NorthWest Fine Woodworking | 101 S Jackson St | 206-625-0542 |
| Pacini Lubel Gallery | 207 2nd Ave S | 206-326-5555 |
| Platform Gallery | 114 3rd Ave S | 206-323-2808 |
| Punch Gallery | 119 Prefontaine Pl S | 206-621-1945 |
| Soil Art Gallery | 112 3rd Ave S | 206-264-8061 |
| Stonington Gallery | 119 S Jackson St | 206-405-4040 |
| The Underground Gallery | 214 1st Ave S, B-12 | 206-340-9395 |

## Map 8 • International District

| | | |
|---|---|---|
| Lawrimore Project | 831 Airport Wy S | 206-501-1231 |

## Map 12 • Queen Anne (North)

| | | |
|---|---|---|
| Fountainhead Gallery | 625 W McGraw St | 206-285-4467 |

## Map 15 • Lower Queen Anne / Seattle Center

| | | |
|---|---|---|
| Pottery Northwest | 226 1st Ave N | 206-285-4421 |
| Judith Kindler | 570 Mercer St | 206-283-5253 |

## Map 18 • Capitol Hill (East) / Madison Valley

| | | |
|---|---|---|
| Lewis/Wara Gallery | 1121 15th Ave E | 206-405-4355 |
| Miner Gallery | 346 15th Ave E | 206-568-7604 |

## Map 24 • Fremont

| | | |
|---|---|---|
| Black Box Gallery | 4911 Aurora Ave N | 206-883-4903 |
| Edge of Glass Gallery | 513 N 36 St | 206-632-7807 |
| TimesInfinity Gallery | 122 NW 36th St | 206-973-4470 |

## Map 26 • U District

| | | |
|---|---|---|
| Henry Art Gallery | 4100 15th Ave NE | 206-543-2280 |
| Jack Straw / New Media Gallery | 4261 Roosevelt Wy NE | 206-634-0919 |
| Kirsten Gallery | 5320 Roosevelt Wy NE | 206-522-2011 |

## Map 28 • Ballard (West)

| | | |
|---|---|---|
| Sev Shoon Arts Center | 2862 NW Market St | 206-782-2415 |

## Map 30 • Greenwood / Phinney Ridge

| | | |
|---|---|---|
| Francine Seders Gallery | 6701 Greenwood Ave N | 206-782-0355 |

## Map 34 • Northeast Seattle

| | | |
|---|---|---|
| Snow Goose Associates | 8806 Roosevelt Wy NE | 206-523-6223 |

## Map 36 • North Delridge

| | | |
|---|---|---|
| Avalon Glassworks | 2914 SW Avalon Way | 206-937-6369 |

## Map 39 • SoDo / Beacon Hill / Georgetown

| | | |
|---|---|---|
| Georgetown Records / Fantagraphics | 1201 S Vale St | 206-762-5638 |
| Mix Lounge | 6006 12th Ave S | 206-767-0280 |
| Western Bridge | 3412 4th Ave S | 206-838-7444 |

## Map 40 • Columbia City / Mount Baker / Seward Park

| | | |
|---|---|---|
| Columbia City Gallery | 4864 Rainier Ave S | 206-760-9843 |

## Map 43 • Bellevue (Southwest)

| | | |
|---|---|---|
| East Shore Gallery | 12700 SE 32nd St | 425-747-3780 |

## Map 45 • Bellevue (West) / Medina

| | | |
|---|---|---|
| Elements Gallery | 10500 NE 8th St | 425-454-8242 |
| Gunnar Nordstrom Gallery | 127 Lake St S | 425-827-2822 |
| Ming's Asian Gallery | 10217 Main St | 425-462-4008 |

## Map 48 • Kirkland

| | | |
|---|---|---|
| Howard/Mandville Gallery | 120 Park Lane | 425-889-8212 |

With literary events cropping up all over Seattle—not just in libraries and bookstores, but in coffee houses, bars, art museums, and rock music venues—it's hardly a shock that each year we rank as highly as we do in CCSU's yearly America's Most Literate Cities study. We love our libraries, devour our newspapers (even online papers!), and keep our bookstores in business. Independent bookstores here, as everywhere, struggle to compete with the big conglomerates. But despite housing Amazon.com headquarters, bookstores in Seattle have maintained a strong presence and a loyal customer base.

## Literary Treasures

**The Elliott Bay Book Company (Map 4)** on Capitol Hill is the favorite son of Puget Sound literati. Established in 1973, the store long ago carved its niche as a cultural gathering place with frequent readings by big-name authors and book groups. It can be argued, however, that the only advantage Elliott Bay really has over the competition (besides all that exposed brick) is killer PR. Ask Seattleites to name the best local bookstore, and you'll rarely hear the same answer twice. Here are some contenders: **Magus Books (Map 26)** in the U-District has a grandpa's attic feel. **Ravenna Third Place Books (Map 32)** offers excellent variety, as does **Twice Sold Tales (Map 4)**, which has several resident cats. **Wessel & Lieberman Booksellers (Map 7)** is ideal for more high-brow browsing, if you will, offering many antiquarian and out-of-print titles as well as prints.

## Books by the Mile

If your true desire is to surround yourself with an immense acreage of reading material (no shame in that), **University Bookstore (Map 26)** has an impressive collection of books including substantial technology, health science, and periodical sections (not to mention an art supply store). **Half Price Books (Map 26, 49)** is a regional chain with locations around Puget Sound and an ever-changing stock of used books, plus deals on CDs, DVDs, and magazines. To satiate your inner Comic Book Guy, check out their disorganized comics bin which is peppered with treasures cast off by boneheads who didn't know what they had.

## Specialty

**Open Books: A Poem Emporium (Map 25)** bravely limits its stock to poetry—one of only two such bookstores in the US. **Cinema Books (Map 26)** is devoted solely to the silver screen. Collectors of art and architecture books should see **Peter Miller Books (Map 3)** downtown. **Seattle Mystery Bookshop (Map 3)** is a paradise for readers of whodunits, thrillers, and true crime, but look to Edge of the **Circle Books (Map 4)** for your pagan and occult literature. **Left Bank Books Collective (Map 3)** is the place for all you lefty-commie-pinkos who still care about the world. May our numbers increase.

For travelers, **Wide World Books & Maps (Map 25)** has all manner of portable goodies in addition to an excellent selection of guidebooks and travel writing. **Metsker Maps of Seattle (Map 3)** in Pike Place Market also carries a variety of travel and recreational guidebooks, as well as carrying our favorite retail item—maps. Birders and botanists will love **Flora & Fauna Books (Map 12)** in Magnolia near Discovery Park. And for young minds, try **Secret Garden Bookshop (Map 23)** and **Alphabet Soup (Map 24)**.

## Map 2 • South Lake Union

| | | | |
|---|---|---|---|
| Kaufer's Religious Supplies | 320 9th Ave N | 206-622-3100 | Religious. |

## Map 3 • Downtown

| | | | |
|---|---|---|---|
| A Literary Saloon - BLMF | 1501 Pike Pl | 206-621-7894 | Used and rare. |
| Art of Illustration | 1301 1st Ave | 206-254-9100 | Gallery of book illustrations/books about illustrators. |
| Arundel Books | 1001 1st Ave | 206-624-4442 | New, used, and rare. |
| Barnes & Noble | 600 Pine St | 206-264-0156 | Chain. |
| Christian Science Downtown Reading Room | 1215 2nd Ave | 206-623-4034 | Christian Science. |
| Eco-Elements | 1530 1st Ave | 206-467-7745 | Mind-body-spirit-earth. |

| | | | |
|---|---|---|---|
| Left Bank Books Collective | 92 Pike St | 206-622-0195 | Leftist slant. |
| Metsker Maps of Seattle | 1511 1st Ave | 206-623-8747 | Maps and travel guides. |
| Peter Miller Books | 1930 1st Ave | 206-441-4114 | Architecture and design. |
| Seattle Mystery Bookshop | 117 Cherry St | 206-587-5737 | Mystery. |
| The White Horse Trading Co | 1908 Post Aly | 206-441-7767 | Pub and bookstore. |
| Zanadu Comics | 1923 3rd Ave | 206-443-1316 | Comics. |

## Map 4 • First Hill / Pike / Pine

| | | | |
|---|---|---|---|
| Barnes & Noble (College Store) | Seattle Central Community College, 1701 Broadway | 206-587-4148 | Chain. |
| City Books | 1305 Madison St | 206-682-4334 | Neighborhood independent. |
| Elliott Bay Books | 1521 10th Ave | 206-624-6600 | The best bookstore in Seattle after Amazon. |
| Spine and Crown Books | 413 E Pine St | 206-322-1227 | Neighborhood independent. |
| Edge Of The Circle Books | 701 E Pike St | 206-726-1999 | Paganism and the occult. |
| Seattle University Bookstore | 823 12th Ave | 206-296-5820 | Text books. |
| Twice Sold Tales | 1833 Harvard Ave | 206-324-2421 | Used. |

## Map 7 • Pioneer Square / SoDo

| | | | |
|---|---|---|---|
| The Globe Bookstore | 218 1st Ave S | 206-682-6882 | Theatre books. |
| Revolution Books | 89 S Washington St | 206-325-7415 | Leftist slant. |
| Wessel & Lieberman | 208 1st Ave S | 206-682-3545 | Rare books. |

## Map 8 • International District

| | | | |
|---|---|---|---|
| Seattle Gospel Center Bookstore | 667 S King St | 206-624-0988 | Spiritual. |

## Map 12 • Queen Anne (North)

| | | | |
|---|---|---|---|
| Flora & Fauna Books | 3212 West Government Wy | 206-623-4727 | Natural history. |

## Map 13 • Upper Queen Anne

| | | | |
|---|---|---|---|
| Armchair Sailor | 2110 Westlake Ave N | 206-283-0858 | Nautical. |
| Queen Anne Avenue Books | 1811 Queen Anne Ave N | 206-283-5624 | Contemporary literature and children's books. |

## Map 17 • Capitol Hill (West)

| | | | |
|---|---|---|---|
| Half Price Books | 115 Belmont Ave E | 206-267-7777 | New and used at half price. |
| Quest Bookshop | 717 Broadway E | 206-323-4281 | Metaphysical. |

## Map 20 • Eastlake / Montlake / Portage Bay

| | | | |
|---|---|---|---|
| Vedanta Society of Western Washington | 2716 Broadway E | 206-323-1228 | Hinduism and Vedanta. |

## Map 23 • Ballard

| | | | |
|---|---|---|---|
| Arcane Comics and More | 5809 15th Ave NW | 206-781-4875 | Comics, games, videos. |
| Art Books Press Bookstore & Gallery | 4703 Ballard Ave NW | 206-285-2665 | Art books and gallery. |
| Secret Garden Bookshop | 2214 NW Market St | 206-789-5006 | Specilizes in kids books. |

## Map 24 • Fremont

| | | | |
|---|---|---|---|
| Alphabet Soup | 1406 N 45th St | 206-547-4555 | Kids books. |
| B Brown & Associates | 3534 Stone Wy N | 206-634-1481 | Used and rare. |
| Episcopal Bookstore | 3837 Stone Wy N | 206-545-0500 | Episcopal. |
| Fremont Place Book Co | 621 N 35th St | 206-547-5970 | Neighborhood independent. |
| Laughing Elephant | 3645 Interlake Ave N | 206-447-9229 | Family oriented religious. |
| Ophelia's Books | 3504 Fremont Ave N | 206-632-3759 | An eclectic mix. |
| Sea Ocean Book Berth | 3534 Stone Wy N | 206-675-9020 | Used maritime books. |
| Seattle Book Center | 3530 Stone Wy N | 206-547-7870 | Used and rare. |

# Arts & Entertainment • **Bookstores**

## Map 25 • Wallingford

| | | | |
|---|---|---|---|
| Comics Dungeon | 250 NE 45th St | 206-545-8373 | Comics and comic-related items. |
| Open Books A Poem Emporium | 2414 N 45th St | 206-633-0811 | Poetry and poetry related. |
| Wide World Books & Maps | 4411 Wallingford Ave N | 206-634-3453 | Travel books. |

## Map 26 • U District

| | | | |
|---|---|---|---|
| Barnes & Noble | 2675 University Way NE | 206-517-4107 | Chain. |
| Cinema Books | 4753 Roosevelt Wy NE | 206-547-7667 | Rare and collectable books on film. |
| Dreaming | 5226 University Wy NE | 206-525-9394 | Comics. |
| Globe Books | 5220 University Wy NE | 206-527-2480 | Used. |
| Half Price Books Records Magazines | 4709 Roosevelt Wy NE | 206-547-7859 | New and used at half price. |
| Magus | 1408 NE 42nd St | 206-633-1800 | Used. |
| University Bookstore | 4326 University Wy NE | 206-634-3400 | U of Washington. |
| Zanadu Comics | 1307 NE 45th St | 206-632-0989 | Comics. |

## Map 29 • Ballard / Loyal Heights

| | | | |
|---|---|---|---|
| Crown Hill Stamp & Coin | 8343 15th Ave NW | 206-789-5363 | Comics and collectables. |

## Map 30 • Greenwood / Phinney Ridge

| | | | |
|---|---|---|---|
| Couth Buzzard Used Books | 8310 Greenwood Ave N | 206-436-2960 | Used. |
| Dreamstrands Comics & Such | 115 N 85th St | 206-297-3737 | Comics. |
| Harvest Logos Bookstore | 115 N 85th St | 206-781-8725 | Faith and religion. |

## Map 31 • Green Lake / Roosevelt

| | | | |
|---|---|---|---|
| East West Bookshop Of Seattle | 6500 Roosevelt Wy NE | 206-523-3726 | Spiritual and metaphysical. |

## Map 32 • Ravenna

| | | | |
|---|---|---|---|
| Ravenna Rare Books | 5639 University Wy NE | 206-525-3737 | Rare books. |
| Renaissance Books | 5554 27th Ave NE | 206-523-1712 | Rare books. |
| Ravenna Third Place Books | 6504 20th Ave NE | 206-525-2347 | Neighborhood independent. |

## Map 33 • Northwest Seattle

| | | | |
|---|---|---|---|
| Balderdash Books & Art | 8536 Greenwood Ave N | 206-784-4660 | Used. |
| Barnes & Noble (College Store) | North Seattle Community College Campus, 9600 College Way N | 206-527-3637 | Chain. |
| Gary's Games & Hobbies | 8539 Greenwood Ave N | 206-789-8891 | Books on chess, bridge and other nerd pursuits. |

## Map 34 • Northeast Seattle

| | | | |
|---|---|---|---|
| Barnes & Noble | 401 NE Northgate Wy | 206-417-2967 | Chain. |

## Map 35 • Alki / West Seattle / North Admiral

| | | | |
|---|---|---|---|
| Leisure Books | 4537 California Ave SW | 206-935-7325 | New and used. |
| Pegasus Book Exchange | 4553 California Ave SW | 206-937-5410 | Used. |
| Square One Books | 4724 42nd Ave SW | 206-935-5764 | Neighborhood Independent. |

## Map 37 • Fauntleroy / Arbor Heights

| | | | |
|---|---|---|---|
| Barnes & Noble | 2600 SW Barton St | 206-932-0328 | Chain. |

## Map 40 • Columbia City / Mount Baker / Seward Park

| | | | |
|---|---|---|---|
| Books4Cars | 4850 37th Ave S | 206-721-3077 | Automotive books and manuals. |

## Map 41 • Rainier Valley / Rainier Beach

| | | | |
|---|---|---|---|
| Aviation Book Company | 7201 Perimeter Rd S | 206-767-5232 | Aviation. |

## Map 42 • Mercer Island

| | | | |
|---|---|---|---|
| Island Books | 3014 78th Ave SE | 206-232-6920 | Neighborhood independent. |

## Map 44 • Bellevue (South)

| | | | |
|---|---|---|---|
| Deseret Book | 3080 148th Ave SE | 425-747-7475 | Mormon. |

## Map 45 • Bellevue (West) / Medina

| | | | |
|---|---|---|---|
| Barnes & Noble | 626 106th Ave NE | 425-451-8463 | Chain. |
| University Book Store | 990 102nd Ave NE | 425-462-4500 | UW text books and general. |

## Map 46 • Bellevue (Central)

| | | | |
|---|---|---|---|
| Stargazers | 12727 NE 20th St | 425-885-7289 | Spiritual. |

## Map 47 • Bellevue (East) / Redmond

| | | | |
|---|---|---|---|
| Barnes & Noble | 15600 NE 8th St | 425-644-1650 | Chain. |
| Half Price Books | 15600 NE 8th Ave | 425-747-6616 | Used |
| Lake Hills Book Exchange | 523 156th Ave SE | 425-746-0354 | Used. |

## Map 48 • Kirkland

| | | | |
|---|---|---|---|
| Family Christian Stores | 12602 Totem Lake Blvd NE | 425-821-1281 | Christian. |
| Parkplace Books | 348 Central Wy | 425-828-6546 | Geared towards suburban families, selection is disappointing for an independent bookstore. |
| Stonehouse Bookstore & Growth Center | 10600 NE 68th St | 425-889-5106 | Spiritual. |

## Map 49 • Redmond

| | | | |
|---|---|---|---|
| Half Price Books | 7805 Leary Wy NE | 425-702-2499 | Used. |
| Soulfood | 15748 Redmond Wy | 425-881-5309 | Mind/body/spirit. |

One of the truer stereotypes about Seattle is our intense love for the brown stuff. No, I don't mean heroin (although that cruel mistress has certainly claimed plenty of our own). I'm talking about coffee.

We owe much of Seatown's coffee omnipresence to that little-mermaid-that-could. Starbucks mass-produced our obsession to the whole of the First World. But it doesn't take much effort to find something better. All over the city, independent coffee shops compete for the expendable income of our resident caffeine junkies. Many places even seem justified in charging $4+ for their artwork in mug. Some NFT neighborhood favorites: **Joe Bar (Map 17)** has been a Capitol Hill staple since 1997. That's like 100 years in Seattle restaurant time. **Vivace (Map 2, 17)** uses their old-world coffee knowledge to make a perfecto cappuccino. **Fuel (Map 18, 21, 25)** is one of the more welcoming spots for long-term table residents. (Seattle etiquette dictates that you must order something for every hour that you occupy your seat). **Verite Coffee (Map 4, 6, 23, 35)** diabolically teamed up with Cupcake Royale to ensure you put on that winter weight. **Caffe Vita (Map 4, 15, 24, 30, 40)** boasts 10 original blends including one co-created with Theo Chocolate. **Seattle Coffee Works (Map 3)** has an express bar for normal coffee consumption and a slow bar, which is more like an inclusive club for coffee nerds.

## Hipster Country

If you like your coffee with a side of scene, try **Bauhaus (Map 4)** which is probably better known for its people watching than for the coffee it sells. At the Portland-based **Stumptown (Map 4)**, our frenemies from the south do a great job showing us up with their singular roasts and it feels as though Carrie Brownstein and Fred Armisen could walk in at any minute. **Victrola (Map 4, 18, 39)** is for the more high-end hipsters, **Analog Coffee (Map 17)** for the mustachioed pseudo-luddite and **Zeitgeist Kunst & Kaffee (Map 7)** for the revolution-through-philosophy-degree types.

## Entertain Me

Sometimes you don't just want to sit quietly on your laptop. For live music, **Tiny Ninja (Map 25)**, **Café Racer (Map 31)**, **Forza (Map 31)** and **Sureshot (Map 26)** have got you covered. Exercise the pop culture lobe of your brain with trivia nights at **Neptune Coffee (Map 30)**.

## Take a Load Off, Annie

Say you're on rugrat duty but you also need to get some work done or catch up with your long-lost friend. These places have decked-out play areas that will keep your offspring distracted while you enjoy some adult conversation and sneak that extra cookie. **Mosaic (Map 25)** has the mother of play areas with a clubhouse, slide and a blocked off corner for accident-prone crawlers. **Twirl's (Map 13)** play area is also pretty sick and features a giant treehouse and an epic train table. The play corners at **Tougo (Map 5)**, **Cloud City (Map 34)**, **Green Bean Coffeehouse (Map 30)**, and **Ballard Coffee Works (Map 23)** pale in comparison, but still get the job done.

## Two for Tea

Preferring tea to coffee won't get you voted out of the Emerald City. Overachievers that we are, we have to do it TO THE MAX. At **Panama Hotel Tea & Coffeehouse (Map 8)**, they serve their large international selection of loose-leaf teas with an hourglass timer so you know exactly how long to steep. At **Pearl's Tea & Coffee (Map 35)**, you can get all the usual bubble tea flavors plus house-created flavors like Taro and Avocado. **Roy Street Coffee & Tea (Map 17)** treats their tea like their coffee, using flowery language to describe their flavors which, fortunately, live up to their own hype.

## Flavor Country

If you're tired of the same-old-same-old, you should head to the **Moore Coffee Shop (Map 3)** for their Nutella Latte, which is exactly as delicious as it sounds and comes with some of the best foam art around. **El Diablo's (Map 13)** Cubano espresso is a must try as is their Mexican Hot Chocolate. **Kitanda's (Map 48, 49)** Brazilian Latte is one of the better reasons to visit Kirkland or Redmond.

With such an embarrassment of riches in the coffee department, we hope you'll forgive us a little discernment. We're not trying to be dicks. But when you're born with a silver coffee stir in your mouth, it's hard to abide whatever it is that passes for joe at Dunkin' Donuts. You'll be one of us soon enough (gobble gobble).

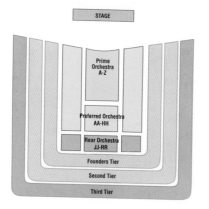

## General Information

NFT Map: 3
Address: 200 University St
Seattle WA 98101
Website: www.seattlesymphony.org
Phone: 206-215-4800
Tickets: www.seattlesymphony.org; 206-215-4747
or www.ticketmaster.com; 206-292-2787

## Overview

Rising up out of an entire city block in the heart of downtown, Benaroya Hall, home to the Seattle Symphony, opened in September 1998. The venue boasts the best balance between acoustic technology and luxurious ambience that 120 million dollars could provide. Taking full advantage of the astounding acoustics, local band Pearl Jam recorded and released *Live at Benaroya Hall* in 2004—but this is not the typical venue of rock musicians. In addition to the symphony, other art performances and lectures are offered in two halls, the S. Mark Taper Foundation Auditorium (capacity 2,500) and the Illsley Ball Nordstrom Recital Hall (capacity 540). Great glass flows of light and color fashioned by the renowned Dale Chihuly are featured in the lobby, which also houses a small café and a surprisingly good gift shop. Be forewarned when choosing your seat location—the front row seats in the upper tiers give the sensation that absolutely nothing is between you and the performance, including any protection from plunging over the edge. Nearby parking is plentiful, but if you arrive late, you can sip a glass of wine while you whisper to your fellow latecomers about the increasingly horrible Seattle traffic and watch the concert on a large screen television in the lobby until being seated at intermission.

## How to Get Tickets

In addition to the cost of the ticket, you'll pay hefty fees for the dubious distinction of buying tickets through Ticketmaster at www.ticketmaster.com. Skip the fees, and buy your tickets directly from the Benaroya Box Office at the corner of Third Avenue and Union, visit their website at www.seattlesymphony.org, or call them at 206-215-4747. The ticket office is open 10 am to 6 pm weekdays, Saturday 1 pm to 6 pm, and 2 hours before performances begin.

## How to Get There—Driving

Benaroya Hall occupies the block between 2nd and 3rd Avenue, and Union and University Streets. The main public entrances are on 3rd Avenue.

Southbound I-5: Take the Union Street exit (#165B) and proceed five blocks to 2nd Avenue. Turn left onto 2nd Avenue. The Benaroya Hall parking garage will be on your immediate left, with the garage entrance on 2nd Avenue just south of Union Street.

Northbound I-5: Exit left onto Seneca Street (exit #165). Proceed two blocks and turn right onto 4th Avenue. Continue two blocks and turn left onto Union Street. Continue two blocks and turn left onto 2nd Avenue. The Benaroya Hall parking garage will be on your immediate left, with the garage entrance on 2nd Avenue just south of Union Street.

## Parking

Your best bet is the 430 car garage located beneath Benaroya Hall. The entrance is off of 2nd Avenue. If it is full, there is metered street parking and more garages nearby. Street parking is free after 6 pm and on Sundays.

## How to Get There—Bus

Numerous bus routes serve Benaroya Hall. For details, call Metro Rider Information at 206-553-3000 (voice) or 206-684-1739 (TDD). Reach metro online at http://transit.metrokc.gov.

## General Information

NFT Map:     15
Address:     321 Mercer St
             Seattle WA 98109
Website:     www.siff.net
Phone:       206-684-7200
Tickets:     206-684-7200; www.ticketmaster.com;
             www.pnb.org; www.seattleopera.org;
             www.seattlefilm.org

## Overview

Marion Oliver McCaw Hall at Seattle Center, the state-of-the-art performance hall our reliance on cell phones helped finance, opened in June 2003. Of course, cell phones are strictly verboten during performances—there's just no place for your rap ringin', video camera of a cell phone during *Swan Lake* or *La Boheme*. Put the technology aside, relax, and enjoy yourself in this splendid venue. Besides being the home of the Pacific Northwest Ballet and Seattle Opera, McCaw Hall can be booked for weddings, conventions, and receptions if you have a pretty penny and need over-the-top accommodations. McCaw Hall houses a 2,900-seat auditorium, a 400-seat Lecture Hall, a café, a five-story serpentine glass Grand Lobby, and a 17,800-square-foot public plaza (the Kreielsheimer Promenade) that serves as an entry into McCaw Hall and the Seattle Center Campus. True to the eco-sensibilities of Seattle, McCaw Hall was built with green technology, featuring the use of recycled materials and energy-efficient theatrical lighting. Seattle opera and ballet-goers keep up the green theme—Dansko clogs are more common than Jimmy Choos, polar fleece wins out over cashmere. Even if you aren't an opera or ballet buff, it's worth a stroll through the promenade to experience just what money can buy, but if you want to be blown away by lavish productions in the extreme, splurge on the ballet and an opera and dress up—at least once. You might fall in love.

The Seattle International Film Festival recently opened a repertory movie house which, in addition to being a SIFF destination, programs retrospectives and cult films year round. In their first year they honored the great Stanley Kubrick by devoting a week to each of his films. Check out www.siff.net for more info.

## How to Get Tickets

Pacific Northwest Ballet tickets can be purchased directly by calling 206-441-2424 or online at www.pnb.org. For the Seattle Opera call 206-389-7676 or visit www.seattleopera.org. You can also purchase tickets for performances at McCaw Hall online at www.ticketmaster.com or by calling the Ticketmaster Fine Arts Line at 206-292-2787. The box office for McCaw Hall events opens two hours before performances, and during normal weekday hours, but weekend hours vary, so call first. For a last minute option, you can also try the Craigslist tickets section. You might luck out, but beware of being scammed.

## How to Get There—Driving

From I-5: Take the Mercer Street exit. At the first light, turn right. At the next light turn left on to Valley Street. Follow Valley Street as it turns into Broad Street, turn right immediately after the underpass. Take a right on 5th Avenue. Turn left on Roy Street, and then turn left onto 2nd Avenue. Turn left onto Mercer Street. McCaw Hall is directly on your right at 321 Mercer Street (Mercer & 3rd Ave N). If you think these directions sound confusing–you've understood them perfectly, it can be tricky to navigate around the perimeter of the Seattle Center. If you get lost, just head toward the Space Needle—McCaw Hall is located just north of the Space Needle on the grounds of the Seattle Center.

## Parking

Your best bet is the parking garage located across Mercer Street from McCaw Hall. A skybridge connects the garage to the Hall. Or you can park in one of the several open-air lots surrounding the Seattle Center. Street parking is scarce and at night, Queen Anne neighborhood streets are reserved for residents with zone passes.

## How to Get There— Bus or Monorail

Several Metro Transit bus routes provide service close to McCaw Hall, located on the north edge of Seattle Center. For the best route, call Metro's 24-hour Rider Information Line at 206-553-3000 or visit their website at metro.kingcounty.gov. The Monorail? It's probably out of service, but you can try the information line at 206-905-2620 to see if it's back shuttling the short stretch of track between downtown and the Seattle Center.

**BALCONY**

**MAIN FLOOR**

## General Information

NFT Map:   3
Address:    1932 Second Ave
              Seattle, WA 98101
Website:   www.stgpresents.org/moore
Phone:     206-467-5510

## Overview

The distinctive title of the country's oldest theater goes to Philadelphia's Walnut Street Theatre, but Seattle is quite proud of its own historic "walnut," the Moore Theatre. Celebrating its centennial in 2007, the Moore was the culmination of effort and vision by developer James A. Moore, a Canadian who arrived in Seattle around 1886. The theater remains the oldest still operating within the city.

Its deceptively shoddy exterior and tacky marquee belie the grandeur and opulence within its walls, embellished with chandeliers, frescoes, mosaics, and marble. Its foyer was once noted for being the largest of any theater in the country. The majestic hall retains its striking elegance while continuing to be a relevant venue for music and other performances. Over the years, some of the most celebrated and talented actors, musicians, and entertainers have played the Moore—from Ethel Barrymore, Vaslav Najinsky, the Marx Brothers, and Harry Houdini, to Sonic Youth, Nirvana, and Pearl Jam. The Moore was on the vaudeville circuit in the 1920s and hosted the first annual Seattle International Film Festival (SIFF) in 1976. History has been made here and the future looks bright for the venue. In 2013, a fundraising campaign for capital improvements to the interior will give this beauty the TLC she deserves.

## How to Get Tickets

You can no longer purchase tickets during the day at the Moore box office. Instead, go to the ticket kiosk at the corner of 2nd and Virginia which is open 24 hours, seven days a week. Other options include the website STGPresents.org or the Paramount Theatre Box Office which handles ticket sales for the Moore Theatre as well. The Moore Box Office still opens one hour prior to show time for Will Call and walk up sales. Tickets may also be purchased through Ticketmaster for a higher service charge, with rates varying by performance. Season ticket packages are also available on the theater's website.

## How to Get There—Driving

From I-5 North, take the Seneca Street exit; from I-5 South take the Stewart Street exit. Turn right onto First Avenue and head north to Virginia Street. Turn right onto Virginia Street and go one block to Second Avenue. Cross your fingers and hope to find parking.

From I-90 take the Madison Street exit. Turn left onto Madison, turn right onto Sixth Avenue, and head north to Stewart Street. Turn left onto Stewart Street, go down to First Avenue, turn right on First. Go north one block to Virginia Street, turn right onto Virginia, and go one block to Second Avenue.

## Parking

The Moore Theatre is located downtown at the corner of Second Avenue and Virginia Street, four blocks from Pike Place Market. Parking is available in nearby pay lots and metered parking along the street, but is nearly impossible to find on a Friday or Saturday night. If you really must park, do your best to find street parking northeast of Fourth Avenue.

## How to Get There—Bus

Take any Metro bus to the heart of downtown. The theater is just a short walk away.

**BALCONY**

**MAIN FLOOR**

**CABARET**

## General Information

NFT Map:        3
Address:        911 Pine St
                Seattle, WA 98101
Website:        www.stgpresents.org/paramount
Phone:          206-467-5510
Tele-charge:    For art events, 206-292-ARTS
                (2787). For concert events call
                Ticketmaster, 206-628-0888 or visit
                www.tickemaster.com

## Overview

In the 1920s, Paramount Pictures built a movie house in nearly every major city, and Seattle was no exception. To make up for the fact that the land they bought was less than prime, Paramount Pictures built the grandest movie house Seattle had ever seen. Modeled after the Palace of Versailles, it boasted a four-tiered lobby, a player piano, grand chandeliers, and original paintings in gilded frames. Those paintings have since been stolen, but nothing could steal the Paramount's dignity. Even after the Depression when people couldn't afford luxuries like movies, The Paramount employed ushers, including famous Seattle native Bruce Lee. In the early days, The Paramount hosted movies and vaudeville, then just first run movies, then second run movies and eventually, it was barely scraping by. It wasn't until 1971 when the Clise Corporation came along and recognized its potential as a live performance hall that things started to pick up again. After changing hands a few more times and undergoing some serious renovations, the Paramount stands again as a Seattle jewel. It even has a fully automated convertible floor system that can turn the theater into a ballroom. It was the first in the country to do so. Besides concerts, the Paramount also hosts a silent movie series on Mondays. The breathtaking lobby also has a bar to hide in when you realize you are the only person at the concert old enough to drink.

## How to Get Tickets

You can get tickets at The Paramount box office Monday through Friday, 10 a.m.–6 p.m. There is a ticket facility fee that ranges from $1-$3.75 (per ticket), depending on the event. You can also get tickets online at Tickets.com or by calling 1-877-784-4849.

## How to Get There—Driving

Coming north on I-5, take the Olive-Denny exit. Go one block to Melrose Street and turn right. The Paramount will be three blocks down on the corner of 9th Avenue and Pine Street.

Coming south on I-5, take the Stewart Street exit. Take Stewart to 9th Avenue and turn left. Follow 9th two blocks to Pine Street. The Paramount will be on your left.

## Parking

The Paramount Theatre does not have its own parking lot, so you are stuck with paying for an expensive lot or trying to find street parking. If it's after 6 pm or a Sunday, it's worth circling the blocks to find a spot on the street. If you don't have that kind of patience, try Pacific Place Mall parking (7th Ave & Pine St) which is the cheapest in the area. You can also try the Washington State Convention Center or the Grand Hyatt's garage (7th & Pike St). There is a loading zone on 9th Avenue and Pine Street to drop off passengers.

## How to Get There—Mass Transit

From downtown, take MT 10, 11, 14, 43, 49, or 84. From the University District, MT 43 or 44. From Capitol Hill, MT 10. From Northgate, take the express MT 66. Because the Paramount Theatre is so close to the Washington State Convention Center, and in a prime downtown location, there are over twenty bus routes that will get you within .1 miles of the theater. Your best bet is to http://visit transit.metrokc.gov or call 206-553-3000 to plan your route.

No doubt about it, Seattle is a cinephile's city. Cutting edge film from around the world screens daily, and even chain video stores stock adventurous fare. Each spring for over thirty years the Seattle International Film Festival has summoned the best and brightest talent from Hollywood and beyond for a month-long movie binge to rival Sundance and Cannes. The non-profit organization Northwest Film Forum offers film production workshops, equipment rentals, and funding grants to local filmmakers. And while there's no shortage of mainstream multiplexes for the latest big-budget snooze, Seattle also boasts many moviehouses that are exceptional not only in architecture and ambiance but also in their programming choices. The result is a consistent flow of cult favorites, foreign cinema, and rarely screened classics from the past.

Over in Capitol Hill, exciting, obscure cinema is the norm at **Northwest Film Forum (Map 4)**, and **Harvard Exit (Map 17)** boasts the most elegant lobby in town—complete with a grand piano, chandelier, and even a fireplace. In the University District, **Seven Gables (Map 26)** welcomes foreign film buffs with a bit of romantic atmosphere, aided and abetted by downstairs neighbor **Mamma Melina Ristorante**—a perfect first date package. **The Varsity (Map 26)** isn't as glamorous, but the sixty-year-old theater offers three screens on three floors connected by a staircase that claustrophobics should avoid. Employee-owned non-profit **The Grand Illusion (Map 26)** (a dentist's office in a former life) only seats 70, but it's one of the best movie-going experience in the city—a cozy, intimate space to enjoy films handpicked by the cineastes on staff.

There are only two places left in the world equipped to properly show films shot in the Cinerama three-screen format, and we got one. A local billionaire (his name escapes us) saved **Cinerama (Map 1)** from extinction in 1998 by kicking in for much-needed technological upgrades while preserving the retro charms of the house itself. Along with rare showings of 70mm classics, this is the place to experience big Hollywood special effect spectaculars like *Indiana Jones* or *The Dark Knight* and classics like *Lawrence of Arabia*.

By contrast, the tiny **Jewel Box Theatre (Map 1)** seats even fewer than The Grand Illusion, but the advantage (or disadvantage, depending on one's attitude toward alcohol) is its location within Belltown's **Rendezvous**—a speakeasy and burlesque stage during Prohibition. Now the Jewel Box features live bands and fringe theater events, as well as occasional special film presentations. Centrally located in the Central District, **Central Cinema (Map 5)** gives pizza, beer, and movies equal weight, serving hungry film fans who love their themed programs, making it a better choice for regular drunken cinema binges. Central's more sophisticated sister is **Big Picture (Map 1)**, which pairs first-run films with classy cocktails. When you purchase your tickets, you can order a drink (or several) to be brought to you mid-movie.

Last, but not least, is the **SIFF Cinema (Map 15)** at McCaw Hall in Seattle Center and the **SIFF Cinema Uptown (Map 15)** in Lower Queen Anne. Here, the Seattle International Film Festival lasts all year. SIFF also completed their decades-in-the-making SIFF Film Center, located a stone's throw away from the Seattle Center cinema in what was formerly the Alki Room. Not ones to miss an opportunity to ask for money, they will hold special screenings there as well.

## Movie Theaters

| | Address | Phone | Map |
|---|---|---|---|
| Admiral Theater | 2343 California Ave SW | 206-938-0360 | 35 |
| AMC Cinerama 1 | 2100 4th Ave | 206-441-3080 | 1 |
| AMC Loews Factoria 8 | 3505 Factoria Blvd SE | 425-641-9206 | 43 |
| AMC Loews Oak Tree 6 | 10006 Aurora Ave N | 206-527-3117 | 33 |
| AMC Loews Uptown 3 | 511 Queen Anne Ave N | 206-285-1022 | 15 |
| AMC Pacific Place 11 | 600 Pine St | 206-652-8908 | 3 |
| Big Picture Seattle | 2505 1st Ave | 206-256-0566 | 1 |
| Broadway Performance Hall | 1625 Broadway | 206-325-3113 | 4 |
| Central Cinema | 1411 21st Ave | 206-328-3230 | 5 |
| Cinemark Lincoln Square Cinemas | 700 Bellevue Wy NE | 425-454-9100 | 45 |
| Cinerama | 2100 4th Ave | 206-448-6680 | 1 |
| Fremont Outdoor Movies | 3501 Phinney Ave N | 206-767-2593 | 24 |
| The Grand Illusion | 1403 NE 50th St | 206-523-3935 | 26 |
| iPic Theatre | 16451 NE 74th St | 425-636-5601 | 49 |
| Jewel Box Theatre | 2322 2nd Ave | 206-441-5823 | 1 |
| Kenyon Hall | 7904 35th Ave SW | 206-937-3613 | 37 |
| King Cat Theatre | 2130 6th Ave | 206-448-2829 | 1 |
| Kirkland Parkplace Cinema 6 | 404 Park Pl | 425-827-9000 | 48 |
| Landmark Egyptian Theatre | 805 E Pine St | 206-781-5755 | 4 |
| Landmark Guild 45th | 2115 N 45th St | 206-547-2127 | 25 |
| Landmark Harvard Exit | 807 E Roy St | 206-323-0587 | 17 |
| Landmark Metro Cinemas | 4500 9th Ave NE | 206-781-5755 | 26 |
| Landmark Seven Gables | 911 NE 50th St | 206-632-8821 | 26 |
| Landmark Varsity | 4329 University Wy NE | 206-632-6412 | 26 |
| Majestic Bay Theatres | 2044 NW Market St | 206-781-2229 | 23 |
| Movies at Marymoor | 6046 W Lake Sammamish Pkwy NE | 360-733-2682 | 49 |
| Movies at the Mural | 305 Harrison St | 206-684-7200 | 15 |
| Northwest Film Forum | 1515 12th Ave | 206-829-7863 | 4 |
| Pacific Science Center IMAX | 200 2nd Ave N | 206-443-4629 | 15 |
| Regal Bella Bottega Stadium 11 | 8890 161st Ave NE | 425-861-6880 | 49 |
| Regal Crossroads Stadium 8 | 1200 156th Ave NE | 425-562-6596 | 47 |
| Regal Meridian 16 | 1501 7th Ave | 206-622-2434 | 3 |
| SIFF Cinema | 321 Mercer St | 206-324-9996 | 15 |
| SIFF Cinema Uptown | 511 Queen Anne Ave | 206-285-1022 | 15 |
| SIFF Film Center | 305 Harrison St | 206-464-5830 | 15 |
| Totem Lake Cinemas | 12232 NE Totem Lake Wy | 425-820-5929 | 48 |

## Art

The **Seattle Art Museum (SAM) (Map 3)** traces its beginnings to the early 20th century, and has grown and expanded as the city came into its own. In 2007 the museum's main downtown space was renovated, adding 70 percent more gallery space to show off its extensive collections of Pacific Northwest art. It also opened a new and improved museum store along First Avenue. Its sister gallery, the **Seattle Asian Art Museum (SAAM) (Map 17)** is located in idyllic Volunteer Park, with its sweeping city, water, and mountain views, and bad-boy reputation. The **Olympic Sculpture Park (Map 1)**, also a SAM project, showcases 22 monumental sculptures in a nine-acre park located on Seattle's waterfront. The **Frye Museum (Map 4)**, founded by a former meat packing executive, shows fairly traditional late 19th-, early 20th-century art in its elegant and contemporary building, although new curators have pushed the institution in a more cutting edge direction. Oh, and since Mr. Frye sold so much meat, it's always free admission.

The **Henry Art Gallery (Map 26)** is the University of Washington's gallery-cum-museum (or the other way around). On permanent display is James Turrell's Skyspace, a very cool enclosed light chamber. **Bellevue Art Museum (Map 45)** was once housed in a chi-chi mall, until it moved across the street into Steven Holl's architectural wonder where it promptly folded. BAM only reopened after reinventing itself as a crafts museum.

## Historic Seattle

**Wing Luke Museum (Map 8)**, located in the heart of the International District, is better than ever after its fantastic renovation. Its primary emphasis is on the cultural history of Asian Pacific Islanders, and the museum invites the community to participate in its exhibitions. The **Burke Museum (Map 26)** is the University of Washington's archaeological and ethnographic museum. Here you can see the notorious Kennewick man. The **Nordic Heritage Museum (Map 28)** is dedicated to the history of immigrant Scandinavians—free your inner Norwegian. The **Museum of History and Industry (Map 16)** is a city history museum for Seattle aficionados.

## Allentown

Ever wonder what billionaires keep in the basements of their mansions? Paul Allen puts his personal collection on display at two museums in the giant titanium blob at Seattle Center. The **Experience Music Project (Map 15)** invites you to free your inner Jimi with lots of interactive music exhibits; it almost justifies the inflated admission when you get a little percussion or guitar time in. Right next to EMP, the **Science Fiction & Fantasy Hall of Fame (Map 15)** houses Planet of the Apes memorabilia and appeals to Seattle's geek-chic set (read: former Microsoft executives).

## Plane Fun

In Boeing-obsessed Seattle, airplanes are serious business and **The Museum of Flight (Map 41)** has this topic covered. This is the place to tour the now-defunct Concorde and JFK's Air Force One.

| Museums | Address | Phone | Map |
|---|---|---|---|
| Burke Museum | 17th Ave NE & NE 45th St | 206-543-5590 | 26 |
| The Center for Wooden Boats | 1010 Valley St | 206-382-2628 | 16 |
| Center on Contemporary Art (CoCA) | 6413 Seaview Ave NW | 206-728-1980 | 2 |
| Chihuly Garden and Glass | 305 Harrison St | 206- 753-4940 | 15 |
| The Children's Museum | 305 Harrison St | 206-441-1768 | 15 |
| Experience Music Project (EMP) | 325 5th Ave N | 206-367-5483 | 15 |
| Frye Art Museum | 704 Terry Ave | 206-622-9250 | 4 |
| The Henry Art Gallery | 15th Ave NE & NE 41st St | 206-543-2280 | 26 |
| Klondike Gold Rush Museum | 319 Second Ave S | 206-220-4240 | 7 |
| Log House Museum | 3003 61st Ave SW | 206-938-5293 | 35 |
| Museum of Flight | 9404 E Marginal Wy S | 206-764-5720 | 41 |
| Nordic Heritage Museum | 3014 NW 67th St | 206-789-5707 | 28 |
| Pacific Science Center | 200 2nd Ave N | 206-443-2001 | 15 |
| Science Fiction Museum & Hall of Fame | 325 5th Ave N | 206-770-2700 | 15 |
| Seattle Art Museum Downtown | 1300 1st Ave | 206-654-3100 | 3 |
| Seattle Asian Art Museum | 1400 E Prospect St | 206-654-3100 | 17 |
| Seattle Metropolitan Police Museum | 317 3rd Ave S | 206-748-9991 | 7 |
| Seattle's Museum of History & Industry | 860 Terry Ave | 206-324-1126 | 16 |
| Wing Luke Asian Museum | 719 S King St | 206-623-5124 | 8 |

Seattle may be small by metropolis standards, but we use our space very efficiently. From quaint dives to swanky Belltown wine bars, punk rock to hipster kitsch, in Seattle, anyone can find their scene.

## Find Your Thrill on the Hill

If you don't know what kind of vibe you're in the mood for, Capitol Hill has a wide range of destinations, from the sexy red lighting of **Cha Cha (Map 4)** to the hunting lodge chic of **Redwood (Map 4)**, you'll find a cool place to hang out. The Hill is often pigeon-holed as a hipster/homo ghetto, but as long as you're open minded, it really can be all things to all people. At **Pony (Map 4)** every day is Pride Day, meaning you're probably going to see a lot of genitalia and party your ass off. The wing to Pony's wang is the **Wild Rose (Map 4)**, a fun and inclusive lesbian bar with plenty of love for both genders and a haunted bathroom. **Smith (Map 4)** is another hunting lodge-style bar with an enterprising gastropub menu. Seattle loves its speakeasy-style bars what with cagey entrances and enthusiastic cocktails. They're like well-decorated clubhouses. **Knee High Stocking Co (Map 4)** is in an unmarked building on a weird triangular island between two busy streets. But if you feel like making the effort, your palette will be richly rewarded. There are only a handful of tables so reservations (by text) are recommended. **Tavern Law (Map 4)** has a speakeasy-within-a-speakeasy called Needle & Thread with extra hoops to jump through for entry. **Pie Bar (Map 4)** wants you to have your pie and drink it too. **Sun Liquor (Map 17)** and **Sun Liquor Distillery (Map 4)** will serve you the greatest cocktails of your life using fresh squeezed juices and their own hooch and they are more than happy to customize. The **Unicorn (Map 4)** is a carnival-themed den of iniquity with an adult arcade called Narwhal in the basement. Both floors serve sugary beverages, an array of corn dogs (with veg options) and more deep-fried junk food than you can shake meat on a stick at. Experience Steampunk salvage chic at **Grim's (Map 4)** and soak up your mason jar cocktails with inventive and reasonably-priced sandwiches. After last call, on the weekends, find the Off the Rez food truck squeezed into a doorway on Pike and they will hook you up with some incredible hangover prevention in the form of frybread tacos.

## It's a Live!

The grunge days of flannel and hype may be long gone (thank goodness), but Seattle still has a thriving live music scene. Ground zero for alt-country and twang fans can be found at the **Tractor Tavern (Map 23)**, but if you prefer turntables over pedal steel, then make it over to **Chop Suey (Map 4)** for "live" music. Nearby, **Neumo's (Map 4)** rivals the **Showbox (Map 3, 39)** for booking the latest indie rock sensations, but their sound is definitely more on the dirty side. **The Crocodile (Map 1)** features shows small in size but big in rock. **The Sunset Tavern (Map 23)** is Seattle's best small venue, a friendly joint with red velvet interior that consistently books great up and coming local acts plus a succession of superior touring rockers from abroad. Try **Shadowland's (Map 35)** Tuesday open-mic night to be the first to discover the next Bon Iver. The bands at **Slim's Last Chance (Map 39)** are eclectic and smalltime but usually play something to get you up and dancing off that bowl of chili. **Blue Moon Tavern (Map 25)** conveys a down-and-dirty vibe, booking punk, honky tonk and everything in between. Fremont's **High Dive (Map 24)** is another good spot to check out new (though not necessarily stellar) local talent.

## Dive On In

Whether ironic or earnest, one thing Seattle excels in is dive bars. We really know how to make the best of a dark drink hole. Coney Island-themed pinball bar, **Shorty's (Map 1)**, is on the NFT shortlist. Its hot dogs and boozy slushies have the Anthony Bourdain stamp of approval. **The Kraken Bar & Lounge (Map 26)** is very metal, very dirty and your best bet on the Ave for avoiding students. Ballardites would love to keep the **Tin Hat (Map 30)** to themselves, but the word is out about this marvelously mellow bar home to a handful of regulars and some of Sea-towns best tater tots. **The Comet (Map 4)** has been the Prom King of dives since 1948. They have live music and karaoke, but the real show comes from the customers. The only thing you can expect there is a memorable night. **Eastlake Zoo (Map 20)** is perhaps so called because of the eclectic clientele it attracts. Every inch of this vast space is covered in kitch, making it the perfect place for a smashed scavenger hunt. Georgetown's diamond in the rough is the **9lb. Hammer (Map 39)** offering free pool and a peanut shell-covered floor for added authenticity. The same owner also graced South Park with **Loretta's (Map 38)**, a cozy, friendly and economical restaurant and bar with an air of grandpa's rec room. West Seattle's best kept secret is the pirate/nautical themed **Benbow Room (Map 35)** which is tucked into the back of a mid-western comfort food restaurant.

## Make Your Own Kind of Music

Seattle is filled with wannabe rock stars, some of which lack the wherewithal to form a band. That's where karaoke comes in handy. And we're not talking about that Gwyneth Paltrow "Duets" crap. Our karaoke is balls out. Some folks even occasionally don costumes add a little choreography to the mix. Often, this sort of dedication makes even the most tone-deaf performances entertaining as hell. Bachelorette parties and other karaoke dabblers usually start at **Ozzie's (Map 15)** or **Hula Hula (Map 1)**. But if you can't stand to hear "Love Shack" one more time, head to **Spectator (Map 15)**, a sports bar that is transformed into a die-hard karaoke singer's paradise every Thursday-Saturday thanks to the mind-blowing selection by Baby Ketten. They make their own tracks so if you don't find that favorite b-side or deep album cut, they just might have it for you the next time you come. Capitol Hill's **Crescent Lounge (Map 4)** has one of the more colorful crowds and sings it loud and proud every damn night of the week, much to their neighbors' chagrin. Everybody loves a karaoke room, but **Rock Box (Map 4)** takes it to the next level with their clean and classy rooms to accommodate nearly any party size from a huge birthday gathering to a single, solitary crooner. Whet your whistle with their Japanese-themed food and drink menu and don't forget to make advanced reservations, especially on the weekends. West Seattle's go-to is **Tug Inn (Map 37)**. Sing at **Monkey Pub (Map 26)** every Tuesday, Friday and Sunday. This beloved dive has a gritty, punk rock vibe and is refreshingly light on student infiltration. The **Twilight Exit (Map 5)** has moved their 70s dive shtick three times and their loyal patrons have always moved with them, singing their hearts out every Sunday night. For a truly erratic time, Greenwood's **Yen Wor Garden (Map 33)** and **Baranof (Map 33)** have competing karaoke every night of the week, attracting ironic amateurs, intense regulars and everyone in between. If you get hungry, they have jello shots.

## Pleased to Meat You

Do you love waiting in line while a power-mad bouncer hold the fate of your evening in his hands? Does your idea of a good time involve bumping genitals with strangers and rolling the dice on roofied drinks? In that case, you'll want to head straight to the breeding grounds of Pioneer Square where any bar can turn into a club at the drop of a white baseball cap. **The Last Supper Club (Map 7)** is the destination for plenty of sweaty radio hits. For those who prefer dancing on a bar or table top, check out **Cowgirls, Inc (Map 7)** or any number of bars in the dude-happy Pioneer Square triangle. The other white stretch-hummer lined strip is along 1st Avenue in Belltown. **Tia Lou (Map 1)** and **Foundation Nightclub (Map 1)** will make sure you don't go home alone, even if you want to. The newest kid on the block is **Aston Manor (Map 39)**, which brings Vegas nightclub elitism to SoDo.

## Come Dancing

If the frat party annex isn't your scene, but you still have happy feet, join the welcoming party scene at **Neighbours (Map 4)** This captain of the Capitol Hill Old Guard breaks out 80s, house, funk and mashups providing the opportunity to get your freak on any night of the week. **ReBar (Map 2)** has some very sexy dance nights in addition to cabaret, fringe theater and other alternative variety shows so check their calendar for details. **Mercury @ Machinewerks (Map 4)** is a private, invite-only goth club. So if your feet only get happy to Joy Division or Skinny Puppy, you might want to strike up a conversation with that pierced-up guy on the bus who wears his black trench coat year-round. **Lo-Fi (Map 2)** has a non-exclusive goth night on occasion but is best known for its super fun Emerald City Soul Club on second Saturdays. Want to hone your skills before hitting the town? You can take tango or swing lessons at the **Century Ballroom (Map 4)**.

## The Kids Are Alright

When your old uncle NFT was a youth, there wasn't much in the way of an all-ages scene. But thanks to the efforts of The Vera Project (www.theveraproject.org), the oppressive Teen Dance Ordinance was repealed in 2002 and since then, the under 21 crowd has been able to enjoy a nightlife outside of their dorm room or house party. **The Vera Project (Map 15)** has its own venue with shows as well as arts programs and plenty of other activities that keep little hands from getting idle. Major venues like **Key Arena (Map 15)** and the **CenturyLink Field Event Center (Map 7)** are always open to all ages as are **The Moore Theatre (Map 3)** and **Paramount Theatre (Map 3)**, but their calendar isn't always geared toward a younger crowd. Bumbershoot (bumbershoot. org) is an annual music and arts fest that allows you to get in a year's worth of live music over Labor Day weekend. **El Corazon (Map 2)**, **Neumo's (Map 4)** and the **Showbox (Map 3, 39)** have loads of all ages shows, putting the grumpy legal drinkers in booze-dispensing bullpens while the kids have direct access to the stage. **The Crocodile (Map 1)**, **Dimitriou's Jazz Alley (Map 2)**, and **Skylark (Map 36)** have occasional all-ages shows as well. **Neptune Theatre (Map 26)** adds alternative comedy shows to their terrific entertainment calendar. Of course there's always a wealth of good cinema, make-out opportunities at the **Seattle Laser Dome (Map 15)** and allowance squandering at **GameWorks (Map 3)** to make keeping curfew a challenge.

## 24-Hour Party People

Seattle can be tough on night owls. But if you're still raring to go at three am, there are a few options, most of which involve greasy spoon grub. **The Hurricane Café (Map 2)** has a decent jukebox and a separate bar so that seasoned drunks can keep to themselves while the loud whippersnappers enjoy their late-night pancakes in the main dining room. The **5 Point (Map 1)** has a solid 24-hour breakfast menu as well as a famous view of the Space Needle from the men's room urinal. The **Mecca (Map 15)** is the 5 Point's nearby little sister. Georgetown's **Square Knot Diner (Map 39)** isn't the best breakfast food you can get at 3 a.m., but it'll do in a pinch. **Beth's (Map 30)** 12-egg omelets and bottomless hash browns might make you sicker than the booze you're trying to soak up, but you'll have fun drawing dirty pictures on their paper tablecloths. For a classier after-hours meal, try **13 Coins (Map 2)** for some surf-and-turf that is guaranteed to bring on weird dreams. **Lost Lake Cafe & Lounge (Map 4)** is Capitol Hill's long overdue replacement to Minnie's, serving an incredibly diverse menu with a Twin Peaksian ambiance.

Seattle's standing in the country's culinary pantheon has ascended in recent years. All the big 'hoods are littered with casually upscale affairs—from the farm-to-plate genius of **Terra Plata (Map 4)** to the cozy and inventive flavors of Belltown's **Tilikum Place Cafe (Map 1)**. Thanks to Seattle's appearance on TV's "Top Chef", several local chefs have earned national recognition and are busy building their restaurant empires. Tom Douglas (**Dahlia Lounge (Map 1); Lola (Map 1); Serious Pie (Map 1, 2);** Cuoco **(Map 2); Palace Kitchen (Map 1)**—the list goes on and on), **Ethan Stowell (How to Cook a Wolf (Map 13); Tavolata (Map 1); Staple & Fancy (Map 23))**, Maria Hines' (**Agrodolce (Map 24); Tilth (Map 24); Golden Beetle (Map 23))** and Matt Dillon (**Sitka & Spruce (Map 4); Bar Sajor (Map 7); Bar Ferd'nand (Map 4))** are the reigning gods. And every single one of their creations deserves the hype. Some will cost you but are worth it and others are shockingly affordable. Many won't bat an eyelash at your fleece and toe shoes. The recent eco-friendly sustainable, free-range organic craze has always been a founding principle of Northwest cuisine, which relies on and reveres locally sourced ingredients. Flavor profiles range from Pan-Asian flair to rustic Italian to provincial French. But often, it's a pick n' mix of vivacious victuals. Our food is accessible. And that's how we like it. It makes it a whole lot easier to get it into your mouth that way.

## Seafood

Because of Seattle's proximity to the Pacific, it's clear why seafood seems to wiggle its way onto every menu in town. But not all of it is first-rate. Selectivity is key. **Ray's Boathouse (Map 28)** is a venerable waterfront institution that's been nailing it for decades, with a prime waterfront location and a slightly older crowd (including, yes, lots of tourists). **Ivar's Salmon House (Map 25)** is the classic place to take out of town guests because the only thing better than the chowder is the view. Downtown, endearingly Bacchanalian chef Tom Douglas serves up calamari and Copper River salmon for his adoring fans at **Etta's Seafood (Map 3)**. For a true taste of Pike Place, go straight to **Matt's in the Market (Map 3)**. If you get a jonesing for lubrication by fish and chips, **Spud on Alki (Map 35)** is classic, but **Pike Street Fish Fry (Map 4)** ups the ante with late-night hours, jars of homemade pickles, and fancy-schmancy sauces. **Emerald City Fish & Chips (Map 40)** injects a Cajun flare into their eclectic offerings. **The Walrus and the Carpenter (Map 23)** has garnered many a devoted follower, not unlike the subjects of Lewis Carol's famous poem.

## Seafood, Nippon-style

Hardcore Pescatarians like their fish raw and there's no shortage of sushi restaurants to accommodate them. It's rumored that Trey Parker bought a condo in Belltown just so he could take sushi-eating mini vacations whenever he wanted. Purists swear by **Nishino (Map 19)**, the eponymous establishment of Tatsu Nishino (a former disciple of famed Nobu Matuhisa). Put your meal in his skilled hands omakase-style for a spectacular experience. The unassuming **Aoki (Map 17)** on Broadway is a little more affordable but still pulls off good quality sushi and a wide selection of sakes. In West Seattle, get to try the chef specials at **Mashiko (Map 35)**. **Chiso (Map 24)** and **Liberty (Map 18)** take sushi for a spin in hip, modern settings, inventing new rolls that are, more often than not, very oishii indeed. The ID offers more traditional sushi experiences, particularly at **Maneki (Map 8)**—Seattle's oldest sushi bar. The U District's **Village Sushi (Map 26)**, gives a solid performance on the cheap, complete with an on-the-ball sake sommelier. For the newly initiated, or those who consider California rolls exotic, **Blue C Sushi (Map 24, 26)** rolls out cheap and accessible dishes on a gimmicky (though admittedly fun) conveyor belt system. The proprietor of self-titled **Shiro's (Map 1)** literally wrote the book on sushi (it's titled Shiro: Wit, Wisdom and Recipes from a Sushi Pioneer) and the dude knows his shoyu.

## Classy Joints

Seattle is infamous for its constant state of casual dress. But you can still find establishments that request a bit more refinement from their diners, and sometimes, it's just dang refreshing to step out of the Birks and into leathered, crystalline luxury. The grand champion is **Canlis (Map 13)**, a Seattle fixture since 1950 with a view to die for, impeccable formal service (crumb brush, dude), and spectacular food. Canlis is the ultimate Treat Yo Self. Not too far behind in impeccability is **Book Bindery (Map 13)**, which resides in (you guessed it) an old book bindery. Chef Shaun McCrain creates a masterpiece with each of his New American dishes and the digs couldn't be more romantic. For **Art of the Table (Map 24)**, what started as a weekend supper club has grown into a hospitable and unforgettable celebration of food. **Miyabi 45th (Map 25)** is a fine dining soba noodle house where you can feel comforted and pampered simultaneously. **Nell's (Map 31)** is proof that greatness can come in an unassuming package. The non-descript beige storefront is one of Seattle's best secrets: pitch-perfect Euro/New American dishes, that are elegant but not ostentatious.

## No Animals, Please

If your dietary preferences don't involve any fuzzy animals, or even their byproducts, you're not alone. As it happens, Seattle does meat-free so well, even the carnivorous have been known to relish the cruelty free options. The cream of the crop is the fine dining at **Plum Bistro (Map 4)**. Their creamy mac & yease could only be the result of a nefarious supernatural bargain. When you really want to indulge the herbivore in your life, drop some coin on the prix-fixe menu at **Sutra (Map 25)**, where the seasonal dishes seem right out of a culinary school text book (if that's a thing). **Café Flora (Map 19)** is slightly less polished, but nonetheless a very pleasant place to take your veggie-skeptical great aunt for brunch (they also cater to the gluten-free crowd). The U-District is an oasis for the penny-pinching vegan. **Wayward Vegan Café (Map 32)** (no relation to Roosevelt's vegan coffee shop) is run by semi-militants, but if you can get past the gruesome pamphlets, they will treat you to the best tofu scramble and biscuits n' gravy in the city. The college crowd loves **Araya's Vegetarian Place (Map 26)**, a tasty faux-meat Thai joint with an excellent lunch buffet and Asian-inspired breakfast pastries. Vegans needn't be deprived of the late-night joys of pizza: **Pizza Pi (Map 32)** has somehow cracked the dairy-free cheese code. The vegan donuts at **Mighty-O (Map 31)** rival anything on the Top Pot roster. Find them at their flagship store or in pastry cases around the city. Even die-hard meat lovers can't stop talking about the faux meat delights at **Bamboo Garden (Map 15)**. The sweet and sour "pork" or anything deep-fried are a safe bet. For the comfort that only bar food provides, head to the gritty **Georgetown Liquor Company (Map 39)**, where you can dig into flavor-packed meatless sandwiches and Super Nintendo, quite literally, on the wrong side of the tracks. Farther south, the animal lovers of Columbia City have **St. Dames (Map 40)**, which proves that gastropubs don't have to be houses of death to be good.

## More Meat, Please

If you find yourself agreeing with Ted Nugent on food matters, Seattle has you covered there too. Prefer to roast your beasts at home? Tromp on down to Pioneer Square, which is a meat market in more ways than one. If you aren't lucky enough to work downtown, it's worth a personal day to grab a glorious sandwich and stock up on Armando Batali's amazing pork products at **Salumi (Map 7)**. While you're shopping be sure to hit **Rain Shadow Meats Squared (Map 7)**, the quintessential Northwest meat emporium with a deli so that you don't have to wait till you get home to chow down. **Rainshadow's (Map 4)** flagship store is the sort of place Sam the Butcher would have been proud to work. West Seattle's **The Swinery (Map 35)** possesses a similar shop-and-dine business model but adds burgers and brunch to the mix. **Quinn's (Map 4)** was at the forefront of the foie gras revival. They might not have invented Upscale Rustic Cuisine, but it sure feels like it. To help you reach artery blockage bliss, order the double bacon deluxe at **Red Mill Burgers (Map 30)**. **Rancho Bravo (Map 25)** makes the most delicious brain, tripe, or tongue tacos this side of the border (though if you're in mixed company, they have a terrific veggie menu too). **Ezell's Famous Chicken (Map 5)** is so good that Oprah literally has it flown from the Emerald City straight to her constantly fluctuating waistline. At the much-lauded fine dining establishment, **Madison Park Conservatory (Map 22)**, they sneak dead animals into just about everything and take offense at substitution requests. Carnivores will be in hog heaven. Vegetarians will leave hungry.

## Eating Ethnic

Like most U.S. metropolitan cities, the cuisines of Mexico, Italy, Thailand, China, Vietnam, and Japan are well-represented. However, the adventurous foodie can find plenty of other cultures to sample from. At **Vostok Dumpling House (Map 4)**, you'll feel like you're back in the USSR (minus the oppressive influence of Putin). **Mamnoon (Map 4)** will get you hooked on their Syrian and Lebanese flavors. Dress up and dine in or do takeaway to enjoy in your pajamas. **Tempero do Brasil (Map 32)** bestows Brazilian favorites in an authentic atmosphere in the University District, while in West Seattle the **Salvadorean Bakery (Map 37)** specializes in fast food from waaaaaay south of the border. Save room for their decadent tres leches cake. Fans of Malaysian fare will find satisfaction at the International District's **Malay Satay Hut (Map 8)**. Wanna try Cambodian? Head to **Phnom Penh (Map 8)** for some tasty noodles. The mysterious Marrakesh **Moroccan Restaurant (Map 1)** is housed in a dusty-pink, windowless Belltown building, but inside all the romance and intrigue of Morocco comes alive. There are numerous Ethiopian spots clustered around Seattle University, but two places stand well above the rest: **Enat Ethiopian (Map 34)** is widely considered the city's best but **Café Selam (Map 5)** has rightfully earned a legion of devotees including a disproportionate number of cabbies.

## Cheap Eats

A high concentration of higher learning institutions means droves of intoxicated and hungry students prowling for food they can buy with their Coinstar winnings and leftover laundry change. Fortunately, there is an endless supply of local restaurants for the hard-up, hungry, or hung over—with no unnecessary sacrifice in taste. At **Aladdin Gyro-Cery (Map 26)**, soak up booze the British way with a lovely kebab or falafel. (Be sure not to confuse this prince of kebab shops with the inferior **Aladdin Falafel Corner** a couple blocks north.) Hill trolls swear by **Hot Mama's Pizza (Map 4)**, where a gargantuan, foldable slice costs less than a bus ride. Even in Seattle, pizza proprietors endeavor to be the most New York-style, and **Big Mario's (Map 4)** makes a strong case. A native Neapolitan, the Vellotti family business gained notoriety in the Big Apple before bringing their bona fide pies westward. On the lighter side, Pho (pronounced "fuh") is one of the cheapest and most mouthwatering meals you can get for a scant $5 or so. Seattleites couldn't face the winter without this eminently filling and fragrant Vietnamese noodle soup. **Pho Cyclo (Map 17, 39)** ladles out a most intriguingly flavored version, but the ubiquitous **Than Brothers' (Map 17, 23, 26, 30, 35)** chain does it a little more cheaply and sweetly (free cream puff with every bowl). For unique gourmet sandwiches on the cheap, stop by **Baguette Box (Map 4)** for their bread-blanketed miracles or queue up at **Paseo (Map 24, 28)** for their cherished Cuban sammies, chicken thighs and the best damn tofu platter in history. And if a late-night craving for the lovably limp burgers you downed as a kid proves unshakable, local institution **Dick's (Map 15, 17, 25, 33, 34)** will sling you a paper sack full of 'em for not much more than your leftover change from that evening's bar-hopping.

## Take Out

With about 140 days of measurable rain each year, it's surprising Seattle has woefully few food delivery options. Agonized East Coasters are usually appalled. Without a multitude of doorstep-delivered, we usually just sigh and order a pizza. Without a multitude of doorstep delivery, you'll still need to muster up enough energy to pick up food, so we often resort to pizza. Unless, of course, you really do want pizza, in which case local chains **Pagliacci (Map 15, 17, 36 35, 45)** or **Flying Squirrel (Map 23, 31, 40)** are your best bets. In the U District **Thai Tom (Map 26)** is usually packed, but you can always call in an order. The crack-like sauces at **Taste of India (Map 31)** will make you a regular (and they'll sometimes throw in a free brick of halva). Luckily, Seattle isn't completely devoid of delivery. Some of Seattle's best Thai restaurants will provide dinner without the need for pants. A lot of Thai food is created equal, but **Savatdee (Map 31)**, serving the U District and surrounding areas, is unmatched in its awesomeness and even has a special Laotian menu to expand your horizons. **Judy Fu's Snappy Dragon (Map 34)** will bring UD and Maple Leaf residents their divine dumplings and hand-shave noodles, but be prepared to wait as long as 90 minutes for your food. **In the Bowl (Map 4)**, will also deliver its delectable vegetarian noodle bowls—good thing, because it's usually impossible to find a seat.

## Food Trucks

Time was some silly law made it prohibitive as hell to open a food truck in Seattle. Until 2011, sidewalk vendors could serve only hot dogs, popcorn and espresso unless they wanted to shell out a ton of cash and jump through some daunting hoops. But thanks to new regulations, our very own mobile food scene has emerged and now there are so many trucks (over 150 at press time) that someone had to make a website (www.seattlefoodtruck.com) to keep track of them all. There are sweet and savory options and every kind of taco and sandwich imaginable. Some of the more successful trucks have opened brick-and-mortar restaurants to keep up with the demand (**Skillet, El Camion, Marination Mobile**) while several popular established restaurants (**Plum, Ezell's, Top Pot**) have taken to the streets to spread the love a little further. Other favorites include the life-changing fry bread tacos of **Off the Rez** (available for lunch or the perfect weekend drunk snack). **314 Pie** bakes locally sourced ingredients into savory pies with cinnamon sugar "fries" (more pie crust!) for dessert. **Where Ya At Matt** peddles authentic and lovingly made Cajun cuisine. **Maximus/ Minumus** slings epic BBQ sandwiches, some of which involve **Beecher's (Map 3)** cheese to brilliant effect

## Essential Mobile Food Trucks

**Beloved Mexico** (Mexican)
www.belovedmexico.com
**Box Nature Sushi** (Sushi)
boxnaturesushi.com
**Brass Tacks** (Comfort Food)
www.georgetownbrass.com
**BUNS** (Burgers)
www.bunsonwheels.com
**Chopstix** (Asian Fusion)
www.chopstixmobile.com
**Cheese Wizards** (Sandwiches)
wizardsofcheese.com
**Cotigo** (Mexican )
www.contigoseattle.com
**Crisp Creperie** (French)
www.crispseattle.com
**Curb Jumper Street Eats** (Sandwiches/Burgers)
www.curbjumperstreeteats.com
**Curry Now** (Indian)
www.iwantcurrynow.com
**Dante's Inferno Hot Dogs** (Hot Dogs)
dantesinfernodogs.com
**Diablo Food Truckz** (Asian)
twitter.com/DiabloFood
**Evolution Revolution** (Global Comfort Food)
evolutionfoodtruck.com
**Ezell's Express** (Fried Chicken)
twitter.com/EzellsExpress1
**Fez!** (Mediterranean)
twitter.com/fezonwheels
**Fish Basket** (Fish & Chips)
www.fishbasketnw.com
**Fusion on the Run** (Hawaiian/Vietnamese)
fusionontherun.com
**Grilled Cheese Experience** (Sandwiches)
twitter.com/wheelsofcheesxp
**Hallava Falafel** (Mediterranean)
www.hallavafalafel.com
**Happy Grillmore** (Sandwiches)
www.happygrillmore.com
**How Pickle Got Out of a Jam** (Comfort Food)
howpicklegotoutofajam.com
**I Love My GFF** (Gluten Free)
www.ilovemygff.com

**Jemil's Big Easy** (Cajun)
jemilsbigeasy.com
**Kaosamai Thai Cook Truck** (Thai)
www.kaosamai.com
**Lumpia World** (Filipino)
www.lumpiaworld.com
**Marination Mobile** (Hawaiian/Korean)
www.marinationmobile.com
**Nosh** (Eclectic)
www.noshthetruck.com
**Now Make Me a Sandwich** (Sandwiches)
www.nowmakemeasandwich.com
**Off the Rez** (Native American)
www.offthereztruck.com
**Outside the Box** (Paleo)
www.eat-otb.com
**Papa Bois** (Carribean)
www.papaboisfood.com
**Plum Vegan Burgers + More** (Vegan)
www.plumbistro.com
**Raney Brothers BBQ** (BBQ)
www.raneybrothersseattle.com
**Six Coins** (Japanese)
www.sixcoinsmobile.com
**Snout & Co** (Cuban)
www.snoutandco.com
**Skillet** (Seasonal)
skilletstreetfood.com
**Skinny Phoenix** (Breakfast/Sandwiches)
www.skinnyphoenix.com
**Street Treats** (Sweets)
www.streettreatswa.com
**Streetzeria** (Pizza)
www.streetzeria.com
**The Sammich Truck** (Sandwiches)
www.thesammichtruck.com
**Where Ya At Matt** (Cajun)
www.whereyaatmatt.com
**Xplosive Truck** (Vietnamese/Filipino)
www.xplosivemobilefoodtruck.com

We weren't always known for our food but we've grown up and struck out on our own. Now, not only are we playing with the big boys, we might even win a couple rounds. But with all this awesome grub around, you might want to start biking to work.

Seattle is nothing if not eclectic, and that's good news for all you shopaholics. Whether you're named in the Gates family trust or scrounging for dollars, Seattle provides plenty of opportunities for retail therapy. If you're looking to do some one-stop shopping, but can't stand the soul-killing atmosphere of a mall, there are a number of funky and/or chic commercial strips in Seattle. Get yourself to: the Pike/Pine Corridor (**Map 4**), Broadway on Capitol Hill (**Map 17**), Ballard Avenue (**Map 23**), 36th Street & Fremont Avenue (**Map 24**), University Way ("The Ave") in the U District (**Map 26**), and pretty much anywhere in Belltown (**Map 1**).

## Look Sharp

Some people think Seattle dresses too casually and perhaps they're correct. But what we lack in formality, we make up for in style. No matter where you are in this city, you will never be far from a cute boutique or funky thrift shop. If money is no object, you'll find some hip duds at **Mishu Boutique (Map 17, 24)** and **Ian (Map 3)**. Fellas will want to check out the post-mod threads **Kuhlman (Map 1)**, **Blackbird (Map 23)** and **Recess (Map 32)**. It's **Leroy Men's Wear (Map 3)** all the way for fedoras and Zoot suits in every color of the rainbow. Rebels without a cause will not want to miss the jackets and boots at **Insurrection (Map 30)**. For a more mainstream look, it's all about the original **Nordstrom (Map 3)**. When you find a hole in the crotch of your bike shorts, you'll want to head to **Hub and Bespoke (Map 24)** for a replacement pair. Do moths fly out of your wallet whenever you open it? Try **Buffalo Exchange (Map 23, 26)** and **Crossroads Trading Company (Map 17, 26)**, where you can buy and sell used, fashionable clothes from name brand designers. It's never too early to get your baby into Johnny Cash. You can score hipster-themed clothing in baby and toddler sizes at **Bootyland (Map 4)** and the slightly more affordable **Boston St (Map 1)**.

## Play that Funky Music

Some cities have let the Internet render their music stores obsolete. But in Seattle, independent record shops are thriving. Maybe that whole grunge thing wasn't so bad after all. Those who know the sound of a record scratch outside of movie trailers may be interested in **Spin Cycle (Map 17)**, **Georgetown Records (Map 39)** and **Jive Time Records Records (Map 24)**. **Bop Street Records (Map 23)** is known for its amazing selection at exorbitant prices. Discover further relics at **Golden Oldies Records Tapes and CDs (Map 23)**. **Sonic Boom (Map 3)** and **Easy Street Records (Map 35)** are great places to see a live band and buy their music simultaneously. **Singles Going Steady (Map 1)** and **Everyday Music (Map 20)** specialize in bands from a time when things like record labels and "selling out" mattered. If you prefer to make your own music, you can get your gear cheap at **Trading Musician (Map 31)**.

## Don't Toy with Me

We take a lot of things seriously in the Emerald City, but we're never too old for fun and games. Quality baubles and gadgets for the pre-pubescent crowd are easy to score in Seattle, thanks to progressively minded toy stores like **Magic Mouse (Map 7)** and **Top Ten Toys (Map 3, 30)**, where cheap plastic crap is an endangered species. **Dragon's Toy Box (Map 3)** boasts noteworthy customer service from people who can hardly believe they get to play with toys all day for a living. If you dream of space exploration but Huntsville, AL seems impossibly far, **Greenwood Space Travel Supply (Map 30)** is a fine substitute. Providing all of your tiny cosmonaut needs are an enthusiastic crew of folks still sore about that whole Pluto demotion thing. Best of all, proceeds go entirely to tutoring non-profit, 826 Seattle. If you think toys were better in the past, **Max and Quinn's Atomic Boy's Shop-O-Rama (Map 35)** agree with you. Stock up on potato guns, slingshots and other wholesome toys for the child in your life, instead of that iPad they asked for. But forget about those unappreciative money drains. This is a city full of adults in various stages of arrested development and they demand to be catered to. Enter **Schmancy (Map 3)**, a cozy boutique for vinyl and plush toys made for whimsical folk of voting age who need a cuddly T-bone steak doll or a sock monkey to get them through the night. Head out to Wallingford to **Archie McPhee's (Map 24)**, a veritable supermarket of kitschy gag gifts and other wacky wares for adults who miss the thrill that only whoopee cushions and potato guns can provide. **Card Kingdom (Map 23)**—"the ultimate in lawful good times"—is the ultimate for anyone who owns dice with more than six sides. You can test any game in their adjacent Cafe Mox or become King of the Elves in a D&D tournament in their back room. Speaking of adults and toys, **Babeland (Map 4)** up on Capitol Hill offers an utterly shame-free zone to casually shop for all manner of stimulating marital (or otherwise) aids—dildos, vibrators, leather whips, silicone sleeves, and how-to books are available in a clean, well-lit atmosphere with helpful sex-positive salespeople. Oh, didn't think we'd go there, did you?

## Eat, Drink, and Spend Money

**Pike Place Market (Map 3)** is unbeatable when it comes to fresh seafood; just don't go to the guys throwing fish around. That's for tourists, which you are not. Go to Harry at **Pure Food Fish (Map 3)**. While you're down in the market load up on cheese at **Beecher's (Map 3)** and the myriad fresh dairy products at **Pike Place Creamery (Map 3)**. Save room for a craft soda (with or without booze) from **Rachel's Ginger Beer (Map 3)**. If you don't eat your meat, you can't have any pudding. **Salumi Artisan Cured Meats (Map 7)** does a fine job of keeping your carnivorous cravings at bay. Around here, we like to keep our fridges and cellars stocked with alcohol to get us through the long, wet winters. **Vino Verite (Map 17)** has the best wine selection. **Bottleworks (Map 25)** specializes in beer, filling every nook and cranny of their small store with international options. **Wine World and Spirits (Map 25)** is your one-stop shop for all things inebriating including an impressive locally distilled liquor section and all the accoutrements you can shake a swizzle stick at. Got a sweet tooth? **The Confectionary (Map 26)** in U Village is your upscale candy boutique with a mouthwatering hand-made chocolate case, the underrated joys of salted black licorice and even some lowbrow favorites. That long line at Molly Moon's isn't worth it, especially when some of the best gelato in town is just up the road at **Fainting Goat (Map 25)**. They do gelato the Turkish way. Don't knock their signature flavor, made from goat milk, until you try it. Pig's Peace Sanctuary owns **Vegan Haven (Map 32)** a small store that is packed to the gills with cruelty-free goods from frozen pizza to lip balm and even the means to enforce your beliefs onto your pets. **Uwajimaya (Map 8, 46)** is a wonderland of Asian food and gifts that can't be missed. **Rising Sun Farms (Map 32)** brings the rural roadside produce stand to the big city. Speaking of farms, there's a farmer's market in pretty much every neighborhood but the standouts are the **University District Farmers Market (Map 26)** on Saturdays and the **Ballard Farmers Market (Map 23)** on Sundays. Both happen year-round, rain or shine. **Melrose Market (Map 4)** made the smart play and put a roof over their vendors. Among those keeping the residents of Capitol Hill stocked up on locally sourced, organic foodstuffs: The Calf and Kid, Rain Shadow Meats, Marigold and Mint flowers and produce.

## They Don't Make 'Em Like They Used To

Let's face it. Things were better in the past. Fortunately, many Seattle shop owners agree with you. Find Formica galore and your new favorite old easy chair at **Fremont Vintage Mall (Map 24)** or **Space Oddity Vintage Furniture (Map 23)**. If Mad Men has got you longing for golden age fashions, try **Pretty Parlor (Map 17)**, carefully curated by Ms. Anna Banana with a bonus section for the men folk. She supplements her always-impressive inventory with clothes from some of Seattle's best vintage-style designers. **Diva Dollz (Map 3)** is where Bettie Page would have shopped and they also have cute designs in plus sizes. **Valley of Roses (Map 26)** has threads for men and women, and frequently cycles through their inventory. The customer service oriented owner hides treasures all over the store, including the clearance rack. **Vintage Angel Company (Map 24)** spans several decades. Try not to get too depressed about the 90s section. Accessorize that 60s mini dress with baubles from **Lil Paisley (Map 30)** vintage jewelry store. If you prefer quantity to quality or are looking for pieces for a Halloween costume, **Atlas Clothing Co (Map 4)** or **Red Light (Map 17, 26)** are your best bets.

## Mallrats

If you must patronize a mall, it's good to know which to hit and which to avoid. Let's start with the malls to avoid. **Westlake Center (Map 3)** is well known as the most useless mall in Seattle. It is one of the two stops on the monorail, which makes it a bona fide tourist trap. Pacific Place is your other downtown option, but with all the Tiffanys, Club Monacos, and J. Jills, really only Amazon and Microsoft executives can afford to shop there. The mall for the masses is **Northgate (Map 34)**, appealing to the simple folk who enjoy the mainstream pleasures of The Gap, Macy's, JC Penney, and Express. Somewhere in between Northgate and Pacific Place is **University Village (Map 26)** with shops like the Apple Store, Eileen Fisher, and Lululemon. It is outdoors, but they provide shoppers with free yellow umbrellas while they stroll around.

**Departures**

```
NFT-NEW YORK CITY
NFT-BROOKLYN
NFT-LONDON
NFT-CHICAGO
NFT-LOS ANGELES
NFT-BOSTON
NFT-SAN FRANCISCO
NFT-SEATTLE
NFT-WASHINGTON DC
```

# Tired of your own city?

You buy the ticket, we'll be the guide.

# Street Index

# Street Index

# Street Index

| Street (Range) | Page | Grid |
|---|---|---|
| **NE 46th St** | | |
| (100-199) | 25 | A2 |
| (2200-2299) | 26 | A2 |
| (4000-4099) | 27 | C1 |
| (10500-10699) | 45 | A2 |
| (16200-16699) | 47 | A1 |
| **NW 46th St** | | |
| (100-599) | 24 | A1 |
| (600-1599) | 23 | C1/C2 |
| **SE 46th St** | | |
| (8300-9499) | 42 | B1/B2 |
| (11600-13399) | 43 | B2/C1/C2 |
| (13900-17699) | 44 | — |
| **SE 46th Way** | 44 | C1/C2 |
| **47th Ave NE** | 27 | A1/B1/C1 |
| **47th Ave S** | | |
| (3900-6499) | 40 | B1/C1 |
| (7946-11099) | 41 | A2/B2/C2 |
| **47th Ave SW** | | |
| (1700-5999) | 35 | A2/B2/C2 |
| (6000-9799) | 37 | A1/B1 |
| **47th Ave W** | 11 | A1 |
| **NE 47th Ct** | 47 | A1 |
| **SE 47th Ct** | 44 | C1/C2 |
| **SE 47th Ln** | 44 | C1/C2 |
| **47th Pl NE** | 27 | C1 |
| **47th Pl SW** | 37 | A1 |
| **NE 47th Pl** | 45 | A2 |
| **SE 47th Pl** | | |
| (8400-8599) | 42 | B2 |
| (11614-13099) | 43 | C1/C2 |
| (14469-17299) | 44 | C1/C2 |
| **N 47th St** | | |
| (100-1599) | 24 | A1/A2 |
| (1600-2099) | 25 | A1 |
| **NE 47th St** | | |
| (200-899) | 25 | A2 |
| (900-2499) | 26 | A1/A2 |
| (3500-4899) | 27 | B1 |
| (9000-10999) | 45 | A1/A2 |
| (13200-13499) | 46 | A1/A2 |
| **NW 47th St** | | |
| (100-599) | 24 | A1 |
| (600-899) | 23 | B2/C2 |
| **SE 47th St** | | |
| (8400-9499) | 42 | B2 |
| (11600-13156) | 43 | C1/C2 |
| (13900-17699) | 44 | C1/C2 |
| **SE 47th Way** | 44 | C2 |
| **48th Ave NE** | | |
| (3700-7499) | 27 | A1/B1/C1 |
| (9400-10499) | 34 | B2/C2 |
| **48th Ave S** | | |
| (3900-7099) | 40 | B2/C2 |
| (7100-10899) | 41 | A2/B2/C2 |
| **48th Ave SW** | | |
| (1900-5999) | 35 | A2/B2/C2 |
| (6000-9799) | 37 | A1/B1 |
| **NE 48th Ct** | 47 | A1 |
| **SE 48th Ct** | 44 | C2 |
| **SE 48th Dr** | 44 | C1/C2 |
| **48th Pl NE** | 27 | C1 |
| **NE 48th Pl** | | |
| (10400-11199) | 45 | A2 |
| (11700-13899) | 46 | A1/A2 |
| **SE 48th Pl** | | |
| (12500-12999) | 43 | C2 |
| (16400-16799) | 44 | C2 |
| **N 48th St** | | |
| (100-1599) | 24 | A1/A2 |
| (1600-2099) | 25 | A1 |
| **NE 48th St** | | |
| (800-899) | 25 | A2 |
| (2300-2399) | 26 | A2 |
| (3600-3899) | 27 | B1 |
| (10800-11098) | 45 | A2 |
| (16400-19199) | 47 | A1/A2 |
| **NW 48th St** | | |
| (2-599) | 24 | A1 |
| (600-1699) | 23 | B1/B2 |
| **SE 48th St** | | |
| (8100-9099) | 42 | B1/B2 |
| (11600-12299) | 43 | C1/C2 |
| (16100-16399) | 44 | C2 |
| **49th Ave NE** | | |
| (3624-7399) | 27 | A1/B1/C1 |
| (9000-10299) | 34 | C2 |
| **49th Ave S** | | |
| (4000-6699) | 40 | B2/C2 |
| (7900-11399) | 41 | A2/B2/C2 |
| **49th Ave SW** | | |
| (2100-5999) | 35 | A2/B2/C2 |
| (6000-9999) | 37 | A1/B1 |
| **NE 49th Ct** | 47 | A1 |
| **NE 49th Pl** | 47 | A1/A2 |
| **SE 49th Pl** | | |
| (11800-11899) | 43 | C2 |
| (14000-17299) | 44 | C1/C2 |
| **N 49th St** | | |
| (100-1599) | 24 | A1/A2 |
| (1600-2099) | 25 | A1 |
| **NE 49th St** | | |
| (2500-2599) | 26 | A2 |
| (10900-11099) | 45 | A2 |
| (15800-15899) | 47 | A1 |
| **NW 49th St** | | |
| (100-599) | 24 | A1 |
| (600-1599) | 23 | B1/B2 |
| **SE 49th St** | | |
| (11600-13299) | 43 | C1/C2 |
| (14300-16799) | 44 | C1/C2 |
| **50th Ave NE** | 27 | A1/B1/C1 |
| **50th Ave S** | | |
| (4000-5399) | 40 | B2/C2 |
| (7900-11199) | 41 | A2/B2/C2 |
| **50th Ave SW** | | |
| (2100-5199) | 35 | A2/B2/C2 |
| (6000-9999) | 37 | A1/B1 |
| **NE 50th Ct** | 47 | A1 |
| **NE 50th Pl** | 46 | A1/A2 |
| **SE 50th Pl** | | |
| (8100-8399) | 42 | B1 |
| (1100-1199)* | 43 | C1 |
| (11600-13609) | 43 | C1/C2 |
| (16500-16699) | 44 | C2 |
| **N 50th St** | | |
| (100-1499) | 24 | A1/A2 |
| (1500-2599) | 25 | A1/A2 |
| **NE 50th St** | | |
| (100-899) | 25 | A2 |
| (900-3450) | 26 | A1/A2 |
| (3451-5399) | 27 | B1 |
| (13200-13599) | 46 | A1/A2 |
| (16201-19831) | 47 | A1/A2 |
| **NW 50th St** | | |
| (100-620) | 24 | A1 |
| (621-1699) | 23 | B1/B2 |
| **SE 50th St** | | |
| (4845-9099) | 42 | B2 |
| (12000-12199) | 43 | C2 |
| (14000-15899) | 44 | C1/C2 |
| **NE 50th Way** | 47 | A1 |
| **51st Ave NE** | | |
| (3800-7599) | 27 | A1/B1/C1 |
| (9000-9299) | 34 | C2 |
| **51st Ave S** | | |
| (4000-6999) | 40 | B2/C2 |
| (9200-11399) | 41 | B2/C2 |
| **51st Ave SW** | | |
| (2300-5211) | 35 | — |
| (9623) | 37 | B1 |
| **NE 51st Ct** | 47 | A2 |
| **51st Pl S** | 40 | C2 |
| **51st Pl SW** | 35 | C1 |
| **NE 51st Pl** | 46 | A1/A2 |
| **SE 51st Pl** | | |
| (9000-9049) | 42 | B2 |
| (12600-13299) | 43 | C2 |
| (13600-14199) | 44 | C1 |
| **N 51st St** | | |
| (100-1599) | 24 | A1/A2 |
| (1600-2399) | 25 | A1 |
| **NE 51st St** | | |
| (100-499) | 25 | A2 |
| (2200-2399) | 26 | A2 |
| (3900-3999) | 27 | B1 |
| (14800-15543) | 46 | A2 |
| (15600-19199) | 47 | A1/A2 |
| **NW 51st St** | | |
| (100-599) | 24 | A1 |
| (600-1699) | 23 | B1/B2 |
| **SE 51st St** | | |
| (12000-13399) | 43 | C2 |
| (14100-15099) | 44 | C1 |
| **52 Ave SW** | 35 | C1 |
| **52nd Ave NE** | 27 | A1/B1/C1 |
| **52nd Ave S** | | |
| (4500-6999) | 40 | B2/C2 |
| (7700-9699) | 41 | A2/B2 |
| **52nd Ave SW** | 35 | — |
| **52nd Pl SW** | 35 | — |
| **NE 52nd Pl** | 27 | B1 |
| **SE 52nd Pl** | | |
| (8700-8799) | 42 | B2 |
| (13200-13399) | 43 | C2 |
| (13800-14399) | 44 | C1 |
| **N 52nd St** | | |
| (100-1599) | 24 | A1/A2 |
| (1600-2399) | 25 | A1 |
| **NE 52nd St** | | |
| (100-499) | 25 | A2 |
| (1000-2999) | 26 | A1/A2 |
| (3500-5199) | 27 | B1 |
| (10201-10799) | 45 | A2 |
| (15400-15599) | 46 | A2 |
| **NW 52nd St** | | |
| (100-599) | 24 | A1 |
| (600-1699) | 23 | B1/B2 |
| **SE 52nd St** | | |
| (9400-9599) | 42 | B2 |
| (11600-13599) | 43 | C1/C2 |
| **52nd Ter S** | 40 | C2 |
| **53rd Ave NE** | | |
| (4200-7399) | 27 | A1/B1/C1 |
| (8500-8599) | 34 | C2 |
| **53rd Ave S** | | |
| (4600-4999) | 40 | B2 |
| (8600-11788) | 41 | B2/C2 |
| **53rd Ave SW** | 35 | A1/B1 |
| **53rd Ct NE** | 34 | C2 |
| **NE 53rd Pl** | 46 | A2 |
| **SE 53rd Pl** | | |
| (8391-9399) | 42 | B2 |
| (13600-15356) | 44 | C1 |
| **53rd St SE** | 42 | B2 |
| **N 53rd St** | | |
| (300-1599) | 24 | A1/A2 |
| (1600-2299) | 25 | A1 |
| (2300-2399) | 31 | C1 |
| **NE 53rd St** | | |
| (100-899) | 25 | A2 |
| (900-2924) | 26 | A1/A2 |
| (10400-11219) | 45 | A2 |
| (11220-11451) | 46 | A1 |
| (15600-18699) | 47 | A1/A2 |
| **NW 53rd St** | | |
| (100-599) | 24 | A1 |
| (600-1699) | 23 | B1/B2 |
| **SE 53rd St** | | |
| (8800-8999) | 42 | B2 |
| (12500-13499) | 43 | C2 |
| (15300-15510) | 44 | C1 |
| **54th Ave NE** | | |
| (4300-7399) | 27 | A1/B1/C1 |
| (8500-8599) | 34 | C2 |
| **54th Ave S** | | |
| (4700-6599) | 40 | B2/C2 |
| (7200-11851) | 41 | A2/B2/C2 |
| **54th Ave SW** | 35 | B1/C1 |
| **SE 54th Ct** | 44 | C1 |
| **54th Pl SW** | 35 | A1 |
| **NE 54th Pl** | | |
| (13200-15525) | 46 | A2 |
| (18700-18799) | 47 | A2 |
| **SE 54th Pl** | | |
| (9160-9170) | 42 | B2 |
| (11700-13399) | 43 | C2 |
| (13600-17399) | 44 | C1/C2 |
| **N 54th St** | | |
| (100-1599) | 24 | A1/A2 |
| (1600-2399) | 31 | C1 |
| **NE 54th St** | | |
| (100-499) | 31 | C1/C2 |
| (2000-2999) | 32 | C1/C2 |
| (4500-5499) | 27 | B1 |
| (15400-15436) | 46 | A2 |
| **NW 54th St** | | |
| (100-599) | 24 | A1 |
| (600-2599) | 23 | B1/B2 |
| (2600-3499) | 28 | C1/C2 |

# Street Index

# Street Index

# Street Index

# Street Index

# Street Index

# Street Index

# Street Index

# Street Index

# Street Index

# Street Index

# We'll map your world.

### Need a custom map?

T will work with you to design a custom map that promotes your company or event. T's team will come up with something new or put a fresh face on something you eady have. We provide custom map-making and information design services to fit ur needs—whether simply showing where your organization is located on one of existing maps, or creating a completely new visual context for the information you sh to convey. NFT will help you—and your audience—make the most of the place u're in, while you're in it.

For more information, call us at 212-965-8650 or visit
www.notfortourists.com/custommapping.aspx

# Customize your NFT.

We can put **your organization's logo or message** on NFT using custom foil stamps of your (or our) design. Not For Tourists Guidebooks make **great gifts** for employees, clients, and promotional events.

For more information, call us at 212-965-8650, or visit www.notfortourists.com/corporatesales.aspx